Adventures in Japanese 3

Textbook

アドベンチャー

日本語 3

Adventures
in Japanese 3
Textbook

Hiromi Peterson and Naomi Omizo

Illustrated by Michael Muronaka & Emiko Kaylor

Cheng & Tsui Company

09 08 07 06 05 04 03 02   12 11 10 9 8 7 6 5 4 3 2

Published by

Cheng & Tsui Company
25 West Street
Boston, MA 02111-1213 USA
Fax (617) 426-3669
www.cheng-tsui.com
"Bringing Asia to the World"™

Printed in the U.S.A.

Library of Congress Control Number: 2001092701

Hardcover Edition: ISBN 0-88727-399-8
Paperback Edition: ISBN 0-88727-396-3

Companion textbooks, workbooks, hiragana/katakana workbooks, flashcards, and audio products,
for this and for other levels of the *Adventures in Japanese* series,
are also available from the publisher.

ADVENTURES IN JAPANESE 3 TEXT
CONTENTS

FOREWORD

As a recent author of an elementary Japanese textbook for college students I am keenly aware of the difficulty of writing an elementary textbook. It is time-consuming, energy-consuming and creativity-consuming. Writing an elementary Japanese textbook for high school students must be much harder than writing the counterpart for college students, because it involves a host of age-adequate considerations peculiar to high school students.

Adventures in Japanese has been prepared by highly experienced and knowledgeable high school teachers of Japanese, Hiromi Peterson and Naomi Omizo, who know exactly what is teachable/learnable and what is not teachable/learnable for high school students. They know how to sustain the students' interest in the Japanese language and its culture by employing so many age-adequate, intriguing activities with a lot of fun illustrations. The grammar explanations and culture notes provide accurate and succinct pieces of information, and each communicative activity is well designed to assist the students in acquiring actual skills to use grammar and vocabulary in context. In short, *Adventures in Japanese* is an up-to-date high school Japanese textbook conceived and designed in a proficiency-based approach. Among many others, it comes with a teacher's manual which is intended to help a novice high school teacher of Japanese teach Japanese in a pedagogically correct manner from day one.

I am pleased that at long last we have a high school textbook that is both learnable and teachable, and very importantly, enjoyable. I endorse *Adventures in Japanese* wholeheartedly.

Seiichi Makino
Professor of Japanese and Linguistics
Department of East Asian Studies
Princeton University

TO THE STUDENT

Welcome to the third volume of *Adventures in Japanese*! We congratulate you on your progress in the study of Japanese language and culture!

In Volume 1, you learned to express your basic needs in Japanese. In Volume 2, you expanded your skills by learning how to use Japanese in your own community. In Volume 3, you will actually be experiencing Japan with Ken as he spends time living in Tokyo with a host family. You will learn about high school life in Japan, talk about your Japanese language studies, write letters in Japanese, read about and experience the entertainment world in Japan, learn about the Japanese home, learn to maneuver around Tokyo on the train system, and even learn more about Japanese foods! This volume truly takes you on an exciting adventure to Japan!

Our general goals for students in this volume align closely with the National Standards in Foreign Language:

1. Students will effectively communicate in Japanese through interpersonal exchange of information, opinions and expressions of feelings and emotions.
2. Students will understand and interpret written and spoken Japanese on many topics related to contemporary life in Japan.
3. Students will present information, concepts and ideas to an audience of listeners or readers on many topics about contemporary life in Japan.
4. Students will demonstrate an understanding of culture by studying certain common Japanese practices, perspectives and products and how they relate to one another.
5. Students will demonstrate an understanding of the nature of language through comparisons between the Japanese and English languages.
6. Students will participate in activities that will enable them to connect to other disciplines, access information through authentic sources and interact in multicultural settings.

Let us preview this volume by discussing the following aspects related to it.

Topics

The topics for Volume 3 were again carefully considered from the point of view of a young first-time traveller to Japan. Ken, the central character throughout *Adventures in Japanese*, arrives in Tokyo for the first time and is greeted by his Japanese host family. Students will learn about appropriate language and behavior in these usually tense first-time meetings. Ken introduces himself and talks about his family in a much more sophisticated way than in past volumes. Through Ken, you will become acquainted with high schools in Japan and learn about some of the special annual events that occur in schools. During the early weeks of Ken's stay in Japan, he writes a letter home to his former Japanese teacher to report about his life in Japan, thus giving you essential skills in traditional letter writing. One of the most difficult aspects of Ken's life in Japan is studying the language. The fourth lesson equips you to discuss your experiences in learning Japanese at this intermediate level and teaches you how to use a *kanji* dictionary, a necessary skill by the time you reach this stage in your study of Japanese. Ken's life in Japan, however, is not entirely consumed by studies. You will be exposed to some of the common forms of entertainment for Japanese high school students, namely popular music, movies and television. As a homestay student, you will become very intimate with living Japanese style in a modern Japanese home. You will learn about the structure of the typical modern Japanese home. Ken and his host family discuss Ken's stay over the dinner table. This favorite lesson introduces you to many of the basic foods and methods of preparation in Japanese cooking. Another essential part of living in an urban city such as Tokyo is knowing how to use public transportation. Finally, you will be given a thorough tour of Tokyo through your study of the train system there.

Tasks

As in previous volumes, each lesson is prefaced by oral tasks that you will be expected to successfully complete at the lesson's end. This task is intentionally placed at the start of each lesson so that you will have a good idea of what you should be able to accomplish by the end of the lesson.

Dialogues/Narratives

In this volume, you will find dialogues or narratives that serve as the core of the lesson. You are expected to study these carefully, as these incorporate all of the new *kanji*, vocabulary and grammar in the lesson, and also provide you with some interesting insights into Japanese life. Use your dialogues and narratives as well to help you review as you conclude each lesson.

Vocabulary

In order to communicate successfully, it is imperative that you retain a rich and abundant vocabulary. This volume continues to provide you with many useful vocabulary items that will be particulary helpful as you describe the Japanese language, people, society and culture. Each vocabulary item is still accompanied by cartoon-like illustrations, which often help to define words better than English explanations can. As in previous volumes a list consisting of previously learned vocabulary words that reappear in the new lesson is provided for each lesson.

Grammar

We have continued the tradition set in earlier volumes of keeping our grammatical explanations simple and understandable. You will learn to distinguish various speech styles and forms, such as the plain and polite styles, and male and female speech. You will learn to use noun clauses; several kinds of conditionals (if...); express time sequences (when, before, after, while, during); state reasons and regrets; give advice; express beginning, concluding and continuation of actions; justify your actions or statements overtly and by implication; and express ease or difficulty of certain actions. In addition, you will be able to express information through hearsay; indicate doubt and lack of knowledge about situations; compare things, actions or situations to other similar things, actions or situations; state plans you are considering and how you prepare for an impending activity; and express how you deal with a situation even if it is not what you had expected. These cover some of the major grammatical areas - - others are introduced as well.

Writing

Adding to the 121 *kanji* you have already learned in Volumes 1 and 2, this volume introduces 12 to 13 new *kanji* every lesson. In addition, new readings for previously learned *kanji* are listed. You will learn 98 additional new *kanji*. Fifty three additional *kanji* are included for recognition only. The student will have learned to write 219 *kanji* by the end of this volume. Early in the volume, the lesson on using a *kanji* dictionary will provide you with a solid base for understanding the construction, meanings and readings of *kanji*. We hope this lesson will help you to better decipher and appreciate *kanji*!

Culture

You will notice that the culture notes in this volume are far more extensive. It is with good reason, of course, as you (through Ken) are now experiencing the true Japan. Through these culture notes, you will be prepared to use a few Japanese proverbs well, write letters and address Japanese letters properly, appreciate Japanese entertainment, get around Tokyo, feel comfortable visiting a Japanese home and eating a Japanese meal.

Class Activities

Your teacher may use some of the activities provided in each lesson. They are designed for you to practice grammatical structures and vocabulary in fun, communicative ways. Some activities will reinforce your understanding of the cultural aspects introduced in the lesson. Even if these activities are not all done in class, they can serve as good practice for you as you progress through the lesson. Give them a try!

Good luck as you enter the third phase of your studies of the fascinating world of Japanese language and culture! Enjoy your adventure to Japan! がんばりましょう！

ACKNOWLEDGMENTS

Adventures in Japanese was developed through the contributions of our current and former colleagues at Punahou School and beyond, feedback from thousands of students who have spent time in our classrooms, and the support of administration and staff of Punahou School. We gratefully express our appreciation to all who contributed in any way, even if we may have failed to mention them below.

First and foremost, we express our warm thanks to all of our students who have contributed directly and indirectly to the development of the text. They provided us with a purpose, motivated us to continue, taught us, gave us ideas, suggestions and even criticism, and encouraged us in many ways.

We acknowledge Professor Seiichi Makino of Princeton University who wrote the foreword, conducted workshops for us and offered us much support and encouragement. We thank Professor Masako Himeno of the Tokyo University of Foreign Studies' Japanese Language Institute for her guidance over many portions of the text and for her valuable suggestions and support throughout the project. We express our gratitude to our illustrators, Punahou graduate Michael Muronaka, former colleague Emiko Kaylor and Masumi Takabayashi. We thank all of our Japanese language colleagues at Punahou. In particular for this volume, we extend our appreciation to Junko Ady and Jan Asato, who created many of the ancillaries such as audio recordings, listening exercises, exams, worksheets and the anticipated CD-ROMs. We also thank former Japanese language colleagues Naomi Okada and Kazuko Love for their substantial contributions to Volume 3. We express our appreciation to Miyoko Kamikawa for her assistance with the lessons on Japanese proverbs. We thank Kazutou Ishida for his assistance with the audio recordings, and student assistants Kohei Itokawa and Motoya Nakamura as well. We acknowledge the Tokyo Denki Daigaku Shashin-bu and its president Kazuyuki Uchida, Tokyo Johnan High School and Jan Asato for their photo contributions. We thank Tamako Takehara of the Tokyo Denki Daigaku for coordinating and expediting the acquisition of many of our photos. As always, we are appreciative of Wes Peterson for generously sharing his technological expertise and support throughout the project.

We also thank Carol Loose, Michele Morikami, Linda Rucci, Martha Lanzas, Susan Oi and the staff at the Punahou Visual Production Center for their years of assistance with the compilation of the early versions of the text. In addition, we recognize Mike Dahlquist and his staff at the Punahou Instructional Television for their help in the production of most of the preliminary audio materials.

Our gratitude is also extended to Harry Kubo, Shoji Oi, Junko Ady, Mia Tanaka, Jean Colburn and Yuto Kakuta, who produced the final version of the audio recordings. We extend our thanks to Mr. Takuro Ichikawa, a leader of the Japanese Traditional Performing Arts Society, for the use of the flute and drum sounds.

We thank all of the administrators at Punahou School for their support in our textbook effort.

Finally, we express our appreciation to our families for their patience and unwavering support of our efforts throughout our many years of work on the *Adventures in Japanese* series.

Hiromi Peterson and Naomi Hirano-Omizo

REFERENCES

Hello Japan. Tokyo: メイクフレンズ・フォー・ジャパン・キャンペーン事務局, 1991.92

岩波現代用字辞典　第二版　岩波書店, 1989

Japan: An Illustrated Encyclopedia. Tokyo: Kodansha Ltd., 1993

Japan: A Bilingual Encyclopedia, Tokyo: Kodansha Ltd., 1998

Japanese In Modules Book 1 & Book 2. Tokyo: ALC Press Inc., 1993

JTB's Illustrated Book Series. Tokyo: Nihon Kotsukosha Shuppan Jigyokyoku

Joya, Mock. *Things Japanese.* Tokyo: Tokyo News Service, 1960

Kawashima, Masaru. 漢字をおぼえる辞典.. Tokyo: Obunsha, 1975

Katsumata, Senkichiro. *Kenkyusha's New Japanese-English Dictionary,* Tokyo: Kenkyusha, 1954

Makino, Seiichi and Tsutsui, Michio. *A Dictionary of Basic Japanese Grammar.* Tokyo: The Japan Times, 1998

Nagara, Susumu. *Japanese For Everyone.* Tokyo: Gakken Co. Ltd., 1991

Otsuka T., Yoshikawa Y. & Kawamura J. *Sanseido's College Crown English-Japanese Dictionary.* Tokyo: Sanseido, 1964

Sato, Esther and Sakihara, Jean. *Japanese Now,* Vols. 1 - 4. Honolulu: University of Hawaii Press, 1982

Schilling, Mark. *The Encyclopedia of Japanese Pop Culture.* Weatherhill, 1997

Seki, Kiyo and Yoshiki, Hisako. *Nihongo Kantan.* Tokyo: Kenkyuusha, 1988

書の年賀状. Tokyo: 日貿出版社, 1989

スクールカット図典学校生活編 & 家庭生活編. Tokyo: 東陽出版, 1997

Tohsaku, Yasuhiko. *Yookoso.* New York: McGraw-Hill, 1994

藤堂方式／小学生版漢字なりたち辞典, 藤堂明保監修教育社編, Tokyo: 教育社, 1997

東京外国語大学附属日本語学校, 初級日本語. Tokyo: 三省堂, 1990

Young, John and Nakajima-Okano, Kimiko. *Learn Japanese: New College Text,* Vols. 1 - 4. Honolulu: University of Hawaii Press, 1985

USEFUL EXPRESSIONS

1. おはよう。*
   Good morning. [informal]

2. おはようございます。*
   Good morning. [formal]

3. お願いします。*
   [Used when one asks a favor of someone.]

4. もう一度お願いします。* or もう一度言って下さい。*
   One more time please.   Please say it one more time.

5. どうぞ。*
   Please.

6. すみません。遅くなりました。*
   I am sorry to be late. [lit., I am sorry. I have become late.]

7. ロッカーへ行ってもいいですか。*
   May I go to my locker? [Asking for permission.]

1

8. すみません。鉛筆（えんぴつ）を貸（か）して下さい。 *
   Excuse me, please lend me a pencil. [request]

9. すみません。紙（かみ）を一枚（まい）下さい。 *
   Excuse me, please give me one sheet of paper. [request]

10. いいですねえ。 *
    How nice!
    [Used when one receives good news of something that will soon occur.]

11. 良かったですねえ。 *
    How nice!
    [Expression of happiness or support on a past event.]

12. 残念（ざんねん）ですねえ。 *
    How disappointing! Too bad!
    [Expression of disappointment at something that will not happen.]

13. 残念（ざんねん）でしたねえ。 *
    How disappointing! Too bad!
    [Expression of disappointment at an unfortunate past occurrence.]

14. いいですよ。 *
    It is good, you know.
    [The sentence-ending particle よ expresses emphasis or exclamation.]

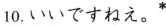
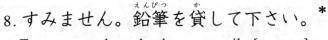

15. いいですね。 *

    It is good, isn't it?

    [The sentence ending particle ね is used when the speaker wishes to
    seek agreement or confirmation from the listener.]

16. いいですねえ。 *

    It is good! How nice!

    [The sentence ending particle ねえ expresses exclamation and surprise.]

17. そうですねえ . . . ええと . . . あのう . . . *

    Let me see . . . Well . . .

    [Used when one needs time to think and pause in search of the right
    thing to say.]

18. （はい、）そうです。 *

    Yes, it is.

    [Expression of agreement. Used as a response.]

19. そうですか。 *

    Is that so?

    [Used very often by a listener as a response to new information he/she
    receives, often used as one nods.]

20. 本当<ruby>とう</ruby>ですか。 *

    Is it true? Really?

21. お先<ruby>さき</ruby>に。

Excuse me for going/doing something first.

22. 失礼します。

> Excuse me, I must be going now.
> [Used when one must leave a place. lit., I will be rude.]
>
> Excuse me, I am about to interrupt.
> [Used to apologize before interrupting another person.]

23. 失礼しました。

> I am sorry to have inconvenienced you
> or for a rude act I have committed.

* Previously introduced.

（かん　じ　ふくしゅう）

I	一 いち, ひと(つ)	二 に, ふた(つ)	三 さん, みっ(つ)	四 し, よ, よん, よっ(つ)	五 ご, いつ(つ)			
	六 ろく, むっ(つ)	七 なな, しち, なな(つ)	八 はち, やっ(つ)	九 きゅう, く, ここの(つ)	十 じゅう, とお			
	日 [に], にち, ひ, [び], か	月 がつ, げつ	火 か	水 みず, すい	木 き, もく	金 かね, きん	土 ど	
II 2 課	口 くち, [ぐち]	目 め	人 ひと, にん, じん	本 もと, ほん, [ぽん], [ぼん]	今 いま, こん	年 とし, ねん	私 [わたし], わたくし	曜 よう
II 3 課	上 うえ	下 した, くだ(さい)	大 おお(きい), たい, だい	小 ちい(さい), しょう	夕 ゆう	何 なに, なん	中 なか, ちゅう	外 そと, がい
II 4 課	行 い(く), こう	来 き(ます), く(る), こ らい	子 こ	車 くるま, しゃ	学 がく, [がっ]	校 こう	見 み(る)	良 よ(い)	食 た(べる), しょく
II 5 課	川 かわ, [がわ]	山 やま, さん	出 で(る), だ(す)	先 せん	生 う(まれる), せい	父 ちち, [とう]	母 はは, [かあ]	毎 まい	書 か(く), しょ
II 6 課	手 て	耳 みみ	門 もん	聞 き(く), ぶん	女 おんな	好 す(き)	田 た, [だ]	男 おとこ	
II 7 課	言 い(う)	語 ご	寺 てら, [でら], じ	時 とき, じ	間 あいだ, かん	分 わ(かる), ふん, [ぶん], ぶん	正 ただ(しい), しょう	家 いえ, か	々 [repeat]

II 9課	白 しろ, はく	百 ひゃく, [びゃく], [びゃく]	千 せん, [ぜん]	万 まん	方 かた, ほう	玉 たま, [だま]	国 くに, [ぐに] こく, [ごく]	安 やす(い)	高 たか(い), こう	
II 10課	牛 うし, ぎゅう	半 はん	*手 て, しゅ	友 とも	帰 かえ(る)	待 ま(つ)	持 も(つ)	米 こめ	番 ばん	事 こと, [ごと], じ
II 11課	雨 あめ	電 でん	天 てん	気 き	会 あ(う), かい	話 はな(す), はなし, [ばなし], わ	売 う(る)	読 よ(む)		
II 13課	右 みぎ	左 ひだり	入 い(れる), はい(る), [いり]	物 もの, ぶつ	名 な, めい	前 まえ, ぜん	戸 と, [ど]	所 ところ, [どころ] しょ, [じょ]	近 ちか(い)	
II 14課	立 た(つ), りつ	作 つく(る), さく	肉 にく	魚 さかな	多 おお(い), た	少 すく(ない), すこ(し)	古 ふる(い)	新 あたら(しい), しん	*生 う(まれる), せい, なま	
II 15課	才 さい	心 こころ, しん	思 おも(う)	休 やす(み)	買 か(う)	早 はや(い)	自 じ	犬 いぬ	太 ふと(る)	屋 や

* Previously introduced.

A. クラスワーク　（じこしょうかい）

Students form two circles of equal number, one circle inside the other. The students in the inner circle face partners in the outer circle and at the teacher's signal, begin to introduce themselves to one another in Japanese, including as much information as possible. At the teacher's signal, the students stop and students in the outer circle move one position to the right and again introduce themselves to their new partner. Continue until the teacher ends the activity.

B. ペアワーク→クラスワーク

だれでしょう。

Interview a partner by asking Questions 1 to 5. Fill in the form for Questions 1 to 5 with your partner's answers in Japanese at the right. For Questions 6 and 7, circle the correct words, and for Question 8, fill in the (　). The teacher collects all the forms and reads them one by one. Match the descriptions with the correct person in your class.

1. お名前は？	
2. 何年生ですか。	
3. とくいなかもくは？	
4. しゅみは？	
5. 上手なスポーツは？	
6.	（男／女）
7. せが	（高い／ひくい）
8. シャツのいろは	（　　　　　）

C. ペアワーク （Useful Expressions）

Role play the following situations using appropriate expressions. Act each out with your partner.

1. A student needs to get a permission slip signed by the teacher. He/She goes to the teacher's office/classroom.

Student:	Excuse me.	Teacher:	Yes, come in.
Student:	Good morning, teacher.	Teacher:	Good morning.
Student:	Ask for a favor.	Teacher:	(Teacher signs.)
	(Hands over the pen & paper.)		Here (you are).
Student:	Thank you very much.	Teacher:	No problem.
Student:	Excuse me for having been rude.		

2. Class is in session. A student has a permission slip to leave class early for a school athletic game.

Student:	(Raises hand.) Excuse me.	Teacher:	Yes.
Student:	(Shows the permission slip.)		
	Is it okay ?	Teacher:	Yes, you may go (you know).
Student:	(Gathers things, bows to the class.)	Teacher:	Yes.
	Excuse me for leaving first.		

3. A student is late to class.

Teacher:	You're late!	Student:	I'm sorry for being late.
Teacher:	What happened?	Student:	Well... (Stall until you can think of a good reason... then give your reason.)
Teacher:	I see. Hurry and sit.	Student:	Yes.

4. Class is in session. The teacher is handing out a one-page quiz. A student doesn't get a quiz sheet and doesn't have anything to write with.

Student:	Excuse me, please give me one sheet.	Teacher:	Here you are.
Student:	Excuse me, may I borrow a pencil ?	Teacher:	No, I do not have one.
Student:	Excuse me, may I go to my locker ?	Teacher:	Yes, go quickly.
	Excuse me. (Leaving the class.)		
	(Student goes to his/her locker and gets a pencil.)		
Student:	Excuse me for interrupting the class.		

5. There is a poster on the wall for a lottery. Both students take a lottery ticket and open them.

Student 1 :	I won!	Student 2:	Really ?
Student 1 :	Yes, it's really true, you know.	Student 2:	How nice !
Student 1 :	How about you ? (Use name.)	Student 2:	I lost.
Student 1 :	Is that so ? That's too bad.		

The teacher gives the prize to the winning student. Everyone in the class says, "HOW NICE!"

D. ペアワーク（かんじ）

Copy and cut these cards out along the lines. Place all these *kanji* cards in the correct spaces on the chart on the following pages.

一	年	夕	六	近	水	良	私	四	母
下	月	目	先	来	金	時	持	読	土
口	戸	男	本	半	名	新	曜	二	今
何	人	八	小	行	聞	中	天	屋	日
門	立	子	作	学	左	見	書	食	事
川	山	家	五	生	父	万	毎	木	七
手	待	番	車	言	好	田	出	三	上
百	語	寺	外	話	分	正	大	々	白
帰	友	千	間	方	女	国	安	高	校
牛	右	早	肉	犬	耳	米	古	所	休
雨	魚	才	気	会	入	売	少	思	多
玉	心	電	物	買	前	自	火	九	太
十									

I									
	いち, ひと(つ)	に, ふた(つ)	さん, みっ(つ)	し,よん, よっ(つ)	ご, いつ(つ)	★	★	★	★
	ろく, むっ(つ)	なな, しち, なな(つ)	はち, やっ(つ)	きゅう, く, ここの(つ)	じゅう, とお	★	★	★	★
	[に], にち, ひ, [び], か	がつ, げつ	か	みず, すい	き, もく	かね, きん	ど	★	★
II 2課	くち, [ぐち]	め	ひと, にん, じん	もと ほん, [ぼん], [ぽん]	いま こん	とし, ねん	[わたし], わたくし	よう	★
II 3課	うえ	した, くだ(さい)	おお(きい), たい, だい	ちい(さい), しょう	ゆう	なに, なん	なか, ちゅう	そと, がい	★
II 4課	い(く), こう	き(ます), く(る), こ らい	こ	くるま, しゃ	がく, [がっ]	こう	み(る)	よ(い)	た(べる), しょく
II 5課	かわ, [がわ]	やま, さん	で(る), だ(す)	せん	う(まれる), せい, なま	ちち, [とう]	はは, [かあ]	まい	か(く), しょ
II 6課	て, しゅ	みみ	もん	き(く), ぶん	おんな	す(き)	た [だ]	おとこ	★
II 7課	い(う)	ご	てら, [でら] じ	とき, じ	あいだ, かん	わ(かる), ふん, [ぷん], ぶん	ただ(しい), しょう	いえ, か	[repeat]

課										
II 9課	しろ, はく	ひゃく, [びゃく], [ぴゃく]	せん, [ぜん]	まん	かた, ほう	たま, [だま]	くに, [ぐに], こく, [ごく]	やす(い)	たか(い), こう	★
II 10課	うし, ぎゅう	はん	★	とも	かえ(る)	ま(つ)	も(つ)	こめ	ばん	こと, [ごと], じ
II 11課	あめ	でん	てん	き	あ(う), かい	はな(す), はなし, [ばなし], わ	う(る)	よ(む)	★	★
II 13課	みぎ	ひだり	い(れる), はい(る), [いり]	もの, ぶつ	な, めい	まえ, ぜん	と, ど	ところ, [どころ], しょ, [じょ]	ちか(い)	★
II 14課	た(つ), りつ	つく(る), さく	にく	さかな	おお(い), た	すく(ない), すこ(し)	ふる(い)	あたら(しい), しん	★	★
II 15課	さい	こころ, しん	おも(う)	やす(み)	か(う)	はや(い)	じ	いぬ	ふと(る)	や

★ Previously introduced.

11

By the end of this lesson, you will be able to communicate the information below in the given situation. Complete the following tasks with a partner. You are expected to conduct a natural conversation using as many new vocabulary and grammatical structures as you can, while appropriately incorporating vocabulary and structures you have learned previously. Use the appropriate speech style (plain or polite) and male/female speech if appropriate. Practice the dialogue with your partner; the aim is not to memorize a dialogue, but to communicate meaningfully with your partner on the topics below.

【 III - 1 トピック 1 】

Partner **A**: *High school student from the U. S. visiting Japan for the first time*
Partner **B**: *A's host older brother/sister in Japan*

Situation: *A has just settled into his/her host family's home, and B has just returned from school before dinner. A and B get acquainted in the living area.*

A and **B** introduce themselves to one another with all the introductory greetings. **B** asks questions about **A**, while volunteering similar information about him/herself such as age, grade, family: parents, siblings, grandparents (names, jobs, grade [if applicable], likes/dislikes). **A** also volunteers information and asks **B** questions. **B** asks **A** what **A** wants to do in Japan. **A** responds.

【 III - 1 トピック 2 】

Partner **A**: *High school student from the U. S. visiting Japan for the first time*
Partner **B**: *A's host father/mother in Japan*

Situation: *A has just been introduced to his /herhost parent (B) on the first day of A's arrival to Japan. They get acquainted before they set off for the host family's home.*

A and **B** introduce themselves to one another with all the introductory greetings. **B** asks **A** many questions about **A**'s age, grade, family, likes and dislikes. **A** also volunteers some information about him/herself. After some conversation, **B** compliments **A** on his/her skill in Japanese, and asks briefly about **B**'s studies in Japanese (*kanji* writing ability) and favorite subjects. **A** responds appropriately. **B** advises **A** to let him/her know if there is anything **B** can do to help **A**. **A** thanks **B** and they decide to go.

【会話１】

＜日本のホストファミリーの家でお母さんと＞

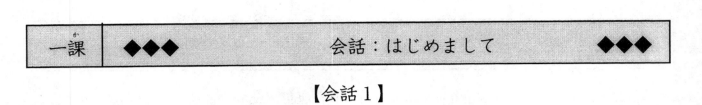

ケン　　　：はじめまして。ケンです。どうぞよろしく。

お母さん：こちらこそ。よろしくね。ケンは、何才？

ケン　　　：十六才です。高校の二年です。

お母さん：そう。日本語が上手ねえ。

ケン　　　：いいえ、とんでもないです。まだ下手です。

お母さん：漢字も書けるの？

ケン　　　：ええ。でも、五十ぐらいしか書けません。

　　　　　　漢字を書くのは苦手(にが)です。

お母さん：ご家族は何人？

ケン　　　：五人です。父と母と姉と妹とぼくです。

お母さん：お父様(さま)のお仕事は？

ケン　　　：父は医者(いしゃ)をしていて、母は銀行で働(はたら)いています。

お母さん：そう。ご兄弟は？

ケン　　　：姉のジーナは、去年高校を卒業(そつぎょう)して、今、カリフォルニアの大学

　　　　　　に行っています。物理を専攻(せんこう)(り)しています。妹のミリーはまだ

　　　　　　幼稚園(ようちえん)です。

お母さん：そう。ケンはどんなことが好きなの？

ケン　　　：そうですねえ...　ぼくはスポーツをすることとギターを

ひくことが好きです。特にサッカーが得意です。

お母さん：何かきらいな食べ物、ある？

ケン　　　：だいたい何でも食べられますが、人参が苦手です。

お母さん：そう。だめよ。日本で一番何をしたいって思ってるの？

ケン　　　：さあ...　何でもしてみたいです。

お母さん：何かあったら、いつでも言ってね。さあ、夕食を食べましょう。

ケン　　　：はい、いただきます。

【会話２】

<日本のホストファミリーの家でお父さんと>

ケン　　　：はじめまして。ケンです。どうぞよろしく。

お父さん：こちらこそ。よろしく。ケンは、何才？

ケン　　　：十六才です。高校の二年です。

お父さん：そうか。日本語が上手だねえ。

ケン　　　：いいえ、とんでもないです。まだ下手です。

お父さん：漢字も書けるかい？

ケン　　　：ええ。でも、五十ぐらいしか書けません。

　　　　　　漢字を書くのは苦手です。

お父さん：ご家族は何人？

ケン　　　：五人です。父と母と姉と妹とぼくです。

お父さん：お父さんのお仕事は？

ケン　　　：父は医者をしていて、母は銀行で働いています。

お父さん：そうか。兄弟は？

ケン　　　：姉のジーナは、去年高校を卒業して、今、カリフォルニアの大学
　　　　　　に行っています。物理を専攻しています。妹のミリーはまだ
　　　　　　幼稚園です。

お父さん：そうか。ケンはどんなことが好きかい？

ケン　　　：そうですねえ ...　 ぼくはスポーツをすることとギターを
　　　　　　ひくことが好きです。特にサッカーが得意です。

お父さん：何かきらいな食べ物、あるかい？

ケン　　　：だいたい何でも食べられますが、人参が苦手です。

お父さん：そうか。だめだよ。日本で一番何をしたいって思ってる？

ケン　　　：さあ ...　 何でもしてみたいです。

お父さん：何かあったら、いつでも言ってくれよ。さあ、夕食、食べよう。

ケン　　　：はい、いただきます。

A. ことわざ Proverbs

Japanese proverbs reflect Japanese people's values and their way of thinking. Here are some common Japanese proverbs.

1.「十人十色」_{じゅうにん と いろ} ＊

じゅうにん refers to 10 people. といろ is an abbreviated form of とおいろ which means 10 colors. 「じゅうにんといろ」 literally means "Ten men, ten colors" and may be interpreted as "Many men, many tastes."

2.「かえるの子はかえる」＊

「かえるの子はかえる」 means "A frog's child is a frog." A child resembles his/her parents and will have a life like his/her parents. A child has the same kind of abilities as his/her parents. Therefore, parents should not expect more of their children than they themselves could achieve. There is the similar Western expression: "The apple doesn't fall very far from the tree."

3.「猫に小判」_{ねこ　こ ばん} ＊

ねこ is a cat. こばん is a gold coin used during the Tokugawa period. 「ねこにこばん」 means "to give a gold coin to a cat." It is used when someone receives something and cannot or does not appreciate its value. This is similar to the Western expression "To cast pearls before swine."

4.「猿も木から落ちる」_{さる　　　　お} ＊

さる is a monkey. も means "even." 木 is a tree. から means "from." おちる means "to fall." 「さるも　木から　おちる」 translates as, "Even monkeys fall from trees." It suggests that even skillful people sometimes make mistakes.

5. 「三日ぼうず」 *

みっか means "three days" and ぼうず means "a monk."
「みっかぼうず」 is used to describe one who does not
persevere or one who is not a steady, reliable worker.

6. 「ばかにつける薬はない」 *

ばか is an idiot. つける means "to apply." くすり is "medicine."
ない means "does not exist." 「ばかに つける くすりは ない」
is translated as "There is no medicine for stupidity" or "There is no cure
for an idiot."

7. 「石の上にも三年」 *

いし means "a stone." This proverb means that (sitting) on a stone for as
long as three years makes anything possible. If you sit on the stone as long
as three years, even the stone becomes warm. This proverb suggests that
perseverance overcomes all things.

8. 「となりの花は赤い」 *

となり means "next door." Translated, this proverb means "Flowers next door are red." It is
equivalent to the English saying, "The grass is greener on the other side of the fence." This proverb
is used when someone feels that things he/she does not own look attractive, but once he/she obtains
them, they are not so attractive any more.

9. 「花より団子」 *

だんご means "sweet rice dumplings." When translated, this proverb
means "Sweet rice dumplings rather than flowers." It is similar to the
English proverb "The belly is not filled with fair words." In other
words, one's physical needs take precedence over more lofty ideals.

10.「負けるが勝ち」*

This proverb means "Defeat is a win." An equivalent English proverb is "Losers gainers."

11.「海より深い母の愛」*

ふかい means "deep." This proverb translates as "Mother's love is deeper than the ocean." A mother is always thinking about her children and will do anything for their sake.

12.「ちりもつもれば山となる」

ちり means "dust." つもれば means "if it amasses or if it accumulates."
This proverb translates as "Even dust amassed will make a mountain."
If you do something a little at a time, someday you will be able to
achieve your lofty goal.

*Previously introduced.

一課

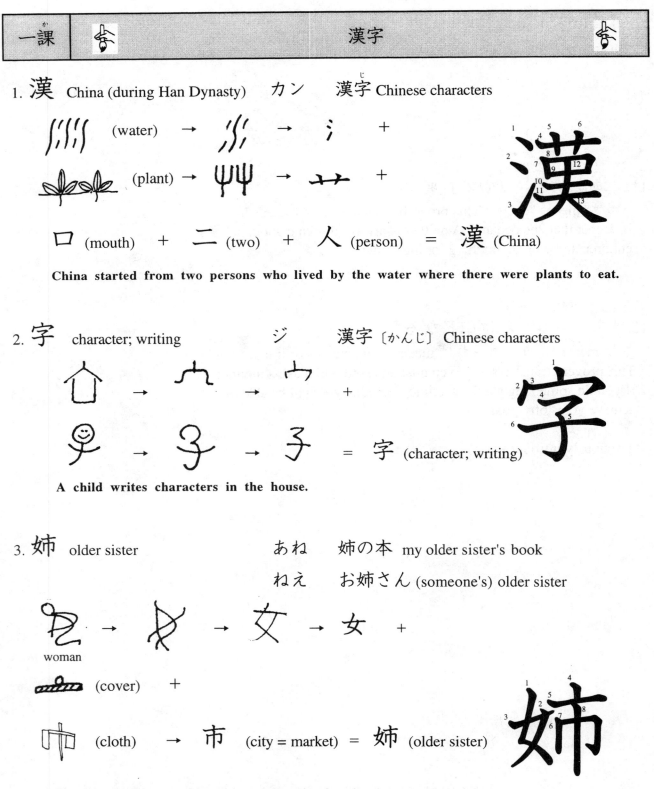

1. 漢　China (during Han Dynasty)　カン　漢字 Chinese characters

‖‖‖ (water) → 〳〵 → 氵 +

🌿 (plant) → 屮屮 → 艹 +

口 (mouth) ＋ 二 (two) ＋ 人 (person) ＝ 漢 (China)

China started from two persons who lived by the water where there were plants to eat.

2. 字　character; writing　ジ　漢字〔かんじ〕Chinese characters

⌂ → ⌂ → 宀 +

☺ → 子 → 子 ＝ 字 (character; writing)

A child writes characters in the house.

3. 姉　older sister　あね　姉の本 my older sister's book
　　　　　　　　　　　ねえ　お姉さん (someone's) older sister

woman → → 女 → 女 +

🗹 (cover) +

巾 (cloth) → 市 (city = market) ＝ 姉 (older sister)

The female person who wants to live in the city is my older sister.

4. 妹 younger sister   　　　　いもうと   　　妹の名前 my younger sister's name

   　　　　　　　　　　　　　　　　　　　　妹さん someone else's younger sister

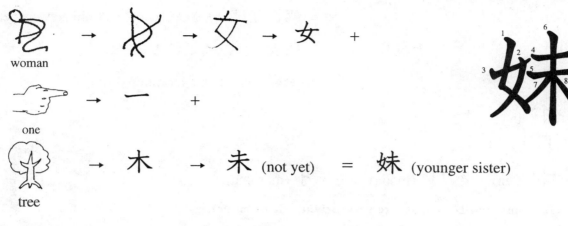

woman

one

tree

未 (not yet)   =   妹 (younger sister)

The female who is not grown-up yet is my younger sister.

5. 兄 older brother   　　　　あに   　　　兄の車 my older brother's car

   　　　　　　　　　　　　　　にい   　　　お兄さん someone's older brother

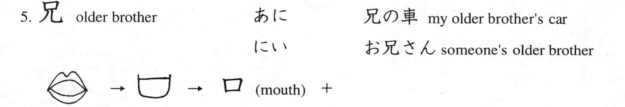

(mouth) +

(legs)   =   兄 (older brother)

**My older brother is the mouthpiece (spokesman) of the family
and does all the family's legwork.**

6. 弟 younger brother   　　　おとうと   　弟の本 my younger brother's book

   　　　　　　　　　　　　　　　　　　　　弟さん someone else's younger brother

   　　　　　　　　　　　　　☆   　　　　　兄弟 〔きょうだい〕 siblings

   弟 = 弟 (younger brother)

**Younger brother is tied up to the lower part of the
tree and is marked.**

一課

7. 朝　morning　　　　　あさ　　　　　朝御飯〔あさごはん〕breakfast

〔ごはん〕

　　　　　　　　　　　　　　　　　　毎朝〔まいあさ〕every morning

　　　　　　　　　　　　　　　　　　朝日新聞〔あさひしんぶん〕Asahi Newspaper

　　　　　　　　　チョウ　　　　　　朝食〔ちょうしょく〕breakfast

　　　　　　　　　☆　　　　　　　　今朝〔けさ〕this morning

十 (ten) ＋

日 (sun) ＋

十 (ten) ＋ 月 (moon) ＝ 朝 (morning)

Ten suns and 10 moons are very bright. It is morning.

8. 昼　daytime　　　　　ひる　　　　　昼御飯〔ひるごはん〕lunch

〔ごはん〕

　　　　　　　　　チュウ　　　　　　昼食〔ちゅうしょく〕lunch

尸 (roof) ＋

丶 (cover) ＋

日 (sun) ＋

一 (one) ＝ 昼 (daytime)

**It is just right to take a nap under the roof because the sun
at one o'clock in the daytime is just too hot.**

9. 明　is bright　　　　あか（るい）　明るい所〔あかるいところ〕a bright place

　　　　　　　　　☆　　　　　　　　明日〔あした〕tomorrow

⊙ (sun) ＋ ☽ (moon) ＝ 明 (is bright)

The sun and moon together are bright.

10. 去 past　　　　キョ　　　　　　去年〔きょねん〕 last year

土 (soil) → 土 → 土 ＋

(cut wood with a knife) → ㇄ → ム ＝ 去 (past)　　去

You planted a tree last year, so you can have free wood this year.

11. 銀 silver　　　　ギン　　　　　　銀行〔ぎんこう〕 bank

銀のネックレス a silver necklace

→ 金 (gold; metal) ＋

→ 良 → 良 (good) 一 ▼ ＝ 銀 (silver)　　銀

a grain of rice and a person (This *kanji* alone means "good.")

After gold, silver is the best metal.

12. 仕 to serve　　　　シ　　　　　　仕事〔しごと〕 job

仕方〔しかた〕がない It cannot be helped.

→ イ ＋

a person

→ 士 → 士 ＝ 仕 (to serve)　　仕

samurai

A *samurai* is a person who serves the lord.

【読みかえの漢字】

1. 父 father ちち＊ 父の仕事〔しごと〕 my father's job

      とう＊ お父さん someone else's father

      フ   祖父 my own grandfather

2. 母 mother はは＊ 母の名前〔なまえ〕 my mother's name

      かあ＊ お母さん someone else's mother

      ボ   祖母 my own grandmother

3. 先 first; previous セン＊ 先生〔せんせい〕 teacher

          先月〔せんげつ〕 last month

      さき   お先に。 Excuse me for going/doing something first.

【読めればいい漢字】

1. 家族 かぞく family
2. 友達 ともだち friend
3. 質問 しつもん question
4. 答え こたえ answer
5. 宿題 しゅくだい homework
6. 試験 しけん exam
7. 昨日 きのう yesterday

Let's review previous vocabulary!

A. めいし Nouns

1.	ホストファミリー	host family	16.	お仕事 [しごと]	job [polite]
2.	家	house	17.	いしゃ	doctor [informal]
3.	お母さん	(someone's) mother	18.	銀行 [ぎんこう]	bank
4.	何才？	how old?	19.	ご兄弟 [きょうだい]	siblings [polite]
5.	高校	high school	20.	去年 [きょねん]	last year
6.	二年	second year	21.	今	now
7.	五十ぐらい	about 50	22.	カリフォルニア	California
8.	(ご)家族 [かぞく]	(someone's) family	23.	どんなこと？	what kind of thing?
9.	何人 [なんにん]？	how many (people)?	24.	スポーツ	sports
10.	五人	five people	25.	ギター	guitar
11.	父	(one's own) father	26.	サッカー	soccer
12.	母	(one's own) mother	27.	食べ物	food
13.	姉 [あね]	(one's own) older sister	28.	何か	something
14.	妹 [いもうと]	(one's own) younger sister	29.	物	thing [tangible]
15.	お父さま	father [polite]	30.	一番	No. 1; most

B. どうし Verbs

31. 書ける〔G1かく／かきます〕 — can write [potential form]

32. 書けません〔G1かく／かきます〕 — cannot write [potential form]

33. 書くの〔G1かく／かきます〕 — to write [noun form]

34. はたらいています〔G1はたらく／はたらきます〕 — is working

35. 行っています〔G1いく／いきます〕 — is going; is attending

36. すること〔IRします／して〕 — to do [noun form]

37. ひくこと〔G1ひきます／ひいて〕 — to play (a string instrument) [noun form]

38. ある？〔G1あります／あって〕 — is there? [informal form]

39. 食べられます〔G2たべる／たべます〕 — can eat [potential form]

40. したい〔IRする／します〕 — want to do [informal form]

41. 思っています〔G1おもう／おもいます〕 — is thinking

42. してみたいです〔IRする／します〕 — want to try to do

43. あったら〔G1ある／あります〕 — if there is [TARA form]

44. 言って 〔G1 いう／いいます〕   please say [informal form]
45. 食べましょう 〔G2 たべる／たべます〕   let's eat [formal form]

C. | な けいようし   NA Adjectives |

46. 上手	skillful		50. とくい	be strong at
47. 下手	unskillful		51. きらい	dislike
48. にが手	be poor at		52. だめ	no good
49. 好き	like			

D. | ふくし   Adverbs |

53. まだ ＋ Aff.	still		55. だいたい	generally; roughly
54. とくに	especially			

E. | Expressions |

56. はじめまして	How do you do?
57. どうぞよろしく	Nice to meet you.
58. そう？	Is that so? [informal]
59. とんでもないです	Far from it! [strong denial]
60. そうですねえ . . .	Let me see . . .
61. さあ . . .	Well . . .
62. いただきます	[Used before meals.]

F. | その他   Others |

63. でも、	However,

Activity A

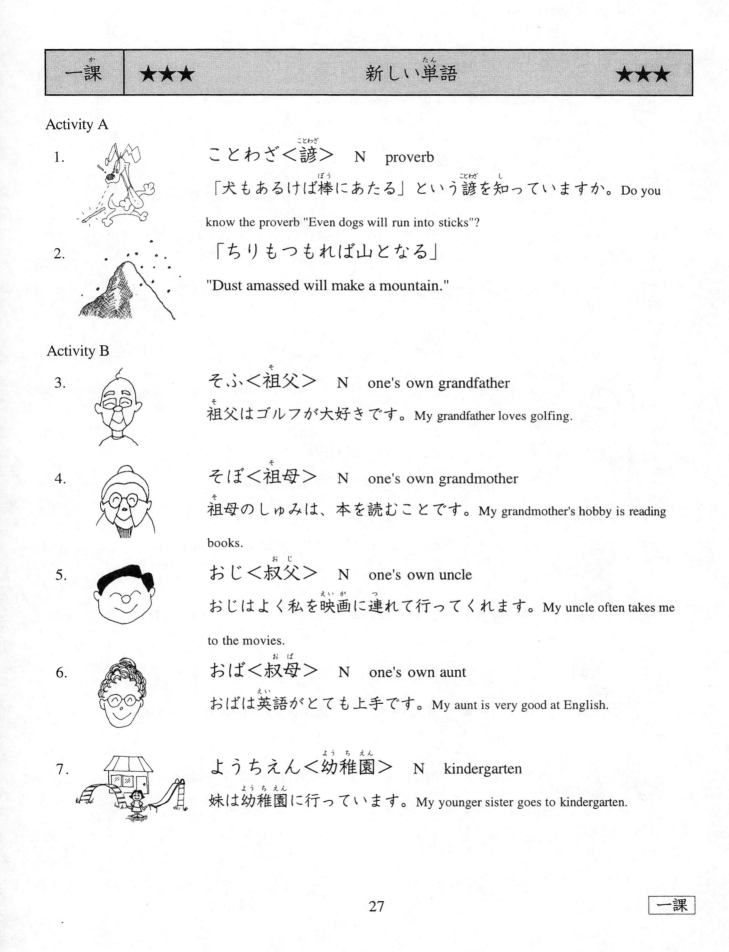

1. ことわざ＜諺＞　N　proverb

「犬_{いぬ}もあるけば棒_{ぼう}にあたる」という諺_{ことわざ}を知_しっていますか。 Do you know the proverb "Even dogs will run into sticks"?

2. 「ちりもつもれば山_{やま}となる」

"Dust amassed will make a mountain."

Activity B

3. そふ＜祖父_そ＞　N　one's own grandfather

祖父_そはゴルフが大好_{だいす}きです。 My grandfather loves golfing.

4. そぼ＜祖母_そ＞　N　one's own grandmother

祖母_そのしゅみは、本_{ほん}を読_よむことです。 My grandmother's hobby is reading books.

5. おじ＜叔父_{お じ}＞　N　one's own uncle

おじはよく私_{わたし}を映画_{えい が}に連_つれて行_いってくれます。 My uncle often takes me to the movies.

6. おば＜叔母_{お ば}＞　N　one's own aunt

おばは英語_{えい ご}がとても上手_{じょうず}です。 My aunt is very good at English.

7. ようちえん＜幼稚園_{よう ち えん}＞　N　kindergarten

妹_{いもうと}は幼稚園_{よう ち えん}に行_いっています。 My younger sister goes to kindergarten.

8. ぶつり＜物理＞　N　physics

物理が苦手です。I am poor at physics.

9. かがく＜化学＞　N　chemistry

化学はおもしろいと思います。I think that chemistry is interesting.

10. りか＜理科＞　N　science

兄は理科が大好きです。My older brother loves science.

11. ぶんがく＜文学＞　N　literature

アメリカ文学のクラスを取っています。I am taking an American literature

class.

12. れきし＜歴史＞　N　history

日本の歴史はとても古いです。Japanese history is very old.

13. (school を) そつぎょうする＜卒業する＞　V3　to graduate from

(school)

姉は去年、高校を卒業しました。 My older sister graduated from high school

last year.

14. せんこうする＜専攻する＞　V3　to major (in)

姉は大学で科学を専攻しています。My older sister is majoring in science at

college.

15. ～しか + Neg.　Nd　only ～ [emphasis]　→ Grammar C.

やさいしか食べません。I eat nothing but vegetables.

日本語が少ししか分かりません。I only understand a little Japanese.

Activity C

16.  こちらこそ。　Exp.　It is I, (not you.)　[emphasis]

こちらこそ、どうぞよろしく。　It is I who should say, "Nice to meet you."

17.  行って来ます。　Exp.　[Used by a family member who leaves home for the day.]

18.  行ってらっしゃい。　Exp.　[Used by a family member who sees off another family member for the day.]

19. ただいま。　Exp.　I'm home. [Used by a family member who has come home.]

20. お帰りなさい。　Exp.　Welcome home. [Used by a family member who welcomes another family member home.]

21. おやすみ（なさい）。　Exp.　Good night.

22. おさきに。＜お先に。＞　Exp.　Excuse me for going/doing something first.

23.  しつれいします。＜失礼します。＞　Exp.　Excuse me, I must be going now.　[Used when one must leave a place. lit., I will be rude.]

Excuse me, I am about to interrupt.　[Used to apologize before interrupting another person.]

一課

24.  しつれいしました。＜失礼しました。＞　Exp.　I am sorry to have inconvenienced you or for a rude act I have committed.

Activity D

25.  にんじん＜人参＞　N　carrot

私は人参がきらいです。I do not like carrots.

Activity E

26.  食べよう　V2 Let's eat [informal form of 食べましょう]

→ Grammar D.　さあ、食べよう。Well, let's eat.

27.  だろう　C　probably is [informal form of でしょう]

日本旅行は楽しいだろう。The Japan trip will probably be enjoyable.

Activity F

28. ちょうしょく＜朝食＞　N　breakfast

私の朝食はパンとコーヒーです。My breakfast is bread and coffee.

29. ちゅうしょく＜昼食＞　N　lunch

昼食をカフェテリアで食べました。I ate lunch at the cafeteria.

30. ゆうしょく＜夕食＞　N　dinner; supper

夕食を一人で食べました。I ate dinner alone.

31. 何でも　Ni+P　anything

ぼくは何でも食べられます。I can eat anything.

32.  いつでも　Ni+P　anytime

もんだい
問題があったら、いつでも言って下さい。　If you have a problem, please tell

me (about it) anytime.

33. どこでも　Ni+P　anywhere

どこでもいいですよ。 Anywhere is fine.

Activity G

34. 一の？　SP　[female sentence ending particle]　→ Grammar F.

漢字が書けるの？ Can you write *kanji*?

35. 一なの？　SP　[female sentence ending particle]　→ Grammar F.

何が好きなの？ What do you like?

36. 一か／かい？　SP　[male informal sentence ending particle]

→ Grammar F.　漢字も書けるかい？ Can you write *kanji* too?

37. 一てくれ　SP　[male informal form of 一て下さい]　→ Grammar F.

何でもぼくに言ってくれ。　Please tell me anything.

38. 一って　P　[informal form of quotation particle と]

はな
花子はパーティーに行くって言っていました。Hanako was saying that she

will go to the party.

39.  かえる＜変える＞　V2　to change (something)

か
MASU form を OO form に変えよう。 Let's change the MASU form to

the OO form.

40.  つかう＜使う＞　V1　to use

おはしを使って、食べよう。 I will eat it using chopsticks.

A. 姉のジーナ　Noun 1 の Noun 2

The particle の normally separates a modifier from the noun it modifies, i.e., アメリカの車. の may also be used in situations where the first noun clarifies or helps to define the second noun. For example, いもうとのみちこ means my younger sister Michiko. いしゃの 山田さん means Yamada, who is a doctor. It does not mean Yamada's doctor.

1. 妹のケリーはまだ小学生です。　　　　　My younger sister Kelly is still an elementary student.

2. 兄の大輔は銀行に勤めています。　　　　My older brother Daisuke is employed at the bank.

B. 父はいしゃをしています　Occupation をしている。

When one describes a person's occupation, one may simply say, 今田さんは先生です。 However, many Japanese would also say, 今田さんは先生をしています。 Literally, this could be interpreted to mean that Imai is doing the work of a teacher.

1. 母は高校で先生をしています。　　　　My mother is a teacher at a high school.

2. 前、父はカイザー病院で医者をしていました。　My father was a doctor at Kaiser Hospital.

C. 〜しか + Neg. Predicate。　　　　　　　nothing/nobody/no 〜 but 〜; only 〜

しか is a particle that means nothing but 〜, nobody but 〜, no one but 〜, etc. しか always occurs with negative predicates. しか replaces particles を, が, は, replaces or follows へ and に, and follows the particles で, と, から, まで, etc. しか must immediately follow the word which is receiving the "nothing but" emphasis. だけ also means "only." Compare だけ and しか:

a. しか suggests fewness or exclusiveness, while だけ describes the situation in a neutral context.

    1. 私だけ行きました。　　　　　Only I went.

    2. 私しか行きませんでした。　　　Nobody but I went.

b. しか occurs only with negative predicates.

c. The verb かかる "it takes (time)" may be used with しか, but not with だけ.

    1. 学校まで五分しかかかりません。　　It takes only five minutes to go to school.

1. 家族では父しか日本語を話しません。　　No one but my father speaks Japanese in my family.

2. 山本さんは野菜しか食べません。　　　Ms. Yamamoto eats nothing but vegetables.

3. 漢字は百ぐらいしか知りません。   I know only about 100 *kanji*.

4. 兄は東京(に)しか行きませんでした。   My older brother went nowhere but to Tokyo.

5. 弟は学校でしか勉強しません。   My younger brother studies nowhere but at school.

6. あなたとしか話したくないんです。   I do not want to talk to anybody but you.

D. Interrogative Noun (+ へ, に, で, と, から etc.) + でも + Affirmative predicate。

When でも is attached to an interrogative (question word) and is accompanied by an affirmative ending, the particles を, が and は are not used. Other particles へ, に, で etc. precede でも.

何でも   食べる。   I eat anything.
いつでも   いい。   Anytime is fine.
どこででもべんきょう出来る。   I can study anywhere.

Interrogative Noun (+ へ, に, で, と, から etc.) + も + Negative predicate。

When an interrogative (question word) is followed by も and is accompanied by a negative predicate, only the particles listed above appear before も.

何も   食べなかった。   I didn't eat anything.
どこへも   行かなかった。   I didn't go to anywhere.

---

1. 何でも言って下さい。   Please tell me anything.

2. いつでも言って下さい。   Please tell me anytime.

3. どこでもいいですよ。   Anywhere is fine.

4. 家からどこへでも電車で行けます。   You can go anywhere by electric train from our house.

5. どこからでも電話して下さい。   Please call me from anywhere.

6. 今日はまだ何も食べていません。   I have not yet eaten anything today.

7. 昨日はどこへも行きませんでした。   I didn't go anywhere yesterday.

E. Quotation + って + 言う／思っている

In the previous volume, you learned the quotation pattern in which と followed the quote. This new form is simply a more conversational and informal way of quoting someone or expressing one's thoughts.

---

1. 友達はその映画に行くって言ってました。   My friend said that she will go to that movie.

2. 日本で何をしたいって思っていますか。   What are you thinking of doing in Japan?

F. The Verb OO Form   "Let's do ～."   "Shall we do ～?"

This is the informal plain equivalent of the -ましょう form. For Group 1 verbs, the final sound of the verb stem is changed to its corresponding お sound, then lengthened with う. Group 2 - OO verbs are formed by attaching よう to the verb stem.

	MASU form	Dictionary form	OO form
Group 1	のみます (nom-imasu) しにます (shin-imasu) あそびます (asob-imasu) かいます (ka-imasu) まちます (mach-imasu) かえります (kaer-imasu) かきます (kak-imasu) およぎます (oyog-imasu) はなします (hanash-imasu)	のむ (nom-u) しぬ (shin-u) あそぶ (asob-u) かう (ka-u) まつ (mats-u) かえる (kaer-u) かく (kak-u) およぐ (oyog-u) はなす (hanas-u)	のもう (nom-oo) しのう (shin-oo) あそぼう (asob-oo) かおう (ka-oo) まとう (mat-oo) かえろう (kaer-oo) かこう (kak-oo) およごう (oyog-oo) はなそう (hanas-oo)
Group 2	みます (mi-masu) たべます (tabe-masu)	みる (mi-ru) たべる (tabe-ru)	みよう (mi-yoo) たべよう (tabe-yoo)
Irregular	します (shi-masu) きます (ki-masu)	する (su-ru) くる (ku-ru)	しよう (shi-yoo) こよう (ko-yoo)

1. たかし：「今、行こうか。」   "Shall we go now?"

    まり：「ええ、いいわよ。」   "Yes, it's o.k."

2. たかし：「さあ、お昼を食べよう。」   "Well . . . let's eat lunch."

    まり：「うん、行こう。」   "Yes, let's go."

G. 思ってる
い of います／いる is often dropped in informal speech when it follows the verb TE form. This form should not be used in formal writing.

1. 今、何してる？   What are you doing now?

2. 毎日テニスをしてるよ。   I play tennis every day.

一課

H. Speech Styles

A conversation between two people in Japanese can reveal much about the relationship between them. The form of the sentence endings tells us about the degree of closeness between the listener and speaker.

If the formal (polite) form is being used, it is an indication that the speaker and listener do not share a close relationship. The formal (polite) form is represented by です/ます forms, and is used by an inferior in formal situations, such as from student to teacher or salesperson to customer. The formal speech style is also used among adults who do not know each other well or at ceremonies and public speeches and announcements.

If the speaker and listener use informal (plain) sentence endings, they share a close relationship, i.e., good friends or family. The informal (plain) style is also used in specific grammatical positions, such as before extenders つもりです "intend to" and はずです "be expected to." Japanese write diaries in the informal (plain) speech style too. Sometimes, when the speaker addresses himself/herself instead of his/her listener, he/she switches from a formal to informal speech style, even in a formal situation. For example, a student speaking with his/her teacher would use the formal style during the conversation. But if he/she suddenly hurt himself/herself while talking, he/she would use the informal いたい "ouch," rather than the formal form いたいです, because the statement is not directed to the teacher.

Other features of speech change when one uses informal language. One is that certain particles may be omitted. The particles は and を are frequently dropped. Other particles (で, に, へ, から, まで, etc.) are usually not dropped. Another change that occurs with the use of informal speech is that forms of male and female speech (discussed later) often appear. Male and female speech are not generally used in formal speech.

When one speaks formally, one is often more polite in one's use of vocabulary and expressions. See the following pages to see how certain words are made more polite by the addition of prefixes, or with completely different forms.

Students who study Japanese as non-native speakers learn the formal (polite) speech style first because it is a "safer" form to use with teachers and Japanese adults. Japanese children, however, master the informal (plain) speech style before the formal (polite) speech style in Japan. It is important to use the correct style, as it can be offensive or rude to use style incorrectly.

Compare the informal (plain) speech style with each です/ます form in the following chart.

Compare:
A. Conversation between friends.

| ゆき：今日は何曜日？ | What day is today? |
| みか：今日は金曜日よ。 | Today's Friday! |

B. Conversation between a customer and cashier.

| Customer：今日は何曜日ですか。 | What day is today? |
| Cashier： 今日は金曜日です。 | Today is Friday. |

Conjugations

	Formal Speech Style	Informal Speech Style	Functions
1. Verb conjugation	のみます のみません のみました のみませんでした のみますか のんでください のめます のみましょう のんでいます のんでみましょう のまなければなりません	のむ のまない のんだ のまなかった のむ？ のんで のめる のもう のんで(い)る のんでみよう のまなければならない or のまなければいけない	non-past (Dictionary form) neg. non-past (NAI form) past (TA form) neg. past (NAKATTA form) question request (TE form) potential form volitional form [OO form] is drinking let's try to drink have to drink; must drink
2. いAdjective conjugation	おいしいです おいしくないです or おいしくありません おいしかったです おいしくなかったです or おいしくありませんでした おいしいですか	おいしい おいしくない おいしかった おいしくなかった おいしい？	non-past neg. non-past past neg. past question
3. なAdjective conjugation	好きです 好きではありません or 好きじゃありません 好きでした 好きではありませんでした or 好きじゃありませんでした 好きですか	好き<u>だ</u> 好きではない or 好きじゃない 好き<u>だった</u> 好きではなかった or 好きじゃなかった 好き？	non-past neg. non-past past neg. past question
4. Noun + Copula conjugation	今日です 今日ではありません or 今日じゃありません 今日でした 今日ではありませんでした or 今日じゃありませんでした 今日ですか	今日<u>だ</u> 今日ではない or 今日じゃない 今日<u>だった</u> 今日ではなかった or 今日じゃなかった 今日？	non-past neg. non-past past neg. past question

一課

Words (Review):

	Formal Speech Style	Informal Speech Style	Meaning
1. Yes, No	はい, ええ [less formal] いいえ	うん ううん	Yes No
2. Particles		を, が, は are omitted.	
3. Quotation particle	と	って	
4. Expressions	おはようございます。 ありがとうございます。 おめでとうございます。 お休みです。 おげん気ですか。 お好きですか。	おはよう。 ありがとう。 おめでとう。 休み げん気？ 好き？	Good morning. Thank you. Congratulations. ~ is absent. How are you? Do you like it?
5. Sentence 　　Conjunctions	ですから しかし 〜が、〜	だから でも 〜けど、〜	Therefore, However, ~, but ~

	Politeness	Informal Speech Style	Meaning
6. Nouns	ご家族〔かぞく〕 ごりょうしん お名前 お仕事〔しごと〕 おいしゃさん お昼ごはん おトイレ おたんじょう日 おいくら？ お金〔かね〕 おかんじょう	家族〔かぞく〕 りょうしん 名前 仕事〔しごと〕 いしゃ 昼ごはん トイレ たんじょう日 いくら？ 金〔かね〕 かんじょう	family parents name job doctor lunch toilet birthday how much? money a check, a bill
7. Pronouns	こちら そちら あちら どちら？ どちら？ いかが？ どなた？	これ、ここ、　こっち それ、そこ、　そっち あれ、あそこ、あっち どれ？、どこ？ どっち？ どう？ だれ？	this one; here that one; there that one over there; over there which one?; where? which one (of two)? how? who?

	Out-group family terms	In-group family terms	Meanings
8. Family terms * New vocabulary for this lesson.	お父〔とう〕さん お母〔かあ〕さん おじいさん おばあさん おじさん おばさん お兄〔にい〕さん お姉〔ねえ〕さん 弟〔おとうと〕さん 妹〔いもうと〕さん	父〔ちち〕 母〔はは〕 祖父〔そふ〕＊ 祖母〔そぼ〕＊ おじ＊ おば＊ 兄〔あに〕 姉〔あね〕 弟〔おとうと〕 妹〔いもうと〕	father mother grandfather grandmother uncle aunt older brother older sister younger brother younger sister

	Respect	Informal Speech Style	Meaning
9. Dependent Nouns	-さま, -さん [less formal] -方〔かた〕 　[dependent noun]	-くん [Attached to boy's names] ひと	Mr.; Mrs.; Ms. person
10. Verbs	さしあげます いらっしゃいます	あげる いる	to give (someone) to exist; to be (for animate)

I. Male and Female Speech Styles. (Recognition only)

In Japanese, there is a male speech style and a female speech style. Often male or female speech style can be identified by the final particle of a sentence. Some of these particles are used exclusively by male or female speakers, and, therefore, mark the speaker's sex. Recently, some young Japanese deliberately mix male and female speech styles. Young Japanese females are less likely to use female speech than older females. Male and female speech markers are generally used only with informal speech. Male and female speech are not used in writing. Instead, the plain form (without male/female speech) is used.

Male Speech	Female Speech
1. When asking a question, a male speaker may use the question particle か or かい at the end of an informal sentence. か or かい question markers are not used when speaking to superiors. だ before the particle か or かい is omitted. Ex. これ、食べるか（い）？ 　　Will you eat this? 　　おいしいか（い）？ 　　Is it tasty? 　　これ、好きか（い）？ 　　Do you like this? 　　しあいは今日か（い）？ 　　Is the game today?	1. わ is used to add a softness to the message of the sentence and may express light assertion. It may be used in both formal and informal speech. Ex. 今日、おすしにするわ。 　　I will have *sushi* today! 　　私、かなしいわ。 　　I am sad! 　　これ、好きだわ。 　　I like this! 　　試験、明日だわ。 　　The exam is tomorrow!
2. ぞ, ぜ, さ and よ express assertion and mean, "I tell you," "you know." だ is used after nouns and NA adjectives before よ, ぞ, ぜ. They are used in informal male speech only. Ex. 今日はかつぞ。 　　I'll win today! 　　これはいいぜ。 　　This is good! 　　とてもきれいだよ。 　　It is very pretty! 　　好きさ。 　　I like it! 　　試験は明日だよ。 　　The exam is tomorrow!	2. の is used by female speakers and children, and is used when giving an explanation or expressing emphasis or emotion. It is also used as a question marker in place of か when uttered with a rising intonation. It is used with informal speech. な replaces だ (after nouns and NA adjectives) when used with の. Ex. 手がみを書くの。 　　I am going to write a letter. 　　うれしいの。 　　I am happy. 　　好きなの。 　　I like it. 　　明日なの。 　　It is tomorrow. 　　今日、行くの？ ↗ 　　Are you going today? 　　それ、おいしいの？ ↗ 　　Is that tasty? 　　好きなの？ ↗ 　　Do you like it? 　　今日なの？ ↗ 　　Is it today?

Male Speech	Female Speech
3. てくれ is an informal request form, used instead of Verb -TE KUDASAI. It is used almost exclusively by males, and not used toward superiors. Ex. 新聞を持って来てくれ。 　　Bring me a newspaper. 　　ぼくのこと、分かってくれよ。 　　Please understand me.	3. わ and の may precede よ and ね in informal female speech. They add a degree of softness to the sentence. Ex. 今、帰るわよ。 　　I'll go home now! 　　これ、安いわね。 　　This is cheap, isn't it? 　　むずかしいのよ。 　　It is difficult! 　　これ、安いのね。 　　This is cheap, isn't it?

A. ペアワーク→クラスワーク （ことわざ）

The teacher gives a different Japanese proverb to each pair of students. The pair is given five munutes to create a skit illustrating the proverb. The pairs present their skits in front of the class, and the class must guess the proverb.

B. ペアワーク： （家族インタビュー）

Imagine that you are a student and your partner is a Japanese adult. The family tree below is your family tree. Your partner asks you the questions listed on the following page. You answer the questions based on the information given below. Use the correct family terms. Take turns being the student and adult.

Cultural Note: In Western diagrams of family trees, the eldest family member appears to the left and younger family members appear to the right. In Japanese, they are positioned in the opposite manner.

Ex. 質問：お兄さんは何才ですか。

答え：兄のいちろうは２５才です。

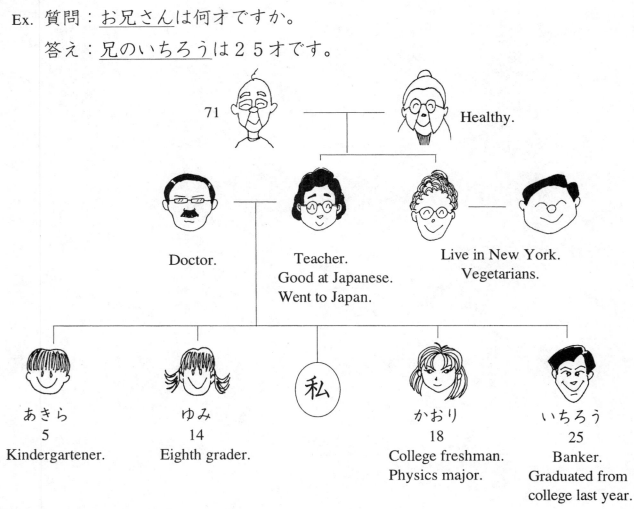

質問

1. ご兄弟は、何人ですか。
2. お父さんは、どんなお仕事をしていらっしゃいますか。 （いらっしゃいます is a polite equiv. of います）
3. お母さんも、お仕事をしていらっしゃいますか。 [If yes, 何のお仕事をしていらっしゃいますか。]
4. おじいさんは、おいくつですか。
5. おばあさんは、おげん気ですか。
6. お兄さんは大学生ですか？ [Use 兄のいちろう.]
7. お兄さんは、いつ大学をそつぎょうしましたか。 [Use 兄のいちろう.]
8. お兄さんは、どこではたらいていますか。 [Use 兄のいちろう.]
9. お姉さんは大学生ですか。何年生ですか。 [Use 姉のかおり.]
10. お姉さんは、大学で何をせんこうしていますか。 [Use 姉のかおり.]
11. 妹さんは何才ですか。何年生ですか。 [Use 妹のゆみ.]
12. 弟さんは何才ですか。何年生ですか。 [Use 弟のあきら.]
13. おじさんとおばさんは、どこにすんでいらっしゃいますか。
14. おじさんとおばさんは、どんな方ですか。 [Use しか.] （方 is a polite equiv. of 人）
15. ご家族のみなさんは、日本語が上手ですか。 [Use しか.]
16. ご家族のみなさんは、日本へ行ったことがありますか。 [Use しか.]

C. ペアワーク（あいさつ）

Ask your partner which Japanese greeting is used in the following situations. Your partner gives the correct greeting in Japanese. Take turns.

1. 出かける時、うちの人に何と言いますか。	
2. 出かける時、うちの人は何と言いますか。	
3. うちに帰った時、うちの人に何と言いますか。	
4. うちに帰った時、うちの人は何と言いますか。	
5. ねる時、うちの人に何と言いますか。	
6. 朝、先生に会った時、先生に何と言いますか。	
7. お昼に、先生に会った時、先生に何と言いますか。	
8. よる、先生に会った時、先生に何と言いますか。	
9. 食べる時、何と言いますか。	
10. ほかの人より早く何かをする時、何と言いますか。	
11. へやから出る時、へやにいる人に何と言いますか。	
12. 先生とながく話して先生のオフィスから出る時、先生に何と言いますか。	
13. はじめての人に会って、その人がじこしょうかいして「どうぞよろしく」と言った時、その人に何と言いますか。	

D. ペアワーク （好き／きらい）

Ask your partner about his/her likes and dislikes from among the following categories.

Ex. 質問：<u>好きなやさい</u>は何ですか。

答え：そうですねえ... <u>好きなやさい</u>は～です。

	好き	きらい
やさい		
くだ物		
食べ物		
のみ物		

E. ペアワーク （食べよう）

You and your partner are friends. You suggest doing the following activities. Your partner answers based on his/her opinions. Check "Yes" or "No" according to your partner's answers. Take turns.

Ex. 　　質問：今、ちょっと休もうか。

YESの答え：うん、休もう。

NOの答え：ううん、休まない。

質問	YES	NO
1. ジュースをのもうか。		
2. ピザを食べようか。		
3. 漢字のべんきょうをしようか。		
4. 図書館〔としょかん〕へ行こうか。		
5. 土曜日いっしょにえいがを見ようか。		
6. 明日、昼食をいっしょに食べようか。		
7. (your own)		

F. ペアワーク （朝食）

Your friend is visiting you. Make plans for your meals. Ask your friend for his/her preferences about the type of foods, the locations and the times for each meal.

Ex. 質問：朝食は （何料理を／どこで／何時ごろ） 食べようか。

答え： If you prefer another choice:

そうねえ．．． (female) ／そうだねえ．．． (male)

（～を／～で／～時ごろ） 食べよう。

Or if you don't mind the suggestion:

（何でも／どこでも／いつでも） いいよ。

	料理 〔りょうり〕 どんなりょうりを？	場所 〔ばしょ〕 どこで？	時間 何時ごろ？
今日の昼食			
今日の夕食			
明日の朝食			

G. ペアワーク （Speech Styles）

Here are the dialogues from the previous lesson. Change the dialogues to the correct speech style, based on the relationships between the speakers.

1. ＜レストランで＞

ケン：いただきます。うどんは　はしで　食べなければ　なりませんか。

まり：いいえ、おはしで　食べなくても　いいですよ。

　　　ケンさん、にぎりずしを　一つ　食べて　みませんか。

　　　おいしいですよ。

ケン：いいえ、けっこうです。ぼくは　魚が　好きじゃないんですよ。

　　　＜After the meal.＞　ごちそうさま。おいしかったですね。

　　　おなかが　いっぱいです。今日は　ぼくが　ごちそう　しますよ。

まり：ありがとう。じゃ、私が　チップを　払いましょう。

　　　いくらぐらい　置かなければ　なりませんか。

ケン：だいたい　十五パーセントぐらいです。

　　　＜He calls the waitress.＞　すみません。

　　　ウェイトレスさん、お勘定を　お願いします。

一課

2. ＜Ｔシャツの　お店で＞

まり：ケンさん、こんにちは。二階に　来ましたから、寄って　みました。

ケン：こんにちは。今晩　バスケットの　試合が　ありますが、見に　行き

　　　ませんか。大事な　試合ですから、応援に　行きましょう。

まり：始まる　時間や　場所は？

ケン：試合の　時間は　午後七時で、場所は　学校の　体育館です。

　　　六時半ごろに　車で　迎えに　行きますよ。

まり：ありがとう。じゃ、その頃に　家の　外で　待って　いますね。

　　　夜は　十一時までに　帰らなければ　なりません。

＜体育館で＞

まり：どっちの　方が　強いですか。

ケン：もちろん　ぼく達の　チームですよ。あの　五番の　ユニフォームの

　　　選手は　ぼくの　友達です。

まり：あの　背が　高い　選手ですか。足が　速そうですね。

　　　今、スコアーは？

ケン：５５対５４で　負けて　います。あと　一点。あと　三分だけです。

　　　ぼく達は　ぜったい　勝ちますよ。

　　　今　ぼくは　ドキドキして　います。

　＜試合の　終わりに＞

ケン：やったあ！　勝った、勝った！　すごい！　ばんざ～い！

まり：良かったですねえ。

アドベンチャー日本語3
OPI単語&文法チェックリスト
1課：はじめまして

名前：＿＿＿＿＿＿＿＿＿＿＿＿＿

クラス：＿＿＿＿＿＿＿＿

たんご	Check	Major Error	Minor Error
祖父〔そふ〕			
祖母〔そぼ〕			
おじ			
おば			
ようちえん			
物理〔ぶつり〕			
化学			
りか			
文学			
れきし			
そつぎょうする			
せんこうする			
こちらこそ			
人参〔にんじん〕			
朝食			
昼食			
夕食			
何でも			
いつでも			
どこでも			
かえる to change			
つかう			
Others			
Others			
Others			

ぶんぽう	Check	Major Error	Minor Error
NのN			
～をしている			
～しか + Neg.			
～って言う			
～という～			
V (- oo)			
だろう			
Others			
Others			
Others			
Plain form Polite form			
Male　- か			
- かい			
- てくれ			
Others			
Female - の			
- なの			
Others			

49

一課

By the end of this lesson, you will be able to communicate the information below in the given situation. Complete the following tasks with a partner. You are expected to conduct a natural conversation using as many new vocabulary and grammatical structures as you can, while appropriately incorporating vocabulary and structures you have learned previously. Use the appropriate speech style (plain or polite) and male/female speech if appropriate. Practice the dialogue with your partner; the aim is not to memorize a dialogue, but to communicate meaningfully with your partner on the topics below.

【 III - 2 トピック 1 】

Partner **A**: *High school student in the U. S.*
Partner **B**: *High school student from Japan*

Situation: *A is hosting B at his/her school in the U. S. Imagine that A's school is yours.*

A and **B** introduce themselves to one another. **A** explains his/her school to **B**: private/public, coed or not, name of school, tuition (if private). **B** makes observations about the school grounds (size, physical appearance) and asks about uniforms, school rules and school commutes. **A** responds. **B** comments, and makes one or two comparative remarks about **B**'s school and **A**'s school in Japan. **B** asks about school problems. **A** responds. They enter **A**'s Japanese classroom and **A** introduces **B** to his/her teacher.

【 III - 2 トピック 2 】

Partner **A**: *High school student from the U. S. studying in Japan*
Partner **B**: *Host older sister/brother in Japan*

Situation: ***B** is curious about **A**'s school in the U. S. **A** responds and asks questions about **B**'s school, since **A** will soon be attending **B**'s school. Imagine that **A**'s school is yours.*

B asks **A** about **A**'s extra-curricular activities in school. **A** responds and explains some of the extra-curricular activities at his/her school in the U. S. and some of the activities he/she does on weekends and after school hours. **B** talks about some of the activities he/she participates in and mentions some of the yearly events held at Japanese high schools. **A** describes some of the school events at his/her school as **B** asks questions about them. **A** talks about which activities occur when (by semester), and they both discuss when the semesters in Japan and the U. S. begin and end. **A** and **B** give opinions about each other's schools.

　今、ぼくは東京の私立の男女共学の高校に留学している。戸田高校という学校だ。授業料はアメリカの高校ほど高くない。

　この高校はアメリカの高校よりずっとせまい。木とか花とか草とか緑も少ない。芝生もほとんどない。

　この学校には制服があって、ぼくも制服を着て、学校へ通っている。自動車で学校へ通う生徒はいなくて、ほとんど電車やバスなどで通っている。この学校の規則はきびしくて、女子生徒はパーマをかけたり、化粧をしたりしてはいけない。学校に着いて、建物の中に入る時、外の靴をぬいで、中の靴にはきかえなくてはいけない。

　日本の学校は四月に始まって、三月に終わる。三学期あって、入学式とか卒業式とか式が多い。学校の行事は運動会とか文化祭とか修学旅行とか、いろいろある。この学校では高二の時に修学旅行として海外旅行をする。

　学校が終わった時、生徒は教室とかトイレとかそうじしなければならない。放課後、部活をする生徒も多い。塾に通う生徒もいる。ぼくは一学期にテニス部に入っていたけど、やめて、二学期から剣道をやっている。日本の文化が分かっておもしろい。

　日本の学校にもいじめとかいろいろ問題があるけど、アメリカの銃や麻薬の問題にくらべたら、とても平和な所だと思う。

　　　　　　　　　　　　　　　　　　　　　　　　　ケン

A. ことわざ Proverb 「二度あることは三度ある」

This is a common proverb among Japanese that literally means, "If something happens twice, it will happen three times." In other words, whether good or bad, when two things occur in fairly close sequence, one can expect another similarly good or bad occurrence soon afterwards. Japanese believe that good and bad events occur in threes.

For example, if one's car stalls on the highway, and sometime after, one is in a car accident, a Japanese would typically prepare himself for another bad thing to occur soon.

B. だるま *Daruma*

Daruma is the Japanized word for "Dharma," a famous Buddhist Indian priest who is said to have lost his legs after sitting on a stone in the mountains for many years in meditation. He came to be represented as a stubby, legless figure wearing loosely draped clothing covering his head, shoulders and body, with only his face showing. A doll called "*daruma*" was designed after this figure. It was perfect for the traditionally common toy called "*okiagari-koboshi*," which was a tumbling doll. The doll, made with a rounded, weighted base, always returned to its upright position even after it was rolled or pushed in different directions. Because of its ability to always return to its upright position, it was also regarded as a symbol of good luck. In fact, there is a common Japanese proverb, "七転び八起き *Nana korobi, ya oki*" which is equated to this determined, persevering spirit. The proverb means, "Fall seven times, get up eight times."

The doll comes in a variety of sizes, shapes and designs. Most commonly, however, it is made from paper-mache or clay and painted red all over except for a grotesque face. Although *daruma* can be purchased at many places at all times of the year, sales of *daruma* are most common around New Year's, as it can potentially bring good luck for the New Year. Certain cities in Japan are known for huge *daruma* markets at this time of the year. In most cases, *daruma* dolls are eyeless at the time of purchase. It is said that it is good luck to paint in one eye when one good event happens. When a second happy event occurs, it is believed that the *daruma* can finally see and will bring more good luck.

だるま *Daruma*

Sing this *Daruma* Song:

だ　る　ま　さん　　だ　る　ま　さん　　に　らめっ　こ　し　ましょ

わ　ら　う　　と　だ　め　よ　　　あっ　ぶっ　ぶ

C. あいづち *Aizuchi*

Aizuchi is a form of feedback one gives as one listens to a person speaking. *Aizuchi* is much more frequently used in Japanese than in English conversations. English examples of *aizuchi* are response words such as "Oh?" "Really?" "You're kidding!" "Uh-huh." In Japanese, they are responses such as, "そう？" "そうですね。" "ほんとうに?" "へえ..." "はい." These responses tell the speaker that you are following the conversation, that you are agreeing with the speaker, that you did not know about the piece of information the speaker is talking about, or that you are encouraging the speaker to continue. Particularly in Japanese, the intonation one uses as one utters *aizuchi* can change the meaning of the response. *Aizuchi* may not necessarily be uttered verbally; it may come in the form of laughter, facial expressions, or nodding. *Aizuchi* is helpful in making communication flow more smoothly and contributes to building good relationships between speaker and listener. Listen carefully to two native speakers talk to each other without actually paying attention to the content of their conversation. You will definitely notice how frequently Japanese use *aizuchi*. Or, attend a lecture or talk given to native Japanese speakers. You will notice how often Japanese will nod their heads in agreement with the speaker as they quietly sit listening. In order to use *aizuchi* effectively, one must be careful about the timing of one's *aizuchi*. It is said that the word *aizuchi* originally referred to the sound of a blacksmith and his assistant as they alternated (matched - *ai*) the striking sounds of their hammers (*tsuchi*).

D. 剣道 *Kendo*

けんどう *Kendo*

Kendo, along with *aikido, judo* and *karate*, is a popular Japanese martial art form. *Kendo* (the way of the sword), is Japanese fencing that involves spiritual discipline. The tradition of *kendo* goes back to China. It is believed that the Japanese adopted Chinese fencing, which used a single-edged, straight-blade sword sometime between 500 and 700 A. D. During the feudal period in Japan, the art of sword fighting was cultivated, though during the subsequent times of peace, the art of *kenjutsu* became less popular. The study of *kenjutsu* was infused with moral and spiritual aspects and focus was put on training the mind and body through the use of the sword. In the late 18th century, protective gear for the head, face, chest, hands, shoulders and hips, as well as bamboo training swords, became standard. The popularity of *kendo* rose and fell throughout recent history. During World War II, it was completely banned, but was eventually restored, even to schools, in 1957. For students of *kendo*, there are 10 ranks and three ranks for teachers.

E. 日本の高校 High School in Japan

a. The Japanese high school campus.

While the structure and layout of high school campuses, particularly private high schools, recently deviate from the norm, most high schools in Japan look somewhat similar. They are enclosed by clearly marked boundaries, and have entrances/exits that are gated. The buildings are often light colored, rather stark in appearance, and several stories high. While one may find occasional small gardens dressing up the appearance of the main building, for the most part, the grounds of Japanese high school are not covered by lawns, but by dirt. Japanese are often struck by the spaciousness and greenery of school campuses in the U. S.

Front gate of a high school

Changing shoes

Classroom

Athletic grounds

Cleaning after school

二課

コンピューターラボ
Computer laboratory

ふゆのせいふく
Winter uniform

なつのせいふく
Summer uniform

b. Extra-curricular activities and school events of Japanese high schools students:
Clubs (部活)

Clubs are a vital part of a Japanese high school student's life. Often, students belong to one club, which serves as the hub of their school social activities. Many clubs meet several times a week. Most schools do not have sports teams as in the U. S. Instead, students belong to the tennis club, or basketball or swimming club, which meet regularly all year to practice and compete. Other common types of clubs in Japanese high schools are the English-speaking club, music/performance clubs, or clubs that focus on certain aspects of Japanese culture (flower arranging, tea) or the martial arts (*aikido, kendo*). Recently, however, more high school students work part-time, and as a result, fewer students belong to clubs.

剣道部 〔けんどうぶ〕 Kendo club

茶道部 〔さどうぶ〕 Tea ceremony club

バスケット部 〔ぶ〕 Basketball club

チアリーダー Cheerleading club

Bunkasai (文化祭)

This annual event is held at high schools and colleges throughout Japan. Various clubs participate through exhibits, performances, demonstrations or other hands-on activities. The school campus is transformed into a fair-like atmosphere, with food, music and people leisurely milling about as they enjoy the various festivities. Activities are usually initiated and organized by students.

文化祭〔ぶんかさい〕
Culture festival

Undokai (運動会) and *Taiikusai* (体育祭)

Students at all levels participate in an all school athletic meet once a year. In most cases, *undokai* (at elementary and junior high schools) and *taiikusai* (at high schools and colleges) occur in the fall. This recreational event emphasizes exercise and cooperation rather than competition. Students, teachers and parents are involved in the meet, which often includes events such as tug-of-war, relay races and ball-throwing games. All participants are divided into two teams, red and white. Sometimes, folk dance performances are also organized. Parents will often show up to cheer their children on, and bring delicious packed lunches (*obento*) and drinks to share with their tired but happy children.

体育祭〔たいいくさい〕
Athletic meet

Shugakuryoko (修学旅行)

School trips are a tradition at most Japanese elementary, junior high schools and high schools. These trips are taken once a year by an entire grade level. They are usually several days long, and thus involve much preparation for transportation, lodgings and meals. Popular destinations are historical and culturally rich cities in Japan, though recently, more schools are taking students to foreign countries. Parents are expected to fund the trips, whether the school is public or private.

修学旅行
〔しゅうがくりょこう〕
School trip

Nyugakushiki (入学式)

For the Japanese, entrance into a school is a significant event. Held on the first day of school, the opening day ceremony, called *nyugakushiki*, is a time when students gather together in the school's auditorium to be officially welcomed to school. There, they sit quietly in their crisp new uniforms as

二課

they listen to speeches and announcements from school administrators and sing the national anthem *Kimigayo* and their school song. Since the Japanese school year begins in April, students often arrive at school near the height of spring, when cherry blossoms are in full bloom. For Japanese, memories of the first day of school often include visions of trees laden with pink blossoms, which signifiy a new beginning.

Sotsugyoshiki (卒業式)

卒業式〔そつぎょうしき〕
Graduation ceremony

As significant as *nyugakushiki* is *sotsugyoshiki* (graduation ceremonies). Graduation ceremonies in Japan occur in February or early March, which is the end of the school year. In formal ceremonies similar to the opening ceremonies, students gather in the school's auditorium with their parents in attendance.   They sing the national anthem and their school song and listen to speeches given by administrators and teachers. Student representatives also give speeches. Students wear their school uniforms and are recognized individually as they are called to the stage to receive their graduation certificates. The event is a solemn affair, with no spontaneous outbursts or expressions of jubilance as sometimes witnessed at graduation ceremonies in the U. S.

Note: For American students, the word "school event" evokes thoughts of social events such as formal dances, homecomings, carnivals, or special pageants or performances. For Japanese, 学校行事 includes many of the activities listed above, such as *nyugakushiki* and *sotsugyoshiki*. Many of the social events associated with high school life in the U. S., i. e., formal dances, are non-existent in Japanese schools.

c. Cram schools.

Juku (塾)

塾〔じゅく〕
Cram school

Juku, known as "cram schools," are privately run schools that offer intensive lessons in various academic areas solely for students to prepare for entrance exams. Although *juku* exist for young children as well, most *juku* accommodate high school students who are intent on scoring well on entrance examinations for prestigious colleges. Students attend *juku* after their regular school day is over and will sometimes stay at the *juku* until 8:00 or 9:00 at night, return home, and continue with their regular studies. Some students attend *juku* on Saturdays as well. Often, Japanese students find their classes and teachers at the *juku* far more stimulating than at their regular day schools.

1. 公 public コウ 公園 park

公立 〔こうりつ〕 public

八 (eight) +

し → ㇄ → ム = 公 (public)

When eight people claim it is theirs, it belongs to the public.

2. 文 writing; composition ブン 文化 〔ぶんか〕 culture

作文 〔さくぶん〕 composition

文学 〔ぶんがく〕 literature

(cover) → 亠 +

(cross lines) → 乂 = 文 (writing; composition)

Under the roof (cover), one makes letters by crossing two lines.

3. 化 to take the form of カ 化学 〔かがく〕 chemistry

文化 〔ぶんか〕 culture

ケ 化粧する to apply make-up

彳 → イ → イ +

匕 → 匕 = 化 (take the form of)

A person changes the form (of his body) by standing and sitting.

59

4. 花 flower

はな   花屋〔はなや〕flower shop

（plant）→ ψψ → 艹 +

化 （to take the form of）

= 花 （flower）

The flower changes the form of the plant.

5. 海 ocean; sea; beach

うみ   海へ行く go to the beach

カイ   海外〔かいがい〕overseas

日本海〔にほんかい〕Sea of Japan

（water）→ 氵 → 氵 +

毎 （every）

= 海 （ocean）

The water everyone enjoys every day is the ocean.

6. 旅 travel

リョ   旅行〔りょこう〕travel

海外旅行〔かいがいりょこう〕overseas travel

修学旅行〔しゅうがくりょこう〕study tour

方 （direction）   +

彳 彳 彳   = 旅 （traveling）

Three people are traveling in the same direction.

7. 教　to teach　　　おし（える）　　　教えて下さい。　Please teach me.

キョウ　　　　　教室 classroom

教科書〔きょうかしょ〕textbook

教会〔きょうかい〕church

キリスト教 Christianity

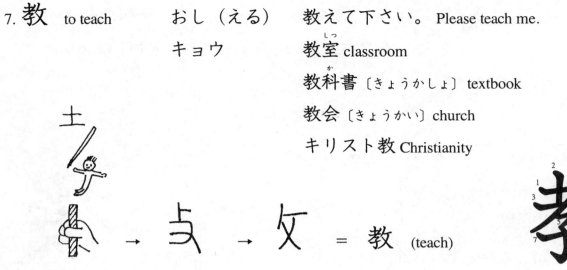

work with hands

= 教 (teach)

On Saturdays, teachers must carry whips in order to teach children how to work with their hands.

8. 室　room　　　シツ　　　教室〔きょうしつ〕classroom

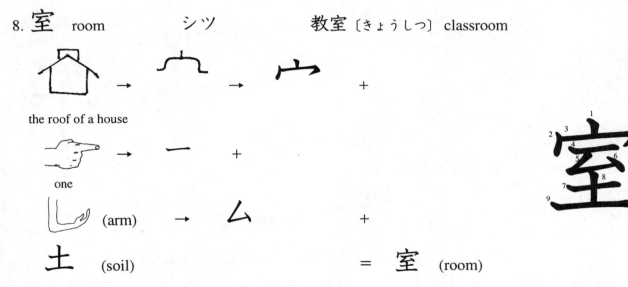

the roof of a house

one

(arm)

土 (soil)

= 室 (room)

The space under the roof and above the soil is my room. I can show it to you with a sweep of my arm.

二課

9. 後　behind; after　　　うし（ろ）　車の後ろ〔くるまのうしろ〕behind the car

　　　　　　　　　　　　あと　　　学校の後で〔がっこうのあとで〕after school

　　　　　　　　　　　　ゴ　　　　午後 p. m.

　　　　　　　　　　　　　　　　　放課後 after school

十 (to go) → ⺅ → 彳 +

8 (string) → 8 → 幺

(dragging feet) → → 夂 ＝ 後 (behind)

When one goes with string tangled around his feet, he drags his feet and falls behind.

10. 午　noon　　　　　　ゴ　　　　午前一時〔ごぜんいちじ〕1:00 a.m.

　　　　　　　　　　　　　　　　　午後一時〔ごごいちじ〕1:00 p.m.

ㄱ (the sound) +

二 (two) +

十 (ten) = 午 (noon)

Gongg!　It is 12 o'clock.　It is noon.

11. 着　to wear　　　　き（る）　シャツを着る wear a shirt

　　　　　　　　　　　　　　　　　着物〔きもの〕Japanese traditional *kimono*

　　　to arrive　　　　　つ（く）　学校に着く arrive at school

(sheep) → 𦍌 → 𦍌 +

丿 (knife)

(eye) → → 目 ＝ 着 (to wear; to arrive)

When you put the sheepskin on, you cut off the sheep's eyes.

12. 知　to get to know　　　し（る）　　　　　知りません。 I do not know.

（arrow） → ⤒ → 矢

（mouth） → ⊔ → 口 ＝ 知 (to get to know)

When you know the target, you shoot and shout with joy.

知

【読みかえの漢字】

1. 私　I; private　　わたし＊　　　　私は山本です。 I am Yamamoto.

　　　　　　　　　シ　　　　　　　私立 〔しりつ or わたくしりつ〕 private

2. 男　male　　　　おとこ＊　　　　男の子 〔おとこのこ〕 boy

　　　　　　　　　　　　　　　　　男の人 〔おとこのひと〕 man

　　　　　　　　　ダン　　　　　　男子 〔だんし〕 boy

3. 女　female　　　おんな＊　　　　女の子 〔おんなのこ〕 girl

　　　　　　　　　　　　　　　　　女の人 〔おんなのひと〕 woman; lady

　　　　　　　　　ジョ　　　　　　女子 〔じょし〕 girl

　　　　　　　　　　　　　　　　　男女共学 〔だんじょきょうがく〕 co-ed

4. 子　child　　　　こ＊　　　　　　子供 child(ren)

　　　　　　　　　シ　　　　　　　男子 〔だんし〕 boy

　　　　　　　　　　　　　　　　　女子 〔じょし〕 girl

5. 入　to enter;　　はい（る）＊　　入って下さい。 Please enter.

　　　to put in　　い（れる）＊　　さとうを入れる put sugar in

　　　　　　　　　いり＊　　　　　入口 〔いりぐち〕 entrance

　　　　　　　　　ニュウ　　　　　入学 〔にゅうがく〕 enter a school

6. 行　to go　　　　い（く）＊　　　学校へ行く go to school

　　　　　　　　　コウ＊　　　　　旅行 〔りょこう〕 travel

　　　　　　　　　ギョウ　　　　　行事 〔ぎょうじ〕 event

＊ Previously introduced.

63

二課

【読めればいい漢字】

1. 生徒　　　せいと　　　　　　student [non-college]
2. 問題　　　もんだい　　　　　problem
3. 教科書　　きょうかしょ　　　textbook
4. 公園　　　こうえん　　　　　park
5. 一度　　　いちど　　　　　　one time; once
6. 図書館　　としょかん　　　　library

Let's review previous vocabulary!

A. めいし Nouns

1. 今	now		15. きそく	rules
2. とうきょう	Tokyo		16. たて物	building
3. 高校	high school		17. 中	inside
4. 戸田 〔とだ〕	Toda		18. 時 〔とき〕	when
5. 学校	school		19. 外	outside
6. アメリカ	U.S.		20. くつ	shoes
7. 木	tree		21. 三月	March
8. 花 〔はな〕	flower		22. 四月	April
9. みどり	green		23. 高二 〔こうに〕	high school junior
10. せいふく	school uniform		24. 教室 〔きょうしつ〕	classroom
11. 自動車 〔じどうしゃ〕	car		25. トイレ	toilet
12. 生徒 〔せいと〕	student		26. 問題 〔もんだい〕	problem
13. 電車	electric train		27. 所	place
14. バス	bus			

B. どうし Verbs

28. 着て 〔G2きる／きます〕　　　　to wear
29. 着いて 〔G1つく／つきます〕　　to arrive
30. 入る 〔G1はいる／はいります〕　to enter
31. はじまって 〔G1はじまる／はじまります〕　to begin; start
32. あって 〔G1あります／あって〕　there is
33. おわる 〔G1おわります／おわって〕　to end; finish
34. 旅行をする 〔IR りょこうをします／りょこうをして〕　to travel
35. おわった 〔G1おわる／おわります〕　to end; finish
36. そうじしなければならない 〔IR そうじする／そうじします〕　have to clean
37. 分かって 〔G1わかる／わかります〕　to understand
38. くらべたら 〔G2くらべる／くらべます〕　if (you) compare
39. 思う 〔G1おもいます／おもって〕　to think

C. いけいようし I Adjectives

40. 高くない	not expensive	43. きびしくて	is strict
41. せまい	is narrow; small	44. 多い	are many
42. なくて	there is not	45. おもしろい	interesting

D. ふくし Adverbs

46. ずっと	by far	47. いろいろ	various

E. その他 Others

48. ～ほど + Neg.　　　　　　　not as ～ as
49. ～より　　　　　　　　　　than ～
50. ～や～など　　　　　　　　～ and ～, etc.
51. ～たり～たりしてはいけない　not allowed to do such things as ～, ～
52. ～けど、　　　　　　　　　　Although ～; Though ～

Activity A

1.

N1 という N2　P+V　N2 called N1

スタンフォードという大学はどこにありますか。Where is the college called Stanford University?

2.
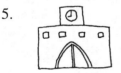

へいわ＜<ruby>平和<rt>へいわ</rt></ruby>＞　N　peace　　NA　peaceful

日本は<ruby>平和<rt>へいわ</rt></ruby>な国だと思いますか。Do you think that Japan is a peaceful country?

3.

「にどあることはさんどある＜二度あることは三度ある＞」

Proverb　"If something happens twice, it will happen three times."

Activity B

4.

N1 とか N2（とか）　P　N1 and N2 (among others)

バスケット<ruby>部<rt>ぶ</rt></ruby>とかバレーボール<ruby>部<rt>ぶ</rt></ruby>とかあります。There is a basketball club and a volleyball club, etc.

Activity C

5.

しりつ＜私立＞　N　private

私立の学校に行っています。I go to (attend) a private school.

6.

こうりつ＜公立＞　N　public

ケネディー高校は公立です。Kennedy High School is public.

7.

だんしこう＜男子校＞　N　boy's school

あの学校は男子校です。That school is a boy's school.

二課

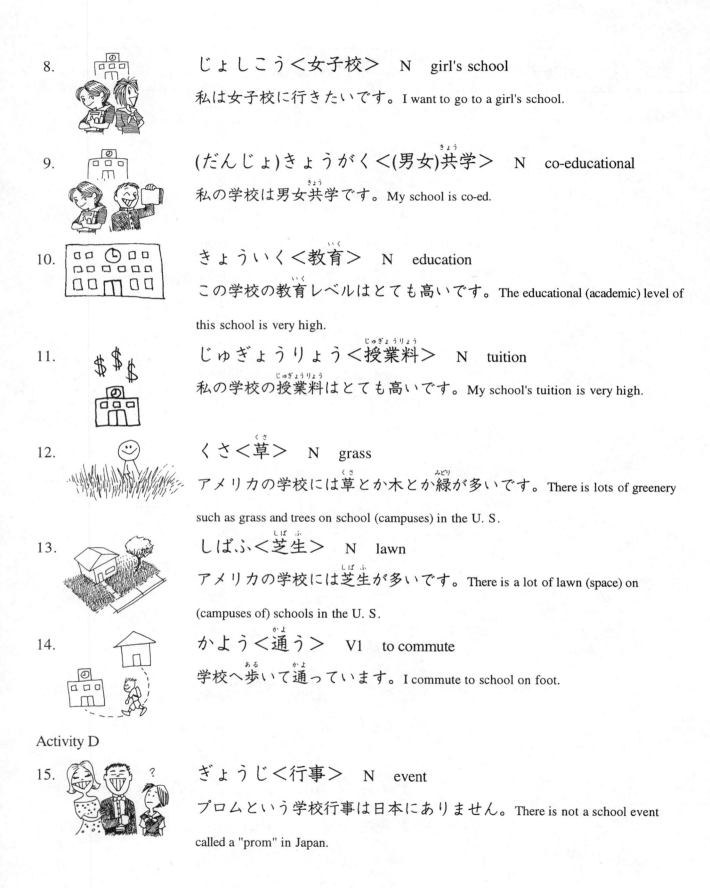

8. じょしこう＜女子校＞　N　girl's school

私は女子校に行きたいです。I want to go to a girl's school.

9. (だんじょ)きょうがく＜(男女)共学＞　N　co-educational

私の学校は男女共学です。My school is co-ed.

10. きょういく＜教育＞　N　education

この学校の教育レベルはとても高いです。The educational (academic) level of

this school is very high.

11. じゅぎょうりょう＜授業料＞　N　tuition

私の学校の授業料はとても高いです。My school's tuition is very high.

12. くさ＜草＞　N　grass

アメリカの学校には草とか木とか緑が多いです。There is lots of greenery

such as grass and trees on school (campuses) in the U. S.

13. しばふ＜芝生＞　N　lawn

アメリカの学校には芝生が多いです。There is a lot of lawn (space) on

(campuses of) schools in the U. S.

14. かよう＜通う＞　V1　to commute

学校へ歩いて通っています。I commute to school on foot.

Activity D

15. ぎょうじ＜行事＞　N　event

プロムという学校行事は日本にありません。There is not a school event

called a "prom" in Japan.

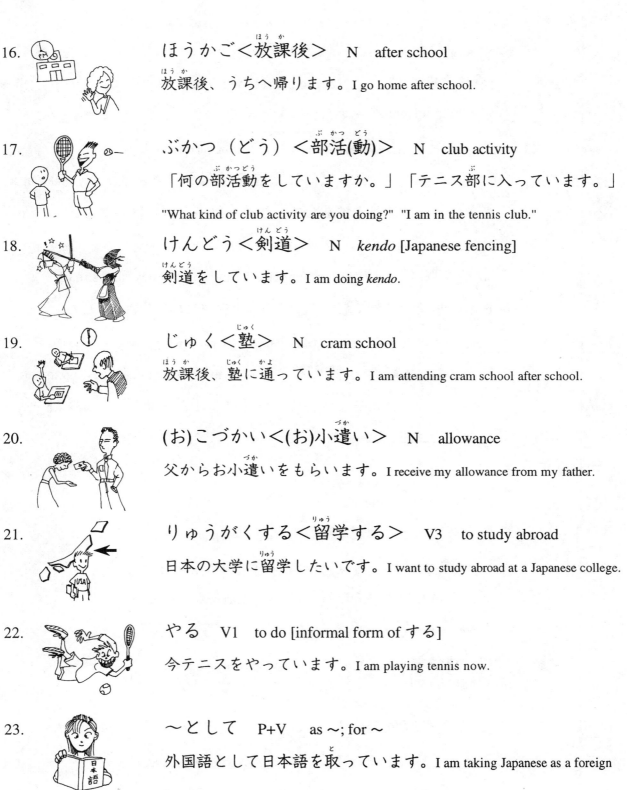

16. ほうかご＜放課後＞　N　after school

放課後、うちへ帰ります。I go home after school.

17. ぶかつ（どう）＜部活(動)＞　N　club activity

「何の部活動をしていますか。」「テニス部に入っています。」

"What kind of club activity are you doing?"　"I am in the tennis club."

18. けんどう＜剣道＞　N　*kendo* [Japanese fencing]

剣道をしています。I am doing *kendo*.

19. じゅく＜塾＞　N　cram school

放課後、塾に通っています。I am attending cram school after school.

20. (お)こづかい＜(お)小遣い＞　N　allowance

父からお小遣いをもらいます。I receive my allowance from my father.

21. りゅうがくする＜留学する＞　V3　to study abroad

日本の大学に留学したいです。I want to study abroad at a Japanese college.

22. やる　V1　to do [informal form of する]

今テニスをやっています。I am playing tennis now.

23. ～として　P+V　as ～; for ～

外国語として日本語を取っています。I am taking Japanese as a foreign language.

Activity E

24.
パーマをかける　V2　to perm (one's hair)

日本の学校ではパーマをかけて、学校へ行ってはいけません。

In Japanese schools, you are not allowed to have your hair permed.

25.
(お)けしょうをする＜(お)化粧をする＞　V3　to apply make-up

日本の学校ではお化粧をして、学校へ行ってはいけません。

In Japanese schools, you are not allowed to wear make-up to school.

26.
ぬぐ＜脱ぐ＞　V1　to remove clothing [i.e., shoes, dress, hat]

日本の学校では外で履いていた靴を脱がなければなりません。

In Japanese schools, you have to take off the shoes that you were wearing outdoors.

27.
はきかえる＜履き替える＞　V2　to change [i.e., shoes, pants, etc.]

日本の学校では靴を履き替えなければなりません。In Japanese schools,

you have to change your shoes.

Activity F

28.
いじめ　N　bullying

いじめは大きい問題です。Bullying is a big problem.

いじめる　V2　to bully; to treat someone harshly

ぼくをいじめないで下さい。Please don't be so mean to me.

29.
じゅう＜銃＞　N　gun

家に銃がありますか。Do you have guns at your home?

30.
まやく＜麻薬＞　N　drugs

けっして麻薬を使ってはいけません。Never use drugs.

31.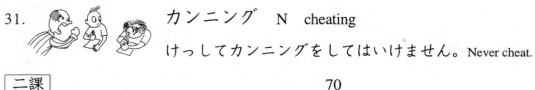
カンニング　N　cheating

けっしてカンニングをしてはいけません。Never cheat.

32. ほとんど　Adv.　almost; mostly

漢字はほとんどおぼえました。I memorized most of the *kanji*.

お金がほとんどありません。I have almost no money.

Activity G & H　　　No new vocabulary.

Activity I

33. 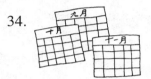 ところ　N　point

この学校のいいところは授業料<ruby>授業料<rt>じゅぎょうりょう</rt></ruby>が安いことです。The good point of this

school is that the tuition is low.

Activity J

34.  がっき＜学<ruby>期<rt>き</rt></ruby>＞　N　semester

いちがっき＜一学<ruby>期<rt>き</rt></ruby>＞　N　first semester

こんがっき＜今学<ruby>期<rt>き</rt></ruby>＞　N　this semester

らいがっき＜来学<ruby>期<rt>き</rt></ruby>＞　N　next semester

せんがっき＜先学<ruby>期<rt>き</rt></ruby>＞　N　last semester

まいがっき＜毎学<ruby>期<rt>き</rt></ruby>＞　N　every semester

今学期の成績は先学期の成績より悪かった。My grades this semester were

worse than last semester.

35.  そつぎょうしき＜卒業式＞　N　graduation ceremony

卒業式に出たことがありますか。Have you ever attended a graduation

ceremony?

36. ぶんか＜文化＞　N　culture

日本の文化はおもしろいと思う。I think Japanese culture is interesting.

37.  かいがいりょこう＜海外旅行＞　N　overseas (foreign) travel

海外旅行に行こう。Let's travel overseas.

Activity K　　　No new vocabulary.

　二課

Activity L

38.  やめる＜止める＞　　V2　to quit; discontinue

たばこを止めて下さい。Please stop smoking.

Others

39. 一かな。　　SP　I wonder if ～　[used by males and females]

明日の試験はむずかしいかな。I wonder if tomorrow's exam is difficult.

40. 一かしら。　　SP　I wonder if ～　[used by females]

明日の試験はむずかしいかしら。I wonder if tomorrow's exam is difficult.

【オプショナル単語】

1.  にゅうがくしき＜入学式＞　N　school entrance ceremony

日本では、四月に入学式があります。In Japan, there is a school entrance

ceremony in April.

2. うんどうかい＜運動会＞　N　sports meet (elementary and

intermediate school)

運動会で玉入れをしました。We did the "ball throw" game at the sports meet.

3. たいいくさい＜体育祭＞　N　sports meet (high school)

高校では体育祭が十月にあります。There is a sports meet at the high school

in October.

4. ぶんかさい＜文化祭＞　N　cultural festival

文化祭で劇をしました。I participated in a play at the cultural festival.

5. しゅうがくりょこう＜修学旅行＞　N　study tour

修学旅行で中国へ行きました。We went to China on a study tour.

A. Noun 1 という Noun 2　　　Noun 2 called/ named Noun 1

Noun 1 identifies or clarifies Noun 2. Recall that 「Tree は日本語で何といいますか。」 means "How do you say 'tree' in Japanese?" Noun 1 という Noun 2 is a modifying clause derived from Noun 2 は Noun 1 といいます.

1. 「トトロ」という映画を見たことがありますか。

Have you ever seen the movie called "Totoro"?

2. 田中花子という人を知っていますか。　　Do you know a person named Hanako Tanaka?

3. 何という学校に行っていますか。　　What school are you attending?

4. 「いえ」という漢字が書けますか。　　Can you write the kanji "ie"?

B. Noun 1 とか Noun 2 （とか）　　　Noun 1 and Noun 2 (among others)

とか is similar in meaning and usage to や, and is therefore used to name several nouns as samples of other similar nouns.

1. 化学とか物理（とか）は苦手です。

I am poor at chemistry and physics (among other subjects).

2. 日本とか中国（とか）に行ってみたいです。

I want to try to go to Japan and China (among other places).

3. 家とか学校（とか）で新聞を読みます。

I read the newspaper at home and at school (among other places).

C. はきかえる

This compound verb consists of the stem form of the verb はきます "to wear (shoes)" and かえます "to change" means "change (shoes)." It is formed by taking the verb stem of the main verb and attaching かえます. Adding かえます to the main verb suggests that an action is being redone. Do not attach かえます to any verb. Use this compound verb only when you have seen it being used previously.

はきます "to wear (shoes, etc.)"	＋かえます	→はきかえます	"to change (shoes, pants, etc.)"
着ます　"to wear (shirt, etc.)"	＋かえます	→着かえます	"to change (shirt, dress, etc.)"
のります "to ride"	＋かえます	→のりかえます	"to transfer (vehicles)"
書きます "to write"	＋かえます	→書きかえます	"to rewrite"
入れます "to put in"	＋かえます	→入れかえます	"to replace"

1. 私は家へ帰ると、服を着かえます。　　　　When I return home, I change my clothes.

2. 東京駅で乗りかえて、上野へ行きました。　I transferred at Tokyo Station and went to Ueno.

3. レポートを書きかえなければなりません。　I have to rewrite the paper.

4. 日本の学校では、くつをはきかえるんですか。

Do you change your shoes at Japanese schools?

D. Modifying Sentence

As is the case with all modifiers in Japanese, clauses also immediately precede the nouns they modify. Verb-ending clauses are formed by using the plain (dictionary, -NAI, -TA, -NAKATTA) forms. い Adjective-ending modifiers also appear in the plain forms preceding the nouns they modify. Elsewhere, な Adjective-ending modifiers take な in the affirmative non-past form and plain forms (-NAI, -TA, -NAKATTA) before the noun being modified.

　Clauses may modify any noun within a sentence. If it modifies the subject or topic of the sentence, the clause generally appears at the beginning of the sentence. If the clause modifies the direct object of the sentence, it may appear in the middle. Some clauses include their own subjects. When there is a subject within a clause, the subject takes the particles が or の, never は. は only appear in a clause when it is the same as the subject of the main sentence. This distinguishes the subject of the clause from the subject or topic of the main sentence, which takes は.

　Clauses are much more common in Japanese, both in speaking and writing, than in English.

1. Verb + Noun

食べる		person who eats/will eat
食べない		person who does not eat/will not eat
食べた		person who ate
食べなかった		person who did not eat
食べている		person who is eating
食べていない		person who is not eating
食べたことがある		person who has eaten
食べたことがない		person who has never eaten
食べてもいい		person who may/is allowed to eat
食べてはいけない	＋人	person who may not/is not allowed to eat
食べなければいけない		person who has to eat
食べてみた		person who tried to eat
食べられる		person who can eat
食べられない		person who cannot eat
食べることが出来る		person who can eat
食べることが出来ない		person who cannot eat
食べてしまった		person who has eaten (something) completely
食べすぎる		person who eats too much
食べすぎた		person who ate too much

2. い Adjective + Noun

高い		expensive book
高くない	+ 本	inexpensive book
高かった		book that was expensive
高くなかった		book that was not expensive

3. な Adjective + Noun

好きな		book I like
好きじゃない or 好きではない	+ 本	book I do not like
好きだった		book I liked
好きじゃなかった or 好きではなかった		book I did not like

1. 試合が（or の）始まる時間は、四時です。 The time the game will start is 4:00.

2. おすしを食べない人は、だれですか。 Who are the people who don't eat *sushi*?

3. ケンが（or の）行っている学校は、どんな学校ですか。

What kind of school is Ken attending?

4. 背が（or の）高い選手は、山田君です。 The tall player is Yamada.

5. 高くないレストランを教えて下さい。 Please tell me about a restaurant that is not expensive.

6. クッキーが（or の）好きな人は、だれですか。 Who is the person who likes cookies?

7. やきゅうが（or の）上手な人は、だれですか。 Who is the person who is good at baseball?

E. Noun 1 として Noun 2 . . .　　　　　as 〜; for 〜;

The noun that precedes として represents a category to which the noun immediately following belongs. When one uses a として sentence, one comments about the second noun as a representative of a larger category (the first noun).

---

1. 私は外国語として日本語を取っています。

I am taking Japanese as a foreign language.

2. 毎朝、朝ご飯としてシリアルを食べています。

I eat cereal for breakfast every morning.

3. 私達の学校では日本語の教科書としてアドベンチャー日本語を使っています。 We are using *Adventures in Japanese* as the Japanese language textbook at our school.

F. Clause + 時（に）　　　　　When...

The word とき used independently, means "time." When it is used after a clause or phrase, it means "at the time when" or "when." The particle に after とき is generally used when the speaker or writer wishes to point out the specificity of the time.

The following rules for the clauses preceding とき apply:

(1) The subject of the とき clause is followed by が if it is different from the subject of the main clause.

　　　　Ex: あなたが行く時、私も行きます。 When you go, I will go too.

(2) Plain (informal) forms precede とき with the exception of the non-past forms of the な adjectives, which take な and nouns, which take の. See below.

Verb	食べる		When (one) eats, will eat
	食べない		When (one) does not eat, will not eat
	食べた		When (one) ate
	食べなかった		When (one) did not eat
い Adjective	高い		When (something) is expensive
	高くない		When (something) is not expensive
	高かった		When (something) was expensive
	高くなかった	＋ 時(に)、	When (something) was not expensive
な Adjective	好きな		When (one) likes
	好きじゃない or 好きではない		When (one) does not like
	好きだった		When (one) liked
	好きじゃなかった or 好きではなかった		When (one) did not like
Noun	学生の		When (one) is a student
	学生じゃない or 学生ではない		When (one) is not a student
	学生だった		When (one) was a student
	学生じゃなかった or 学生ではなかった		When (one) was not a student

(3) Unlike English, the とき construction is not used to express conditionals. In Japanese, the ーたら, ーと or ーば constructions must be used instead.
　　　When you go outside, you can see the mountains.
　　　O　外に行ったら、山が見えます。
　　　O　外に行けば、山が見えます。
　　　O　外に行くと、山が見えます。
　　　X　外に行く時、山が見えます。

(4) The use of the past or non-past い adjectives, な adjectives and nouns preceding とき is generally flexible. If the sentence ending is in the non-past tense, the とき clause should also be non-past. If the tense of the main clause (sentence ending) is past, however, either the past or non-past forms may be used in the とき clause. Generally, though, the non-past

form is more common.

There is no difference in meaning between the two sentences below.

子どもの時、日本にすんでいました。　　　　When I was a child, I lived in Japan.

子どもだった時、日本にすんでいました。　　　　〃

(5) When the とき clause contains a verb, the use of the correct tense of the verb preceding とき is crucial.

a.) If the verb in the とき clause is an existence verb, either the past or non-past form may be used when the ending of the entire sentence is past. If the sentence ending is non-past, the とき clause should also be non-past.

私は日本にいる／いた時、秋田さんに会った。

　　　When I was in Japan, I met Ms. Akita.

b.) When the verb in the とき clause expresses an action, it is important that the correct past or non-past form is used. The sequence of the two actions listed in the とき clause and the main clause must always be considered. Study the examples below. Although a loose translation of all of the sentences is, "When I eat/ate a meal, I wash(ed) my hands," note the subtle differences in the sequencing of events depending on the tense of the verbs in the とき clause.

1. ごはんを食べる時、手をあらう。

　　　I wash my hands (just) before I eat my meal.

2. ごはんを食べた時、手をあらう。

　　　I wash my hands (just) after I eat my meal.

3. ごはんを食べる時、手をあらった。

　　　I washed my hands (just) before I ate my meal.

4. ごはんを食べた時、手をあらった。

　　　I washed my hands (just) after I ate my meal.

For further clarification, compare the examples below:

X　1. 朝、おきる時、かおをあらう。

O　2. 朝、おきた時、かおをあらう。

　　　When I get up in the morning, I wash my face.

Example #1 is incorrect because it implies that one washes his face before getting up in the morning.

(6) When the actions in the main clause and the とき clause occur together, the past or non-past forms may be used if the main sentence ends in a past tense. If the main sentence ends in a non-past form, the verb in the とき clause should also be in the non-past form.

1. ほっかいどうへ行く時、ひこうきで行く。

　　　When I go to Hokkaido, I go by plane.

2. ほっかいどうへ行く時、ひこうきで行った。

　　　When I went to Hokkaido, I went by plane.

3. ほっかいどうへ行った時、ひこうきで行った。

　　　When I went to Hokkaido, I went by plane.

二課

1. 日本レストランへ行った時に、おすしを食べました。

    When I went to a Japanese restaurant, I ate *sushi*.

2. 中学一年生の時に、私はぜんぜん日本語を話せませんでした。

    I could not speak Japanese at all when I was in the seventh grade.

3. その時、どうしましたか。

    What did you do at that time?

4. ひまな時に、家へ来て下さい。

    Please come to my house when you are free.

5. 私は小さい時に、よく父と映画を見に行きました。

    When I was small, I often went to watch movies with my father.

6. 家に帰った時、服を着かえます。

    I change my clothing when I go home.

A. ペアワーク：〜という〜

Ask your partner the following questions. Your partner should answer in Japanese using complete sentences. Expand your conversation beyond yes/no answers. Take turns.

質問	はい	いいえ
1. 「山本」という人を知っていますか。		
2. 「富士山〔ふじさん〕」という山を知っていますか。		
3. 「カルピス」という日本ののみ物をのんだことがありますか。		
4. 「いえ」という漢字が書けますか。		
5. 「慶応〔けいおう〕」という日本の私立大学を知っていますか。		
6. 「竜安寺〔りょうあんじ〕」というお寺を知っていますか。		
7. 「トトロ」という日本のアニメを見たことがありますか。		
8. 「おや子どんぶり」という日本りょうりを食べたことがありますか。		
9. 「お正月」という日本のうたを知っていますか。		
10. 「桃太郎〔ももたろう〕」というお話を知っていますか。		
11. 「せんそう(war)とへいわ」という本を知っていますか。		
12. 「二度あることは三度ある」ということわざを知っていますか。		

B. ペアワーク（かもく）

Ask your partner what subjects he/she is taking this semester. Fill in the blanks with the subjects your partner is taking. Use the chart below as a reference for vocabulary words. Then ask your partner which subjects he/she is strong and poor at, and fill in the blanks below.

質問：「今学期、何の科目を取っていますか。」

答え：「〜とか〜とか〜とか（を）取っています。」

1.	4.
2.	5.
3.	6.

英語〔えいご〕 English	小説〔しょうせつ〕novel, 詩〔し〕poetry, アメリカ文学, American literature, ヨーロッパ文学 European literature, アジア文学 Asian literature, 作文 composition, スピーチ speech
社会〔しゃかい〕 Social Studies	歴史〔れきし〕history, アメリカ史〔アメリカし〕American history, 世界史〔せかいし〕World history, アジア史〔アジアし〕Asian history, ヨーロッパ史〔ヨーロッパし〕European history, 政治〔せいじ〕politics/government, 経済〔けいざい〕economics
理科〔りか〕 Science	生物〔せいぶつ〕biology, 化学 chemistry, 物理〔ぶつり〕physics
数学〔すうがく〕 Math	代数〔だいすう〕algebra, 幾何〔きか〕geometry, 微分積分〔びぶんせきぶん〕calculus, コンピューターcomputer
外国語 Foreign Languages	日本語, 中国語, フランス語, スペイン語, ドイツ語, ラテン語, ギリシャ語
体育〔たいいく〕 Physical Education	
美術〔びじゅつ〕 Art	図画〔ずが〕drawing, 絵画〔かいが〕painting, ガラス細工〔ガラスざいく〕glass blowing, 陶芸〔とうげい〕ceramics, 彫金〔ちょうきん〕jewelry, 写真〔しゃしん〕photography, 書道〔しょどう〕calligraphy
音楽〔おんがく〕 Music	オーケストラ orchestra, バンド band , シンフォニー symphony , コーラス chorus/choir
演劇〔えんげき〕 Drama	
その他〔た〕 Others	タイプ typing on a keyboard, 予備士官訓練〔よびしかんくんれん〕ROTC, カウンセラー counseling, 家庭科〔かていか〕home economics, 商業〔しょうぎょう〕business

とくいなかもく		にが手なかもく	

C. ペアワーク （学校についてインタビュー）

Interview your partner about his/her school. Jot down your partner's responses.

1. 公立ですか。私立ですか。	
2. 男女きょう学ですか。男子校ですか。女子校ですか。	
3. じゅぎょうりょうは一年間いくらですか。	
4. 学校は大きいですか。	
5. 生徒は何人ぐらいいますか。	
6. 何年生から何年生までいますか。	
7. せいふくがありますか。	
8. 学校のきそくはきびしいですか。	
9. 学校に木とか花とかくさとかみどりが多いですか。	
10. 校庭 〔こうてい〕 (school grounds) はしばふですか。	
11. 生徒は学校へ何でかよっていますか。	
12. 学校の教育 〔きょういく〕 レベルは高いと思いますか。	

D. ペアワーク （インタビュー）

Interview your partner. Jot down your partner's responses.

1. ほうか後、ぶかつをやっていますか。	
2. 学校行事の中で、何が一番好きですか。	
3. 学校行事の中で、何が一番きらいですか。	
4. じゅくに行っていますか。	
5. おこづかいは一か月にいくらもらいますか。	
6. 高校生としては、あなたのおこづかいは多いですか。	
7. 将来 〔しょうらい〕 日本の大学に留学 〔りゅうがく〕 してみたいと思いますか。	

二課

E. ペアワーク （学校のきそくについてインタビュー）

Interview your partner about his/her school. Jot down your partner's responses.

1. 学校でせいふくを着なければなりませんか。	
2. 女子生徒はパーマをかけてもいいですか。	
3. 化粧〔けしょう〕をしてもいいですか。	
4. ピアスをしてもいいですか。	
5. 教室をそうじしなければなりませんか。	
6. トイレはだれがそうじをしますか。	
7. 教室の中でぼうしをぬがなければなりませんか。	
8. 学校のたて物に入る時、くつをはきかえなければなりませんか。	

F. ペアワーク （学校の問題についてインタビュー）

Interview your partner for his/her opinions about the following school problems at his/her school. Check the correct column.

質問：学校にいじめの問題があると思いますか。

答え： （多い／少ない／ほとんどない） と思います。

	多い	少ない	ほとんどない
1. たばこ			
2. アルコール			
3. いじめ			
4. まやく			
5. 銃〔じゅう〕			
6. カンニング			

G. ペアワーク (Modifying Sentence)

Interview your partner and identify a classmate who fits each of the following descriptions. Write the person's name in the space.

Ex. 野球〔やきゅう〕が上手な人

質問：「野球〔やきゅう〕が上手な人は、だれですか。」

1	テニスが上手な人	
2	ピアノがひける人	
3	学校へバスで来る人	
4	映画〔えいが〕が好きな人	
5	日本へ行ったことがある人	
6	中国語が話せる人	
7	うんてんめんきょを持っている人	
8	やさいしか食べない人	
9	今、アルバイトをしている人	
10	漢字をよく知っている人	

二課

H. ペアワーク (Modifying Sentence)

On this and the next page, you will find two identical pictures with some different names missing on each. You will look at one picture and your partner will take the other. Find out each person's name by asking the question below. Your partner's picture has the answers. Write the names in the correct brackets. Take turns. After you have both completed your pictures, compare the names in the your brackets. Are they accurate?

Person A

質問：「（～を―て）いる人は、だれですか。」

答え：「（～を―て）いる人は、～さんです。」

Person B

質問：「（〜を―て）いる人は、だれですか。」
答え：「（〜を―て）いる人は、〜さんです。」

二課

I. ペアワーク

Hanako Yamamoto is an 11th grade student in Japan. The chart below is her weekly school schedule. Answer the questions on the next page after studying Hanako's schedule.

高2山本花子さんの時間割(わり) (schedule)

Note: In Japan, you will often encounter military times, as in the afternoon hours below.

	月	火	水	木	金
8:30 〜 8:35	ホームルーム	ホームルーム	ホームルーム	ホームルーム	ホームルーム
1時間目 8:40 〜 9:30	古典〔こてん〕 Japanese classics	げんだい 国語 Modern language	古典〔こてん〕 Japanese classics	げんだい 国語 Modern language	げんだい 国語 Modern language
2時間目 9:40 〜 10:30	英語〔えいご〕	英語〔えいご〕	英語〔えいご〕	英語〔えいご〕	英語〔えいご〕
3時間目 10:40 〜 11:30	地理〔ちり〕 Geography	日本史〔にほんし〕 Japanese history	地理〔ちり〕 Geography	日本史〔にほんし〕 Japanese history	道徳〔どうとく〕 Morals/Ethics
4時間目 11:40 〜 12:30	数学〔すうがく〕	数学〔すうがく〕	数学〔すうがく〕	化学	数学〔すうがく〕
昼食	昼食	昼食	昼食	昼食	昼食
5時間目 13:15 〜 14:05	音楽〔おんがく〕	家庭科〔かていか〕 Home Economics	音楽〔おんがく〕	家庭科〔かていか〕 Home Economics	音楽〔おんがく〕
6時間目 14:15 〜 15:05	体育〔たいいく〕	保健〔ほけん〕 Health	体育〔たいいく〕	体育〔たいいく〕	ホームルーム
15:10 〜 15:30	ホームルーム そうじ	ホームルーム そうじ	ホームルーム そうじ	ホームルーム そうじ	ホームルーム そうじ

山本さんの時間割 (schedule) について、質問に答えて下さい。

1. 毎日、何時に学校へ行かなければなりませんか。　_____

2. 毎日、何時に学校が終わりますか。　_____

3. 昼食時間は何分ありますか。　_____

4. クラスは何分ですか。　_____

5. 一週間に何日、学校がありますか。　_____

6. 毎日、いくつ授業がありますか。　_____

7. 毎日ある授業は、何と何ですか。　_____

8. 一週間に何日、体育の授業がありますか。　_____

9. 授業の後で、何がありますか。　_____

10. あなたの時間割 (schedule) とちがうところはどこですか。

　三つ書いて下さい。

1. _____

2. _____

3. _____

J. | ペアワーク （一年の行事） |

Hanako Yamamoto is a Japanese 11th grade student. The chart below shows her school calendar.
Compare it with your school calendar and answer the questions on the next page in Japanese.

高２山本花子さんの一年の学校行事とテスト

月	学校行事	テスト
４月６日 ４月１０日	始業式〔しぎょうしき〕 Opening ceremony 入学式〔にゅうがくしき〕 Entrance ceremony	実力〔じつりょく〕テスト Scholastic aptitude test
５月		中間試験〔ちゅうかんしけん〕 Mid-term exam
６月１５日	夏服〔なつふく〕 Change to summer uniform 合唱祭〔がっしょうさい〕 Song festival/competition	
７月２０日	終業式〔しゅうぎょうしき〕 Closing ceremony	期末試験〔きまつしけん〕 Final exam
８月	補習授業〔ほしゅうじゅぎょう〕 Supplementary lessons 修学旅行〔しゅうがくりょこう〕 　オーストラリア Study tour	
９月１日	始業式〔しぎょうしき〕 Opening ceremony	実力〔じつりょく〕テスト Scholastic aptitude test
１０月１０日	冬服〔ふゆふく〕 Change to winter uniform 体育祭〔たいいくさい〕 Sports meet	中間試験〔ちゅうかんしけん〕 Mid-term exam
１１月３日	文化祭〔ぶんかさい〕 Cultural festival	
１２月２４日	終業式〔しゅうぎょうしき〕 Closing ceremony	期末試験〔きまつしけん〕 Final exam

| 二課 |
88

1月8日	始業式〔しぎょうしき〕 Opening ceremony	実力〔じつりょく〕テスト Scholastic aptitude test
2月1日 2月10日	マラソン大会 Marathon 入学試験〔にゅうがくしけん〕 Entrance exam	
3月10日 3月20日	卒業式〔そつぎょうしき〕 Graduation ceremony 修了式〔しゅうりょうしき〕 Closing ceremony	学年末〔がくねんまつ〕テスト Final (end of the year) exam

質問

1. 日本の学校が始まるのは、いつですか。 ＿＿＿＿＿＿＿＿

2. 日本の学校は、何学期ありますか。 ＿＿＿＿＿＿＿＿

3. 修学旅行は、海外旅行ですか。 ＿＿＿＿＿＿＿＿

4. 山本さんの学校に制服がありますか。 ＿＿＿＿＿＿＿＿

5. 夏服に着かえるのは、いつですか。 ＿＿＿＿＿＿＿＿

6. 冬服に着かえるのは、いつですか。 ＿＿＿＿＿＿＿＿

7. 一年の行事の中で、何が一番おもしろそうですか。 ＿＿＿＿＿＿＿＿

8. 山本さんの学校では試験が多いと思いますか。 ＿＿＿＿＿＿＿＿

9. あなたの学校と一番ちがうところはどこですか。 ＿＿＿＿＿＿＿＿

10. あなたの学校と同じところはどこですか。 ＿＿＿＿＿＿＿＿

K. ペアワーク

For each of the situations below, ask your partner what Japanese expression is most appropriate to use. Take turns asking and answering questions.

Ex. 朝、先生に会った時に

質問：<u>朝、先生に会った時に</u>、何と言いますか。

答え：<u>朝、先生に会った時に</u>、「おはようございます」と言います。

1. 食べる時に	
2. はじめて人に会った時に	
3. うちを出かける時に	
4. 朝、友達に会った時に	
5. プレゼントをもらった時に	
6. 友達がうるさい時に	
7. 友達が大事なしあいに行く時に	
8. 友達がしあいにかった時に	
9. ねる時に	
10. 日本人の日本語がはやすぎて分からない時に	

L. ペアワーク

Ask your partner the following questions. Your partner will answer based on fact. Take turns.

1. どんな時、ドキドキしますか。	
2. どんな時、友達に電話しますか。	
3. どんな時、お母さんはあなたをしかりますか。	
4. どんな時、学校をやめたいと思いますか。	
5. どんな時、かなしいですか。	
6. どんな時、うれしいですか。	

アドベンチャー日本語3
ＯＰＩ単語＆文法チェックリスト
２課：日本の高校生

名前：＿＿＿＿＿＿＿＿＿＿＿

クラス：＿＿＿＿＿＿

たんご	Check	たんご	Check
へいわ		いじめ	
私立		じゅう	
公立		まやく	
男子校		カンニングする	
女子校		ほとんど	
男女きょう学		ところ	
教いく		学期〔がっき〕	
じゅぎょうりょう		一学期	
くさ		二学期	
しばふ		先学期	
かよう		今学期	
行事		来学期	
ほうか後		毎学期	
ぶかつ		入学しき	
けんどう		そつぎょうしき	
じゅく		文化	
お小づかい		文化さい	
りゅう学する		海外旅行	
やる		やめる	
～として		～かな	
パーマをかける		～かしら	
お化しょうをする		Others	
ぬぐ		Others	
はきかえる		Others	

ぶんぽう	Check	Error
NのN		
～をしている		
～しか + Neg.		
V (- oo)		
～という～		
～とか～		
～かえる		
～時（に）		
Noun Modifiers		
～って言う		
Others		
Others		
Plain Polite		
Male Female		

91

二課

By the end of this lesson, you will be able to communicate the information below in the given situation. Complete the following tasks with a partner. You are expected to conduct a natural conversation using as many new vocabulary and grammatical structures as you can, while appropriately incorporating vocabulary and structures you have learned previously. Use the appropriate speech style (plain or polite) and male/female speech if appropriate. Practice the dialogue with your partner; the aim is not to memorize a dialogue, but to communicate meaningfully with your partner on the topics below.

【Ⅲ-3 トピック 1】

Partner **A** : *High school student*
Partner **B**: *Friend of A*

Situation: **A** *has a problem he/she discusses with a close friend.*

A explains his/her problem at school. **A** is troubled since his/her grades are not good, and is worried because there are so many exams to take and a project presentation next week. School life is not good either, since **A** is not participating in any club activities. **A** is also concerned about his/her friends, who ordinarily have positive traits but recently do not call. **A** asks for **B**'s advice. **B** tries to help by asking many questions and giving advice for each of **A**'s problems. **A** responds to the advice.

【Ⅲ-3 トピック 2】

Partner **A**: *High school student studying Japanese*
Partner **B**: *Another high school student studying Japanese*

Situation: *Two classmates discuss a person they each respect.*

Partner **A** and **B** discuss persons they respect. They discuss how they know/are related to the people, physical characteristics of the person, some biographical information and personality traits of the people they admire and the person's hobbies/interests. They discuss the reasons they respect the individuals. **A** and **B** comment and ask questions and opinions of each other.

はいけい

　秋になって、ずい分さむくなって来ました。おひさしぶりです。お元気ですか。ぼくは、おかげ様で元気でやっています。ホストファミリーのみなさんは、とてもしんせつで、ぼくをよく世話して下さいます。

　さて、日本の学校生活は楽しいですが、大変なことも多いです。一クラスに四十人も生徒がいるので、自分のいけんをはっぴょうする時は、ほとんどありません。ぼくは日本語がよく分からないから、音楽とか体育のじゅぎょうは楽ですが、ほかのじゅぎょうはつらいです。試験をうける時、先生はぼくにとくべつの試験を作って下さいます。ぼくの問題を聞いて下さい。一生けんめいべんきょうしているのに、日本語が分からないんです。よるもよくねられないので、こまっています。どうしたら、いいですか。アドバイスをおねがいします。

　では、お元気で。

　　　　　　　　　　　　　　　けいぐ

十月二十日

川口秋子先生

　　　　　　　　　　　　　　ケン・スミス

A. Writing Traditional Japanese Letters.

When writing formal Japanese-style letters, a definite format must be followed. In addition to the parts of the letter, pay close attention to the relative positioning of each part of the letter on the page.

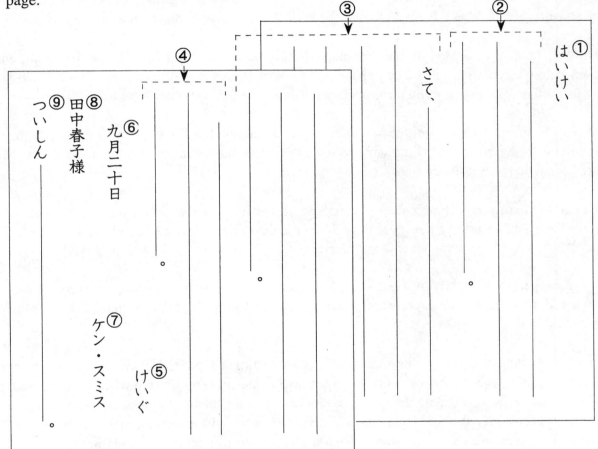

① **Opening**. 拝啓 (はいけい), 前略 (ぜんりゃく), etc. These are set expressions used to open all traditional Japanese letters. 前略 (ぜんりゃく) suggests that you will dispense with opening formalities. Note that this appears near the top right side of the page. Also note that all letters must be surrounded by margins.

② **Preliminary greetings**. Generally, greetings referring to the current season or climate and inquiries about the receiver's health are included in this first portion of the letter. Note that each new paragraph is indented.

③ **Body**. The main message of the letter is conveyed here. Almost always, the new paragraph begins with the words さて or ところで.

④ **Final greetings**. This final paragraph expresses wishes for the good health of the receiver, that one is waiting for a response, and/or apologies for the poor writing or penmanship of the author of the letter.

⑤ **Closing**. Note the position of the closing remark. It appears very low on the page on a separate line from the final greeting paragraph. When one uses 拝啓 (はいけい) at the beginning, one generally closes with 敬具 (けいぐ). If one begins one's letter with 前略 (ぜんりゃく), one closes with 草々 (そうそう). In more informal letters, one may even close with さようなら. Females may close with かしこ, also in more informal contexts.

⑥ **Date**. The date is written on the next line, slightly below the top of the of the main text, and even below the normal indentation space. When written in the traditional vertical letter writing format, all dates must be written completely in *kanji*. The year does not have to be written.

⑦ **Writer's name**. This is written on the next line, about one-third of the way down on the page. Foreigners may write their first name followed by their family name, but Japanese write their last name, then their first name.

⑧ **Receiver's name**. The receiver's name should appear near the top of the page at about the same level as the start of a new paragraph. The receiver's name should be followed by 様 (さま) or 先生 (せんせい), whichever is appropriate.

⑨ **Postscript**. (P.S.) This is to be avoided in letters to superiors or very formal letters. If it is included, it appears after the receiver's name, near the top of the page, slightly higher than the receiver's name.

Other notes: As indicated earlier, the format is fixed in writing a Japanese letter. Observing spacing and positioning is very important. One must also avoid breaking up words in columns. Also, one should be generous with the use of stationery. Do not attempt to "squeeze" your letter on a page. It is considered much better etiquette to be generous with spacing, especially at the end of the letter. Sometimes, Japanese will attach a blank page to a letter that ends at the end of the previous page. In traditional and formal letters, black pen is generally used. Crossing out and correction fluid are also generally taboo in formal letters. Observing these rules shows that one has respect for the receiver of the letter.

B. Addressing Envelopes in Japanese.

Envelopes sent within Japan are longer and slimmer than Western envelopes. They are used vertically and the opening flap is on the top side of the envelope.

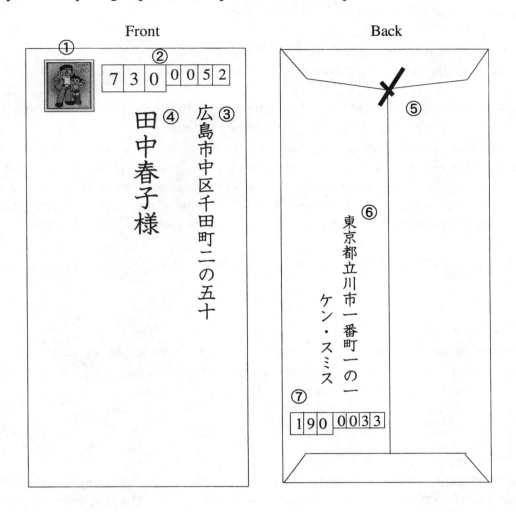

Front Back

① Stamps are placed on the upper left hand side of the envelope.

② Small blocks situated horizontally next to the stamp are for zip codes. Zip codes have seven digits.

③ On the right side of the envelope, from top down, the address of the person receiving the letter is written. Begin fairly high on the envelope, so that most of the address will fit in one line. When writing addresses in Japanese, the largest geographical unit is written first. In most cases, it is the prefecture, unless it is a major city such as Tokyo. The next largest unit may be a city or district, then something equivalent to a street address.

④   At the upper center part of the envelope, write the last name of the person, then the first name, if the person is Japanese. In the case of foreigners, the first name may appear first. After the receiver's name, one must attach the polite suffix -SAMA or SENSEI, whichever is appropriate. Often, the name of the receiver is also written larger.

⑤   On the back of the envelope, you will notice that many Japanese will mark an X or place a seal on the flap after the envelope has been sealed. This is to ensure security.

⑥   The writer's name and return address is written on the left half of the back of the envelope. The address is written first, again beginning with the largest unit. Note the position of the address. It appears about two-thirds of the way down on the envelope. If the entire return address does not fit, it is permissible to continue the address on the next line, but at a lower level. Do not break up individual units of the address. The writer's name appears to the left of the address. Usually, the name is written slightly lower than the first line of the address. If the writer's name is Japanese, the last name is written first. Foreigners may write their first name first.

⑦   In the lower left corner of the envelope are small boxes in which the writer's zip code is written.

C. Fortune Telling in Japan （日本のうらない）

Many forms of fortune-telling（うらない）exist in Japan. They include 十二し, the 12-animal cycle zodiac described in an earlier volume of this text, palm reading（てそううらない）, blood-type fortune telling, and Western astrology（ほしうらない）, which has recently become very popular.

1. Palm Reading（てそううらない）

Palm reading is similar in the U. S. and Japan. Interpretations vary according to different schools, but they are based on the eight basic lines etched on human hands. The first is the life line （せいめいせん）, which refers to one's physical health and life span. The second is the fate line （うんめいせん）, which tells of one's walk through life and turning points in work, marriage and homelife. The intellect line（ちのうせん）reveals one's character, talents, decision-making tendencies and powers of understanding. Those with short lines are active and decisive, while those with long lines tend to be cautious. The heart line（かんじょうせん）describes one's personality and love and married life. Those with long or curvy heart lines are said to be passionate; those with short lines are cool and rational. Not every person possesses a sun line （たいようせん）. Having one indicates that one will be famous, successful and wealthy. A sharp, strong marriage line（けっこんせん）suggests that one will enjoy strong and happy love or marriage relationships. The health line（けんこうせん）is said to appear when one's health is not good. This line may appear or disappear according to one's physical condition. A sharp fortune line（ざいうんせん）indicates that one is prosperous and successful in business.

三課   98

Palm Reading (てそううらない)

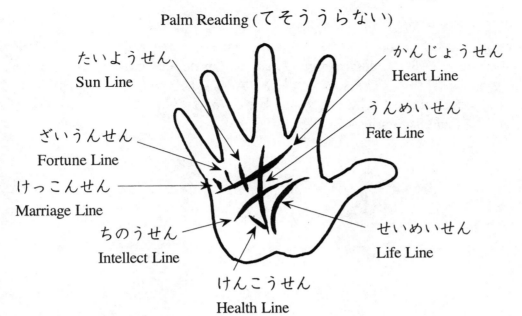

たいようせん
Sun Line

かんじょうせん
Heart Line

うんめいせん
Fate Line

ざいうんせん
Fortune Line

けっこんせん
Marriage Line

ちのうせん
Intellect Line

せいめいせん
Life Line

けんこうせん
Health Line

2. Blood Type (けつえきがた)

One of the most popular recent forms of fortune telling uses blood type (けつえきがた) as a means to characterize people or to predict their futures. While many Americans may not even be sure of their blood type, all Japanese (especially younger people) know their blood type. The blood types of famous people and entertainers are always included as part of their "vital statistics."

Type A persons are thought to be private, perfectionists, traditionalists, proper, "rule followers," service-oriented, good team players, mature, pragmatic and diligent. If they are to show negative characteristics, they may be nervous, timid, too eager to please others, distrustful and overly structured.

Type B persons are independent, practical, open, frank, good-natured, decisive, generous, objective, research-oriented and often have many interests, but are not very focused. They may also be considered eccentric, willful, rude and not very resourceful.

Type AB persons are rational, analytical, politically and socially concerned, focused, dependable, business-minded, congenial, fair, hopeful and possess many interests. Sometimes, however, they may be overly cautious, disagreeable, lacking in independence, indecisive, childish and self-centered.

Type O persons are ambitious, determined, decisive, loyal, straightforward, aggressive, confident, independent, strong-willed, passionate, enterprising, action-oriented and romantic. They may also be inconsistent in their work, calculating, self-centered, rebellious and use any means to attain their goals.

三課

3. Western Astrology (ほしうらない)

Western astrology, based on one's birthdate, is the same in Japan and the U.S. Here are the Japanese equivalents of each astrological sign. Learn the Japanese term for yours. Capricorn - やぎざ, Aquarius - みずがめざ, Pisces - うおざ, Aries - おひつじざ, Taurus - おうしざ, Gemini - ふたござ, Cancer - かにざ, Leo - ししざ, Virgo - おとめざ, Libra - てんびんざ, Scorpio - さそりざ, and Sagittarius - いてざ.

1. 春 spring　　　　はる　　　　春休み〔はるやすみ〕spring vacation

春子さん Haruko

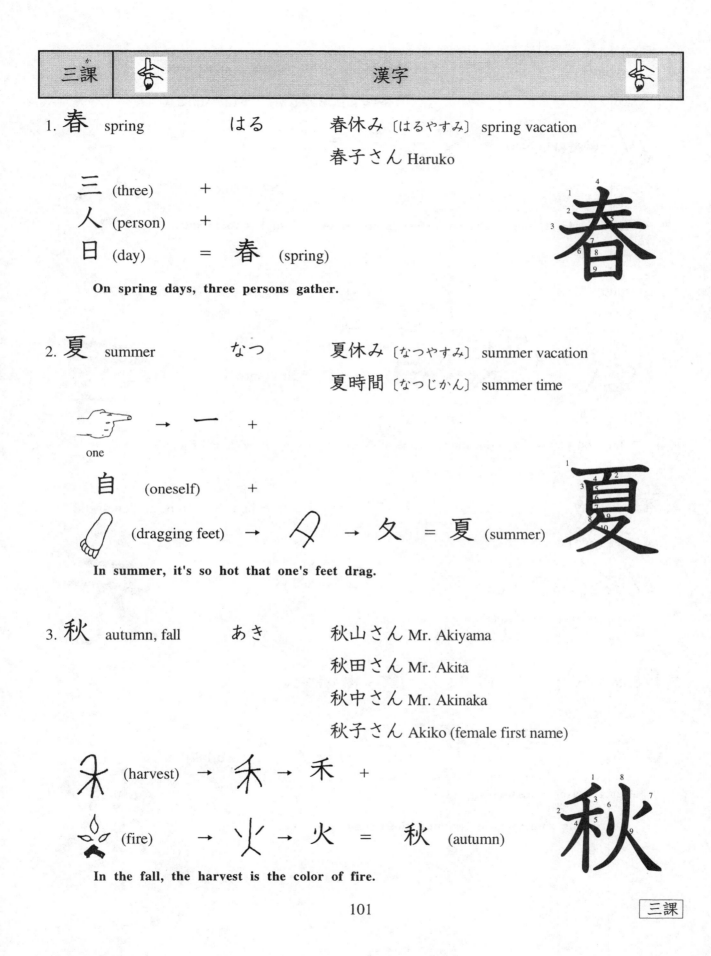

三 (three)　　　+

人 (person)　　+

日 (day)　　　= 春 (spring)

On spring days, three persons gather.

2. 夏 summer　　　　なつ　　　　夏休み〔なつやすみ〕summer vacation

夏時間〔なつじかん〕summer time

one → 一 +

自 (oneself)　　+

(dragging feet) → 夂 → 夂 = 夏 (summer)

In summer, it's so hot that one's feet drag.

3. 秋 autumn, fall　　あき　　　　秋山さん Mr. Akiyama

秋田さん Mr. Akita

秋中さん Mr. Akinaka

秋子さん Akiko (female first name)

禾 (harvest) → 禾 → 禾 +

(fire) → 火 → 火 = 秋 (autumn)

In the fall, the harvest is the color of fire.

101

4. 冬　winter　　　　　　　ふゆ　　　　冬休み〔ふゆやすみ〕winter vacation

冬時間〔ふゆじかん〕winter time

（dragging feet）→ 夂 → 夂 ＋

こ　　　　　　　　　　　　　　　　　　　＝　冬　（winter）

In the winter, one drags one's feet in the snow and makes footprints.

冬

5. 雪　snow　　　　　　　　ゆき　　　　雪がふる to snow

→ 雨 → 雨 ＋

→ ヨ → ヨ ＝ 雪　（snow）

a broom in a hand

Rain falls and turns to snow.　Now we have to sweep it with a broom.

雪

6. 元　healthy　　　　　　　ゲン　　　　元気〔げんき〕fine; be in a good health; energetic

二（two）＋

→ 儿（legs）＝ 元　（healthy）

A healthy person can run on both legs.

元

7. 飲　to drink　　　　　　の（む）　　　飲み物〔のみもの〕a drink

食（to eat）＋

→ 欠 → 欠 → 欠（to lack）＝ 飲（to drink）

a hungry person bends his body and opens his mouth

Drinking something is less nutritious than eating.

飲

三課　　　　　　102

8. 体　body　　　　　　からだ　　　　　大きい体 a big body

タイ　　　　　体育 physical education

体育館 gym

イ (person) → イ → イ ＋

本 (book; origin)

The body is basic (the origin) to one's existence.

9. 音　sound　　　　　　おと　　　　　　うるさい音 noisy sound

オン　　　　　音楽 music

立 (to stand)　＋

日 (sun)　　　＝　音　(sound)

Stand up on Sunday and make good sounds.

10. 楽　enjoyable　　　　たの（しい）　　楽しい is enjoyable

comfortable　　　らく　　　　　楽ないす comfortable chair

ガク　　　　　音楽〔おんがく〕 music

白 (white)　＋

六 (sound)　＋

木 (tree)　＝　楽 (enjoyable)

I hear the sound of a white tree.　It is comforting!

11. 糸　thread, string　　　いと　　　　　糸こんにゃく shredded *konnyaku*

∂ → ∂ → 糸 → 糸 ＝ 糸 (thread)

A string wound around a spindle.

103

三課

12. 紙　paper　　　　　　　　かみ　　　　　　　白い紙〔しろいかみ〕 white paper

　　　　　　　　　　　　　　がみ　　　　　　　手紙〔てがみ〕 letter

糸 (thread)　＋

乆 → 仐 → 氏 → 氏 (family name) ＝ 紙 (paper)

a spoon with a bent handle

(One feeds a baby with a spoon that has a bent handle. This character refers to one's family
name that one passes down through the generations.)

Paper is made from threads on which people write their family names.

【読みかえの漢字】

生　　be born　　う（まれる）　＊　日本で生まれました。 I was born in Japan.

　　　　　　　　なま＊　　　　　生卵〔なまたまご〕 raw egg

　　　person　　セイ　　　　　先生〔せんせい〕 teacher

　　　　　　　　　　　　　　　学生〔がくせい〕 student

　　　　　　　　ショウ　　　　一生懸命〔いっしょうけんめい〕 utmost effort

＊ Previously introduced.

【読めればいい漢字】

1. 世話　　　せわ　　　　　care

2. 生活　　　せいかつ　　　life; living

3. 体育　　　たいいく　　　P.E.

4. 様　　　　さま　　　　　polite equivalent of -さん

5. 変　　　　へん　　　　　strange; weird; unusual

6. 大変　　　たいへん　　　hard; difficult

Let's review previous vocabulary!

A. めいし　Nouns

1. 手紙〔てがみ〕　letter
2. 秋〔あき〕　autumn, fall
3. 二日前〔ふつかまえ〕　two days ago
4. 山　mountain
5. 雪〔ゆき〕　snow
6. ぼく　I [used by males]
7. ホストファミリー　host family
8. みなさん　everyone
9. 日本　Japan
10. 学校　school
11. こと　things [intangible]
12. 一〔ひと〕クラス　one class
13. 四十人　40 people
14. 生徒　students
15. 自分〔じぶん〕　oneself
16. 時〔とき〕　when
17. 日本語　Japanese language
18. 音楽〔おんがく〕　music
19. 体育〔たいいく〕　physical education
20. じゅぎょう　class
21. ほか　other
22. 試験　exam
23. 先生　teacher
24. 問題　problem
25. よる　night
26. 十一月　November
27. 二十日〔はつか〕　20th (of the month)

B. どうし Verbs

28. なって〔G1 なる／なります〕　to become [TE form]
29. 来ました〔IR くる／きて〕　came
30. 雪がふりました〔G1 ふる／ふって〕　snowed
31. いる〔G2 います／いて〕　there are [animate]
32. ありません〔G1 ある／あって〕　there is not [inanimate]
33. 分からない〔G1 わかる／わかって〕　do not understand
34. 作って〔G1 つくる／つくります〕　to make
35. 聞いて下さい〔G1 きく／ききます〕　please listen
36. べんきょうしている〔IR べんきょうする／べんきょうします〕　is studying
37. ねられない〔G2 ねます／ねて〕　cannot sleep
38. いない〔G2 います／いて〕　there is not [animate]

C. い けいようし　I Adjectives

39. 楽しい　is fun; enjoyable
40. さむく　is cold
41. 多い　are many

105

D. な けいようし　NA Adjectives

42. 元気 〔げんき〕　healthy; fine

43. 大変 〔たいへん〕　hard

E. ふくし　Adverbs

44. とても　very

45. よく　well

46. ほとんど　mostly

47. 一生 〔いっしょう〕 けんめい　utmost effort

F. Expressions

48. お元気 〔げんき〕 ですか。　How are you?

49. おねがいします。　I would like to ask you a favor.

50. では、お元気で。　Well, take care!

Activity A   No new vocabulary.

Activity B

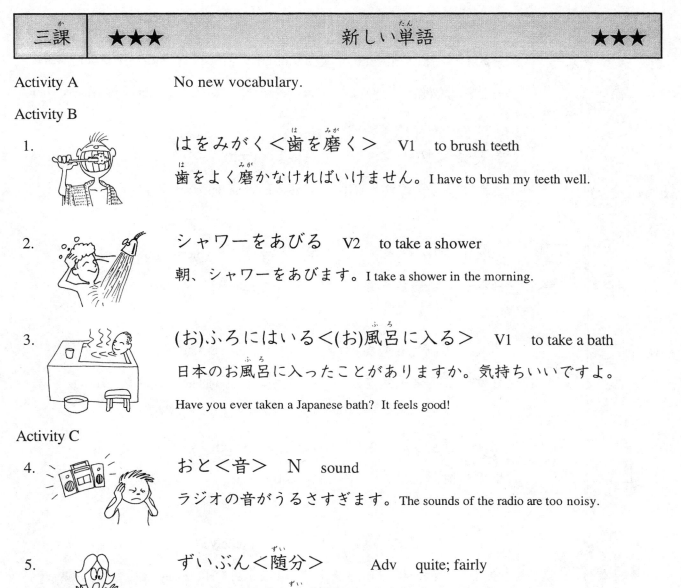

1. はをみがく＜歯(は)を磨(みが)く＞   V1   to brush teeth

   歯(は)をよく磨(みが)かなければいけません。I have to brush my teeth well.

2. シャワーをあびる   V2   to take a shower

   朝、シャワーをあびます。I take a shower in the morning.

3. (お)ふろにはいる＜(お)風呂(ふろ)に入(はい)る＞   V1   to take a bath

   日本のお風呂(ふろ)に入(はい)ったことがありますか。気持(きも)ちいいですよ。

   Have you ever taken a Japanese bath? It feels good!

Activity C

4. おと＜音＞   N   sound

   ラジオの音がうるさすぎます。The sounds of the radio are too noisy.

5. ずいぶん＜随分(ずい)分＞   Adv   quite; fairly

   このおむすびは随分(ずい)大きいですねえ。This rice ball is quite big!

6. ～ので   Rc   since ～; because ～ [expected result] ; so → Grammar A

   ぼくは十六才なので、お酒(さけ)を飲んではいけません。Since I am 16 years

old, I am not allowed to drink alcohol.

Activity D

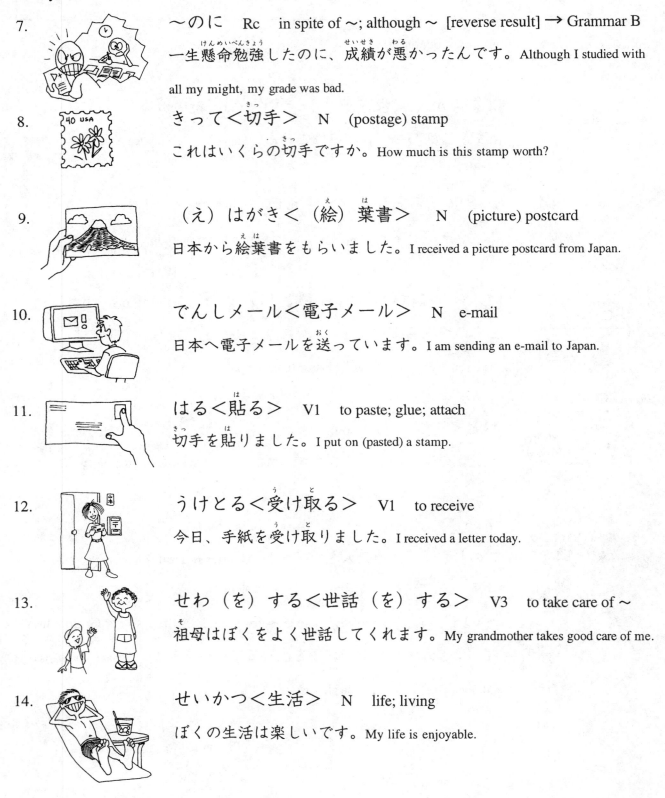

7. 〜のに　Rc　in spite of 〜; although 〜 [reverse result] → Grammar B

一生懸命勉強したのに、成績が悪かったんです。Although I studied with all my might, my grade was bad.

8. きって＜切手＞　N　(postage) stamp

これはいくらの切手ですか。How much is this stamp worth?

9. （え）はがき＜（絵）葉書＞　N　(picture) postcard

日本から絵葉書をもらいました。I received a picture postcard from Japan.

10. でんしメール＜電子メール＞　N　e-mail

日本へ電子メールを送っています。I am sending an e-mail to Japan.

11. はる＜貼る＞　V1　to paste; glue; attach

切手を貼りました。I put on (pasted) a stamp.

12. うけとる＜受け取る＞　V1　to receive

今日、手紙を受け取りました。I received a letter today.

13. せわ（を）する＜世話（を）する＞　V3　to take care of 〜

祖母はぼくをよく世話してくれます。My grandmother takes good care of me.

14. せいかつ＜生活＞　N　life; living

ぼくの生活は楽しいです。My life is enjoyable.

Activity E   No new vocabulary

Activity F

15.  いけん＜意見＞　N　opinion

私の意見を言ってもいいですか。May I give my opinion?

16.  つらい＜辛い＞　A　is hard; bitter; trying

学校の勉強は辛いです。School work is hard.

17.  とくべつ＜特別＞　NA　special

この人は私の特別な人です。This person is a special person to me.

18.  はっぴょうする＜発表する＞　V3　to present; announce

クラスの前でプロジェクトを発表しました。I presented my project in front

of the class.

19.  しけんをうける＜試験を受ける＞　V2　to take an exam

今日、日本語の試験を受けました。I took my Japanese exam today.

20.  そうだんする＜相談する＞　V3　to consult

この問題についてカウンセラーに相談しました。I consulted my counseler

about this problem.

21.  こまる＜困る＞　V1　to be troubled

今、本当に困っているんです。I am really troubled now.

22. 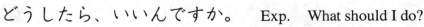 どうしたら、いいんですか。　Exp.　What should I do?

三課

Activity G

23. せいかく＜性格＞　N　personality; character

この人は性格がとてもいいです。This person has a very good personality.

24.  ふつう＜普通＞　N　ordinary; average; regular

ぼくの背の高さ(height)は普通です。My height is average.

25. かっこいい＜格好いい＞　A　is good looking

田中君はとても格好いいです。Mr. Tanaka is good looking.

26. おとなしい　A　is quiet (refers to people only)

山下さんはとてもおとなしいです。Ms. Yamashita is very quiet.

27. しんせつ＜親切＞　NA　is considerate; kind

お医者さんはとても親切な方でした。The doctor was a very considerate

person.

28. まじめ＜真面目＞　NA　is serious (refers to people only)

川口さんはとてもまじめな生徒です。Ms. Kawaguchi is a very serious

student.

Activity H

29.  ゆめ＜夢＞　N　dream

楽しい夢を見ています。He is having an enjoyable dream.

30.  けいたいでんわ＜携帯電話＞　N　cellular phone

ここで携帯電話を使ってはいけません。You are not allowed to use a cellular

phone here.

31.  かじ ＜家事＞　　N　household chore; housework

姉はよく家事を手伝います。 My older sister often helps with the housework.

32.  ペットをかう ＜飼う＞　　V1　to raise a pet

私は犬を飼っています。 I am raising a dog.

33.  そんけいする ＜尊敬する＞　　V3　to respect

私は父を一番尊敬しています。 I respect my father most.

34. ～てくださいます ＜～て下さいます＞ E (superior) do ～ for me

[～てくれます (equal/inferior) do ～ for me]

山田先生は毎日私達に日本語を教えて下さいます。 Mrs. Yamada teaches

us Japanese every day.

35.  らく ＜楽＞　　NA　is comfortable

このソファーはとても楽です。 This sofa is very comfortable.

Activity I

36. おひさしぶりです。　　Exp.　I have not seen you for a long time.

37. おかげさまで。 ＜お陰様で。 ＞　　Exp.　Thanks to you . . .

お陰様で旅行は楽しかったです。 Thanks to you, my trip was enjoyable.

38. おせわになりました。 ＜お世話になりました。 ＞

Exp.　Thank you for your kind help.

三課

39. （お）れい＜（お）礼＞　N　thanks; gratitude; appreciation

先生にお礼を言いました。I thanked my teacher.

40. (お)れいじょう＜(お)礼状＞　N　thank-you letter

友達からお礼状をもらいました。I received a thank-you letter from my friend.

【オプショナル単語】

1. はいけい＜拝啓＞　　　　　　　　Exp.　Dear Sir/Madam [letter]

2. けいぐ＜敬具＞　　　　　　　　　Exp.　Sincerely yours, [letter]

3. さて　　　　　　　　　　　　　　SI　Well; Now,

4. ふうとう＜封筒＞　　　　　　　　N　envelope

5. びんせん＜便箋＞　　　　　　　　N　stationery

6. こうくうびん＜航空便＞　　　　　N　air mail

7. ゆうびんばんごう＜郵便番号＞　N　zip code

8. へんじ＜返事＞　　　　　　　　　N　a reply

9. ごぶさたしています＜御無沙汰しています＞

　　　　　　　　　　　　　　　　　Exp.　I apologize for not being in contact with you for a long time./I apologize for not calling upon you sooner.

A. Sentence 1 (informal ending) [Reason/Cause] ので、 Sentence 2 [Result]。

ので is a mid-sentence conjunction which is used to connect two simple sentences into one. The first of the two clauses expresses a reason or cause for the second. It is often translated as "so," "because" or "since."

　When the word immediately preceding ので is a verb or い adjective, the appropriate plain form is used, i.e., たかいので... If the word immediately preceding ので is a non-past affirmative noun or な adjective, な must appear between that word and ので, i.e., 好きなので... In the negative, past and negative forms, the plain forms of the noun and な adjectives are used.

　Note: The sentence conjoiner から you learned earlier may also be translated as "so," "because" or "since." ので cannot be used when the second portion of the sentence involves the speaker's own conjecture, opinion, command, request, suggestion, invitation or volition. That is, when the second part of the sentence is an expression of one's personal feelings imposed on the listener, から should be used instead. In each of the following examples, ので should not be used.

　a. S1 expresses the speaker's conjecture.

　　日本は寒（さむ）いでしょうから、コートを持って行きましょう。

　　　Since it will probably be cold in Japan, I will take a coat.

　b. S2 is a command, request, suggestion or invitation.

　　土曜日にパーティーをしますから、ぜひ来て下さい。

　　　Because we will have a party on Saturday, please be sure to come.

　c. S2 expresses the speaker's volition or personal opinion.

　　その映画（えいが）はおもしろそうですから、私も行きたいです。

　　　Because that movie looks interesting, I also want to go.

1. 弟はまだ１５才なので、お酒（さけ）を飲んではいけません。

　　Since my younger brother is still 15 years old, he is not allowed to drink alcohol.

2. 明日試験があるので、今晩（ばん）、勉強（べんきょう）しなければなりません。

　　Since I will have an exam tomorrow, I have to study tonight.

3. Ｔシャツがセールで安かったので、三枚（まい）も買ってしまいました。

　　Since T-shirts were on sale (at a cheap price), I bought (as many as) three.

4. ジーンズは、楽なので、私はいつもジーンズをはいています。

　　Since jeans are comfortable, I always wear them.

5. 図書館は、静（しず）かだったので、よく勉強（べんきょう）出来ました。

　　Because the library was quiet, I was able to study well.

B. Sentence 1 (informal ending) [contrary] のに、 Sentence 2 。

The mid-sentence conjunction のに is translated as "In spite of the fact that ..." It is used to join two simple sentences into a more complex one and is used when one wishes to express an unexpected result, usually surprise, discontent, disappointment, regret or disbelief at an occurrence or state. The first of the two clauses appears in the plain form, with the exception of the present noun and な adjective, which take な. The first clause expresses the occurrence and the second main clause expresses the unexpected result. Occasionally, the unexpected result is not stated in words, but is implied. In such cases, the sentence ends with のに.

    a. 毎日練習したのに。

        (lit. Although I practiced every day . . .)

        "Although I really practiced hard every day . . . (something unexpected happened.)"

    b. あの子が好きだったのに。

        (lit., Although I liked him/her.)

        "Although I really liked him/her . . . (something unexpected happened.)"

Note: When the second clause is a request, suggestion, question, command or request for permission, けど or けれど, which means "although" should be used instead of のに. For each of the following examples, のに should not be used.

    c. この本はちょっと高いけど、買いますか。

        This book is a little expensive, but will you buy it?

    d. このケーキはちょっとあまいけど、食べてみて下さい。

        This cake is a little sweet, but please try to eat it.

If a neutral "but" meaning is preferred が should be used instead of けど, けれど or のに.

    e. 昨日、映画を見ましたが、あまりおもしろくなかったです。

        I watched a movie yesterday, but it was not very interesting.

1. 妹は小学生なのに、料理がとても上手です。

    Although my younger sister is an elementary school student, she is very skillful at cooking.

2. 私がケーキを作ったのに、だれも食べてくれませんでした。

    Even though I baked a cake, no one ate it.

3. ゆうべよく勉強したのに、今日の試験はよく出来なかったんです。

    Although I studied hard last night, I did not do well on today's exam.

4. 僕はあの子が好きなのに、あの子はほかの子が好きなんですよ。

    Although I like her, she likes someone else.

5. 日本語を三年も勉強しているのに、まだ上手に話せません。

    Although I have been studying Japanese for three years, I still cannot speak it well.

C. 〜んです，〜のです

The 〜んです and 〜のです endings are frequently used in speaking. When it appears in a statement form, it suggests that the speaker feels obligated to explain him/herself or his/her actions. When it appears in a question form, it serves the purpose of inviting an explanation from the listener. 〜のです is used in formal situations and 〜んです is used in less formal situations. The copula だ changes to な before 〜んです and 〜のです.

1. 友達が麻薬を使っているんですよ。　My friend is using drugs.

2. この本は本当に高かったんですよ。　This book was really expensive, you know.

3. 僕は化学が苦手なんですよ。　I am poor at chemistry.

4. あの人が好きなんです。　I like him/her.

5. ぼくはあの子が好きだったんです。　I liked her.

6. 本当にいいんですか。　Is it really o.k.?

7. なぜ分からないんですか。　Why don't you understand it?

Summary:

Verb	食べる			eat; will eat
	食べない			do not eat; will not eat
	食べた			ate
	食べなかった			did not eat
いAdjective	高い			is expensive
	高くない			is not expensive
	高かった			was expensive
	高くなかった			was not expensive
なAdjective	好きな	+ので、 のに、 んです。 のです。		like
	好きじゃない or 好きではない			do not like
	好きだった			liked
	好きじゃなかった or 好きではなかった			did not like
Noun	学生な			is a student
	学生じゃない or 学生ではない			is not a student
	学生だった			was a student
	学生じゃなかった or 学生ではなかった			was not a student

三課

D. 寒く<ruby>寒<rt>さむ</rt></ruby>くなってきました

When the verbs きます and いきます are attached to -TE forms of verbs that describe a change of state, i.e., なる "to become," こむ "to get crowded," すく "to get less crowded," ふとる "to gain weight," やせる "to lose weight," etc., they suggest a progressive change from one point to another. When くる is attached, it suggests a change of condition from a certain point in time to another point in time that may be perceived as the present. When いく is attached, it suggests a change in condition from some point in time to some future time. In this construction, きます and いきます are not usually written in *kanji*.

～てくる ～ていく

Past ——————→ Point in Time ——————→ Future

1. 寒くなってきました。   It has become cold.

2. 暖かくなっていくでしょう。   It will probably become warm.

3. 道が込んできました。   The streets have become crowded.

4. 日本語が難しくなってきました。   Japanese language has become difficult.

5. 毎年、物が高くなっていきます。   Things become more expensive every year.

E. Verb (TA form) ＋方が　　（いいです）　　It is better for you to ～.

  Verb (NAI form) ＋方が　　（いいです）　　It is better not to ～.

This constuction is derived from the comparative sentence structure introduced in Volume II. With the verb -TA preceding 方がいいです, however, this construction becomes a direct advice-giving construction. It literally means "It is good if you do/do not . . ." いい may be replaced by another い adjective or な adjective.

Compare:　行った方がいい。　　　　It is better for you (or someone) to go.
　　　　　行く方がいい。　　　　　It is better to go.
　　　　　行かない方がいい。　　　It is better not to go.

Using the -TA form makes the advice more direct and personal. Using the dictionary form makes it a more general piece of advice. The -NAI form may be used as the negative form of either.

1. 中山さんに手紙を書いた方がいいです。   It's better for you to write a letter to Mr. Nakayama.

2. 早く寝た方がいいでしょう。   It's probably better for you to go to bed early.

3. 寒いから、セーターを持って行った方がいいよ。

    It's better for you to take a sweater because it is cold.

4. たばこはすわない方がいいと思います。   I think it's better not to smoke.

A. ペアワーク (Time differences)

Look at the world standard time map. When you want to phone or send a fax to a person in Japan, you have to be aware of time differences 時差（じさ）. Fill in the blanks with appropriate responses and circle the correct word in the parentheses.

1. 私達の住んでいる所は、今日、＿＿＿＿＿月＿＿＿＿＿日＿＿＿＿＿曜日です。

2. ここは、今（午前　午後）＿＿＿＿＿時＿＿＿＿＿分です。

3. でも、日本では今日は、＿＿＿＿＿月＿＿＿＿＿日＿＿＿＿＿曜日です。

4. そして、今、日本は　（午前　午後）＿＿＿＿＿時です。

5. 今、アメリカは（夏時間　冬時間）です。

6. （夏時間　冬時間）（だったら　でも）、今、日本は

　　（午前　午後）＿＿＿＿＿時です。

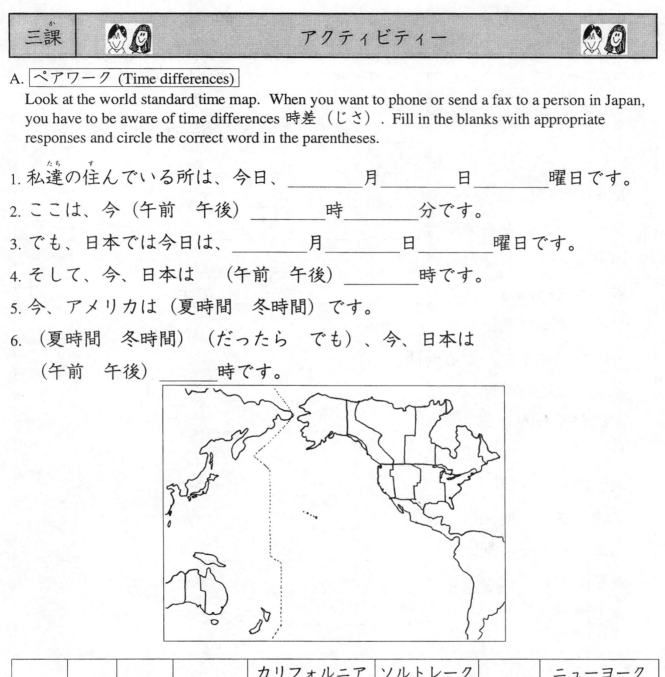

	日本	ハワイ	アラスカ	カリフォルニア ロス バンクーバー	ソルトレーク デンバー フィニックス	シカゴ ダラス	ニューヨーク ボストン モントリオール
	2日	1日	1日	1日	1日	1日	1日
夏時間	7:00	12:00	14:00	15:00	16:00	17:00	18:00
冬時間	7:00	12:00	13:00	14:00	15:00	16:00	17:00

B. ペアワーク

Interview your partner about his/her daily routine. Fill in the blanks with your partner's answers. Then compare it to your own routine and write one similarity and one difference in Japanese.

＿＿＿＿＿＿＿＿＿＿＿さんの一日

起きる時間は ＿＿＿＿＿＿＿＿＿＿＿＿＿ です。

シャワーをあびる時間は ＿＿＿＿＿＿＿＿＿＿＿＿＿ です。

朝食を食べる時間は ＿＿＿＿＿＿＿＿＿＿＿＿＿ です。

家を出る時間は ＿＿＿＿＿＿＿＿＿＿＿＿＿ です。

学校に着く時間は ＿＿＿＿＿＿＿＿＿＿＿＿＿ です。

家から学校までかかる時間は ＿＿＿＿＿＿＿＿＿＿＿＿＿ です。

昼食を食べる時間は ＿＿＿＿＿＿＿＿＿＿＿＿＿ です。

学校が終わる時間は ＿＿＿＿＿＿＿＿＿＿＿＿＿ です。

放課後にやっている部活は ＿＿＿＿＿＿＿＿＿＿＿＿＿ です。

家へ帰る時間は ＿＿＿＿＿＿＿＿＿＿＿＿＿ です。

夕食を食べる時間は ＿＿＿＿＿＿＿＿＿＿＿＿＿ です。

お風呂に入る時間は ＿＿＿＿＿＿＿＿＿＿＿＿＿ です。

歯を磨く時間は ＿＿＿＿＿＿＿＿＿＿＿＿＿ です。

寝る時間は ＿＿＿＿＿＿＿＿＿＿＿＿＿ です。

私とちがうところ Difference	
私とおなじところ Similarity	

C. ペアワーク：〜ので

Match the sentences in the left column with an appropriate ending on the right by filling in the ( ) with the correct letter.

1. 将来〔しょうらい〕、日本に留学〔りゅうがく〕したいので、（　　）	A. 今日の試験はよく出来たんです。
2. テレビの音がうるさいので、（　　）	B. 今おなかがいっぱいなんです。
3. 目がわるいので、（　　）	C. かさを持って来たんです。
4. 夕食をたくさん食べたので、（　　）	D. 今日本語をべんきょうしているんです。
5. あたまがいたいので、（　　）	E. ここで待っていなければいけないんです。
6. やさいしか食べないので、（　　）	F. あなたのこえが聞こえないんです。
7. 毎朝みちがずい分こんでいるので、（　　）	G. 肉も魚も食べないんです。
8. 朝、雨だったので、（　　）	H. めがねがいるんですよ。
9. ゆうべいっしょうけんめいべんきょうしたので、（　　）	I. 学校まで一時間もかかるんですよ。
10. 母がむかえに来るので、（　　）	J. アスピリンを飲んだんです。

D. ペアワーク：〜のに

Match the sentences in the left column with an appropriate ending on the right by filling in the ( )
with the correct letter.

1. 私たちの学校のバスケットの チームをおうえんしたのに、 （　）	A. いつも話し中だったんですよ。
2. ゆうべいっしょうけんめい べんきょうしたのに、 （　）	B. まだおなかがすいているんです。
3. 日本の生活は大変なのに、 （　）	C. 楽しいことも多いです。
4. たくさん食べたのに、 （　）	D. まけてしまったんですよ。
5. 昨日、友達に三度も電話を かけたのに、 （　）	E. かんしゃのことばを言った ことがないんです。
6. シャワーをあびたのに、 （　）	F. 今日の数学〔すうがく〕の試験は よく出来なかったんです。
7. 今日は休みなのに、 （　）	G. 日本の友達は私の手紙を うけとったんです。
8. 日本の友達から電子メールを もらったのに、 （　）	H. 私は日本語でタイプが出来ない から、まだへんじをしていない んですよ。
9. 切手〔きって〕をはらなかったのに、 （　）	I. もう、きたなくなったんですよ。
10. 母は私をよく世話してくれる のに、 （　）	J. 父は会社〔かいしゃ〕に行ったん ですよ。

E. ペアワーク （～てくる／いく）

Ask your partner's opinions. Write the answers in the blanks.

質問：これから寒くなっていくと思いますか。

Yes 答え：はい、寒くなっていくと思います。

No 答え：いいえ、寒くなっていくと思いません。

1. 日本語のべんきょうはむずかしくなってきたと思いますか。	
2. 日本語のべんきょうはこれからやさしくなっていくと思いますか。	
3. あなたは日本語をいっしょうけんめいべんきょうしてきたと思いますか。	
4. 物のねだんは高くなってきたと思いますか。	
5. 物のねだんは安くなっていくと思いますか。	
6. あなたのおこづかいは多くなっていくと思いますか。	
7. この学校のじゅぎょうりょうは高くなっていくと思いますか。	
8. あなたの生活は良くなっていくと思いますか。	

三課

F. ペアワーク→クラスワーク　（～た方がいいです）

You are a peer counselor and receive these questions from students with whom you work. For each, respond by writing your advice in Japanese. Present one case to your class. You may create another problem and use it instead.

問題１

試験や宿題がたくさんあって、ぜんぶ
出来ません。スポーツをしているので、
時間がないんです。明日、日本語の
試験をうけるはずですが、べんきょう
していません。どうしたら、いいですか。

アドバイス：

問題２

私の友達は、うんてんめんきょを
持っていませんが、車を時々うんてん
しています。私はこまっていますが、
そうだんする人もいません。
どうしたら、いいですか。

アドバイス：

問題３

友達がまやくをつかっています。私は
「やめて。」と言いましたが、
やめません。私はとてもつらいんです。
この友達は私のとくべつな友だち
ですから、たすけたいんです。
どうしたら、いいですか。

アドバイス：

問題４

私は人の前で自分のいけんをはっぴょう
することが出来ません。ドキドキして
話せないんです。
どうしたら、いいですか。

アドバイス：

G. ┌──────────────────────────────────┐
   │ ペアワーク→クラスワーク　　（どんな人？）│
   └──────────────────────────────────┘

Bring a picture of a person you admire to class. If you know another student who likes the same person, you may work together. Analyze why he/she is ideal to you. Circle the words that appropriately describe the person. Later, describe the person to the class and have the class guess who it is.

私の好きな人

Category	Choice (Circle)
男/女	男, 女
せ（い）	高い, ふつう, ひくい
体	大きい, ふつう, 小さい
かみのけ	ながい, ふつう, みじかい
かみのけのいろ	くろ, ちゃいろ, ブロンド blond, 白, あか
あたま	いい, ふつう, わるい
めがね	かけている, かけていない
かお	かわいい, ふつう, 良くない ハンサム, きれい
年〔とし〕	私よりわかい, 私とおなじぐらい, 私より上
スタイル style	かっこいい, ふつう, あまり良くない
きん肉 strength	つよい, ふつう, よわい
こえ	大きい, ふつう, 小さい
せいかく	あかるい, ふつう, くらい にぎやか lively, ふつう, おとなしい まじめ, ふつう, ふまじめ not serious
ユーモア humor	ある, ふつう, ない
そのほか others	おもしろい, ひょうきん facetious, はずかしがりや shy, しんせつ, 世話好〔ず〕き likes to do favors

三課

H. ペアワーク

Ask your partner the following questions and write the answers in the blank spaces.

質問	答え
1. 学校へ何でかよっている？	
2. じゅくへ行っている？	
3. ペットをかっている？　どんなペット？	
4. おこづかいは一カ月にいくらぐらいもらう？	
5. 一日に何時間ぐらいべんきょうする？	
6. 家へよる何時に帰らなければならない？	
7. 将来〔しょうらい〕、留学〔りゅうがく〕してみたいと思う？	
8. 大学で何をせんこうしたいと思っている？	
9. 漢字がいくつぐらい書ける？	
10. 海外旅行に行ったことがある？　どこに？	
11. 家事を手つだう？　何を手つだう？	
12. アルバイトをしている？	
13. けいたい電話を持っている？	
14. 車のうんてんめんきょを持っている？	
15. 一週間〔しゅうかん〕に何度お父さんといっしょに夕食を食べる？	
16. 先生は生徒をよく世話して下さる？	
17. 学校で一番楽なじゅぎょうは何？	
18. あなたがそんけいしている人はだれ？	
19. 将来〔しょうらい〕のあなたのゆめは何？	

I. **ペアワーク** (Expressions)

Ask your partner what expression he/she is supposed to use in the following situations. Your partner should answer in Japanese. Take turns.

質問：人に会った時、何と言いますか。

答え：「おはようございます。」と言います。

1. よる、人に会った時、	
2. 人におれいを言う時、	
3. ながく会わなかった人に会った時、	
4. よく世話をしてくれた人におれいを言いたい時、	
5. 先生のオフィスに入る時、	
6. 先生と話をしてオフィスを出る時、	
7. 人より先に何かをする時、	
8. 人が「お元気ですか。」と聞いた時、	

三課

アドベンチャー日本語3
OPI単語＆文法チェックリスト
3課：手紙

名前：＿＿＿＿＿＿＿＿＿＿＿

クラス：＿＿＿＿＿＿＿

たんご	Check	たんご	Check
シャワーをあびる		おとなしい	
はをみがく		しんせつ（な）	
おふろに入る		まじ目（な）	
音		ゆめ	
ずい分		けいたい電話	
切手〔きって〕		家事	
葉書〔はがき〕		ペットをかう	
絵葉書〔えはがき〕		そんけいする	
電子メール		世話をする	
はる		～て下さる	
うけとる		楽（な）	
生活		おひさしぶり	
意見〔いけん〕を言う		おかげ様で	
つらい		お世話になった	
とくべつな		おれい	
はっぴょうする		おれいじょう	
試験をうける		Others	
そうだんする		Others	
こまる		Others	
どうしたらいい？		Others	
せいかく		Others	
ふつう		Others	
かっこいい			

ぶんぽう	Check	Error
～しか + Neg.		
～という～		
～とか～		
～時（に）		
Noun Modifiers		
～ので		
～のに		
～んです		
～て来た		
～た方がいい		
～はじめる ～おわる ～つづける		
～にくい／やすい		
～てから		
～し		
～間に		
～ながら		
～そうだ		
～によると		
～後（あと）で		
～前に		
Others		
Plain Polite		
Male Female		

By the end of this lesson, you will be able to communicate the information below in the given situation. Complete the following tasks with a partner. You are expected to conduct a natural conversation using as many new vocabulary and grammatical structures as you can, while appropriately incorporating vocabulary and structures you have learned previously. Use the appropriate speech style (plain or polite) and male/female speech if appropriate. Practice the dialogue with your partner; the aim is not to memorize a dialogue, but to communicate meaningfully with your partner on the topics below.

【Ⅲ-4 トピック 1】

Partner **A**: *High school student from the U. S. studying in Japan*
Partner **B**: *Japanese high school student*

Situation: **A** *talks about his Japanese language studies in the U. S.* **A** *may use his/her own language studies at his/her own school as a basis for information.*

B compliments **A**'s skill in Japanese. **A** responds appropriately. **B** asks questions about when, where and why **A** began studying Japanese. **A** responds and explains how often his/her class meets and describes his/her Japanese teacher. **A** talks about what he/she has studied in his/her Japanese class. **B** asks what is easiest and most difficult about Japanese. **A** responds. **A** tells **B** how long he/she plans to continue studying Japanese and why. **B** encourages **A**, and **A** thanks **B**.

【Ⅲ-4 トピック 2】

Partner **A**: *High school student from the U. S. studying in Japan*
Partner **B**: *Japanese high school student*

Situation: **A** *and* **B** *talk about* **A** *'s daily lifestyle in the U. S.* **A** *may use his own daily routine as a basis of conversation.*

B is interested in **A**'s daily lifestyle in the U. S. **A** talks about his/her normal school day in the U. S., starting from the minute s/he wakes up. **B** asks **A** questions and adds his/her comments on his/her own school preparation in the morning for school, his/her school day and his/her after school hours and evenings.

＜ケンは漢字辞典を引いて、日本語の文を英語に訳している。＞

ケン：すみません、この漢字は何と読みますか。

お兄さん：「けいざい」と読むよ。

ケン：どういう意味ですか。

お兄さん："Economy"という意味だよ。

ケン：漢字辞典を使って、言葉をさがすのは、大変ですね。

お兄さん：ケンはいつ日本語を勉強し始めた？

ケン：三年前です。中学一年の時に日本語を取り始めました。
まだ日本語の初級のクラスです。

お兄さん：学校では、一週間に何時間ぐらい授業がある？

ケン：一週間に五回ですが、一回の授業は四十分だけです。

お兄さん：日本語は何がむずかしいと思う？

ケン：たくさんあるけど、漢字が一番むずかしいですね。かんたんな漢
字は覚えやすいけど、ふくざつな漢字は覚えにくいです。漢字は
数が多いし、一つの漢字に読み方がたくさんあるし、大変です。

お兄さん：漢字をいくつぐらい知ってる？

ケン：百五十ぐらい習ったと思いますが、百ぐらいしか覚えていません。
それに、ある漢字は形が変で、書きにくいです。たとえば、ぼく
は「家」という漢字をあまり上手に書けません。それに、ぼくの
書き順はめちゃくちゃです。

お兄さん：ぼくもコンピューターを使い始めてから、最近正しい漢字がなか
なか思い出せないよ。いつも、間違えているよ。それに、ケンの
字の方がぼくのよりずっときれいだと思うよ。

ケン：いいえ、とんでもないです。

A. History and Background of *Kanji*

As you have learned in earlier volumes of this text, *kanji* is a writing system borrowed from the Chinese. *Hiragana* and *katakana* were both derived later from *kanji*. *Hiragana* is a stylized version of a *kanji* that represents phonetic sounds. *Katakana* was formed by taking a portion of a *kanji*. The phonetic sound of that *kanji* was adopted for that *katakana*.

There are four main types of *kanji*. First, there are pictographs, 象形文字 (SHOKEIMOJI), which are characters that represent stylized images of an actual object. Examples of pictographic *kanji* are 魚 SAKANA (fish), 山 YAMA (mountain), 木 KI (tree) and 月 TSUKI (moon). The second group is called 指示文字 SHIJIMOJI. They are characters that represent abstract concepts or ideas. 一 ICHI (one), 上 UE (up) and 中 NAKA (inside, center) are examples of this second group. The third and fourth groups of *kanji* are more complex, as they are composed of two or more simpler components. The third group, called 会意文字 KAIIMOJI, are compound ideographs. These *kanji* are combinations of two or more simple characters that are combined, and together, they indicate the meaning of the word. For example, the *kanji* 林 HAYASHI, which means forest, is a combination of two characters that mean "tree." Another example is the *kanji* 明 AKARUI, which means bright, as it is composed of the character 日 HI (sun) and 月 TSUKI (moon), which both provide us with bright light. The fourth category is the most common. Eighty percent of all *kanji* belong in this category called 形声文字 KEISEIMOJI. These *kanji* are compound ideograms. They are composed of two parts: one portion provides the general meaning, and the other indicates how the *kanji* is read. For example, the *kanji* 時 TOKI (time or hour) is composed of two parts: 日 HI, which indicates that the meaning of this *kanji* has to do with time or day, and 寺 TERA, which indicates that at least one of the readings of this *kanji* is 時 JI. Other examples of 形声文字 KEISEIMOJI are 作る TSUKURU, 待つ MATSU and 読む YOMU. Two other less common types of *kanji* are 仮借文字 KASHAMOJI and 転注文字 TENCHUMOJI. *Kanji* in these two categories are extended usages of *kanji* in the first four categories, and may be far removed from the original derivations of the *kanji*.

B. Japanese *Kanji* Dictionaries

There are several types of *kanji* dictionaries. For the Japanese native speaker, there is the 漢和辞典 KANWA JITEN, which is used when one does not know the meaning of a *kanji*. When one knows a word, but does not know how it is written in *kanji*, a Japanese may consult a 国語辞典 KOKUGOJITEN, or any other Japanese dictionary that lists entries in *hiragana*.

For a non-native speaker who is not fluent in the written language, or Japanese learning English, there are Japanese-English (和英辞典 WAEIJITEN) and English-Japanese dictionaries (英和辞典 EIWAJITEN) to look up words. There are also special *kanji* dictionaries for foreigners that can be used to find out how a *kanji* is read, and what it means, either independently or as part of a word combination.

To find information on any given *kanji*: (Example: 休 YASUMU)

1. Isolate the radical (部首 BUSHU), which is the main identifying component of a *kanji*. (イ)
   Note: See the categories and most common radicals in the following section.
2. Count the number of strokes in the radical. (2)

3. Go to the front cover, or to the list of all of the radicals in the dictionary. Look for the number that indicates the number of strokes your radical contains. (2) Find your radical in that section. Under each radical is a radical number.

4. Use the radical number to look up the section of all the *kanji* that use this radical in the dictionary.

5. After you have located the section of the dictionary that is devoted to the radical you are looking up, count the number of remaining strokes in the *kanji*. (4)

6. Flip through the radical section until you get to a sub-section labeled with the number that indicates the number of strokes in the *kanji* other than the radical. (4)

7. Look through the entire subsection until you locate your *kanji*.

8. After you have located your *kanji*, you will find that the *kanji* has an entry number. You will also find other ways in which this *kanji* may be written and the Japanese (訓 KUN) and Chinese (音 ON) readings of the *kanji*. You will also find the definitions of each reading.

9. In this section, you will find a listing of words that are called 熟語 JUKUGO, or *kanji* compounds. Here, you will be able to locate *kanji* compounds that contain the *kanji* you are locating. The readings and meanings of the *kanji* compounds are provided.

C. Common Radical Types (部首 BUSHU) and examples

1. へん **HEN** - Usually appears on the left side.

イ 人	にんべん (person)	：	人, 休, 何, 作, 化, 仕, 体, 今, 会
シ	さんずいへん (water)	：	漢, 海
彳	ぎょうにんべん (moving person)	：	行, 待, 後
日	ひへん (day)	：	日, 曜, 時, 明, 暗
女	おんな (female)	：	女, 好, 姉, 妹, 始
木	きへん (tree)	：	木, 校, 林
牛	うしへん (cow)	：	牛, 物
禾	のぎへん (crop)	：	私, 秋
糸	いとへん (thread)	：	糸, 紙, 終
扌	てへん (hand)	：	手, 持
言	ごんべん (speech)	：	言, 語, 話, 読

2. つくり **TSUKURI** - Appears on the right side.

斤	おのづくり (ax)	：	新, 所

3. かんむり **KANMURI** - Appears at the top.

宀	うかんむり (*u*-crown)	：	家, 字, 安, 室

艹	くさかんむり (grass)	：花, 英, 草
雨	あめかんむり (rain)	：雨, 電, 雪
亠	なべぶた (cover)	：高, 文

4. あし **ASHI** - Appears at the lower half of the *kanji*.

心	こころ (heart)	：心, 思
儿	ひとあし (legs)	：先, 見, 兄, 元

5. かまえ **KAMAE** - Surrounds the *kanji*.

門	もんがまえ (gate)	：門, 間, 聞
囗	くにがまえ (country)	：国, 四
气	きがまえ (steam)	：気
匚	はこがまえ (box)	：区 (district), 医 (medical)

6. にょう **NYO** - Starts at the left and flows under to the right.

辶	しんにょう (road)	：近, 週 (week)

7. たれ **TARE** - Appears at the top and the left of the *kanji*.

广	やまいだれ (sickness)	：病 (illness)

131

四課

1. 英 British,　　　　エイ　　　　英語〔えいご〕English

　　excellent　　　　　　　　　英国〔えいこく〕England

　　　　　　　　　　　　　　　英文学〔えいぶんがく〕British literature

"English" was formally written in kanji as "英吉利(イギリス)."
Thereafter, the *kanji* 英 came to represent England.

艸 (plant) → 屮屮 → 艹 +

呂 (hat)　　+

人 (person)　=　英　(excellent)

The plant that looks like a person wearing a hat is excellent!

英

2. 草 grass　　　　　くさ　　　　みどりの草 green grass

艸 (plant) → 屮屮 → 艹 +

早 (early)　　=　草　(grass)

The plant that grows early is grass.

草

3. 林 small forest　　はやし　　　林〔はやし〕さん

　　　　　　　　　　　　　　　林田〔はやしだ〕さん

　　　　　　　　　ばやし　　　小林〔こばやし〕さん

　　　　　　　　　　　　　　　中林〔なかばやし〕さん

　　　　　　　　　　　　　　　外林〔そとばやし〕さん

(tree)　+　(tree)　=　林　(small forest)

Two trees make a small forest.

林

4. 森 forest　　　　　　もり　　　　森〔もり〕さん

森田〔もりた〕さん

小森〔こもり〕さん

大森〔おおもり〕さん

中森〔なかもり〕さん

森本〔もりもと〕さん

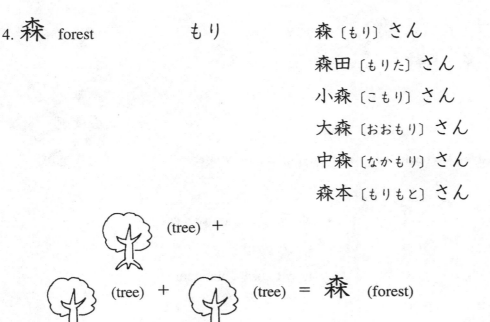

Three trees make a forest.

5. 台 counter　　　　　　タイ　　　　台湾 Taiwan

ダイ　　　　一台の車〔いちだいのくるま〕one car

台所〔だいどころ〕kitchen

(arm) → ム ＋

(mouth) → ロ ＝ 台 (counter)

One feeds oneself at the counter with an arm.

6. 始 start; begin　　　はじ（める）　　始める to begin

(woman) → 女 ＋

台 (counter)　　　　＝ 始 (begin)

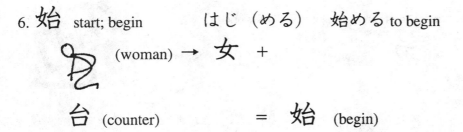

When a woman is at the kitchen counter, she will start something.

133

7. 終 end; finish　　　お（わる）　　　終わりましょう。　Let's finish.

糸 (thread) → 糸　＋

冬 (winter)　　＝　終 (end)

The year is "wrapped up" (concluded) (with thread) in the winter.

8. 使 to use　　　　つか（う）　　　車を使う to use a car
　　　　　　　　　　　　　　　　辞書の使い方〔じしょのつかいかた〕
　　　　　　　　　　　　　　　　how to use a dictionary

(person) → イ　＋

(one) → 一　＋

(mouth) → 口　＋

人 (person)　　＝　使 (to use)

A person uses his one mouth to teach another how to use things.

9. 勉 to endeavor　　　ベン　　　　勉強〔べんきょう〕study
　　　　　　　　　　　　　　　　ガリ勉〔ガリべん〕study fervently

(head)　＋

(windows)　＋

(legs)　→　免 (to escape from)

Put your head first through the window and run to escape from hard work.

an arm　→　力　→　力 (power)

免 (to escape from)　＋　力 (power)　＝　勉 (to endeavor)

You have to endeavor with all your might (power) to escape from hard work.

10. 強　strong　　　　　つよ（い）　　強いチーム　a strong team

キョウ　　　勉強〔べんきょう〕study

(bow) → 彡 → 弓 ＋

(arm) → ム ＋

(insect) → → 虫 ＝ 強 (is strong)

With a bow, I shot an insect and carried it home in my arms.　I am strong!

11. 回　- time(s)　　　　カイ　　　　二回〔にかい〕two times

(mouth) → 口 ＋

(mouth) → 口 ＝ 回 (- time)

How many times do I have to tell you?

12. 週　week　　　　　シュウ　　　今週〔こんしゅう〕this week

先週〔せんしゅう〕last week

来週〔らいしゅう〕next week

毎週〔まいしゅう〕every week

週末〔しゅうまつ〕weekend

一週間〔いっしゅうかん〕one week

冊 (extended rice field) ＋
口 (mouth)　　　　　　＝ 周 (a round) ＋

The extended rice field can produce enough rice to satisfy everyone's mouth (appetite) all year round.

辶 (step forward)　　＝ 週 (week)

I stepped forward and walked around my rice field.　It took a whole week.

135

四課

【読みかえの漢字】

1. 近 near ちか（い）＊ 学校〔がっこう〕に近い close to school

   キン 最近〔さいきん〕recently

2. 間 between; among あいだ＊ 学校〔がっこう〕と家〔いえ〕の間

   between school and my house

   interval カン＊ 時間〔じかん〕time

   ま 間違える to make a mistake

＊ Previously introduced.

【オプショナル漢字】

1. 虫 insect; bug むし 虫がきらいです。 I dislike bugs.

   an insect → = 虫 (insect)

   A funny-looking insect munching something.

2. 弱 is weak よわ（い） 弱いチーム a weak team

   two bows with a funny sound → = 弱 (is weak)

   Two bows still make a weak sound.

【読めればいい漢字】

1. 本当 ほんとう true; real

2. 最近 さいきん recent; recently

3. 違う ちがう is different; is wrong

4. 辞書 じしょ dictionary

5. ～君 ～くん

   [a suffix usually attached to boys' names]

6. 週末 しゅうまつ weekend

四課 136

Let's review previous vocabulary!

A. めいし Nouns

1. 勉強	study	13. 一週間〔いっしゅうかん〕	one week
2. 英語	English	14. 何時間	how many hours?
3. 漢字〔かんじ〕	Chinese character	15. じゅぎょう	class; instruction
4. 何	what?	16. 四十分	40 minutes
5. お兄〔にい〕さん	older brother	17. 一つ	one
6. ことば	word	18. 読み方	how to read
7. いつ	when?	19. いくつぐらい	about how many?
8. 三年前	three years ago	20. 百五十	150
9. 中学一年	seventh grade	21. 百	100
10. 時	when	22. 家	house
11. クラス	class	23. コンピューター	computer
12. 学校	school	24. 字	writing

B. どうし Verbs

25. ～と読みます〔G1 よむ／よんで〕 　　to read ～
26. 使って〔G1 つかう／つかいます〕 　　to use
27. 勉強し〔IR べんきょうする／べんきょうして〕 　　to study
28. とり〔G1 とる／とって〕 　　to take
29. 思う〔G1 おもいます／おもって〕 　　to think
30. ある〔G1 あります／あって〕 　　there is
31. おぼえ〔G2 おぼえる／おぼえて〕 　　to memorize
32. 知ってる〔G1 しる＋G2 いる／しります＋います〕 　　to know
33. ならった〔G1 ならう／ならいます〕 　　learned
34. おぼえていません〔G2 おぼえる／おぼえます〕 　　do not remember
35. 書き〔G1 書く／書きます／書いて〕 　　to write
36. 書けません〔G1 書く／書きます／書いて〕 　　cannot write
37. 使い〔G1 つかう／つかいます〕 　　to use

C. い けいようし I Adjectives

38. むずかしい	is difficult	40. 正しい	correct
39. 多い	are many		

D. な けいようし　NA Adjectives

41. 大変	hard	44. 変	strange; weird
42. たくさん	a lot	45. きれい	pretty
43. 一番	the most		

E. ふくし　Adverbs

46. まだ ＋ Aff.	still	49. いつも	always
47. あまり ＋ Neg.	(not) very	50. ずっと	by far
48. 上手に	well		

F. Expressions

51. すみません。	Excuse me.
52. とんでもないです。	How ridiculous!; It's impossible!

G. そのほか　Others

53. N1 という N2	N2 called N1
54. 〜ぐらい	about 〜
55. 〜だけ	only 〜
56. 〜けど	Although 〜
57. 〜しか ＋ Neg.	nothing but 〜
58. それに	Moreover; Besides,
59. ある〜	certain 〜
60. N1 の方が N2 より〜です	N1 is more 〜 than N2

Activity A

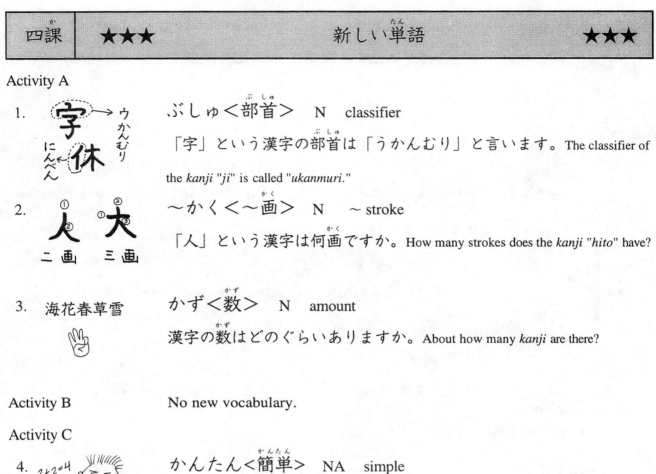

1. ぶしゅ＜部首＞　N　classifier

「字」という漢字の部首は「うかんむり」と言います。The classifier of the *kanji* "*ji*" is called "*ukanmuri.*"

2. 〜かく＜〜画＞　N　〜 stroke

「人」という漢字は何画ですか。How many strokes does the *kanji* "*hito*" have?

3. かず＜数＞　N　amount

漢字の数はどのぐらいありますか。About how many *kanji* are there?

Activity B　　　No new vocabulary.

Activity C

4. かんたん＜簡単＞　NA　simple

これは簡単な問題です。This is a simple problem.

5. ふくざつ＜複雑＞　NA　complicated

これは複雑な問題ですねえ。This is a complicated problem!

6. まちがえる＜間違える＞　V2　to make mistakes

ぼくはよく英語のスペルを間違えます。I often make spelling mistakes in English.　　＊ちがいます＜違います＞　V1　is wrong

7. Verb Stem ＋やすい　A　is easy to do 〜　→ Grammar B

「口」という漢字は覚えやすいです。The *kanji* "*kuchi*" is easy to memorize.

四課

8.  Verb Stem ＋にくい　A　is hard to do ～　→ Grammar B

この漢字は覚えにくいですよ。This *kanji* is hard to memorize, you know.

Activity D

9.  おん（よみ）＜音（読み）＞　N　Chinese reading (of a *kanji*)

「中」という漢字の音読みは「ちゅう」です。The Chinese reading of the

kanji "中" is *"chuu."*

10. 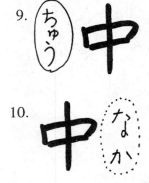 くん（よみ）＜訓（読み）＞　N　Japanese reading (of a *kanji*)

この漢字の訓読みは何ですか。What is the Japanese reading of this *kanji*?

11. いみ＜意味＞　N　meaning

「経済」は economy という意味です。"*Keizai*" means economy.

けいざい＝economy

12.  どういういみ＜意味＞ですか。　Exp　What does it mean?

けいざい

「けいざい」は、どういう（or 何という）意味ですか。

What does "*keizai*" mean?

13. ～といういみ＜意味＞です。　Exp　It means ～.

けいざい
＝
economy

「けいざい」は、economy という意味です。"*Keizai*" means "economy."

Activity E

14.  かんじじてん＜漢字辞典＞　N　*kanji* dictionary

漢字の読み方が分からない時に、漢字辞典を使います。I use the *kanji*

dictionary when I don't know the readings of *kanji*.

15.  （じしょを）ひく＜(辞書を) 引く＞　V1　to look up (a word)

(in a dictionary) 辞書を引くのは時間がかかりますねえ。It takes time to

look up (words in) the dictionary!

四課

140

16. さがす＜探す＞　V1　to look for; search for

寺田さんは眼鏡を探しています。Mr. Terada is looking for his glasses.

17. （～が）みつかる＜見つかる＞　V1　to be found [intransitive]

眼鏡が見つかりました。　My glasses were found.

18. （～を）みつける＜見つける＞　V2　to find [transitive]

眼鏡を見つけました。　I found my glasses.

19. なかなか＋ Neg.　Adv　(not) easily ～

今晩はなかなか寝られない。I cannot sleep easily tonight.

Activity F

20.  Verb Stem ＋はじめる＜始める＞　V2　to begin doing ～

→ Grammar A　花子さんは十二時に昼食を食べ始めました。Hanako started to eat her lunch at 12 o'clock.

21. Verb Stem ＋おわる＜終わる＞　V1　to finish doing ～

→ Grammar A　花子さんは十二時半前に昼食を食べ終わりました。

Hanako finished eating her lunch before 12:30.

22.  Verb Stem ＋つづける＜続ける＞　V2　to continue/keep doing ～

→ Grammar A　花子さんはまだ昼食を食べ続けています。Hanako is still eating her lunch.

Activity G

23.  しょきゅう＜初級＞　N　beginning level

初級のクラスを取っています。I am taking a beginning class.

四課

ちゅうきゅう＜中級＞　N　intermediate level

中級クラスはまだ難しいです。The intermediate level is still hard.

じょうきゅう＜上級＞　N　advanced level

上級クラスの人は本当に上手です。The advanced (level) person is really

skillful.

24. ～かい＜～回＞　Nd　～ time(s)

去年、日本に一年に二回も行ったんですよ。Last year, I went to Japan as

many times as twice a year.

1 いっかい	4 よんかい	7 ななかい	10 じゅっかい
2 にかい	5 ごかい	8 はっかい	? なんかい
3 さんかい	6 ろっかい	9 きゅうかい	

Activity H

25. しらべる＜調べる＞　V2　to check; investigate

インターネットで京都について調べてみました。I tried to find out about

Kyoto on the Internet.

26. わえいじてん＜和英辞典＞　N　Japanese-English dictionary

日本語の意味が分からない時に和英辞典を使います。I use the

Japanese-English dictionary when I don't know the Japanese meanings (of words).

27. えいわじてん＜英和辞典＞　N　English-Japanese dictionary

英和辞典を使って、作文を書きました。I wrote my composition using the

English-Japanese dictionary.

28. 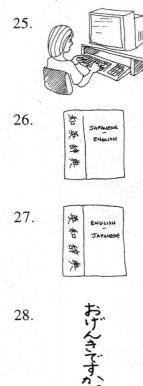　ぶん＜文＞　N　sentence

この文を英語に訳して下さい。Please translate this sentence into English.

29. $ ¥ けいざい＜経済＞　N　economics; economy

今、日本の経済はいいですか。Is the Japanese economy good now?

30. かたち＜形＞　N　shape

ある漢字は形が変です。The shapes of certain *kanji* are strange.

31. かきじゅん＜書き順＞　N　stroke order

「書」という漢字の正しい書き順を教えて下さい。Please teach me the correct stroke order of the *kanji* "*sho*."

32. おもいだす＜思い出す＞　V1　to recall

漢字を思い出せません。I cannot recall *kanji*.

33. やくす＜訳す＞　V1　to translate

school
学校

田中さんは英語を日本語に訳しています。Mr. Tanaka is translating English to Japanese.

やく＜訳＞　N　translation

田中さんの日本語の訳は正しいですか。Is Mr. Tanaka's Japanese translation correct?

34. めちゃくちゃ　NA　messy; confusing; incorrect

机の上はめちゃくちゃです。The top of my desk is messy.

35.  さいきん＜最近＞　Adv　recently

最近、林さんはやせてきました。Recently, Miss Hayashi has lost weight.

36.  たとえば＜例えば＞　SI　For example

例えば、「家」という漢字はとても書きにくいです。For example, the

kanji "ie" is very hard to write.

Activity I

37.  まんが＜漫画＞　N　comics

弟は漫画が大好きです。My younger brother loves comics.

38.  はつおん＜発音＞　N　pronunciation

グレイスさんの日本語の発音はとてもきれいです。Grace's Japanese

pronunciation is very good.

はつおんする＜発音する＞　V3　to pronounce

日本人に英語のLとRは発音しにくいです。It is hard for Japanese to

pronounce the English "l" and "r" (sound).

39.  きょうみ＜興味＞　N　(personal) interest

私はバスケットやテニスに興味があります。I am interested in basketball and

tennis, etc.

Activity J

40.  S1 し、S2。　S1, besides/what's more, S2. → Grammar D

よくジェットコースターに乗ったし、よく食べたし、よく車を運転

しました。I rode the roller coaster a lot, ate a lot, and what's more, I drove the car a lot.

Activity K

41.  S1 て（から）、S2。　After S1, S2. → Grammar C

朝ご飯を食べてから、学校へ出かけました。After I ate breakfast, I left for

school.

四課　144

A. Verb Stem ＋始める〔はじめる〕　　　begin/start to do

Verb Stem ＋終わる〔おわる〕　　　finish doing

Verb Stem ＋つづける　　　　　　continue doing; keep doing

Verb stems are attached to the verbs はじめる, おわる, つづける to extend the meaning of the verb to "begin doing," "finish doing" or "continue doing." Existence verbs are not generally used.

1. 私は三年前に日本語を取り始めました。　I started to take Japanese three years ago.

2. 昨日やっとこの本を読み終わりました。　I finally finished reading this book yesterday.

3. ゆうべ十時に英語のレポートを書き始めて、今朝五時ごろに書き終わりました。　I started writing an English report at 10:00 last night and finished writing it around 5:00 this morning.

4. さあ、食べ始めましょう。　　　　　Well, let's start eating.

5. ピアノはいつ習い始めたんですか。　When did you start learning the piano?

6. 漢字を書きつづけていたので、手が痛くなった。

　Since I kept on writing *kanji*, my hand became sore.

7. どうぞ話しつづけて下さい。　Please continue talking.

B. Verb Stem ＋やすいです　　　　is easy to do 〜

Verb Stem ＋にくいです　　　　is hard/difficult to do 〜

To describe that an action is easy or difficult to do, use the verb stem ＋ やすい or にくい. やすい and にくい conjugate as い adjectives. The original direct object of a sentence becomes either the topic or the subject in this construction. Thus, the particle used after the noun being described is は or が and not を. Other particles do not change to は or が.

Ex. とうふを　はしで　食べます。　　I'll eat *tofu* with chopsticks.

とうふは　はしで　食べにくいです。　*Tofu* is hard to eat with chopsticks.

1. このシャツはとても着やすいです。　This shirt is very easy to wear.

2. このペンは書きにくいですねえ。　This pen is hard to write with, isn't it?

3. 先生の発音はとても聞きやすいです。　The teacher's pronunciation is easy to understand.

145

4. この漢字はとても覚^{おぼ}えにくかったです。　This *kanji* was very hard to memorize.

5. あの大学はあまり入りやすくないです。　That college is not very easy to enter.

6. これは話しにくい問題です。　This is a problem I have difficulty talking about.

7. うどんははしで食べやすいです。　Noodles are easy to eat with chopsticks.

C. S1 て（から）、S2。　　　　　　　　　After doing S1, S2.

This pattern lists two actions that occur in sequential order. It is used when Sentence 1 ends with a verb. The final tense of the sentence determines the tense of the entire sentence. In many cases, the から may be omitted with little change in meaning. Using から, however, emphasizes the sequential time order of the two events listed. Also, から is used when the sentence suggests the speaker's strong will, i.e., suggestion, determination or command. Do not confuse V-てから with V-たから sentence constructions.

　　a. たくさん食べてから、ねました。
　　　　After I ate a lot, I slept.
　　b. たくさん食べたから、ねました。
　　　　I ate a lot, so I slept.

---

1. 昼食を食べてから、映画^{えいが}を見に行こう。　Let's go to watch a movie after eating lunch.

2. 家へ帰ってから、名前を思い出した。　After I returned home, I recalled his name.

3. コンピューターを使い始めてから、漢字がなかなか思い出せなくなった。

　　Since I've started to use computers, I cannot recall *kanji* easily.

4. 日本語を勉強し始めてから、もう三年になる。

　　It's already been three years since I started to study Japanese.

D. S1 し、S2。　　　　　　　S1, and what's more S2.　　Not only S1, but also S2, so . . .

In this sentence structure, the conjunction し is generally used after the plain forms listed below. Occasionally, polite forms are used before し when speaking in formal situations. Using し emphasizes the speaker's desire to indicate that more than one thing has occurred, or is being described. し may occur more than once in a sentence. Sometimes, the final statement of this construction serves as a concluding remark. If a concluding remark is not stated, it is implied. The particle も (also) frequently appears in this sentence construction to serve as reinforcement.

　　All of the sentences should support one another in logic and lead up to a unified conclusion, whether that conclusion is stated or implied.

Plain form Review:

Verb	食べる		eat; will eat
	食べない		do not eat; will not eat
	食べた		ate
	食べなかった		did not eat
いAdjective	高い		is expensive
	高くない		is not expensive
	高かった	＋ し、	was expensive
	高くなかった		was not expensive
なAdjective	好きだ		like
	好きじゃない or 好きではない		do not like
	好きだった		liked
	好きじゃなかった or 好きではなかった		did not like
Noun	学生だ		is a student
	学生じゃない or 学生ではない		is not a student
	学生だった		was a student
	学生じゃなかった or 学生ではなかった		was not a student

1. 森田君は頭(あたま)もいいし、スポーツも上手だ。

   Mr. Morita is smart; what's more, he is also good at sports.

2. 漢字は数(かず)も多いし、読み方も多い。

   There are many *kanji*; what's more, they have many readings.

3. この週末は、映画(えいが)も見たし、テニスもしたし、パーティーへも行ったし、
   とても忙(いそが)しかった。

   This weekend, I saw a movie, played tennis, and what's more, I went to a party, so I was very busy.

4. このジャケットは楽だし、とても安かったのよ。

   This jacket is comfortable; what's more, it was very cheap.

5. ベンさんは宿題もしなかったし、教科書も持って来るのを忘(わす)れました。

   Ben did not do his homework; what's more, he forgot to bring his textbook, too.

6. この台所は広(ひろ)いし、明るいです。

   This kichen is spacious; what's more, it is bright.

7. 私の部屋はせまいし、暗(くら)いです。

   My room is small; what's more, it is dark.

A. ペアワーク（部首、何画）

Write the total number of strokes for each 部首（ぶしゅ）, *kanji* classifier, in the column labelled かく. Select the *kanji* from the box below that contains the same 部首（ぶしゅ）and write them in the column labelled 漢字.

ぶしゅ	ぶしゅの名前	何かく	漢字	ぶしゅ	ぶしゅの名前	何かく	漢字
Ex. イ 人	にんべん	2	使, 何, 休, 作, 今, 会	9. 扌	てへん		
1. 言	ごんべん			10. 牛	うしへん		
2. 糸	いとへん			11. 斤	おのづくり		
3. 彳	ぎょうにんべん			12. 宀	うかんむり		
4. 木	きへん			13. 艹	くさかんむり		
5. 女	おんなへん			14. 雨	あめかんむり		
6. 日	ひへん			15. 門	もんがまえ		
7. 氵	さんずい			16. 囗	くにがまえ		
8. 禾	のぎへん			17. 辶	しんにょう		

漢	字	英	語	行	春	林	紙	問	何	雪	姉	校	休	草
始	終	時	明	家	私	秋	曜	国	安	早	待	持	電	雨
話	読	物	所	近	作	今	新	聞	花	室	会	森	間	週

B. ペアワーク（何画）

Below each *kanji*, write the total number of strokes it takes to write the *kanji*. Compete to see who gets the correct answers first.

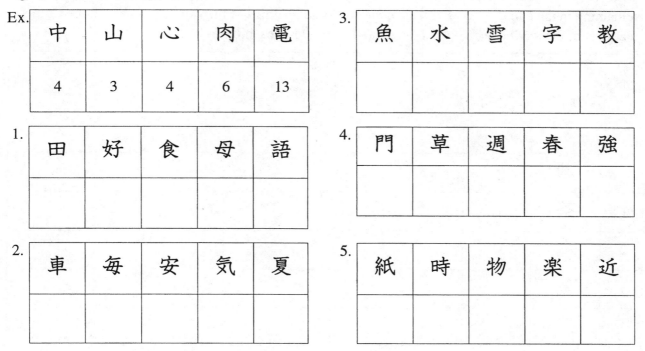

Ex.

中	山	心	肉	電
4	3	4	6	13

1.

田	好	食	母	語

2.

車	毎	安	気	夏

3.

魚	水	雪	字	教

4.

門	草	週	春	強

5.

紙	時	物	楽	近

C. クラスワーク（漢字についてのいけん）

Fill in your own answers on Grid A. Then one student in the class will ask the whole class for their answers and find out the first, second, third most popular answers for each item. Use Grid B to record the results by ranking the *kanji* according to your classmates' responses.

A.

私のいけん	漢字
1.一番かんたんな漢字	
2.一番ふくざつな漢字	
3.一番間違えやすい　漢字	
4.一番おぼえやすい　漢字	
5.一番書きにくい漢字	
6.一番好きな漢字	

B.

クラスのいけん	1い	2い	3い
1.一番かんたんな漢字			
2.一番ふくざつな漢字			
3.一番間違えやすい　漢字			
4.一番おぼえにくい　漢字			
5.一番書きにくい漢字			
6.一番好きな漢字			

D. ペアワーク　（漢字辞典）

Find the following *kanji* in a *kanji* dictionary. Fill in the spaces with the correct *kanji* classifier (ぶしゅ), the total number of strokes in the classifier (ぶしゅのかく), the number of strokes remaining in the *kanji* (のこりのかく), the Japanese readings of the *kanji* (くん読み), the Chinese readings of the *kanji* (音読み) and the meaning (いみ) of each *kanji*.

	漢字	ぶしゅ	ぶしゅの かく	のこりの かく remaining strokes	くん読み	音読み	いみ
Ex.	酒	氵	3	7	さけ	シュ	rice wine
1	茶						
2	海						
3	星						
4	飲						
5	住						
6	絵						
7	悪						
8	遠						

E. クラスワーク　（漢字さがしゲーム）

Form a group of three students. The teacher will write a *kanji* on the board. The first student in the group finds the *kanji* in the dictionary and writes the *ON* and *KUN* readings on a slip of paper and gives it to the teacher. Group members may assist, but only the first person may write the answer. The first group that turns in the correct answer will earn a point. The teacher will write another *kanji* on the board. The second person in the group will find it in the dictionary and write the answer. Then the third person will find his/her *kanji*. Continue this three times.

F. ペアワーク（日本人からの質問）

When American students visit Japan, they are often asked the same kinds of questions by Japanese people. The following questions are quite commonly asked by Japanese. Ask your partner these questions. Your partner will answer based on fact. Take turns.

質問	答え
1. わあ、日本語が上手ですねえ。	
2. どこで日本語を勉強しましたか。	
3. いつ日本語を勉強し始めましたか。	
4. 何年日本語を勉強していますか。	
5. 日本語の新聞が読めますか。	
6. 漢字をいくつぐらい書けますか。	
7. 字がきれいですねえ。	
8. あなたのすんでいる所に日本人は多いですか。	

G. ペアワーク（日本語クラスについての質問）

Ask your partner the following questions about his/her Japanese class. Your partner answers. Take turns.

質問	答え
1. この日本語のクラスはしょきゅうですか。中きゅうですか。上きゅうですか。	
2. 日本語のクラスは一週間に何回ありますか。	
3. 日本語のクラスは一回何分ですか。	
4. 日本語のクラスに生徒が何人いますか。	
5. 日本語のクラスに男子生徒と女子生徒とどちらの方が多いですか。	
6. 日本語の生徒はよく勉強していますか。	

四課

H. ペアワーク（日本語の勉強についての質問）

Ask your partner the following questions about his/her Japanese study. Your partner answers.
Take turns.

1. 漢字のいみをしらべたい時、何辞典〔じてん〕を使いますか。	
2. 日本語の文を英語にやくす時、何辞典〔じてん〕を使いますか。	
3. 英語の文を日本語にやくす時、何辞典〔じてん〕を使いますか。	
4. あなたの漢字の書きじゅんは、だいたい正しいですか。めちゃくちゃですか。	
5. 日本語を勉強し始めた時、ひらがなはやさしいと思いましたか。思い出しますか。	
6. どんなかたちの漢字は書きやすいですか。たとえば、「山」という漢字は、書きやすいですか。	
7. どんなかたちの漢字は書きにくいですか。たとえば、「近い」という漢字は書きにくいですか。	
8. 来年も日本語を勉強しつづけるつもりですか。	
9. 日本のけいざいがわるくなったら、日本語の勉強をやめますか。	
10. 今漢字辞典〔じてん〕を買いたいと思いますか。どんな辞典〔じてん〕がほしいですか。	

I. 一人ワーク→クラスワーク（日本語の勉強についてアンケート）

Answer the following questions individually first. Then one student will ask the whole class about their opinions and find out the majority opinion of the class.

1. 日本語の勉強が好きですか。	-はい -ふつう -いいえ
2. 日本語の勉強で何が一番むずかしいと思いますか。	-漢字 -たん語 -どうしのへんか　Verb conjugation -じょし　Particles
3. 日本語ははつ音しやすいですか。 はつ音しにくいですか。	-はつ音しやすい -ふつう -はつ音しにくい
4. 漢字を今いくつぐらい知っていますか。	-２５ぐらい　　-５０ぐらい -７５ぐらい　　-１００ぐらい -１２５ぐらい　-１５０ぐらい -１７５ぐらい　-２００ぐらい
5. 日本語を英語にやくすのと英語を日本語にやくすのと、どちらの方がむずかしいですか。	-日本語を英語にやくす方がむずかしい -英語を日本語にやくす方がむずかしい -りょう方やさしい -りょう方むずかしい
6. 日本語の何に一番きょうみがありますか。	-日本人と日本語を話すこと -日本語のテレビを見ること -日本語のまんがを読むこと -日本の文化を知ること

153

四課

J. ペアワーク （〜てから、〜）

What is your morning daily routine? Write your morning routine in the chart below marked "My routine." Explain your routine to your partner using the pattern of 〜てから、 〜 and have your partner write your morning routine sequence in English. After both of you write each other's routine, check to see whether you communicated correctly.

Ex. 「朝おきてから、シャワーをあびます。シャワーをあびてから、着かえます。 ． ． ． 」

| A. | B. | C. |

起きる　　　　　　歯を磨く　　　　　　出かける

| D. | E. | F. |

着かえる　　　　　朝食を食べる　　　シャワーをあびる

	1	2	3	4	5	6
My routine						
Partner's routine						

四課　　　　　　　154

K. ペアワーク （〜し、〜）

Ask your partner the questions below. Your partner will respond by finding two appropriate
answers to the following questions from the lists below and filling in the letters in the ( ).
Then verbally join them into an appropriate response using 〜し、〜.

質問	答え
1. なぜつかれているんですか。	（　）（　）
2. なぜ漢字はむずかしいんですか。	（　）（　）
3. なぜおばあさんは花子さんが好きですか。	（　）（　）
4. なぜ女の生徒は林くんが好きですか。	（　）（　）
5. なぜあなたは最近やせてきましたか。	（　）（　）
6. なぜあなたはその車が好きじゃないんですか。	（　）（　）
7. なぜお父さんをそんけいしていますか。	（　）（　）

A. かずが多いし、	H. スポーツも上手です。
B. せいかくがいいし、	I. よく家族の世話をして くれます。
C. あまり食べないし、	J. かたちも好きじゃないんです。
D. よく仕事をするし、	K. とてもしんせつです。
E. 昨日パーティーがあったし、	L. よくうんどうをしています。
F. かっこういいし、	M. レポートも書かなければ なりませんでした。
G. いろも良くないし、	N. 読み方も多いです。

四課

名前：＿＿＿＿＿＿＿＿＿＿

クラス：＿＿＿＿＿＿

たんご	Check	たんご	Check
ぶしゅ		シャワーをあびる	
～かく		はをみがく	
かず		おふろに入る	
かんたん		けいざい	
ふくざつ		かたち	
間違える		書きじゅん	
音読み		思い出す	
くん読み		やくす	
いみ		めちゃくちゃ	
どういういみ？		最近	
～といういみ		たとえば	
漢字じてん		まんが	
英わじてん		はつ音（する）	
わ英じてん		きょうみ	
ひく		しょう来	
さがす			
～が見つかる			
～を見つける			
なかなか + Neg.			
しょきゅう			
中きゅう			
上きゅう			
～回			
文			

ぶんぽう	Check	Error
～しか + Neg.		
～という～		
～とか～		
～時（に）		
N. Modifiers		
～ので		
～のに		
～んです		
～て来た		
～た方がいい		
～始める／終わる		
～つづける		
～にくい／やすい		
～てから		
～し		
～間に		
～ながら		
～そうだ		
～によると		
～後（あと）で		
～前に		
Plain Polite		
Male Female		

I. Sentence Patterns

1課

1. 妹のケリーはまだ小学生です。 My younger sister Kelly is still an elementary school student.

2. 母は高校で先生をしています。 My mother is a teacher at a high school.

3. 家族では父しか日本語を話しません。 No one but my father speaks Japanese in my family.

4. Verb OO form

　今、行こうか。 Shall we go now?

　うん、行こう。 Yes, let's go.

5. Informal/Plain Speech Style

6. Male & Female Speech Style

　これ、食べるか（い）？ Will you eat this? [male]

　今日はかつぞ。 I'll win today! [male]

　新聞を持って来てくれ。 Bring me a newspaper. [male]

　今日、おすしにするわ。 I will have *sushi* today! [female]

　手紙を書くの。 I'm going to write a letter. [female]

　今、帰るわよ。 I'll go home now! [female]

2課

1. 「トトロ」という映画（えいが）を見たことがありますか。

　　　　　　　　　　　　Have you ever seen the movie called "Totoro"?

2. 日本とか中国（とか）に行ってみたいです。

　　　　　　　　　　　　I want to try to go to Japan and China (among other places).

3. 私は、家へ帰ると、服（ふく）を着かえます。 When I return home, I change my clothes.

4. 試合（しあい）が（or の）始まる時間は、四時です。 The game's starting time is 4:00.

5. クッキーが（or の）好きな人は　だれですか。 Who is the person who likes cookies?

6. 日本レストランへ行った時に、おすしを食べました。

　　　　　　　　　　　When I went to a Japanese restaurant, I ate *sushi*.

7. 中学一年生の時に、私は日本語をぜんぜん話せませんでした。

　　　　　　　　　　　I could not speak Japanese at all when I was in the seventh grade.

8. ひまな時に、家へ遊びに来て下さい。 Please come to my house to play when you are free.

3課

1. 私は、まだ１６オなので、お酒を飲んではいけません。

　　　　　　　　　　　Since I am still 16 years old, I am not allowed to drink alcohol.

2. 明日試験があるので、今晩、勉強しなければなりません。

　　　　　　　　　　　Since I will have an exam tomorrow, I have to study tonight.

3. ジーンズは楽なので、私はいつもジーンズをはいています。

　　　　　　　　　　　Since jeans are comfortable, I always wear them.

4. 妹は、小学生なのに、料理がとても上手です。

　　　　　　Although my younger sister is an elementary school student, she is very skillful at cooking.

5. 私がケーキを作ったのに、だれも食べてくれませんでした。

　　　　　　　　　　　Even though I baked a cake, no one ate it.

6. 友達が麻薬を使っているんですよ。　　　My friend is using drugs.

7. あの人が好きなんです。　　　I like him/her.

8. 寒くなってきました。　　　It has become cold.

9. 暖かくなっていくでしょう。　　　It will become warm.

10. 早く寝た方がいいでしょう。　　　It's probably better to go to bed early.

11. たばこはすわない方がいいと思います。　　　I think it's better not to smoke.

4課

1. 私は三年前に日本語を取り始めました。　　　I started to take Japanese three years ago.

2. 昨日やっとこの本を読み終わりました。　　　I finally finished reading this book yesterday.

3. 漢字を書きつづけていたので、手が痛くなりました。

　　　　　　　　　　　Since I kept writing *kanji*, my hand became sore.

4. このシャツはとても着やすいです。　　　This shirt is very easy to wear.

5. このペンは書きにくいですねえ。　　　This pen is hard to write with, isn't it?

五課　　　　　　158

6. 昼食を食べて<u>から</u>、映画を見に行こう。   Let's go to watch a movie after eating lunch.

7. 森田君は頭もいい<u>し</u>、スポーツも上手です。

Mr. Morita is smart; what's more, he is also good at sports.

8. このジャケットは楽だ<u>し</u>、とっても安かったのよ。

This jacket is comfortable; what's more, it was very cheap.

9. ベンさんは宿題もしなかった<u>し</u>、教科書を持って来るのも忘れました。

Ben did not do homework; what's more, he also forgot to bring his textbook.

五課

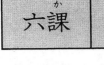

By the end of this lesson, you will be able to communicate the information below in the given situation. Complete the following tasks with a partner. You are expected to conduct a natural conversation using as many new vocabulary and grammatical structures as you can, while appropriately incorporating vocabulary and structures you have learned previously. Use the appropriate speech style (plain or polite) and male/female speech if appropriate. Practice the dialogue with your partner; the aim is not to memorize a dialogue, but to communicate meaningfully with your partner on the topics below.

【Ⅲ-6 トピック1】

Partner **A**: *High school student from the U. S.*
Partner **B**: *Japanese high school student*

Situation: *A and B are discussing their favorite musicians and songs.*

A asks **B** if songs from foreign countries are popular in Japan. **B** responds that they are and tells **A** about his/her favorite songs from the U. S. **A** talks about his/her favorite songs and favorite singers. **A** provides information about the singers and asks **B** about his/her favorite singers. They share comments and opinions about each of their favorite singers and reasons they like/do not like them (personality, physical characteristics, biographical background). They agree to go to a concert together some time (いつか).

【Ⅲ-6 トピック2】

Partner **A**: *High school student from the U. S.*
Partner **B**: *Japanese high school student*

Situation: *A and B discuss their favorite TV/movie stars and favorite TV programs/movies.*

B invites **A** to see a movie with him/her this weekend. They begin to talk about their favorite actors/actresses and favorite movies they have seen. They discuss reasons they liked the movies and share opinions about each of the movies they like. They briefly discuss the lives of their favorite actors and actresses. They also discuss at least one TV actor/actress they each like, what TV program they are on, and why they like them. They both agree on a movie they want to see this weekend and **B** says he/she will give **A** a call later.

＜ホームステイのお兄さんは、晩ご飯を食べた後、夜のテレビ番組を見ている。＞

ケン：歌の番組ですね。

　兄：ああ、今人気がある歌手が多く出てるよ。

ケン：この女性歌手はかわいい顔[かお]をしているし、踊り[おど]も上手ですね。よく
　　　あんなに踊り[おど]ながら、歌えますね。

　兄：ぼくはこんな歌、好きじゃないよ。うわさによると、この歌手は最近、
　　　有名なプロ野球[や きゅう]選手とつきあっているそうだよ。

ケン：そうですか。あっ、コマーシャルだ。コマーシャルをやっている間に、
　　　ちょっとトイレに行って来ます。

＜ケンは番組がまた始まる前に、トイレから帰って来る。＞

　兄：このギターの音、いいなあ。ぼくもあんなに弾け[ひ]たら、いいなあ。う
　　　らやましい。

ケン：ぼくは寂[さび]しい曲より、速[はや]くてにぎやかな曲の方が好きだなあ。ロック
　　　のような曲の方が好きです。

＜テレビ番組が終わった後で＞

　兄：ケンは、日本の映画を見たことがある？

ケン：アメリカにいた時、黒沢監督[さわ かんとく]の「七人の侍[さむらい]」を見たことがあります。
　　　とってもおもしろいと思いました。白黒映画でしたよ。

　兄：なつかしい映画だなあ。

ケン：ええ、三船敏郎[み ふね としろう]という俳優[はいゆう]がすごくかっこ良かったです。この映画を
　　　見てから、日本に興味[きょう み]を持ち始めたんです。

A. JAPANESE POPULAR CULTURE: MUSIC

Reigning over all Japanese popular songs is 歌謡曲 *kayokyoku* (popular music). Idol music and *enka* music are both considered *kayokyoku*. *Kayokyoku* is made popular through the medium of television. 美空ひばり Misora Hibari and 石原裕次郎 Ishihara Yujiro are the most famous singers in modern Japanese song history. Commemorative stamps were made in honor of them.

美空ひばり   石原裕次郎

1. アイドル歌手 (Idol Singers)／ポップミュージック (Pop Music)

Every year, cute, young teenagers or groups of teenagers debut in the world of pop music, singing light, bouncy, upbeat tunes. They are cute and have a sense of innocence, but they are not always able to carry a tune. Looks and personality allow them to make the Top 10 charts. They sing and dance on weekly music television programs, and as their popularity grows, they move over into the world of acting. These singers have the biggest influence on young teenagers in Japan who begin to dress and speak like these stars.

2. 演歌 (Modern Folk Music)

Although often translated as "modern folk music," *enka* is different from American country-western folk music. It is considered to be the most "Japanese-sounding" of all genres of Japanese music and the songs are often about the pain of loneliness and loss of a loved one. *Enka* music is usually slow in tempo. To bring about a Japanese mood, many *enka* singers wear traditional *kimono* when they perform.

3. ニューミュージック (New Music)

"New Music" is a genre of music somewhat between ポップミュージック (pop music) and 演歌 *enka* (folk music). Originating in the 1970s, it is quite similar to rhythm and blues. Many new music performers are composers and lyricists as well. These musicians appeal more to an older audience than アイドル歌手 *aidoru kashu* (idol singers) do, and the music style is much closer to music from the West. "New Music" is just as popular as ポップミュージック (pop music) and 演歌 *enka* (folk music), but New Music performers do not appear as often on weekly television music programs.

4. カラオケ (*Karaoke*)

Karaoke today is a favorite pastime for Japanese and foreigners of all ages. Literally, it means "empty" (から) and "orchestra" (オケ). The singer sings *karaoke* into a microphone and is accompanied by instrumental recorded music. The lyrics appear on a television screen that the singer may read as he sings. In the 1980's, the *karaoke* box brought a whole new form of entertainment to young teenagers. Charged by the hour, many Japanese have gatherings in a *karaoke* box, where they can have their own private singing parties.

5. 紅白歌合戦 *Kohaku Uta Gassen* (The Red and White Song Contest)

One of the most popular T.V. programs in Japan is NHK's* annual 紅白歌合戦 *Kohaku Uta Gassen*, or the Red and White Song Contest. It is broadcast on New Year's Eve and is very much like Dick Clark's New Year's Eve in Times Square. In recent years, it has become a tradition for many Japanese families to spend New Year's Eve watching this program. The *Kohaku Uta Gassen* features many of the year's top-selling singers and musical groups of all genres. There are two teams: Red (females) and White (males). Originally a radio music contest, it has developed into a television spectacular much like the Academy Awards. The performers are honored to be invited to appear on the show by NHK's selection committee. The performers sing and dance in extravagant, pricey outfits and try to outdo their opponents in every way. Western performers such as Cindi Lauper, Andy Williams, and even the *sumo* wrestler Konishiki have appeared on this program. A few minutes before midnight, the winning team is announced by a panel of celebrity judges. They are handed a trophy and a chorus of 蛍の光 *Hotaru No Hikari*, or "Auld Lang Syne" marks the end of the program as well as the year.

* Japan's nationally operated T.V. station.

B. JAPANESE POP CULTURE: TELEVISION

1. ドラマ "Dramas" (Japanese T.V. Dramas)

Japanese T.V. *dorama,* resemble American soap operas. They air for only 10 - 12 weeks, however, no matter how popular they are or high the ratings. This short-lived air-time allows the program's creators to respond quickly to trends, and thus the term "trendy drama" was developed in the 1990's. These programs reflect the most current stories and issues in contemporary Japan. The appeal lies with the fashionably dressed characters, fancy cars, snazzy hangout scenes, and modern surroundings, whether at the office or the home. The popularity of the dramas also brings many of their theme songs to the Top 10 charts.

2. 時代劇 *Jidaigeki* (Japanese Westerns)

Much like American Westerns, 時代劇 *jidaigeki* or "period dramas" have not changed significantly over the years. Featuring classic *samurai* attire and battles of feudal lords and *shogun*, many of the story lines are similar to the Western "Robin Hood" themes, which pit good against evil. NHK's weekly 大河ドラマ *taiga dorama* is representative of this type of program. *Taiga dorama* attempts to adhere to more historical accuracy than typical 時代劇 *jidaigeki* such as 水戸黄門 *Mito Komon*, one of the longest-running period dramas in Japan. Much of the language used in period dramas is *samurai* language.

C. JAPANESE POP CULTURE: MOVIES

Although there are internationally renowned Japanese directors such as Kurosawa Akira, younger Japanese prefer going to foreign (mostly American) movies with sub-titles. Many of the Japanese movies are written starring roles for アイドル歌手 *aidoru kashu* (idol singers), which appeal to the audience through the singers' popularity. Because of this, however, they have no solid story-lines, and are not as popular as foreign (American) movies.

D. JAPANESE POP CULTURE: JAPANESE CARTOONS

Anime, which may be translated as "Japanese cartoons," has a large cult following in Japan. Even in America, *anime* ranging from classics such as "My Neighbor Totoro" to the popular "Dragon Ball" or "Sailor Moon" are seen and appreciated by audiences for their entertainment and cultural value. *Anime* are not necessarily geared toward a young audience as cartoons are in the United States. In fact, many *anime* contain mature themes that can depict violence and sexual themes. Due to the wide variety of *anime* available, the cartoons can be seen and enjoyed by people of various ages. Some popular *anime* characters are:

鉄腕アトム

ドラえもん

1. 映 reflection; projection   エイ   映画 [が] movie

映画館 [が かん] movie theater

日 (sun)   +

口 (hat)   +

人 (person)   =   映 (reflection; projection)

The person in the hat is projected in the sun.

2. 画 picture   ガ   映画 [えいが] movie

漫画 [まんが] cartoons; comics

stroke(s)   カク   この漢字は何画 [なんかく] ですか。

How many strokes is this *kanji*?

(a brush in one hand)   +

(mark the rice field)   =   画 (picture)

When you mark the rice field with a brush in one hand, you will have a complete picture.

3. 歌 song; to sing   うた   歌を歌う to sing a song

カ   歌手 [かしゅ] singer

校歌 [こうか] school song

哥 → 哥   +

A voice comes from the bottom and turns at a right angle and comes out of the mouth.

→ → 欠   =   歌 (song; to sing)

A hungry person bends his body and opens his mouth.

The person sings a song with a voice from the heart and a bent posture.

4. 晩 evening; night　　　　　　　ばん　　　　　今晩〔こんばん〕 tonight

　　　　　　　　　　　　　　　　　　　　　　　毎晩〔まいばん〕 every night

　　　　　　　　　　　　　　　　　　　　　　　晩ご飯〔ばんごはん〕 dinner

日 (sun)　　　+

刀 (head)　　+

口 (windows) +

儿 (legs)　　　→　免 (to escape from)　=　晩 (evening; night)

Put your head first through the window and run to escape.

In the evening, you can finally escape from the sun.

5. 夜 night　　　　　　　　よる　　　　　　夜 night

夜 (cover)　　　　　+

イ (person)　　　　+

夕 (early evening) +

丶 (one)　　　　　= 夜 (night)

Under the roof (cover), a person has one more thing to do in the early evening before the night comes.

6. 黒 black　　　　　　　くろ　　　　　黒い髪の毛 black hair

　　　　　　　　　　　　　　　　　　白黒映画〔しろくろえいが〕

　　　　　　　　　　　　　　　　　　black and white (lit., white and black) movie

　　　　　　　　　　　コク　　　　　黒人〔こくじん〕 black person

　　　　　　　　　　　　　　　　　　黒板〔こくばん〕 blackboard

田 (rice field)　+　土 (land)　→　里 (measured land)　+

A rice field is used as a measurement for land.

〟〟〟〟 (fire)　　→　　丶丶丶丶　=　黒 (black)

The measured land got burnt black.

167

六課

7. 茶 tea　　　　　　　チャ　　　　　　お茶 tea; tea ceremony

茶色〔ちゃいろ〕 brown

サ　　　　　　喫茶店 coffee shop

艹 (grass)　　　+

𠆢 (person)　　+

ホ (*katakana* HO)　=　茶 (tea)

The plant which people drink and enjoy ("HO HO HO") is tea.

8. 飯 cooked rice　　　　ハン　　　　　ご飯 cooked rice; meal

朝御飯〔あさごはん〕 breakfast

昼御飯〔ひるごはん〕 lunch

晩御飯〔ばんごはん〕 dinner

食 (to eat)　　+

反 → 反 → 反 (to bend; to turn around) = 飯 (cooked rice)

a hand pushing a hanging cloth

To cook rice, one must bend and twist one's hand to wash it.

9. 足 foot; feet　　　　あし　　　　　大きい足 big feet

↓ → ↓ → 足 = 足 (foot)

10. 長 is long   なが（い）   長いお話〔ながいおはなし〕a long story

                                    長山〔ながやま〕さん

    chief   チョウ   校長先生〔こうちょうせんせい〕school principal

                                    社長〔しゃちょう〕company president

    長 (an old man with long hair) → 長 → 長 (is long)

    The old man has long hair.

11. 走 to run   はし（る）   走りました。I ran.

    土 (Saturday; soil)   +

    (to stop) →廿 → 止 → 止 = 走 (to run)

    On Saturdays, I am able to stop while I run.

12. 起 to get up;   お（きる）   六時〔ろくじ〕に起きました。

    to wake up   I woke up at 6:00.

    走 (to run) +

    (to rise) → 己 → 己 = 起 (to get up; wake up)

    Oh, it is time to get up and run to school.

13. 寝 to sleep　　　ね（る）　　早〔はや〕く寝ました。I went to sleep early.

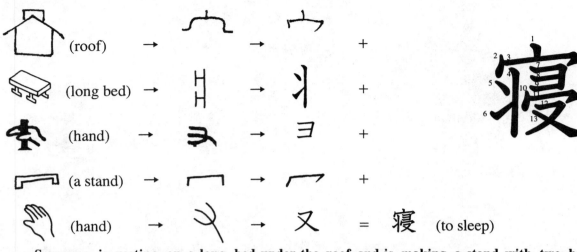

(roof) → → +

(long bed) → → +

(hand) → → +

(a stand) → → +

(hand) → → 又 = 寝 (to sleep)

Someone is resting on a long bed under the roof and is making a stand with two hands from the top and the bottom. He can sleep now.

【読めればいい漢字】

1.	有名	ゆうめい	famous
2.	番組	ばんぐみ	(T.V.) program
3.	女性	じょせい	female
4.	男性	だんせい	male
5.	曲	きょく	musical piece; song
6.	子供	こども	child
7.	選手	せんしゅ	(sports) player
8.	彼	かれ	he; him; boyfriend
9.	彼女	かのじょ	she; her; girlfriend

Let's review previous vocabulary!

A. めいし Nouns

1.	ホームステイ	homestay	11.	前	before
2.	お兄さん	older brother	12.	ギター	guitar
3.	晩ご飯〔ばんごはん〕	dinner	13.	音〔おと〕	sound
4.	夜〔よる〕	night	14.	自分〔じぶん〕	oneself
5.	テレビ	T.V.	15.	アメリカ	U.S.
6.	歌〔うた〕	song	16.	時〔とき〕	when
7.	今	now	17.	七人〔しちにん〕	seven people
8.	最近〔さいきん〕	recent	18.	白黒〔しろくろ〕	black and white
9.	選手〔せんしゅ〕	(sports team) player	19.	きょうみ	an interest
10.	トイレ	toilet			

B. どうし Verbs

20. 食べた〔G2 たべる／たべます〕　ate
21. 見ている〔G2 みる／みます〕　is watching
22. 出てる＝出ている〔G2 でる／でます〕　is participating; is playing
23. 歌えます〔G1 うたう／うたいます〕　can sing
24. やっている〔G1 やる／やります〕　is doing [informal equiv. of している]
25. 行って来ます〔G1 いく＋G3 くる〕　to go and come
26. (〜が) 始まる〔G1 はじまります／はじまって〕　(something) begins
27. 帰って来る〔G1 かえる＋G3 くる〕　to return; come back
28. ひけたら〔G1 ひく／ひきます〕　if I can play [musical instrument]
29. (〜が) 終わった〔G1 終わる／終わります〕　(something) finished
30. 見たことがある〔G2 見る／見ます〕　have seen [experience]
31. いた〔G2 いる／います〕　was; existed
32. 〜と思いました〔G1 おもう／おもって〕　thought that 〜
33. 見てから〔G2 みる／みます〕　After I watched (it)
34. 持ち始めた〔G1 持ちます／持つ〕　started to have

C. | い　けいようし　I Adjectives |

35.	かわいい	cute	38. おもしろい	interesting; funny
36.	いい	good	39. かっこ良かった	was good looking
37.	はやくて	fast		

D. | な　けいようし　NA Adjectives |

40.	上手	skillful	42. 好き	like
41.	こんな〜	this kind of 〜	43. 有名〔ゆうめい〕	famous

E. | Copula |

44. だ　　　　　　　was [plain form of です]

F. | ふくし　Adverbs |

45.	多く	a lot	49. また	again
46.	よく	well	50. とっても	very [informal form of とても]
47.	あんなに	like that	51. すごく	extremely
48.	ちょっと	for a while		

G. | Expressions |

52.	ああ	Yeah
53.	そうですか。	Is that so?
54.	あっ	Oh
55.	ええ	Yes

H. | そのほか　Others |

56.	(sentence) なあ	!
57.	N1 より N2 の方が〜	N2 is more 〜 than N1
58.	N1 という N2	N2 called N1

Activity A

1. 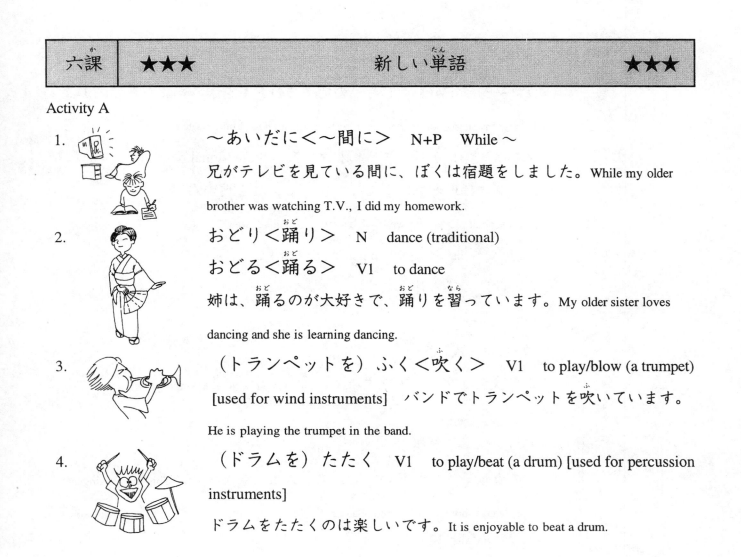 〜あいだに＜〜間に＞　N+P　While 〜

兄がテレビを見ている間に、ぼくは宿題をしました。 While my older brother was watching T.V., I did my homework.

2. おどり＜踊(おど)り＞　N　dance (traditional)

おどる＜踊(おど)る＞　V1　to dance

姉は、踊(おど)るのが大好きで、踊(おど)りを習(なら)っています。 My older sister loves dancing and she is learning dancing.

3. （トランペットを）ふく＜吹(ふ)く＞　V1　to play/blow (a trumpet) [used for wind instruments]　バンドでトランペットを吹(ふ)いています。

He is playing the trumpet in the band.

4. （ドラムを）たたく　V1　to play/beat (a drum) [used for percussion instruments]

ドラムをたたくのは楽しいです。 It is enjoyable to beat a drum.

Activity B

5.  Verb stem form ＋ ながら　Rc　While 〜 [Describes a person's simultaneous or concurrent actions]　ギターを弾(ひ)きながら、歌って います。 He is singing while playing the guitar.

Activity C

6. 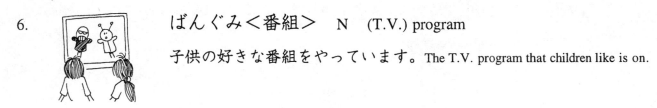 ばんぐみ＜番組＞　N　(T.V.) program

子供の好きな番組をやっています。 The T.V. program that children like is on.

7.
コマーシャル　N　commercial

コマーシャルがおもしろいので、このお茶を飲み始めたんですよ。

Because the (tea) commercial is interesting, I started to drink this tea.

8.
プロやきゅう＜プロ野球＞　N　professional baseball

あのプロ野球選手はよく打つ (hit) し、足も速いんですよ。

That baseball player hits well; what's more, he runs fast.

9.
きょく＜曲＞　N　musical piece; song

この曲はとても弾きやすいです。This piece is very easy to play.

10.
かしゅ＜歌手＞　N　singer

この歌手は歌が上手ですねえ。This singer is good at singing!

11.
じょせい＜女性＞　N　female

この女性歌手はかわいいし、ダンスも上手ですね。This female singer is

cute; what's more, she is a good dancer.

だんせい＜男性＞　N　male

この男性歌手は声がいいですねえ。This male singer has a good voice!

12.
はいゆう＜俳優＞　N　actor

この俳優は歌も歌うんですよ。This movie star also sings!

じょゆう＜女優＞　N　actress

黒川秋子という女優を知っていますか。Do you know the actress named

Kurokawa Akiko?

13.  かんとく＜監督＞　N　(movie) director; (baseball) manager

この方は有名な映画監督です。 This person is a famous movie director.

Activity D

14.  (description of a part of the body を) している

V　have (a description of a part of the body)

この歌手はかわいい顔をしています。 This singer has a cute face.

Activity E

15.  かない＜家内＞　N　(own) wife

ぼくの家内です。 This is my wife.

16.  おくさん＜奥さん＞　N　(someone else's) wife

こちらは秋山さんの奥さんです。 This is Mr. Akiyama's wife.

17.  しゅじん＜主人＞　N　(own) husband

主人の一郎です。 This is my husband, Ichiro.

 ごしゅじん＜ご主人＞　N　(someone else's) husband

春子さんのご主人は医者をしています。 Haruko's husband is a doctor.

18.  さむらい＜侍＞　N　Japanese warrior

侍映画を見たことがありますか。 Have you ever seen a *samurai* movie?

19.  きゅうりょう＜給料＞　N　salary; pay

今日、給料をもらったから、ごちそうしてあげましょう。 Since I

received my pay today, I will treat you.

六課

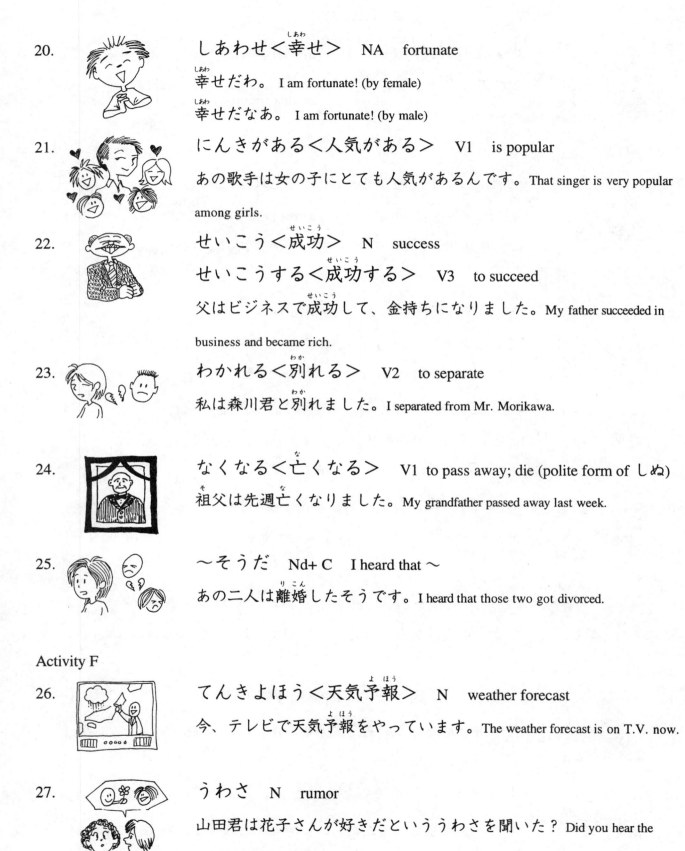

20. しあわせ<幸せ>　NA　fortunate

幸せだわ。　I am fortunate! (by female)

幸せだなあ。　I am fortunate! (by male)

21. にんきがある<人気がある>　V1　is popular

あの歌手は女の子にとても人気があるんです。That singer is very popular among girls.

22. せいこう<成功>　N　success

せいこうする<成功する>　V3　to succeed

父はビジネスで成功して、金持ちになりました。My father succeeded in business and became rich.

23. わかれる<別れる>　V2　to separate

私は森川君と別れました。I separated from Mr. Morikawa.

24. なくなる<亡くなる>　V1　to pass away; die (polite form of しぬ)

祖父は先週亡くなりました。My grandfather passed away last week.

25. ～そうだ　Nd+ C　I heard that ～

あの二人は離婚したそうです。I heard that those two got divorced.

Activity F

26. てんきよほう<天気予報>　N　weather forecast

今、テレビで天気予報をやっています。The weather forecast is on T.V. now.

27. うわさ　N　rumor

山田君は花子さんが好きだといううわさを聞いた？ Did you hear the rumor that Yamada likes Hanako?

28.  ～によると　P+V+P　according to ～

天気予報によると、明日のお天気は晴れです。 According to the news, tomorrow's weather will be sunny.

Activity G

29.  かれ＜彼＞　N　he; him; boyfriend

私の彼です。 He is my boyfriend.

30.  かのじょ＜彼女＞　N　she; her; girlfriend

彼女はとてもかわいいです。 She is very cute.

Activity H

31.  ごらく＜娯楽＞　N　entertainment

どんな娯楽が好きですか。 What kind of entertainment do you like?

32.  さびしい＜寂しい＞　A　is lonely

私は今、友達がいないので、寂しいんです。 Because I do not have any

friends now, I am lonely.

33. なつかしい＜懐かしい＞　A　is nostalgic

子供の時が懐かしいです。 I feel nostalgic about my childhood.

34. にぎやか＜賑やか＞　NA　lively; bustling

にぎやかな音楽ですねえ。 It's lively music!

35.  たのしむ＜楽しむ＞　V1　to enjoy

皆さんはパーティーを楽しんでいます。 Everyone is enjoying the party.

36. Dictionary form + 前に、S2。 Before S1, S2. → Grammar E

食べる前に、「いただきます。」と言います。We say "*Itadakimasu*" before we eat.

37.  TA form + 後（で）、S2。 After S1, S2. → Grammar D

食べた後で、「ごちそうさま。」と言います。We say "*Gochisosama*" after we eat.

Activity I

38.  (Someone) と　つきあっている　V1　to associate with 〜

私は今、森田君とつきあっています。I am associating with (dating) Mr. Morita now.

39.  うらやましい＜羨ましい＞　A　envious

あの二人がとても羨ましいんです。I envy those two a lot.

40. N1のようなN2　P+Nd+C　N2 like N1

イチローのような選手になりたいです。I want to become a player like Ichiro.

【オプショナル単語】

1. ベストテン		N	Best Ten
2. 歌謡曲	かようきょく	N	Japanese modern popular songs
3. 演歌	えんか	N	Japanese modern folk songs
4. ニューミュージック		N	New Music
5. カラオケボックス		N	*karaoke* room
6. チャンネル		N	channel
7. テレビガイド		N	T.V. guide
8. NHK（日本放送協会）		N	NHK (Nihon Hoso Kyokai) [Japan Broadcast System]

A. Subordinate Clause (Plain/Informal form) ＋ 間 あいだ (に)、 Main Clause.

Main Clause <u>while</u> Subordinate Clause; Main Clause <u>during</u> Subordinate Clause

This construction is used when events, actions or states occur within or during an overlapping space of time or activity. Verbs preceding あいだ（に）are usually non-past, and appear either in the V-ている form or as the verb いる. いAdjectives, なadjectives and nouns are also generally in the non-past forms. いadjectives appear in their plain forms, なadjectives take な before あいだ（に）and nouns take の. The final tense determines the tense of the entire sentence.

When the particle に follows あいだ, the implication is that the action or occurrence in the main clause occurs within a specific time span or event named in the あいだ clause. When に does not appear after あいだ, one can assume that the event or occurrence in the main clause generally occurs concurrently for about the same length of time as the time span or event named in the あいだ clause.

As with other sentences with subordinate clauses and main clauses, if the subject of the subordinate clause is different from the subject of the main clause, the subject of the あいだ clause is marked with が and not は. The subject of the main clause is followed by は. If the subject is the same for the subordinate and main clause, the subject takes は, wherever it appears in the sentence.

Plain form Review:

Verb	いる 食べている	＋ あいだ（に）、	While (you) are here, While (you) are eating,
いAdjective	すずしい		While it is cool,
なAdjective	しずか(な)		While it is quiet,
Noun	学生(の)		While (you are) a student,

1. 弟がテレビを見ている<u>間</u>に、私は宿題をしてしまいました。

   I finished doing my homework while my younger brother was watching T.V.

2. 冬休みの<u>間</u>に、日本へ旅行するつもりです。

   I am planning to take a trip to Japan during winter vacation.

3. 私は、本を読んでいる<u>間</u>に、寝てしまいました。

   While I was reading a book, I fell asleep.

4. 長い<u>間</u>、私は日本料理 りょうり を食べていません。

   I have not eaten Japanese food for a long time.

5. 静かな しず <u>間</u>、よく勉強出来ました。

   I could study well while it was quiet.

179

B. Verb 2 [Stem form] + ながら、 Verb 1.

     do (verb 1) <u>while</u> doing (verb 2)

This construction is used when one subject performs two actions concurrently. The first verb is used in its stem form to which ながら is attached. Since the action in the main clause is central, the "while" interpretation is attached to the ながら verb and NOT the verb in the main clause. The tense of the final verb determines the tense of the entire sentence.

    Compare with あいだ（に）：

1. -ながら is generally used only to describe two concurrent ACTIONS.
   あいだ（に）　may be used with existence verbs, nouns that indicate a duration of time, い and な adjectives.

2. -ながら is only used when one subject performs both actions. There may be one or two separate subjects in an あいだ sentence.

3. -ながら almost always describes two actions occurring simultaneously or concurrently for the same duration of time. In the case of あいだ, the main action or event may occur during only a portion of the time or action named in the あいだ clause.

1. 姉は、いつも音楽を聞きながら、勉強しています。

    My older sister always studies while she listens to music.

2. 食べながら、話してはいけません。

    You should not talk while you are eating.

3. 電話で話しながら、車を運転するのは危ないと思います。

    I think it is dangerous to drive a car while talking on the phone.

4. シャワーをあびながら、歌を歌っています。

    She is singing while taking a shower.

5. ギターを弾きながら、歌を歌っていました。

    He was singing while playing the guitar.

C. [Description of a part of the body] + を　している。

   To describe an attribute of a person, a descriptive word (い adjective, な adjective, etc.) preceding the part of the body is followed by 〜を　している. It is more natural to use this construction than to use 〜が　あります.

1. 山口さんはとてもかわいい顔をしています。   Mr. Yamaguchi has a very cute face.

2. この歌手はとてもいい声をしています。   This singer has a very good voice.

3. あの人は長い脚をしていますね。   This person has long legs, doesn't he?

D. Sentence [Plain/Informal form] + そう　です/だ。

     I hear that; I understand that; It is said that...

This construction reports information that the speaker or writer has heard from second-hand sources, i.e., other people, the media, or the beliefs of people in general. The form used before そう is the plain form. な adjectives and nouns in the affirmative non-past forms take だ before そう.

Plain form Review:

Verb	食べる		eat, will eat
	食べない		do not eat, will not eat
	食べた		ate
	食べなかった		did not eat
い Adjective	高い		is expensive
	高くない		is not expensive
	高かった		was expensive
	高くなかった	+ そうです。	was not expensive
な Adjective	好きだ		like
	好きじゃない or 好きではない		do not like
	好きだった		liked
	好きじゃなかった or 好きではなかった		did not like
Noun	学生だ		is a student
	学生じゃない or 学生ではない		is not a student
	学生だった		was a student
	学生じゃなかった or 学生ではなかった		was not a student

Do not confuse this sentence pattern with the other -そう pattern you learned earlier. In the previous volume, you learned a そう construction which meant "to look...", or "to seem..." Compare the forms below.

Verbs:	今日、雨が<u>ふる</u>そうです。	I understand it will rain today.
	今日、雨が<u>ふり</u>そうです。	It looks like it will rain today.
い Adjectives:	<u>おもしろい</u>そうです。	I hear that it is interesting.
	<u>おもしろ</u>そうです。	It seems interesting.
な Adjectives:	<u>元気だ</u>そうです。	I hear (she) is well.
	<u>元気</u>そうです。	(She) seems well.
Nouns:	<u>日本人だ</u>そうです。	I understand (he) is Japanese.
	X　No noun sentence possible in the "seems" construction.	

1. あの俳優(はいゆう)は三度目の結婚(けっこん)をした<u>そうです</u>。   I heard that that actor got married three times.

六課

2. 新聞によると、この冬はとても寒いそうだよ。

      According to the newspaper, (I understand that) it will be very cold this winter.

3. この映画はアメリカでとても人気があったそうだから、ぜひ見たい。

      I heard this movie was very popular in the U.S., so I definitely want to see it.

4. うわさによると、あの二人は別れたそうです。

      According to rumors, (I heard that) those two have separated.

E. Verb TA form ＋後〔あと〕（で）   after doing ～

  ＊Noun ＋の ＋後〔あと〕（で）   after ～

  ＊この ＋後〔あと〕（で）   after this

This construction is used when some state or action takes place at a time (not always immediately) after another state or action has occurred. The TA form is always used before あとで. The tense of the entire sentence is determined by the tense of the final verb. The particle で may be omitted in informal speech.

    −た後〔あと〕で is different from −てから in three ways:

1) −てから should not be used if the main clause expresses something beyond the control of the subject or the speaker of the sentence. 後〔あと〕で should be used in such cases.

    O 私が家を出た後で、雨がふった。

    X 私が家を出てから、雨がふった。

        It rained after I left home.

2) −てから indicates "the space of time following after," but −た後〔あと〕で indicates "any space of time after."

    O 日本に来てから、一年になります。

    X 日本に来た後で、一年になります。

        One year has passed since I came to Japan.

3) The verb used with −たあとで generally cannot be one that suggests a change of state/action that occurs instantaneously.

    O あかちゃんは生まれてから、なき始めた。

    X あかちゃんは生まれた後で、なき始めた。

        The baby started to cry right after he/she was born.

1. 夕食を食べた後で、宿題をしました。

   After I ate dinner, I did my homework.

2. 日本人は食べた後で、「ごちそうさま。」と言います。

   Japanese say "*GOCHISOSAMA*." after eating.

3. このクラスの後で、お昼を一緒に食べましょう。

   Let's eat lunch together after this class.

4. この後で、何をしますか。

   What are you going to do after this?

F. Verb Dictionary form ＋前に　　　　before ～

　　* Noun ＋の ＋前に　　　　before ～

The verb before 前に is always in the non-past form. Nouns take の preceding 前(に). The tense of the final verb determines the tense of the entire sentence.

---

1. ゆうべ寝る前に、コーヒーを飲んだから、なかなか寝られませんでした。

   Since I drank coffee last night before I went to bed, I could not sleep well.

2. 日本人は、食べる前に、「いただきます。」と言います。

   Japanese say "*ITADAKIMASU*" before they eat.

3. 冬休みの前に、ビデオを貸して下さい。

   Please lend me some videos before winter vacation.

4. 食べる前に、手を洗って下さい。

   Please wash your hands before you eat.

G. Noun 2 のような Noun 1　　　　Noun 1 like Noun 2

This construction is used when one wants to provide a context by specifying an example from a larger category. Noun 1 represents a broad category; Noun 2 is the specific example.

スタンフォードのような大学　　　　a university like Stanford

マイクさんのような人　　　　a person like Mike

---

1. 私はスタンフォードのような大学に行きたいです。

   I want to go to a university like Stanford.

2. 私はマイクさんのような人とつきあいたいです。

   I want to associate with a person like Mike.

A. クラスワーク（〜間）

The teacher has 10 cards on which the following sentences are written. A pair of students volunteer to act out what is on one card. The rest of the class guesses which one they are doing. A different volunteer pair acts out another sentence. At the end, the class decides which pair performed best.

1. Aがドラムをたたいている間、Bはおどっています。	
2. Aがトランペットをふいている間、Bは歌っています。	
3. Aがシャワーをあびている間、Bは犬をあらっています。	
4. Aが話している間、Bはないています。	
5. Aがりょうりをしている間、Bはピアノをひいています。	
6. Aが電話で話している間、Bはしゅくだいをしています。	
7. Aがせんたくをしている間に、Bはゴミを出しました。	
8. Aが寝ている間に、Bは家をそうじしました。	
9. Aがふくを着ている間、Bはけしょうをしています。	
10. Aがパーマをかけている間、Bは待っていました。	

B. ペアワーク （〜ながら）

One student acts out one of the sentences from Set 1, while his partner guesses which sentence he/she is acting out. The partner then acts out a sentence from Set 2 and the first student guesses which sentence he/she is acting out. Continue until all sentences have been acted out.

Set 1:

a. おどりながら、歌っています。	
b. 歌を歌いながら、そうじをしています。	
c. 音楽を聞きながら、コンピューターをタイプしています。	
d. りょうりの本を見ながら、おすしを作っています。	
e. コーヒーを飲みながら、新聞を読んでいます。	
f. トランペットをふきながら、あるいています。	

Set 2:

g. アイスクリームを食べながら、テレビを見ています。	
h. 車をうんてんしながら、電話しています。	
i. ポップコーンを食べながら、映画を見ています。	
j. ギターをひきながら、歌を歌っています。	
k. ガムをかみながら、サッカーをしています。	
l. ドラムをたたきながら、歌を歌っています。	

六課

C. ペアワーク

Discuss your favorite singers, songs, movies, T.V. programs, cartoon/comics and commercials as listed below together with your partner. Jot down notes and be ready to share with your class.

質問：あなたの（orが）好きな男性歌手はだれですか。

答え：私の（orが）好きな男性歌手は〜です。

	名前
男性歌手	
女性歌手	
曲／歌	
はいゆう（男ゆう）	
はいゆう（女ゆう）	
映画かんとく	
テレビ番組	
アニメ・まんが	
コマーシャル	
プロやきゅうチーム	

D. ペアワーク （長いかみをしている人）

Ask your partner the following questions. Your partner will answer based on his/her observations of your classmates. Take turns. Expand the conversation about each person you discuss.

1. 長いかみをしている生徒はだれですか。	
2. 黒いかみをしている生徒はだれですか。	
3. 大きい目をしている人はだれですか。	
4. いいこえをしている人はだれですか。	
5. かわいいかおをしている人はだれですか。	
6. 大きい手をしている人はだれですか。	
7. 長いあしをしている人はだれですか。	
8. あおい目をしている人はだれですか。	
9. いつもしあわせそうなかおをしている人はだれですか。	
10. いつも元気そうなかおをしている人はだれですか。	

六課

E. ペアワーク（有名人インタビュー）

The family tree on the next page is the family tree of Fuyuko, a famous singer. Imagine that this information was provided in a popular magazine that you are reading. Your partner asks the following questions about Fuyuko's family tree. Answer in Japanese using ～そうです. Take turns.

1. 冬子さんのご主人〔しゅじん〕はどんな仕事をしていますか。	
2. 冬子さんのご主人〔しゅじん〕はいいきゅうりょうをもらっていますか。	
3. 冬子さんはお子さんが何人いますか。	
4. 冬子さんのむす子さんは何才ですか。	
5. 冬子さんのむすめさんは何才ですか。	
6. 冬子さんの弟さんはどんな仕事をしていますか。	
7. 冬子さんの弟さんのおくさんはどんな仕事をしていますか。	
8. 冬子さんの弟さんとおくさんはりこんしていますか。	
9. 冬子さんのお父さんはお元気ですか。	
10. 冬子さんのお父さんはどんな仕事をしていましたか。	
11. 冬子さんのおじいさんはどんな仕事をしてせいこうしましたか。	
12. 冬子さんのお母さんはどんな仕事をしていますか。	
13. 冬子さんは今、人気がありますか。	
14. 冬子さんは今、しあわせですか。	

Review vocabulary:

お子さん　polite equivalent of 子ども "child(ren)"

むす子さん　polite equivalent of むす子 "son"

むすめさん　polite equivalent of むすめ "daughter"

冬子さんの家族

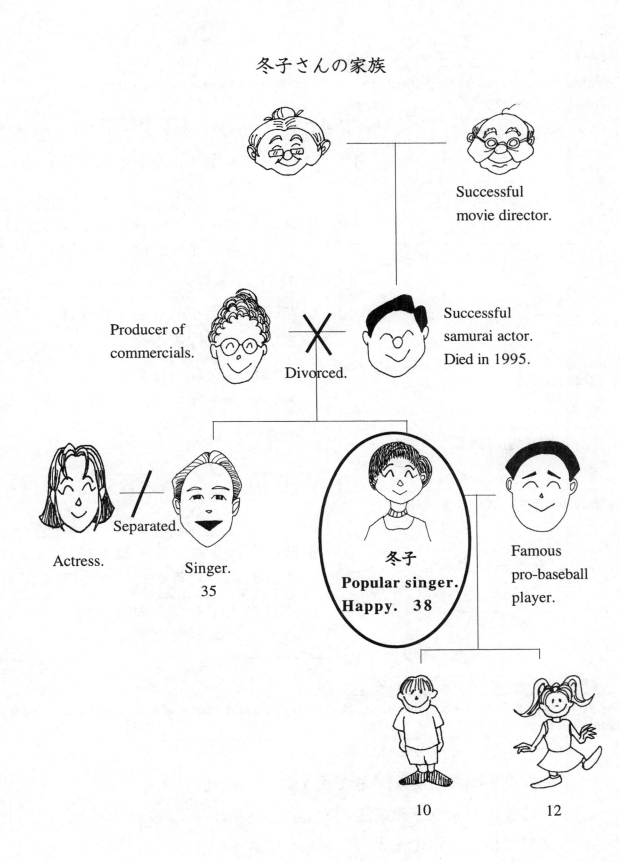

Successful movie director.

Producer of commercials.

Divorced.

Successful samurai actor. Died in 1995.

Separated.

Actress.

Singer.
35

冬子
**Popular singer.
Happy. 38**

Famous pro-baseball player.

10

12

六課

F. ペアワーク（〜によると／〜そうです）

Complete the sentences on the left with the most appropriate sentence endings from the right. Use each ending once only.

1. うわさによると、　（　　）	A. おじさんがビジネスでせいこうして、いいきゅうりょうをもらっているそうです。
2. 天気よほうによると、　（　　）	
3. スポーツニュースによると、　（　　）	B. シェイクスピアのレポートは二十日までに出さなければいけないそうです。
4. 父の話によると、　（　　）	C. 友達は家族といっしょに春休みにカナダに旅行するそうです。
5. 日本の友達の手紙によると、　（　　）	D. あのロック歌手はおくさんとわかれたそうです。
6. クラスの友達の話によると、　（　　）	E. 明日は雪だそうです。
7. 英語の先生の話によると、　（　　）	F. 私の好きなやきゅうチームがまけたそうです。
8. カウンセラーによると、　（　　）	G. 問題がある時、すぐだれかにそうだんした方がいいそうです。
	H. 来週の土曜日に、友達の家でたん生パーティーをするそうです。

G. ペアワーク→クラスワーク（〜そうです）

Ask your partner the following questions. Report to your class what you have learned about your partner using 〜そうです.

1. いい友達がいますか。

2. どんなタイプの友達が好きですか。

3. 子供の時、どんな子供でしたか。

4. 将来何になりたいですか。

5. 週末に、何をしましたか。

H. ペアワーク　（〜後／〜前）

Ask your partner the following questions. Your partner will answer in Japanese. Take turns.

1. 食べる前に、何と言いますか。	
2. 食べた後で、何と言いますか。	
3. 寝る前に、何と言いますか。	
4. 食べた後で、はをみがきますか。	
5. 寝る前に、はをみがきますか。	
6. 朝起きてから、シャワーをあびますか。 　　寝る前に、シャワーをあびますか。	
7. どんな時に、さびしいと思いますか。	
8. どんな時をなつかしく思い出しますか。	
9. あなたの彼（or 彼女）はしずかな人ですか。	
10. どんな娯楽〔ごらく〕が一番好きですか。	
11. にぎやかな音楽が好きですか。それとも、 　　しずかな音楽が好きですか。	

I. ペアワーク　（〜のような〜）

Ask your partner the following questions. Your partner will answer using 〜のような〜. Take turns.

1. どんな人とつきあいたいですか。	
2. どんな曲を聞きたいですか。	
3. どんな人をうらやましいと思いますか。	
4. どんな人をそんけいしますか。	
5. どんな大学へ行きたいですか。	

六課

名前：＿＿＿＿＿＿＿＿＿＿＿＿

クラス：＿＿＿＿＿＿

たんご	Check	たんご	Check
おどり／おどる		うわさ	
ふく		彼	
たたく		彼女	
番組		さむらい	
コマーシャル		うらやましい	
プロやきゅう		さびしい	
曲		なつかしい	
娯楽〔ごらく〕		にぎやか（な）	
歌手		楽しむ	
女性			
男性			
はいゆう			
女ゆう			
かんとく			
家ない／おくさん			
しゅ人／ごしゅ人			
つきあっている			
きゅうりょう			
しあわせ			
人気がある			
せいこうする			
わかれる			
なくなる			
天気よほう			

ぶんぽう	Check	Error
～しか + Neg.		
～という～		
～とか～		
～時（に）		
Noun Modifiers		
～ので		
～のに		
～んです		
～て来た		
～た方がいい		
～始める／終わる		
～つづける		
～にくい／やすい		
～てから		
～し		
～間に		
～ながら		
～そうだ		
～によると		
～後〔あと〕で		
～前に		
Ｎ１のようなＮ２		
～をしている		
Plain Polite		
Male Female		

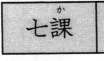

By the end of this lesson, you will be able to communicate the information below in the given situation. Complete the following tasks with a partner. You are expected to conduct a natural conversation using as many new vocabulary and grammatical structures as you can, while appropriately incorporating vocabulary and structures you have learned previously. Use the appropriate speech style (plain or polite) and male/female speech if appropriate. Practice the dialogue with your partner; the aim is not to memorize a dialogue, but to communicate meaningfully with your partner on the topics below.

【III-7 トピック1】

Partner **A**: *High school student from the U. S.*
Partner **B**: *Japanese high school student*

Situation: *A high school student describes his /her home in the U. S. to his Japanese friend.*

A is visiting **B**'s home and admires the Japanese style home. **B** responds appropriately and asks **A** to describe his/her home in the U. S. by talking about whether it is a one/two story home, apartment or condo, number of bedrooms, baths, kitchen, family room, etc.
A describes his/her own bedroom (location, size, carpeting, brightness, furniture/appliances, decorations - posters, pictures, etc.) **A** also talks about whether he/she likes her room or not and why. **B** comments and asks questions.

【III-7 トピック2】

Partner **A**: *High school student from the U. S.*
Partner **B**: *Japanese high school student*

Situation: *A and B discuss their future dream homes.*

B visits **A**'s home in the U. S. and observes some of the differences between Japanese and American homes. **B** asks **A** what kind of home he/she would like to build in the future.
A describes his/her ideal home: location, size, Western/Eastern (Japanese style), type of home (one/two story, apartment, condo), number of bedrooms and baths, types of rooms, kitchen, etc.) and what would be in them. **B** also talks about his/her dream house as **A** describes his/hers. They also discuss the garage, amenities (pool, jacuzzi, tennis courts, etc.) and the exterior or the home: color, yard, landscaping, etc.

　ぼくのホストファミリーの家は二階建ての家だ。玄関に入ると、くつをぬいで内に上がらなければならない。日本にはこの「内と外」の考えがある。

　この家には、東洋的なものと西洋的なものが一緒にある。八畳の畳の部屋は伝統的な和室で、客間として使っている。和室には床の間や仏壇があり、ふすまや障子などもある。床の間には掛け軸がかけてあり、生け花も飾ってある。障子を開けると、美しい庭が見える。この部屋に入ると、いつも心が落ち着く。でも、ぼくは座布団に正座すると、いつも足が痛くなってしまう。将来、ぼくが家を建てたら、こんな部屋を作るかもしれない。

　毎日、生活に使う所は西洋的だ。冷蔵庫、電子レンジなどの電気製品も多い。日本の家ではお風呂とトイレが違う所にある。

　ぼくの部屋は二階の四畳半の小さい部屋だ。ベッドはない。毎日、ふとんに寝ている。ふとんはちょっと重い。ふとんは朝起きたら、押し入れに入れる。部屋を広く使うことが出来て、便利だ。

　「郷に入れば郷に従え」という諺がある。日本の家での生活をけいけんしなければ、日本人が分からないと思う。

* Underlined words are for recognition only.

A. 内 UCHI (in) and 外 SOTO (out)

One of the consistently recurring characteristics of Japanese culture, language and society is the concept of UCHI (in) and SOTO (out). Japanese have a strong sense of belonging (in) or not belonging (out). In language, it is manifested in many ways. A very basic example is the system of family terms in Japanese. In English, there is one word, "father," whether one refers to one's own father or to another person's father. As you studied family terms in Japanese, you learned two words for "father": CHICHI, which is used when you refer to your own father, and OTOSAN, which is used when referring to someone else's father. In the culture, the SOTO and UCHI concept is best exemplified by the Japanese practice of removing shoes, hats, and outerwear (winter coats) which are considered apparel reserved for outdoor wear before entering homes or buildings. Within the society, one is able to witness the UCHI/SOTO system at work when one visits Japan. In public places, such as at rush hour at the station, Japanese can be extremely rude and pushy to people they do not know (SOTO), but when one is on a one-to-one encounter with a Japanese, they are extremely polite and accommodating (UCHI). The Japanese have a celebration called SETSUBUN in early February, which marks the end of winter and the coming of spring. On this day, the head of the household goes around the house calling out, "福は内、鬼は外 FUKU WA UCHI, ONI WA SOTO," which means "In with good fortune, out with the demon (evil)" as he scatters roasted beans throughout the home. By doing so, Japanese believe they will be able to separate the good and evil spirits by keeping all evil outside and insuring good luck within the environs of the home. Examples of UCHI/SOTO practices abound in all aspects of Japanese life.

げんかん　Entrance way

195

B. Japanese measurements: - 畳 -JO and - 坪 -TSUBO

TATAMI (straw mats) came into general use in Japanese homes toward the end of the 11th century. It was not until much later, however, that the entire floor was covered by TATAMI and used to sit and sleep on. TATAMI is a straw mat measuring three inches thick, three feet in width, and six feet in length. The size of the *tatami* may vary slightly by district, though they are becoming more and more standardized, since the sizes of rooms are determined by the number of *tatami* mats arranged on the floor. In Japan, Japanese-style room measurements are given by number of mats, that is, there are three-mat rooms, 4 1/2-mat rooms, six-mat rooms and eight-mat rooms. See the pre-determined arrangement of *tatami* for different sized rooms below. Five- or seven-mat rooms do not exist. The counter -JO is used as a unit of measurement for number of mats. For example, ROKUJO and HACHIJO rooms are considered comfortable-sized rooms.

Another uniquely Japanese unit of measurement is the TSUBO. It is used to measure land area, as square feet or acres would be used in the U.S. It represents a space of roughly 36 square feet (3.35 square meters).

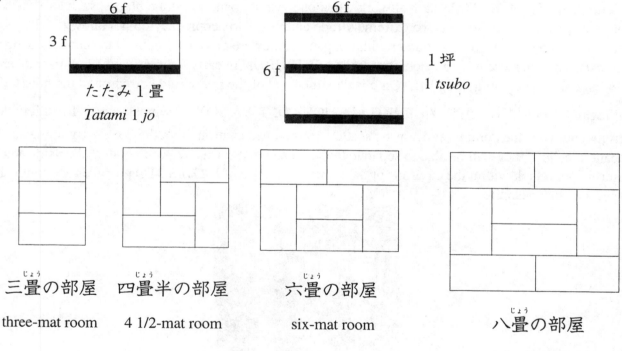

たたみ1畳
Tatami 1 jo

1 坪
1 *tsubo*

三畳の部屋
three-mat room

四畳半の部屋
4 1/2-mat room

六畳の部屋
six-mat room

八畳の部屋
eight-mat room

C. Japanese-style room: 和室 WASHITSU

Most modern Japanese homes are now designed with both Western-style and Japanese-style rooms. If a home has a Japanese-style room, it is most likely the parlor, or room in which guests are received. This room is called the ZASHIKI. The floor is made of *tatami* mats, and the entries to the room are SHOJI (rice paper) sliding doors. Certain walls may be solid, stationary walls while other "walls" may actually be sliding doors (FUSUMA), which are covered with durable, opaque paper. They often are light-colored and may have traditional Japanese designs on them. These "walls" can open up to an adjacent room if the more space is required. Or, FUSUMA doors may open up to closets in which FUTON are stored. An essential feature of the ZASHIKI is the TOKONOMA (alcove). The TOKONOMA is the focal point of this WASHITSU. In the TOKONOMA hangs the KAKEJIKU, which is scroll of a traditional Japanese painting or calligraphic work. A Japanese-style flower arrangement, IKEBANA, also graces the TOKONOMA. When one hosts a party and uses the ZASHIKI, the seat located closest to the TOKONOMA is the seat reserved for the honored guest. Because of the revered nature of the TOKONOMA, it is considered extremely disrespectful to venture inside the alcove area. In the ZASHIKI, there may also be a BUTSUDAN, a small Buddhist altar, which is dedicated to the deceased members of the family. Here, one may find burning incense, small dishes of food such as rice or a recently deceased family member's favorite foods, small cups of drinks, small vases of flowers and a little bell, which may be rung to call the family spirits' attention when one goes there to pray. Photos of recently deceased family members may also stand in this altar.

This ZASHIKI is not only used to formally greet and entertain guests, but it may also serve as a guest bedroom when special guests sleep over. Here, guests sleep Japanese-style on FUTON.

Other WASHITSU in a modern Japanese home may be its bedrooms, though more and more bedrooms are becoming Western style. Western-style rooms in most modern Japanese homes are the kitchen, a living (family) room area, and dining area. Bathrooms take on both Japanese and Western features. In Japan, however, the toilet area and the bathing area are always in separate rooms.

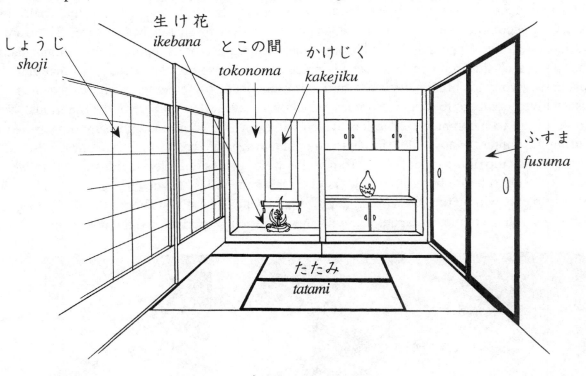

ざしき ZASHIKI
Japanese-style guest room

D. The Bathing Area (FUROBA) and the Toilet (TOIRE) 風呂場とトイレ

One of the most consistently noticeable differences between a Japanese and Western home is the fact that in Japan, the bathing area (FUROBA) and the toilet (TOIRE) are in two separate rooms. In the

七課

U.S., the bathroom usually houses a bathtub, shower, toilet and basin. In Japan, most houses have a FUROBA, which these days also includes a removable hand-held shower. The bathtub is a relatively smaller, more square and far deeper tub than Western tubs. Traditionally, (O)FURO were made from wood, though they are now made from durable synthetic materials. Before bathing at a Japanese home, one usually first goes to the toilet, then, taking one's change of clothes, one goes to the FUROBA where one removes one's clothes and soaps oneself outside the tub with a long bathing towel. One sits on a low plastic stool as one bathes outside the tub. Warm water, taken directly from a faucet, or ladled directly from the tub into large bowls, are used to rinse off the lather. Recently, showers serve this function. After one has soaped, shampooed and rinsed thoroughly, one is finally ready to soak in the tub which has been filled with hot water. When one is sitting in the tub, the water completely immerses the body, often at least to the shoulders. After enjoying the soak, one emerges from the tub, and dries oneself. Since the hot water in the tub is used by the entire family, it is not drained until the last person in the household has bathed. Recently, the temperature of the water is easily monitored automatically, but in the old days, hot water had to be added, or had to be re-heated with fire if the whole family did not hurry and bathe within a short period of time. One person in the family (generally the mother) is often relegated to start the bath and clean up after the entire family bathes.

Toilet etiquette is often very interesting to foreigners. In Japan, toilet space is often small, since the room only accommodates the toilet bowl, and often not even a separate basin space. There are always separate toilet slippers in the bathroom. One must remove one's regular house slippers and slip into the "toilet use" slippers, which are usually made of vinyl or some other waterproof material. Confusing the two kinds of slippers is a common mistake made by foreigners. These days, it is always an adventure to go to Japanese homes, which may have toilets that are of the traditional "squat" type to very high-tech computerized toilets, which will even take your blood pressure or warm your seat during the winter. Many toilets in Japan do not have separate basins to wash your hands, but have built-in basins on top of the toilet fixture from which water rushes out after one flushes the toilet. Often, you can also choose between two ways of flushing the toilet. If you choose the 大 side, your bodily excrements will be flushed with more power and water than if you choose the 小. Whatever kinds of toilet you encounter in Japan, you will find all of your experiences quite interesting!

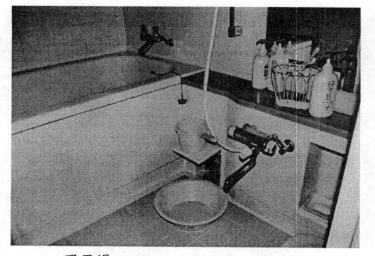
風呂場 (FUROBA)　Bathing Area

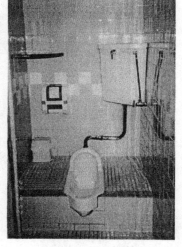
トイレ　Toilet

1. 東 east ひがし 東口〔ひがしぐち〕 East exit

東山〔ひがしやま〕さん

トウ 東京〔とうきょう〕 Tokyo

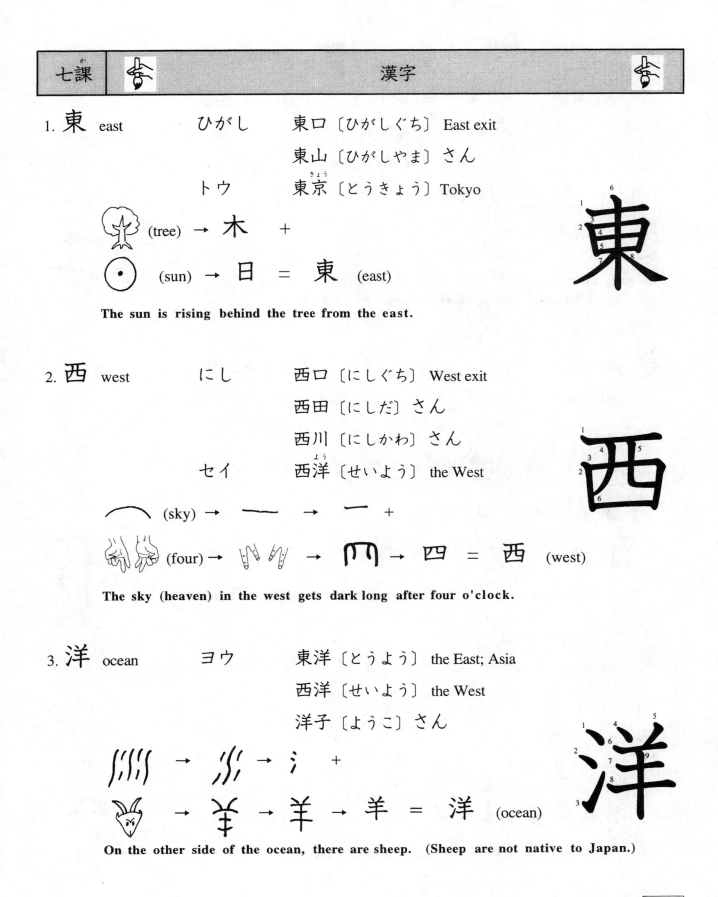

(tree) → 木 +

(sun) → 日 = 東 (east)

The sun is rising behind the tree from the east.

2. 西 west にし 西口〔にしぐち〕 West exit

西田〔にしだ〕さん

西川〔にしかわ〕さん

セイ 西洋〔せいよう〕 the West

(sky) → 一 → 一 +

(four) → → → 四 = 西 (west)

The sky (heaven) in the west gets dark long after four o'clock.

3. 洋 ocean ヨウ 東洋〔とうよう〕 the East; Asia

西洋〔せいよう〕 the West

洋子〔ようこ〕さん

→ → 氵 +

→ 羊 → 羊 → 羊 = 洋 (ocean)

On the other side of the ocean, there are sheep. (Sheep are not native to Japan.)

199

4. 和 Japanese; 　　ワ 　　　　和食〔わしょく〕 Japanese food

　　 harmony 　　　　　　　和室〔わしつ〕 Japanese-style room

　　　　　　　　　　　　　和英辞典〔わえいじてん〕 Japanese-English dictionary

　　　　　　　　　　　　　英和辞典〔えいわじてん〕 English-Japanese dictionary

禾 (harvest) → 禾 → 禾 ＋

口 (mouth) → 口 ＝ 和 (harmony, Japanese)

The more often people eat (put food in their mouths) together after harvests, the more harmony and good will result.

5. 部 part 　　　　ブ 　　　　　　全部〔ぜんぶ〕 all

　　 club 　　　　　　　　　　部活〔ぶかつ〕 club activity

　　　　　　　　ヘ 　　　　　　部屋〔へや〕 room

立 (to stand) → 立 → 立 ＋

口 (mouth) → 口 ＋

阝 (flag) → 阝 → 阝 ＝ 部 (part)

The person standing holds a flag and says "This is my part (territory)."

6. 美 beautiful 　　うつく（しい）　　美しい庭 a beautiful garden

　　　　　　　　ビ 　　　　　　　美術〔びじゅつ〕 fine arts

　　　　　　　　　　　　　　　　美人〔びじん〕 a beautiful woman

羊 (sheep) → 羊 → 羊 ＋

大 (big) → 大 → 大 ＝ 美 (beautiful)

A big sheep offered to the gods is a beautiful sacrifice.

7. 広　is spacious　　　　　ひろ（い）　　　　広い家〔いえ〕a spacious house

広島 Hiroshima

広田〔ひろた〕さん

広中〔ひろなか〕さん

(building roof) → 广 → 广 +

(mine) → ㄥ → ㄙ = 広 (is wide)

My building is spacious.

8. 内　inside　　　　　うち　　　　内に上がって〔あがって〕下さい。

Please step up into the house.

内田〔うちだ〕さん

山内〔やまうち〕さん

ナイ　　　家内〔かない〕one's own wife

(cottage) +

人 (person) = 内 (inside)

A person is inside a cottage.

9. 主　main　　　　　シュ　　　　主人〔しゅじん〕one's own husband

ご主人〔ごしゅじん〕someone else's husband

(a drop) +

(jewel = a symbol of the king) → 王 (king) = 主 (main)

The main person is the crowned king.

201

10. 住　to reside　　す（む）　　　日本に住んでいる。I am living in Japan.

　　　　　　　　　ジュウ　　　　住所〔じゅうしょ〕address

~~~（person）→ イ ＋

◊ （a drop）＋

（jewel = a symbol of the king）→ 王 (king) → 主 (main)

= 住 (to reside)

A person can live as a king wherever spot (drop) he resides.

11. 開　to open　　あ（ける）　　窓を開けて下さい。Please open the window.

門 → 門 → 門 → 門 (gate) ＋

开 → 开 → 开　　　　　= 開 (to open)

The gate opens, and there stands a beautiful Japanese shrine (*torii*).

12. 閉　to close　　し（める）　　戸〔と〕を閉めて下さい。Please close the door.

門 → 門 → 門 → 門 (gate)

才 → 才 (~ year old)

The gate is closed until one reaches a certain age.

【読みかえの漢字】

1. 生　to be born　　う（まれる）＊　日本で生まれました。I was born in Japan.

　　　　　　　　　　なま＊　　　　生卵〔なまたまご〕raw egg

　　　　　person　　セイ　　　　　先生〔せんせい〕teacher

　　　　　　　　　　　　　　　　　学生〔がくせい〕student

		ショウ	一生懸命〔いっしょうけんめい〕 utmost efforts
	to arrange	い（ける）	生け花〔いけばな〕 flower arrangement
2. 上	to go up	あ（がる）	階段を上がる to go up the stairs
	top; above	うえ＊	山の上〔やまのうえ〕 top of the mountain
		ジョウ＊	上手〔じょうず〕 skillful
3. 下	to go down	お（りる）	山を下りる〔やまをおりる〕
			to go down the mountain
	under	した＊	車の下〔くるまのした〕 under the car
	to give	くだ＊	お水を下さい〔おみずをください〕。
			Please give me some water.
		へ＊	下手〔へた〕 unskillful
4. 正	is correct	セイ	正座〔せいざ〕する to sit properly
		ただ（しい）＊	正しいです It is correct.
		ショウ＊	お正月〔しょうがつ〕 New Year's
5. 寝	to sleep	シン	寝室〔しんしつ〕 bedroom
		ね（る）＊	早〔はや〕く寝ました。 I went to sleep early.

＊ Previously introduced.

【読めればいい漢字】

1. ～階	～かい／がい	- floor
2. ～的	～てき	[suffix converting nouns to NA adjectives; translates as "- ic," "-al," "-ish," - style]
3. 全部	ぜんぶ	everything
4. 座る	すわる	to sit
5. 正座する	せいざする	to sit properly

七課

Let's review previous vocabulary!

A. めいし Nouns

1. ホストファミリー	host family	11. しょう来	future
2. 家	house	12. 毎日	every day
3. くつ	shoes	13. 所	place
4. 外	outside	14. トイレ	toilet
5. かんがえ	thought, idea	15. 二階〔にかい〕	second floor
6. もの	thing	16. ベッド	bed
7. 部屋〔へや〕	room	17. 朝	morning
8. にわ	garden	18. ことわざ	proverb
9. 心	heart	19. 日本人	Japanese
10. 足〔あし〕	feet, legs		

B. どうし Verbs

20. 入ると〔G1 はいる／はいります〕 — when (I) enter
21. ぬいで〔G1 ぬぐ／ぬぎます〕 — to take off; remove
22. ある〔G1 あります／あって〕 — there is
23. 使っている〔G1 つかう／つかいます〕 — is using
24. 開けると〔G2 あける／あけます〕 — when (I) open
25. ～が見える〔G2 見えます／見えて〕 — ～ can be seen
26. ～てしまう〔G1 しまいます／しまって〕 — to do ～ completely
27. 作る〔G1 つくります／つくって〕 — to make
28. 違う〔G1 ちがいます／ちがって〕 — different
29. 寝ている〔G2 ねる／ねます〕 — is sleeping
30. 起きたら〔G2 おきる／おきます〕 — when (I) get up
31. 入れる〔G2 いれます／いれて〕 — to put in
32. 使うことが出来て〔G1 つかう＋G2 出来る〕 — can use
33. 分からない〔G1 わかる／わかります〕 — do not understand
34. ～と思う〔G1 おもいます／おもって〕 — to think that ～

C. い けいようし I Adjectives

35. 美〔うつく〕しい	is beautiful	37. 多い	are many
36. いたくなって	(become) painful		

D. ふくし Adverbs

38. いっしょに   together   40. 広〔ひろ〕く   spaciously

39. いつも   always

E. そのほか Others

41. N1 とか N2   N1 and N2, etc. [same usage as や]

42. 〜や〜など   〜 and 〜 etc.

43. でも、   However,

44. こんな〜   this kind of 〜

45. N1 という N2   N2 called N1

七課

Activity A   No new vocabulary.

Activity B

1.  もし　If

もし、明日晴(は)れたら、ピクニックをしましょう。If it is clear tomorrow, let's have a picnic.

2.  けいけんする＜経験(けいけん)する＞　V3　to experience

日本の生活を経験(かつ)(けいけん)しなければ、日本人が分からない。If you do not experience the Japanese lifestyle, you will not understand the Japanese.

Activity C   No new vocabulary.

Activity D

3.  とうようてき＜東洋的＞　NA　Eastern (Asian)-style

だるまは東洋的な絵(え)ですね。The *daruma* is an Asian-style painting, isn't it?

4. せいようてき＜西洋的＞　NA　Western-style

父は西洋的な絵(え)が好きです。My father likes Western-style paintings.

5. かける＜掛(か)ける＞　V2　to hang

玄関(げんかん)の所に絵(え)が掛(か)けてあります。A painting is hung at the entrance.

6. かざる＜飾(かざ)る＞　V1　to decorate

母はいつもお花(か)を飾(かざ)っています。My mother always decorates flowers.

Activity E   No new vocabulary.

Activity F

7.

〜かもしれない／〜かもしれません　might; may

このプレゼントはシャツかもしれません。This present might be a shirt.

Activity G

No new vocabulary.

Activity H

8.

げんかん＜玄関＞　N　entrance way; foyer

日本の家では玄関に入って、くつをぬぎます。In a Japanese house, you

enter the entrance way and then remove your shoes.

9.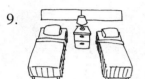

しんしつ＜寝室＞　N　bedroom

家にいくつ寝室がありますか。How many bedrooms are there in your house?

10.

きゃく＜客＞　N　customer; guest; passenger

きゃくま＜客間＞　N　room where guests are received

八畳の和室を客間として使っています。We are using the eight-mat room

to greet guests.

11.

いま＜居間＞　N　living room; family room

家族は夕食後はたいてい居間でテレビを見ます。My family usually

watches T.V. in the living room after dinner.

12.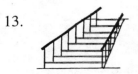

ベランダ　N　veranda

ベランダに花を置いて楽しんでいます。I put flowers on the veranda and am

enjoying them.

13.

かいだん＜階段＞　N　stairs

おばあちゃんは高い階段が嫌いです。My grandmother doesn't like the steep

stairs.

 七課

14. 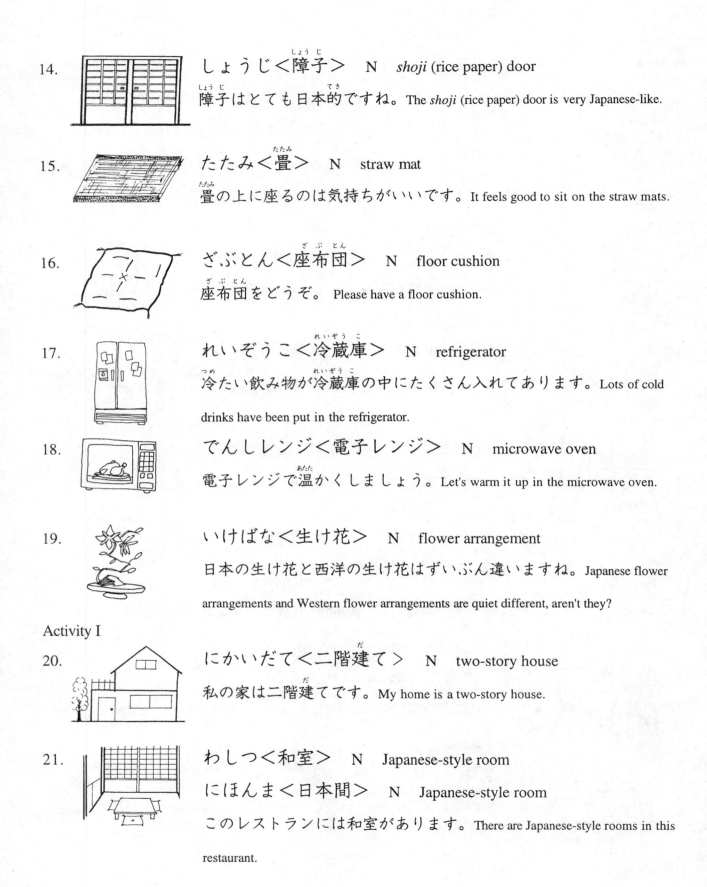 しょうじ<障子> N *shoji* (rice paper) door

障子はとても日本的ですね。 The *shoji* (rice paper) door is very Japanese-like.

15. たたみ<畳> N straw mat

畳の上に座るのは気持ちがいいです。 It feels good to sit on the straw mats.

16. ざぶとん<座布団> N floor cushion

座布団をどうぞ。 Please have a floor cushion.

17. れいぞうこ<冷蔵庫> N refrigerator

冷たい飲み物が冷蔵庫の中にたくさん入れてあります。 Lots of cold drinks have been put in the refrigerator.

18. でんしレンジ<電子レンジ> N microwave oven

電子レンジで温かくしましょう。 Let's warm it up in the microwave oven.

19. いけばな<生け花> N flower arrangement

日本の生け花と西洋の生け花はずいぶん違いますね。 Japanese flower arrangements and Western flower arrangements are quiet different, aren't they?

Activity I

20. にかいだて<二階建て> N two-story house

私の家は二階建てです。 My home is a two-story house.

21. わしつ<和室> N Japanese-style room

にほんま<日本間> N Japanese-style room

このレストランには和室があります。 There are Japanese-style rooms in this restaurant.

22.  ようしつ＜洋室＞　N　Western-style room

ようま＜洋間＞　N　Western-style room

洋室にはソファーやテーブルがあります。 There are a sofa and a table in the Western-style room.

23. でんきせいひん＜電気製品＞ N　electric goods; electric appliances

台所に電気製品がたくさんあります。 There are lots of electric appliances in the kitchen.

24. ふとん＜布団＞　N　Japanese bedding

布団に寝たことがありますか。 Have you ever slept on Japanese bedding?

25.  カーペット　N　carpet

私の部屋のカーペットの色は茶色いです。 The color of the carpet in my room is brown.

26. 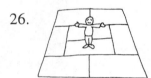 〜じょう＜〜畳＞　C　(counter for *tatami*)

はちじょう＜八畳＞　N　eight-mat room

八畳の和室はちょっと広いです。 The eight-mat Japanese-style room is a little spacious.

よじょうはん＜四畳半＞　N　4 1/2-mat room

私の部屋は四畳半です。 My room is a 4 1/2-mat room.

1 いちじょう	4 よじょう	7 ななじょう	10 じゅうじょう
2 にじょう	5 ごじょう	8 はちじょう	? なんじょう
3 さんじょう	6 ろくじょう	9 きゅうじょう	

27.  べんり＜便利＞　NA　is convenient

この家は駅に近くて、便利です。 This house is close to the station, so it is convenient.

28.  ふべん＜不便＞　NA　is inconvenient

この家は駅に遠くて、不便です。 This house is far from the station, so it is

inconvenient.

Activity J & K　　No new vocabulary.

Activity L

29.  うち＜内＞　N　inside

日本では内と外がはっきり(clear)しています。 In Japan, (the concepts of)

inside and outside are clear.

30.  でんとう＜伝統＞　N　tradition

でんとうてき＜伝統的＞　NA　traditional

京都には伝統的な建物がたくさんあります。 There are many traditional

buildings in Kyoto.

31. 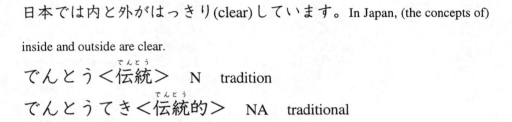 おもい＜重い＞　A　is heavy

ぼくのバッグは重いです。 My bag is heavy.

32. 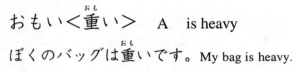 かるい＜軽い＞　A　is light (in weight)

この本は軽いです。 This book is light.

33.  ～が　こわれる＜壊れる＞　V2　to break [intransitive verb]

戸が壊れています。 The door is broken.

～を　こわす＜壊す＞　V1　to break [transitive verb]

戸を壊してしまいました。 I broke the door.

34. なおす＜直す＞　V1　to fix

父は壊れた戸を直してくれました。 My father fixed the broken door for me.

35.  あがる＜上がる＞　V1　to step up

日本の内に上がる時、くつをぬがなければなりません。When you step up into a Japanese house, you have to take off your shoes.

36.  おりる＜下りる＞／おります　V2　to go down; descend

階段を下りました。I went down the stairs.

37.  おちつく＜落ち着く＞　V1　to become calm

座禅をすると、落ち着きます。When I do Zen meditation, I become calm (relaxed).

38.  せいざする＜正座する＞　V3　to sit properly

正座すると、足が痛くなります。When I sit properly, my legs hurt.

39.  たてる＜建てる＞　V2　to build

将来、家を建てたら、和室がほしいです。If I build a house in the future, I want a Japanese-style room.

40.  「ごうにいればごうにしたがえ＜郷に入れば郷にしたがえ＞」　Proverb: When in a village, do as the villagers do.

(When in Rome, do as the Romans do.)

【Recognition 単語】

1. とこのま＜床の間＞　N　alcove

2. ぶつだん＜仏壇＞　N　Buddhist household shrine

3. ふすま　N　opaque sliding door

4. かけじく＜掛け軸＞　N　hanging scroll

5. おしいれ＜押し入れ＞　N　closet

6. げたばこ＜げた箱＞　N　shoe closet

【オプショナル単語】

1. 家具	かぐ	N	furniture
2. 食堂	しょくどう	N	dining room
3. マンション		N	condominium
4. アパート		N	apartment
5. 地下室	ちかしつ	N	basement room
6. 車庫 or ガレージ	しゃこ	N	garage
7. 洗濯機	せんたくき	N	washing machine
8. 掃除機	そうじき	N	vacuum cleaner
9. 皿洗い機	さらあらいき	N	dishwasher
10. 冷凍庫	れいとうこ	N	freezer
11. 炊飯器	すいはんき	N	digital rice cooker
12. オーブン		N	oven
13. レンジ		N	stove
14. 壁	かべ	N	wall
15. 天井	てんじょう	N	ceiling
16. 床	ゆか	N	floor

A. BA form / NAKEREBA form　　　if ～/if not ～

The BA form is a conditional form used to express a hypothetical situation.　"If and only if . . . " is an appropriate English equivalent of the BA form.　The word もし ("If") may appear at the beginning of the - BA clause to emphasize the hypothetical nature of the sentence.　Note the formation of -BA in verbs, いAdjectives, なAdjectives and nouns below.

a. Verbs
Group 1 Verbs

	NAI FORM	MASU FORM	DICTIONARY FORM		BA FORM	NEG. BA FORM
む verbs mu	のまない nomanai	のみます nomimasu	のむ nomu	"drink"	のめば nomeba	のまなければ nomanakereba
ぬ verbs nu	しなない shinanai	しにます shinimasu	しぬ shinu	"die"	しねば shineba	しななければ shinanakereba
ぶ verbs bu	あそばない asobanai	あそびます asobimasu	あそぶ asobu	"play"	あそべば asobeba	あそばなければ asobanakereba
う verbs u	かわない kawanai	かいます kaimasu	かう kau	"buy"	かえば kaeba	かわなければ kawanakereba
つ verbs tsu	またない matanai	まちます machimasu	まつ matsu	"wait"	まてば mateba	またなければ matanakereba
る verbs ru	つくらない tsukuranai	つくります tsukurimasu	つくる tsukuru	"finish"	つくれば tsukureba	つくらなければ tsukuranakereba
く verbs ku	かかない kakanai	かきます kakimasu	かく kaku	"write"	かけば kakeba	かかなければ kakanakereba
ぐ verbs gu	およがない oyoganai	およぎます oyogimasu	およぐ oyogu	"swim"	およげば oyogeba	およがなければ oyoganakereba
す verbs su	はなさない hanasanai	はなします hanashimasu	はなす hanasu	"speak"	はなせば hanaseba	はなさなければ hanasanakereba

Group 2 Verbs (-I RU / -E RU verbs)

	NAI FORM	MASU FORM	DICTIONARY FORM		BA FORM	NEG. BA FORM
-I RU verbs	みない minai	みます mimasu	みる miru	"look"	みれば mireba	みなければ minakereba
-E RU verbs	たべない tabenai	たべます tabemasu	たべる taberu	"eat"	たべれば tabereba	たべなければ tabenakereba

Group 3 Irregular Verbs

	NAI FORM	MASU FORM	DICTIONARY FORM		BA FORM	NEG. BA FORM
きます	こない	きます	くる	"come"	くれば	こなければ
します	しない	します	する	"do"	すれば	しなければ

b. い Adjectives, な Adjectives, Nouns

い Adjective	高い	高ければ	if it is expensive
	高くない	高くなければ	if it is not expensive
	高かった	高かったら	if it were expensive
	高くなかった	高くなかったら	if it were not expensive
な Adjective	好き	好きなら	if (you) like
	好きじゃない or 好きではない	好きじゃなければ	if (you) do not like
	好きだった	好きだったら	if (you) liked
	好きじゃなかった or 好きではなかった	好きじゃなかったら	if (you) did not like
Noun	学生	学生なら	if (you) are a student
	学生じゃない or 学生ではない	学生じゃなければ	if (you) are not a student
	学生だった	学生だったら	if (you) were a student
	学生じゃなかった or 学生ではなかった	学生じゃなかったら	if (you) were not a student

c. Additional notes:

> 1. BA forms can only mean "if ~."
>   It cannot be used to mean "when" as "～たら "and "～と."
> 2. Active verbs used with ～ば **cannot** be followed by commands, requests, suggestions, admonitions, etc.
>
> Example:　　○ 日本へ行ったら、おみやげを買って来て下さい。
>
> 　　　　　　　X 日本へ行けば、おみやげを買って来て下さい。

1. 日本語が話せれば、旅行は楽しいです。　　If you can speak Japanese, the trip will be fun.

2. あなたが行かなければ、私も行きません。　If you won't go, I won't go either.

3. もし、安ければ、買います。　　　　　　　If it is cheap, I will buy it.

4. 映画が好きなら、おもしろい映画をたくさん知っているはずです。

　　　　　　　If he likes movies, he should know lots of interesting movies.

5. 学生なら、安いですよ。　　　　　　If you are a student, it is cheap.

> B. 日本での生活　　　　　　　　　life in Japan
>
> The particle の sometimes follows other particles such as へ, で, から, まで, and indicates that the first noun phrase modifies the second noun.

1. 友子さんからの電話はいつもとても長いんです。

　　A telephone call from Tomoko is always very long.

2. ディズニーランドへの旅行はとても楽しかったです。

　　The trip to the Disneyland was very enjoyable.

3. 日本レストランでの食事はとてもおいしかったけど、高かったです。

The meal at the Japanese restaurant was very delicious, but it was expensive.

C. Transitive verb (-TE form) ＋ ある　　has been done; be done

First, let us review transitive verbs: Transitive verbs are verbs that take direct objects. In the case of Japanese, a transitive sentence contains a direct object that is followed by the particle を. A sentence that does not contain a direct object but suggests one is still transitive.
An intransitive verb is one that does <u>not</u> take a direct object.

In Japanese, certain verbs clearly are always transitive or intransitive. Other verbs take different forms depending on whether the verb is used transitively or intransitively.
Example: はじめる (transitive) and はじまる (intransitive); あける (transitive) and あく (intransitive).
Example sentences:

1. 先生はじゅぎょうを<u>始めました</u>。The teacher started the class.
　じゅぎょうが<u>始まりました</u>。　　The class started.
2. ドアを<u>開ける</u>。　　　　　　(I'll) open the door.
　ドアが<u>開く</u>。　　　　　　　The door will open.

This lesson's new sentence construction employs the TE form of a transitive verb to which ある is attached. It is used to describe an existing state which is the result of an action previously done by someone.

Do not confuse this with a verb *-te iru* construction. The verb *-te iru* form has two interpretations. Usually, a transitive verb *-te iru* suggests an ongoing action. An intransitive verb *-te iru* generally suggests a state as a result of a previous action. The difference between these and the new sentence construction is that the new construction strongly suggests the <u>existence of a current state as a result of a person's previous action</u>. Compare, noting verb forms and particles:

1. 手紙を<u>書いている</u>。(Someone) is writing a letter.
　手紙が<u>書いてある</u>。The letter has been written (by someone).
2. ドアを<u>開けている</u>。(Someone) is opening the door.
　ドアが<u>開いている</u>。The door is open (statement of fact).
　ドアが<u>開けてある</u>。The door has been opened (Is still open and was opened previously by someone.)

Note that this new construction becomes intransitive, though the original verb was a transitive one. Because it becomes intransitive, the word that was originally the direct object loses that function and instead takes a が, as it is now the subject of the sentence.

---

1. 床の間に掛け軸が<u>かけてあります</u>。　　　A scroll has been hung in the alcove.

2. 机の上にいつも花が<u>かざってあります</u>。　　(She) always has flowers decorated on her desk.

3. パーティーについてもう話して<u>あります</u>。　　I have already talked about the party.

4. パーティーの食べ物はもう買って<u>あります</u>。　　Food for the party has already been bought.

D. Plain form ＋ かもしれない／かもしれません　　might ～ ; may ～

Originally, this sentence extender literally meant "I cannot know that . . . " Currently, it is used to express uncertainty. It implies a higher degree of improbability than a "deshoo" sentence. Plain forms precede かもしれない. Note that な adjectives and nouns take nothing before this ending. This ending does not appear in affirmative or past tense forms.

Verb	食べる			might eat
	食べない			might not eat
	食べた			might have eaten
	食べなかった			might not have eaten
い Adjective	高い			might be expensive
	高くない			might not be expensive
	高かった			might have been expensive
	高くなかった	＋ かもしれない		might have not been expensive
な Adjective	好き	かもしれません		might like
	好きじゃない or 好きではない			might not like
	好きだった			might have liked
	好きじゃなかった or 好きではなかった			might not have liked
Noun	学生			might be a student
	学生じゃない or 学生ではない			might not be a student
	学生だった			might have been a student
	学生じゃなかった or 学生ではなかった			might not have been a student

1. 明日雨が降る<u>かもしれません</u>。　　It might rain tomorrow.

2. 試験はむずかしい<u>かもしれません</u>。　　The exam might be difficult.

3. 田中君はあなたが好き<u>かもしれません</u>。　　Tanaka might like you.

4. あの人は歌手だった<u>かもしれない</u>。　　That person may have been a singer.

5. パーティーへ行かない<u>かもしれない</u>。　　I may not go to the party.

E. Sentence 1 (Verb stem form)、 Sentence 2。

To join two sentences with "and" when the first of the two sentences ends with a verb, convert the verb in the first sentence into its stem form and attach the second sentence. A sequence of actions and a listing of actions may be described using this construction. It is a more formal version of the Sentence 1 (Verb-TE form), Sentence 2. The tense of the sentence is determined by the tense of the final verb.

1. 学校に<u>着き</u>、宿題を家に<u>忘</u>れたことを思い出しました。

      I arrived at school, then remembered that I forgot my homework at home.

2. 昨日、おそく家へ<u>帰り</u>、すぐ寝ました。

      I returned home late yesterday and went to bed immediately.

3. 毎朝六時半に<u>起き</u>、朝食を<u>食べ</u>、学校に出かけます。

      Every morning I get up at 6:30, eat breakfast and leave for school.

4. 和室には<u>床</u>の間や<u>仏壇</u>が<u>あり</u>、ふすまや<u>障子</u>などもあります。

      In the Japanese-style room, there is the alcove and the Buddhist household shrine, and there are also opaque sliding doors and paper sliding doors.

A. ペアワーク：Tic Tac Toe ゲーム

Play the Tic Tac Toe game by taking turns changing the MASU form to the correct BA form. The answers are on the next page.

1.

飲みます	しにます	見ます
起きます	寝ます	あそびます
書きます	話します	買います

2.

待ちます	来ます	ふります
あらいます	読みます	食べます
行きます	かします	旅行します

3.

かちます	まけます	出来ます
あります	休みます	会います
間違えます	およぎます	はつ音します

[答え]

1.

のめば [飲みます]	しねば [しにます]	みれば [見ます]
おきれば [起きます]	ねれば [寝ます]	あそべば [あそびます]
かけば [書きます]	はなせば [話します]	かえば [買います]

2.

まてば [待ちます]	くれば [来ます]	ふれば [ふります]
あらえば [あらいます]	よめば [読みます]	たべれば [食べます]
いけば [行きます]	かせば [かします]	りょこうすれば [旅行します]

3.

かてば [かちます]	まければ [まけます]	できれば [出来ます]
あれば [あります]	やすめば [休みます]	あえば [会います]
間違えれば [まちがいます]	およげば [およぎます]	はつおんすれば [はつ音します]

七課

4.

安い	お茶を飲む	けっこんする
日本に住む	好き	むずかしい
太る	明日	ピアノをひく

5.

きらい	車にのる	良くない
家へ来る	行かない	おもしろい
食べる	上手	はたらく

6.

分からない	きびしくない	金曜日
学生じゃない	六時に起きる	よわい
あまい	しずか	まどを開ける

4.

やすければ [安い]	お茶をのめば [お茶を飲む]	けっこんすれば [けっこんする]
日本にすめば [日本に住む]	すきなら [好き]	むずかしければ [むずかしい]
ふとれば [太る]	明日なら [明日]	ピアノをひけば [ピアノをひく]

5.

きらいなら [きらい]	車にのれば [車にのる]	よくなければ [良くない]
家へくれば [家へ来る]	いかなければ [行かない]	おもしろければ [おもしろい]
食べれば [食べる]	上手なら [上手]	はたらけば [はたらく]

6.

分からなければ [分からない]	きびしくなければ [きびしくない]	金曜日なら [金曜日]
学生じゃなければ [学生じゃない]	六時におきれば [六時に起きる]	よわければ [よわい]
あまければ [あまい]	しずかなら [しずか]	まどをあければ [まどを開ける]

B. ペアワーク：私はどこにいるでしょう。Guessing game

You report to your partner what you see in each room/location in a Japanese house. Use the following sentences. Your partner listens and guesses which location you have described. Use 〜ば as in the example below. Take turns.

Ex. 生徒１：ここに、冷蔵庫があります。

生徒２：冷蔵庫があれば、そこは台所でしょう。

1. ここに、ふとんがあります。	
2. ここに、げたばこがあります。	
3. ここに、とこの間があります。	
4. ここに、おきゃくさんのソファーがあります。	
5. ここに、電子レンジがあります。	
6. ここに、テレビがあります。	
7. ここに、スリッパがあります。	

C. ペアワーク：〜からの〜

Ask how your partner feels about the following things/activities. Take turns.

Ex. 質問：友達からの電話はどうですか。

質問	うれしい	かなしい	こわい
1. 友達からの電話			
2. 日本への旅行			
3. 月〔つき〕moon への旅行			
4. 学校からのつうちひょう report card			
5. 好きな人とのデート			

D. ペアワーク （〜てある）

Ask your partner the following questions about your Japanese classroom. Your partner answers.
Take turns.

1. 日本語の教室に日本のポスターがはって あります。か。	（はい　いいえ）
2. 日本語の教室に花がかざってありますか。	（はい　いいえ）
3. 日本語の教室に東洋的な物がおいてありますか。	（はい　いいえ）
4. 日本語の教室に西洋的な絵〔え〕が かけてありますか。	（はい　いいえ）
5. 日本語の教室はよくそうじしてありますか。	（はい　いいえ）

E. ペアワーク （〜かもしれない）

Ask your partner the following questions. Your partner answers. If you are unsure about your
answer, use the pattern of 〜かもしれません. Take turns.

Ex. 質問：今日は早く家へ帰りますか。

答え：今日は早く家へ帰る<u>かもしれません</u>。

or 今日は早く帰らない<u>かもしれません</u>。

1. 今晩、宿題を全部〔ぜんぶ〕しますか。
2. 今晩、友達から電話があると思いますか。
3. この週末に、映画を見に行きますか。
4. 来年、日本語をとりますか。
5. しょう来、日本へ旅行しますか。
6. しょう来、あなたはお金持ちになると思いますか。
7. しょう来、仕事で日本語を使うと思いますか。

F. クラスワーク：Discovery Box　「日本の家で使う物」

In a box provided by your teacher, there are many things that can be found in a Japanese house. A student picks one item from the box and guesses what the item is or what it is used for. Use ～かもしれません.

～かもしれません。

G. ペアワーク（起き、食べ、～　）

What do you do in the morning after you get up? Narrate your daily morning routine as your partner numbers the sequence of events below. Use the ～ (Verb stem)、 ～ pattern. If an activity is not on the list, add it in the blank space at the end.

Ex. 私は朝起き、トイレを使い、～、～、

1	起きる。		ひげをそる。shave
	はをみがく。		かみのけをきれいにする。
	着かえる。		化しょうをする。
	トイレを使う。		朝食を食べる。
	シャワーをあびる。		新聞を読む。
	かおをあらう。		

H. ペアワーク

Label each numbered item or location below by writing the correct letter of the corresponding word
from the box below. [   ] item [   ] room

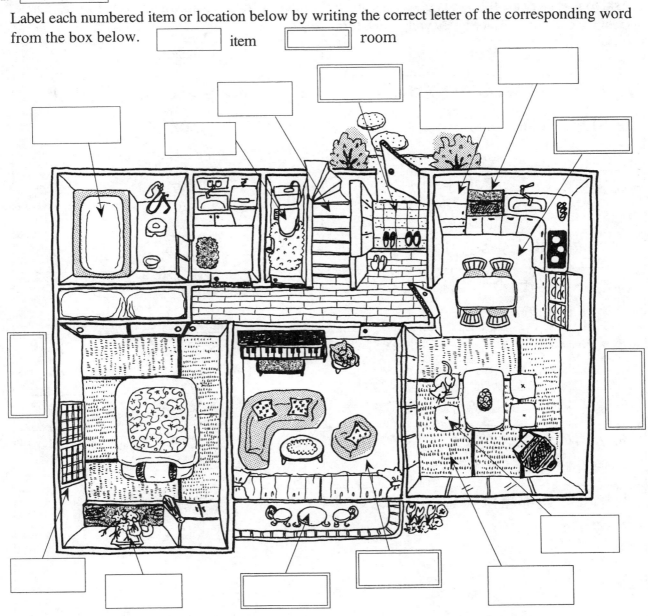

A. ざぶとん

B. 階段〔かいだん〕

C. ベランダ

D. 居間〔いま〕

E. 生け花〔いけばな〕

F. たたみ

G. 風呂〔ふろ〕

H. 台所

I. 冷蔵庫〔れいぞうこ〕

J. 客間〔きゃくま〕

K. 玄関〔げんかん〕

L. 寝室〔しんしつ〕

M. 障子〔しょうじ〕

N. 電子〔でんし〕レンジ

O. トイレ

I. ペアワーク

Ask your partner the following questions about the house and the room where he/she lives. Circle the answers your partner gives you. Take turns.

質問	答え
1. どんな家に住んでいますか。	家、マンション condo、アパート
2. 何階だてですか。	一階だて、二階だて、三階だて（そのほか other：　　　）
3. 寝室がいくつありますか。	＊なし、一つ、二つ、三つ、四つ、五つ
4. トイレがいくつありますか。	一つ、二つ、三つ
5. バス、シャワーがいくつありますか。	一つ、二つ、三つ
6. カーペットは何いろですか。	白、グレイ、茶いろ、あお、あか（そのほか：　　　）
7. 家の場所〔ばしょ〕はどうですか。	べんり、ふべん
8. 台所の電気せいひんの中で何を一番よく使いますか。	れいぞうこ、電子レンジ（そのほか：　　　　）
9. あなたの部屋は何じょうぐらいですか。	三じょうぐらい、四じょう半ぐらい、六じょうぐらい、八じょう、十じょう、（そのほか：　　　）
10. あなたの部屋はどんな部屋ですか。	洋室、和室
11. あなたの部屋にどんなえがかけてありますか。そして、どんなポスターがはってありますか。	東洋的なえ、西洋的なえ、ポスター　（そのほか：　　　）
12. あなたは何に寝ていますか。	ベッド、ふとん

＊なし＝ない

七課

J. ペアワーク

Some physical features of homes in the U.S. and Japan are different. Ask your partner the following questions. Your partner will answer the questions based on the knowledge he/she has. Take turns.

質問	アメリカ	日本
1. どこでくつをぬぎますか。		
2. トイレとおふろはおなじ所にありますか。		
3. 家の中にたくさんカーペットがありますか。		
4. 寝室のドアにかぎがありますか。		
5. ベッドに寝ますか。ふとんに寝ますか。		
6. せっけん(soap)をおふろの中で使いますか。外で使いますか。		
7. トイレを使っていない時、戸が開けてありますか。閉めてありますか。		

K. ペアワーク

What do you do in the following rooms or places? List two activities one can do at each place. Do not list the same activity twice. Write in Japanese.

場所	する事
1. げんかん	1. 2.
2. 台所	1. 2.
3. きゃく間	1. 2.
4. 居間〔いま〕	1. 2.
5. 寝室	1. 2.
6. 風呂〔ふろ〕	1. 2.

L. ペアワーク

Ask your partner the following questions. Your partner will answer based on fact.

質問	
1. おふろに入ったことがありますか。	
2. たたみの上に座ったことがありますか。	
3. 正座することが出来ますか。	
4. ざぶとんに座ったことがありますか。	
5. ふとんに寝たことがありますか。	
6. 日本の生け花を見たことがありますか。	
7. 家にどんな日本のでんとう的な物がありますか。	
8. あなたの家ではうちに入る時に、くつをぬがなければなりませんか。	
9. あなたはどこにいる時、一番おち着きますか。	
10. 家で何かこわれたら、たいていだれがなおしますか。	
11. しょう来、どんな家をたてたいと思いますか。	
12. 大学のりょうに住んだら、自分の部屋にれいぞうこや電子レンジがあると思いますか。	
13. 学校でよくかいだんを上がったり、下りたりしなければなりませんか。	
14. あなたが学校へ持って行くバッグはおもいですか。かるいですか。	
15. 「ごうに入れば、ごうにしたがえ。」ということわざのいみは何ですか。	

名前：＿＿＿＿＿＿＿＿＿＿＿＿＿＿

クラス：＿＿＿＿＿＿＿

たんご	Check	たんご	Check	ぶんぽう	Check	Error
もし		電子レンジ		～しか ＋ Neg.		
けいけんする		れいぞうこ		～という～		
東洋的		居間〔いま〕		～とか～		
西洋的		内		～時（に）		
かける		生け花		Noun Modifiers		
かざる		でんとう的		～ので		
げんかん		おもい		～のに		
寝室		かるい		～んです		
きゃく／きゃく間		～がこわれている		～た方がいい		
ベランダ		～をこわす		～始める／終わる		
かいだん		なおす		～つづける		
しょうじ		上がる		～にくい／やすい		
たたみ		下りる		～てから		
ざぶとん		おち着く		～し		
二階だて		正座する		～間に		
和室		たてる		～ながら		
洋室		ごうに入れば...		～そうだ		
ふとん				～後で／～前に		
カーペット				～かもしれない		
～じょう				～てある		
べんり				～ば		
ふべん				S1 V(stem)、S2。		
電気せいひん				Plain Polite		
				Male Female		

By the end of this lesson, you will be able to communicate the information below in the given situation. Complete the following tasks with a partner. You are expected to conduct a natural conversation using as many new vocabulary and grammatical structures as you can, while appropriately incorporating vocabulary and structures you have learned previously. Use the appropriate speech style (plain or polite) and male/female speech if appropriate. Practice the dialogue with your partner; the aim is not to memorize a dialogue, but to communicate meaningfully with your partner on the topics below.

【 III - 8 トピック 1 】

Partner **A**: *Student from the U.S.*
Partner **B**: *Student from Japan*

Situation: *A describes a Japanese meal to his Japanese friend.*

A tells **B** about a Japanese meal she/he has had in the U.S. **B** asks **A** questions about the meal. They discuss: where and when **A** had the meal, how it tasted, what was included, how the food was prepared (に物, あげ物, etc.), whether it was nutritious, its appearance and how it was eaten (with condiments, spices, garnishes). **A** talks about what kinds of Japanese meal she/he plans to have soon and where. **B** offers to prepare a Japanese meal for **A**. **A** gladly accepts.

【 III - 8 トピック 2 】

Partner **A**: *High school student in the U.S.*
Partner **B**: *High school student from Japan*

Situation: *A, who is studying Japanese, describes his obento to his Japanese friend.*

A describes the *obento* making process in detail and **B** asks questions and comments. They talk about: reason for making the *obento*, preparations (planning, shopping, cooking), what was included in the *obento* and reasons for each item (appearance, taste, texture, shape, smell, nutrition, method of preparation), type of container and carrier. **A** shares his/her impression of *obento*-making. **B** comments on **A**'s work. **A** and **B** talk about whether they will make *obento* in the future, and if so, for whom. If not, why.

＜ホストファミリーの家での夕食だ。食事は和食で、おさしみと焼き魚と竹の子の煮物と酢の物とみそ汁とご飯と漬物だ。＞

お母さん：ご飯ですよ。ケン、冷蔵庫に入れておいた冷たい飲み物をテーブルに持って行って。重いから、気をつけてね。

ケン　　：は〜い。わあ、おいしそう。

お母さん：もうすぐケンがアメリカへ帰ってしまうから、ケンが好きな物ばかり料理したのよ。ごえんりょなく、どうぞ。

お父さん：じゃ、ケンの将来の成功を祈って、乾杯！

ケン　　：本当にお世話になりました。さびしくなるなあ。

お母さん：ケンは何でも食べてくれたから、料理するのも困らなかったわ。でも、納豆だけは好きじゃないらしいわね。健康的なのに。

ケン　　：納豆は苦手です。でも、ぼくは和食が大好きになりました。特に、お母さんのお弁当は最高だった。

お母さん：それはどうも。この竹の子は太いから、ちょっとかたいかしら？

ケン　　：いいえ、やわらかいですよ。でも、ちょっと変わった味ですね。

お母さん：少し苦いでしょうけど、それは竹の子の自然の味だから、心配しないで。今、竹の子の季節だから、一番おいしいはずよ。

ケン　　：おいしいです。ぼくは、この丸くて黄色いたくあんが大好きです。

お母さん：ご飯のおかわりは？お茶漬けを食べる？

ケン　　：いいえ、けっこうです。とてもおいしかったです。ごちそうさまでした。アメリカに帰ったら、日本のレストランで働こうと思っています。そうしたら、日本語も使えるし、和食も食べられるし、一石二鳥でしょう？

お父さん：ケンも日本語が上手になったな。

A. Food Preparation

Western menus are generally organized in the order in which one would eat one's meal: appetizers, soups, salads, entrees and desserts. Side dishes and drinks are also listed.

Japanese menus may also present foods in a similar sequence, but main dishes are also generally broken down into sub-categories according to the way the food is prepared. Common Japanese food preparation styles are やきもの (broiled or grilled food), あげもの (deep fried food), むしもの (steamed food), にもの (food simmered in broth), なべもの (foods prepared and served in a pot), しるもの (soup), すのもの／あえもの (salads and dressed foods).

B. Drinking tea.

Drinking green tea is a part of daily life for most Japanese. As in the case of foods, there are rules on how tea is to be consumed. Here are some pointers to observe as you are offered tea in Japan:

1. Tea cups come in various sizes and shapes. Green tea, however, is generally served in cups with no handles.
2. In most situations, tea cups arrive with a little saucer beneath, which also serves as a coaster.
3. To prepare tea, one boils hot water, allows it to sit for a few minutes, then pours the hot water over the dried tea leaves, which have been placed in a teapot. Allow the tea to steep for a minute or two before pouring it into the tea cups.
4. When tea is served, the person serving the tea holds the handle of the teapot with one hand, and as she pours the tea, gently holds the knob on the cover of the teapot with her other hand to prevent it from dropping off as she pours.
5. When one drinks tea, it is considered good manners to hold the cup with one hand encircling the cup and the other gently supporting the bottom of the tea cup. Only in very informal situations drinking tea with one hand is acceptable.
6. One should not drink tea in a single gulp, but take sips.
7. The host should always keep an eye on her guest's tea cup to be sure that it is filled.
8. In the case of formal tea ceremonies, a different kind of tea called まっちゃ is served. It is a thick, frothy and stronger-tasting tea, which is prepared individually by the host of the tea ceremony. It is served in bowl-shaped tea cups. When consumed, it should be held with both hands supporting the base of the bowl.

まっちゃ
(powdered tea)

C. Place Settings

In Western culture, dishes are set, sometimes on place mats, in a predetermined way. Likewise, there is an accepted presentation of dishes in Japan. Instead of place mats, Japanese often set their dishes on trays, as the Japanese use many separate small dishes when serving their meals. In most cases, Western dishes come in matching sets, that is, all dishes are of the same design. Japanese dishes will generally complement each other, but do not come in sets of the same design. Dishes used together will even be made from different materials such as lacquer, earthenware or porcelain. Since each food is presented in its own container, the placement of dishes on the tray is determined by the type of food the dishes contain. See the sketch below.

AN EXAMPLE OF AN ORDINARY MEAL

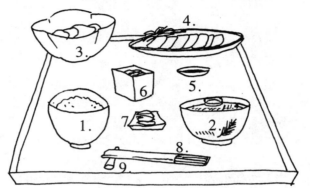

1. cooked rice
2. clear or *miso* soup
3. boiled food
4. broiled or deep-fried food
   or *sashimi* (sliced raw fish)
5. soy sauce for *sashimi*
6. vinegared or dressed food
7. pickles
8. chopsticks
9. chopstick holder

D. Chopstick Etiquette

Chopsticks are placed horizontally at the part of the table or tray closest to the person sitting at the table. The pointed end of the chopsticks faces the left of the setting and the thicker end of the chopsticks lie to the right for the convenience of right-handed people. Under the pointed end of the chopsticks is placed a はしおき, which elevates this part of the chopsticks off the table or tray to keep them clean. はしおき is a small ceramic, porcelain, lacquer or wooden piece usually designed or shaped in an attractive way.

Some rules to remember when using chopsticks:

1. Do not rub your wooden (わりばし) chopsticks together after breaking them apart.
2. Do not stick your chopsticks vertically into your bowl of rice.
3. Do not slide dishes away or toward you on the dining table using chopsticks.
4. Do not pass food to another person chopstick to chopstick.

5. Do not "cut" your food by holding a chopstick in each hand.
6. Do not point your chopsticks to others as you talk.
7. Do not bite, chew or lick your chopsticks.
8. Do not allow your chopsticks to "wander" over dishes of food as you try to decide what to take.
9. Do not "spear" your food.
10. When not at home, turn your chopsticks around when taking food from communal serving dishes. Do not use the end of your chopsticks from which you eat.
11. Even at home, chopsticks must match. Do not use mismatched chopsticks to form pairs.
12. Use chopsticks to lift food up to you. Do not bend over your dishes to eat your food.
13. Return your chopsticks to their original place on the はしおき when you are finished.

E. Other Etiquette Reminders:
1. Do not pour soy sauce, catsup or other condiments over your rice.
2. Napkins are not traditionally used for Japanese meals. This is true largely because foods are generally served in small, bite-sized pieces. Many restaurants will instead offer おしぼり, which are moist, heated towels used to wipe one's hands. It is not to be used to wipe one's face.
3. Hold rice and soup bowls with one hand while eating/drinking out of them. They should be lifted up about halfway off the table.

4. Consume soup and liquid dishes directly from the bowl. Chopsticks may be used to take food out of the bowl.
5. Slurping is acceptable and encouraged while eating noodles.
6. Try to finish your rice "to the last grain."
7. After finishing soup or any other food served in a covered container, always replace the cover on the empty container.
8. Check that your area of the table is tidy before your leave the table.

F. The History of *Obento*.
The term お弁当 （おべんとう） originally referred to the wooden container that held a lunch, and not the lunch itself. According to some accounts, the word first came into use when Oda Nobunaga moved his headquarters to a castle on Lake Biwa near Kyoto in 1576.

In its earliest form, *obento* consisted simply of dried rice, riceballs, or sweet potatoes wrapped in a leaf or in a sheath of a bamboo shoot. At this time, *obento* was mainly eaten by travellers or people who worked outdoors. Most Japanese during this time still ate only two meals a day. Laborers and others who did strenuous work, however, carried their third meal to the fields. This meal was considered a snack, and came to be called *kashi*, which then meant fruit.

In the 1600's, elaborate meals were prepared and carried in tiered lacquered boxes for outings. The *samurai* often ate *obento* on their long journeys, especially since it was not customary for them to eat in public places. These origins explain the distinctive features of *obento*: its portability and its ability not to spoil over periods of time while remaining flavorful even when eaten cold.

By the 19th century, it had become common for people to eat three meals a day. The term *okashi* then came to mean snacks eaten between meals. Today, *okashi* refers to any sort of sweets.

The Japanese custom of taking snacks with them on their travels is a remnant of the old tradition of taking food on trips. Also, the tradition of serving only two meals at Japanese inns originally began with the custom of eating only twice a day.

Presently, *obento* are common sights at theaters, where people look forward to eating their *makunouchi bento* during intermissions. *Makunouchi* literally means "between curtains." Another popular kind of *obento* is the *ekiben,* which are *obento* sold at train stations or on trains that travel long distances. Certain stations are famous for one or two *obento* that represent their region. Of course, "home lunches" as we call them, are also a very common type of *obento*. Japanese mothers take pains to make delicious, nutritious and attractive *obento* for their children and husbands. *Obento* is also now commonly sold at convenience stores or delivered to homes or business establishments. There are also now many shops that feature take-out *obento*.

Obento will very likely continue to be a favorite meal for Japanese on the go.

幕の内弁当 *makunouchi bento*

1. 竹 bamboo　　　　たけ　　　　竹の子〔たけのこ〕 bamboo shoot

竹田〔たけだ〕さん

竹本〔たけもと〕さん

竹内〔たけうち〕さん

(bamboo) → (bamboo) → 竹 (bamboo)

2. 鳥 bird　　　　とり　　　　鳥肉〔とりにく〕 chicken, poultry

焼き鳥〔やきとり〕 grilled chicken on skewers

チョウ　　　　一石二鳥〔いっせきにちょう〕

Kill two birds with one stone.

→ → → → 鳥 (bird)

3. 色 color　　　　いろ　　　　何色〔なにいろ〕？ what color?

茶色〔ちゃいろ〕 brown

刀 (head) + ⊞ (windows) + (snake) = 色 (color)

I can see the head of the snake through the window. What color is it?

4. 赤 red   あか   赤い車〔くるま〕 red car

赤ちゃん a baby

土 (soil) ＋

灬 (fire) → ⟨ ⟩ ⟨ ⟩ → 小 ＝ 赤 (red)

When you burn the soil, it will be red.

5. 青 blue   あお   青い海〔うみ〕 blue ocean

blue-green   青木〔あおき〕さん

青色〔あおいろ〕 blue (color)

(new plant) → 生 → 圭

(moon) → 丹 → 月 ＝ 青 (blue)

A new plant looks blue under the moonlight.

6. 黄 yellow   き   黄色〔きいろ〕 yellow (color)

黄色い花〔きいろいはな〕 yellow flowers

(plant) → 屮屮 → 艹 ＋

一 (one) ＋

(come out from a bottle) → → 由 (a reason) ＋

八 (*katakana* "ha") ＋

The person with one yellow grass hat has a reason to laugh "ha ha ha."

7. 風　wind　　　　　　かぜ　　　　強い風〔つよいかぜ〕strong wind

　　　　～ style　　　　　フウ　　　　和風〔わふう〕Japanese-style

　　　　　　　　　　　　　　　　　　洋風〔ようふう〕Western-style

　　　　　　　　　　　　　　　　　　台風〔たいふう〕typhoon

　　　　　　　　　　　　フ　　　　　風呂〔ふろ〕Japanese bath

→ 風 → 風 = 風 (wind)

an insect blown by the wind

Gone with the wind is the funny, munching insect.

8. 味　flavor, taste　　　あじ　　　　いい味 good taste

　　　　　　　　　　　　　　　　　　味の素 MSG (monosodium glutamate; a

　　　　　　　　　　　　　　　　　　flavor-enhancer for food)

　　　　　　　　　　　　ミ　　　　　趣味はテニスです。　My hobby is tennis.

　　　　　　　　　　　　　　　　　　何という意味ですか。　What does it mean?

口 (mouth) ＋ 一 (one) ＋ 木 (tree) ＝ 味 (taste)

Let's taste one young tree sprout.

9. 料　materials　　　　リョウ　　　料理する　to cook

　　　　　　　　　　　　　　　　　　授業料　tuition

　　　　　　　　　　　　　　　　　　材料〔ざいりょう〕ingredients

　　　　　　　　　　　　　　　　　　調味料〔ちょうみりょう〕seasonings

米 (rice) ＋ 斗 (a measure) ＝ 料 (materials)

→ 斗 → = 斗 (a measure)

a rice measure with a handle

Let's measure rice. Rice is the most important of materials one eats.

10. 理 arrangement　　　り　　　　日本料理〔にほんりょうり〕Japanese cooking

料理屋〔りょうりや〕(Japanese) restaurant

料理人〔りょうりにん〕a cook

田 (rice field) ＋ 土 (land) ＝ 里 (measured land)

A rice field is used as a measurement of land.

王 (king)　　　＋ 里 (measured land) ＝ 理 (arrangement)

A king ordered the land to be measured. It was a good arrangement.

11. 由 a reason　　　ユウ　　　　自由〔じゆう〕free; liberal

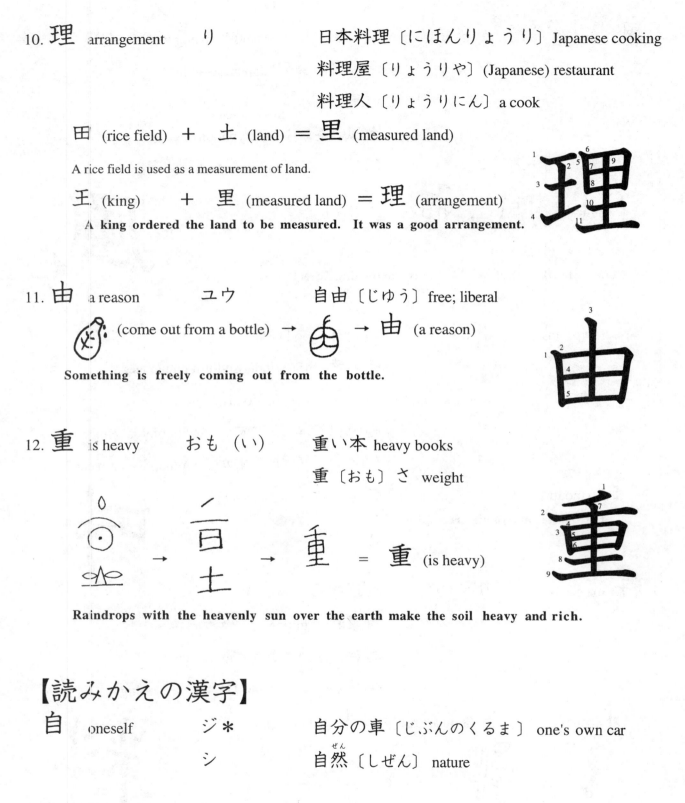 (come out from a bottle) → → 由 (a reason)

Something is freely coming out from the bottle.

12. 重 is heavy　　　おも（い）　　　重い本 heavy books

重〔おも〕さ weight

→ → 重 ＝ 重 (is heavy)

Raindrops with the heavenly sun over the earth make the soil heavy and rich.

【読みかえの漢字】

自 oneself　　　ジ ＊　　　　自分の車〔じぶんのくるま〕one's own car

シ　　　　自然〔しぜん〕nature

＊ Previously introduced.

【読めればいい漢字】

1. 自然　　　しぜん　　　nature
2. 焼く　　　やく　　　　to grill; roast; bake; toast; fry
3. 苦手　　　にがて　　　be weak in
4. 丸　　　　まる　　　　circle
5. 三角　　　さんかく　　triangle
6. 四角　　　しかく　　　square
7. 弁当　　　べんとう　　box lunch
8. 最〜　　　さい〜　　　the most 〜

Let's review previous vocabulary!

A. めいし Nouns

1. 食事〔しょくじ〕	meal	12. アメリカ	U.S.
2. ホストファミリー	host family	13. 物〔もの〕	thing [tangible]
3. 家〔いえ〕	house	14. しょう来	future
4. 夕食〔ゆうしょく〕	dinner; supper	15. せいこう	success
5. さしみ	raw fish	16. 何でも	anything
6. みそしる	*miso* soup	17. お母さん	someone else's mother
7. ご飯〔はん〕	cooked rice; meal	18. お弁当〔べんとう〕	box lunch
8. れいぞうこ	refrigerator	19. 味〔あじ〕	taste
9. 飲み物〔のみもの〕	drink	20. 今	now
10. テーブル	table	21. 日本のレストラン	Japanese restaurant
11. もうすぐ	pretty soon		

B. どうし Verbs

22. 持って行って〔G1 もっていく／もっていきます〕 to take [something]
23. 気をつけて〔G2 きをつける／きをつけます〕 to be careful
24. 帰ってしまう〔G1 かえる＋G1 しまう／かえります＋しまいます〕 return (completely)
25. 料理した〔IR りょうりする／りょうりします〕 cooked
26. 食べてくれた〔G2 たべる＋G2 くれる／たべます＋G2 くれます〕 ate (for me)
27. 心ぱいしないで〔IR しんぱいする／しんぱいします〕 do not worry
28. 食べる？〔G2 たべます／たべて〕 will you eat?
29. 帰ったら〔G1 かえる／かえります〕 when I return home
30. 使えるし〔G1 つかう／つかいます〕 can use (what's more)
31. 食べられるし〔G2 たべる／たべます〕 can eat (what's more)

C. い けいようし I Adjectives

32. つめたい	cold (to the touch)	35. おいしいはず	supposed to be delicious
33. おいしそう	look delicious	36. おいしかった	was delicious
34. さびしくなる	become lonely; miss		

D. な けいようし NA Adjectives

37. 好き　　　　　to like
38. 好きじゃない　do not like
39. 苦手〔にがて〕　poor at; cannot handle
40. 大好きになりました　came to like very much
41. 上手になった　became skillful

E. ふくし Adverbs

42. 本当に　　truly
43. とくに　　especially
44. ちょっと　a little
45. 少し　　a little [formal]
46. また　　again

F. その他 Others

47. じゃ　　　　　　　　　　Then
48. Sentence ＋なあ　　　　　[exclamation]
49. ～だけ　　　　　　　　　only ～
50. Sentence ＋のに　　　　　Although ～
51. Noun/ なAdj. ＋だった　was [plain form of でした]
52. Sentence ＋かしら　　　I wonder if ～ [female]
53. Noun/ なAdj. ＋でしょう　probably is ～
54. そうしたら、　　　　　　If you do so,

G. Expressions

55. は～い。　　　　　　　　Ye～s.
56. わあ。　　　　　　　　　Wow.
57. お世話〔せわ〕になりました。　Thank you for taking care of me.
58. それはどうも。　　　　　Thank you (for saying that).
59. いいえ、けっこうです。　No, thank you.
60. ごちそうさまでした。　　[expression used after meals]

Activity A

1.
~ばかり　Nd　only ~

父は最近ゴルフばかりやっている。My father is only playing golf recently.

Activity B

2. つけもの<漬物(つけ)>　N　pickled vegetable

つける<漬ける(つ)>　V2　to soak; dip

日本人は食事の終わりに、よく漬け物(つ)を食べる。Japanese often eat pickled

vegetables at the end of their meals.

3. たくあん<沢庵(たくあん)>　N　pickled turnip

たくあんという黄色くてくさい漬け物(つ)を食べたことがある？Have you

ever eaten the smelly yellow pickled vegetable called *takuan*?

4. なっとう<納豆(なっとう)>　N　fermented soybeans

納豆(なっとう)だけは好きになれない。It is only *natto* that I cannot come to like.

5. しぜん<自然>　N　nature

美しい自然はまだ残(のこ)っている。Beautiful nature (natural beauty) still remains.

6. きせつ<季節(きせつ)>　N　season

季節(きせつ)の中で、いつが一番好きですか。Among the seasons, which do you like

the best?

7. 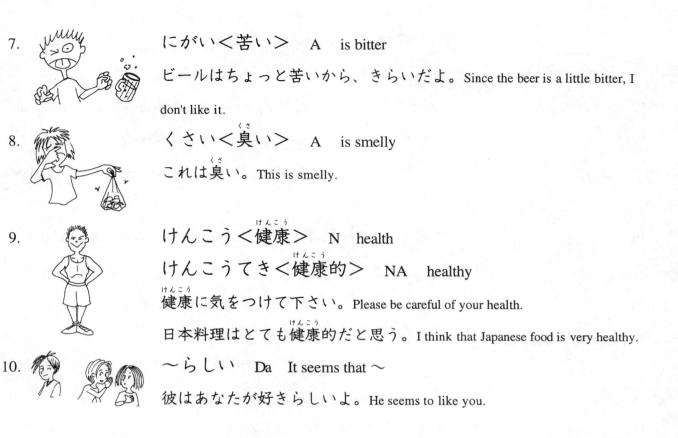 にがい＜苦い＞　A　is bitter

ビールはちょっと苦いから、きらいだよ。Since the beer is a little bitter, I don't like it.

8. くさい＜臭い＞　A　is smelly

これは臭い。This is smelly.

9. けんこう＜健康＞　N　health

けんこうてき＜健康的＞　NA　healthy

健康に気をつけて下さい。Please be careful of your health.

日本料理はとても健康的だと思う。I think that Japanese food is very healthy.

10. ～らしい　Da　It seems that ～

彼はあなたが好きらしいよ。He seems to like you.

Activity C

11. いれておく＜入れておく＞　V2+ V1　place; put in (something somewhere in advance)　飲み物を冷蔵庫に入れておこう。Let's put the drinks in the refrigerator (in advance).

Activity D

12. はたらこうとおもっている＜働こうと思っている＞

V1+P+V1　I am thinking of working.

将来、日本で働こうと思っている。I am thinking of working in Japan in the future.

Activity E

13. たけのこ＜竹の子＞　N　bamboo shoot

竹の子という物を食べたことがない。I have never eaten the thing called *takenoko*.

八課

14. にもの＜煮物＞　N　boiled (in broth) foods

にる＜煮る＞　V2　to boil (in broth); simmer

野菜をさとうとしょうゆで煮ます。Cook the vegetables with sugar and soy sauce.

15. すのもの＜酢の物＞　N　vinegared vegetables

酢の物は少しすっぱいけど、体にいい。The vinegared vegetables are a little

sour, but good for the body.

16. （お）ちゃづけ＜茶漬け＞　N　tea poured over a bowl of rice,

eaten with garnishes

日本人はお茶漬けが大好きだ。Japanese love *ochazuke*.

17. やきざかな＜焼き魚＞　N　grilled fish

やく＜焼く＞　V1　to grill; roast; bake; toast; fry

魚を焼いて、食べよう。Let's grill some fish and eat it.

18. さんかく＜三角＞　N　triangle

三角のおむすびは、伝統的だ。The triangular rice ball is traditional.

19. しかく＜四角＞　N　square

しかくい＜四角い＞　A　square (shaped)

四角い形のむすびは作りやすそうだ。The square rice ball looks easy to make.

Activity F

20. まる＜丸＞　N　circle

まるい＜丸い＞　A　is round

まる＜丸＞をする　V3　to circle

この丸い野菜は何という野菜ですか。What is this round vegetable called?

正しい答えに丸をしましょう。Let's circle the correct answers.

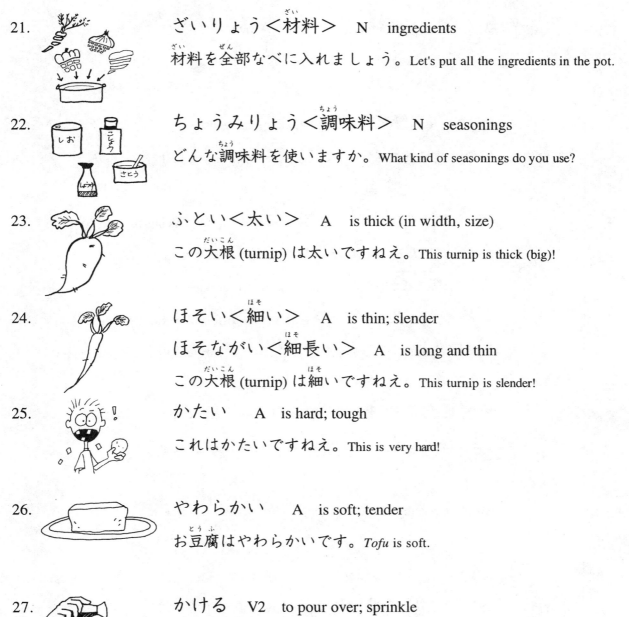

21. ざいりょう＜材料＞　N　ingredients

材料を全部なべに入れましょう。Let's put all the ingredients in the pot.

22. ちょうみりょう＜調味料＞　N　seasonings

どんな調味料を使いますか。What kind of seasonings do you use?

23. ふとい＜太い＞　A　is thick (in width, size)

この大根 (turnip) は太いですねえ。This turnip is thick (big)!

24. ほそい＜細い＞　A　is thin; slender

ほそながい＜細長い＞　A　is long and thin

この大根 (turnip) は細いですねえ。This turnip is slender!

25. かたい　A　is hard; tough

これはかたいですねえ。This is very hard!

26. やわらかい　A　is soft; tender

お豆腐はやわらかいです。Tofu is soft.

27. かける　V2　to pour over; sprinkle

醤油をかけると、おいしいですよ。If you pour shoyu over (it), it's tasty.

Activity G

28. （お）いのり＜（お）祈り＞　N　pray

いのる＜祈る＞　V1　to pray

毎日、あなたの幸せを祈っています。I am praying for your happiness every day.

29. 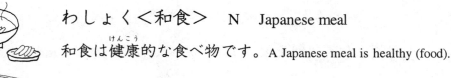 かんぱい！＜乾杯＞　Exp.　Cheers!

Activity H

30. わしょく＜和食＞　N　Japanese meal

和食は健康的な食べ物です。A Japanese meal is healthy (food).

31. せいようりょうり＜西洋料理＞　N　Western-style cooking

ようしょく＜洋食＞　N　Western-style meal

西洋料理は油が多いです。Western-style cooking has lots of oil.

32. かわった＜変わった＞　V1　is different; odd; unusual

これはちょっと変わった味ですねえ。This has slightly unusual flavor!

33. めずらしい＜珍しい＞　A　is rare; unusual

これは珍しい食べ物ですねえ。This is unusual food!

Activity I　　No new vocabulary.

Activity J

34. さいしょ＜最初＞　N　(the) first

さいしょに＜最初に＞　Adv　at first

最初に、ボールの中にさとうを入れます。First, put sugar in the bowl.

35. さいご＜最後＞　N　(the) last; final

さいごに＜最後に＞　N　at last; finally

最後に、卵を入れます。Last, put in the egg.

36. さいこう＜最高＞　N　the best

さいこうに＜最高に＞　Adv　the most

母の作る弁当は最高です。The box lunch my mother makes is the best.

母の弁当は最高においしいです。My mother's box lunch is the tastiest.

Activity K

37. 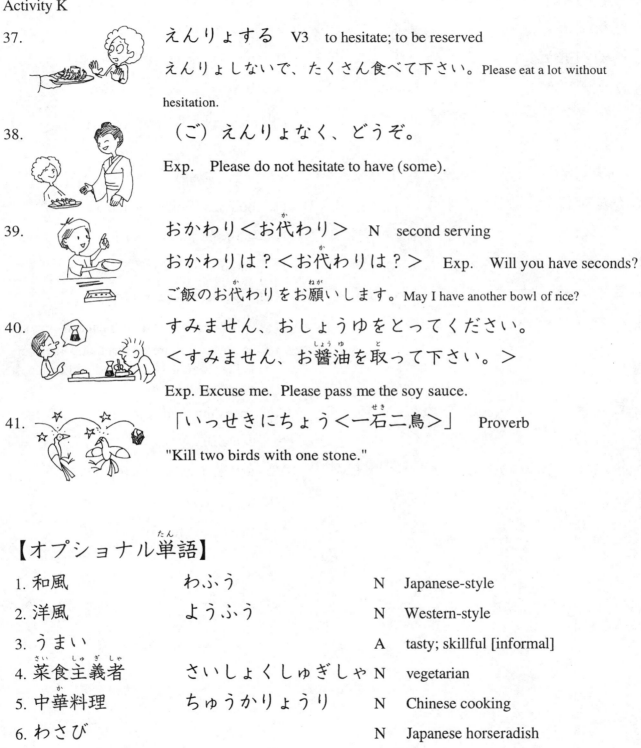 えんりょする　V3　to hesitate; to be reserved

えんりょしないで、たくさん食べて下さい。Please eat a lot without hesitation.

38. （ご）えんりょなく、どうぞ。

Exp.　Please do not hesitate to have (some).

39. おかわり＜お代わり＞　N　second serving

おかわりは？＜お代わりは？＞　Exp.　Will you have seconds?

ご飯のお代わりをお願いします。May I have another bowl of rice?

40. すみません、おしょうゆをとってください。

＜すみません、お醤油を取って下さい。＞

Exp. Excuse me. Please pass me the soy sauce.

41. 「いっせきにちょう＜一石二鳥＞」　Proverb

"Kill two birds with one stone."

【オプショナル単語】

1. 和風	わふう	N	Japanese-style
2. 洋風	ようふう	N	Western-style
3. うまい		A	tasty; skillful [informal]
4. 菜食主義者	さいしょくしゅぎしゃ	N	vegetarian
5. 中華料理	ちゅうかりょうり	N	Chinese cooking
6. わさび		N	Japanese horseradish
7. のり		N	dried pressed seaweed

八課

8. 麦茶	むぎちゃ	N	barley tea (hot or cold)
9. 特別料理	とくべつりょうり	N	specialty dish
10. 定食	ていしょく	N	a set meal
11. 幕の内弁当	まくのうちべんとう	N	popular variety of *bento*
12. うな丼	うなどん	N	flavored grilled eel on rice
13. 〜付き	〜つき	Nd	〜 included
14. AまたはB		P	A or B
15. 長持ちする	ながもちする	V	to last (long)
16. 奇数／偶数	きすう／ぐうすう	N	odd numbered/even numbered
17. 飾り物	かざりもの	N	garnishes; decorations
18. 感触	かんしょく	N	texture
19. 蒸す／蒸し物	むす／むしもの	V1/N	to steam/steamed food
20. バランスがいい		A	well-balanced ["Well-balanced" in the Japanese culture means that something is harmoniously arranged and is not necessarily symmetrical.]
21. 見た目がいい	みためがいい	A	appealing to the eye
22. 入れ物	いれもの	N	container
23. 揚げる／揚げ物	あげる／あげもの	V2	to deep fry/deep fried food
24. 御飯を炊く	ごはんをたく	V1	to cook rice
25. のせる		V2	to place on top (of)

A. Noun ばかり　　　only ～

ばかり is another particle that means 'only.'　Unlike ～だけ and ～しか，～ばかり emphasizes
the preceding noun in a positive tone.　It also suggests that a large quantity of the noun
is involved.　In speech，ばかり is sometimes pronounced ばっかり.

Compare:　　a. ケンは肉ばかり食べました。　　　Ken ate only meat (and a lot).

　　　　　　b. ケンは肉だけ食べました。　　　　Ken ate only meat.

　　　　　　c. ケンは肉しか食べませんでした。　Ken ate nothing but meat.

Note 1:　～ばかり cannot be used if the preceding noun is singular or represents only one entity.

　○　　　　男の子ばかりパーティーに来ました。Only (and many) boys came to the party.

　×　　　　ケンばかりパーティーに来ました。　Only Ken came to the party.

Note 2:　～ばかり cannot be used with negative predicates.

　○　　　　ケンは肉だけ食べませんでした。　Ken did not eat only meat.

　×　　　　ケンは肉ばかり食べませんでした。　Ken did not eat only meat.

1. 今日は日本料理ばかり作りました。

　　　　I made only Japanese food today.

2. 弟は毎日テレビゲームばかりしています。

　　　　My younger brother is playing only computer games every day.

3. あの学生は本ばかり読んでいます。

　　　　That student over there is only reading (lots of) books.

B. Sentence (Plain form) ＋ らしい（です）。　　　It seems that ～

This construction is used to state something that appears true based on information the speaker has read, heard or observed. Although this construction is translated as "seems," the speaker is actually quite sure of his statement when らしい is used. The plain form is used before らしい. Negative forms and tenses are indicated in the plain form before らしい. だ is omitted after な adjectives and nouns.

Verb	食べる 食べない 食べた 食べなかった		eat; will eat do not eat; will not eat ate did not eat
い Adjective	高い 高くない 高かった 高くなかった	＋らしい	is expensive is not expensive was expensive was not expensive
な Adjective	好き 好きじゃない or 好きではない 好きだった 好きじゃなかった or 好きではなかった		like do not like liked did not like
Noun	学生 学生じゃない or 学生ではない 学生だった 学生じゃなかった or 学生ではなかった		is a student is not a student was a student was not a student

1. ベンさんは来年、日本へ行くらしいです。

   It seems that Ben is going to Japan next year.

2. 日本語の試験はむずかしかったらしいです。

   It seems that the Japanese exam was difficult.

3. 妹はジョンが好きらしいです。

   My younger sister seems to like Jon.

4. その話は本当じゃないらしいですよ。

   It seems that story is not true, you know.

C. Verb (TE form) ＋ おく　　　　　doing something in advance/ ahead of time

Independently the verb おく means "to put" or "to place." When おく follows a verb -TE form, it means "do something in advance and leave as is for future convenience." - ておく is often contracted or shortened to - とく in informal conversation.

　　話しておく　→　話しとく　talk in advance
　　読んでおく　→　読んどく　read in advance

1. 明日、パーティーをするので、今日、食べ物を買っておきました。

       Since we are going to have a party tomorrow, I bought food today (for it).

2. いつか日本に留学したいので、日本語を勉強しておきます。

       Since I want to study in Japan someday, I will study Japanese (to prepare for it).

3. 母は、今晩出かけるので、晩ご飯を作っておいてくれました。

       Since my mother is going out tonight, she made our dinner ahead of time for us.

4. あのテーブルに置いておいて下さい。

       Please leave it on that table for future use.

D. Verb (OO form) ＋ と　思っている　　I think that I will do ～ .

This construction is used when the speaker says that he may do or decide to do something in the future. The subject doing the action should be the same as the person who is thinking about doing it. Do not confuse this pattern with the Plain Form ＋ と思います pattern that is used when expressing opinions.

    Compare: 行くと思う。   I think (I/he) will go. (Opinion)
           行こうと思っている。   I am thinking of going. (Intention)

* Review of the verb OO form.

	MASU form	Dictionary form	OO form
Group 1	のみます (nom-imasu) しにます (shin-imasu) あそびます (asob-imasu) かいます (ka-imasu) まちます (mach-imasu) かえります (kaer-imasu) かきます (kak-imasu) およぎます (oyog-imasu) はなします (hanash-imasu)	のむ (nom-u) しぬ (shin-u) あそぶ (asob-u) かう (ka-u) まつ (mats-u) かえる (kaer-u) かく (kak-u) およぐ (oyog-u) はなす (hanas-u)	のもう (nom-oo) しのう (shin-oo) あそぼう (asob-oo) かおう (ka-oo) まとう (mat-oo) かえろう (kaer-oo) かこう (kak-oo) およごう (oyog-oo) はなそう (hanas-oo)
Group 2	みます (mi-masu) たべます (tabe-masu)	みる (mi-ru) たべる (tabe-ru)	みよう (mi-yoo) たべよう (tabe-yoo)
Irregular	します (shi-masu) きます (ki-masu)	する (su-ru) くる (ku-ru)	しよう (shi-yoo) こよう (ko-yoo)

1. 大学に行っても、日本語を<u>勉強しようと思っています</u>。

   I am thinking of studying Japanese even when I go to college.

2. 将来、日本に<u>留学しようと思っています</u>。

   I am thinking of studying abroad in Japan in the future.

3. ケン：「この週末、どこかへ行かない？」

   "Won't you go somewhere (with me) this weekend?"

   まり：「映画に<u>行こうと思っているけど</u>...」

   "I am thinking of going to a movie . . ."

A. 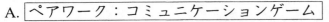 ペアワーク：コミュニケーションゲーム

First, Person A randomly writes a name for each person pictured below in the space above the picture. Then Person B asks Person A for the names that Person A has given to each person by describing the person who is "only" doing a certain action. Use ばかり. See the example below. Partner B writes the person's name below the appropriate picture. Reverse roles. Answer using ～ばかり. After filling in the answers, check to see whether you communicated correctly or not.

Ex. 質問：「ご飯ばかり食べている人は、だれですか。」

　　答え：「マイクさんです。」

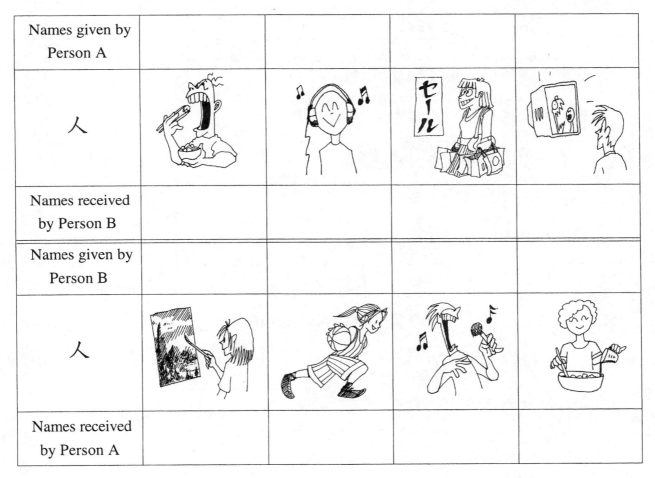

B. ペアワーク

Based on the many cultural notes in this textbook, you have a general idea about Japan and Japanese people. Answer the following questions using 〜らしいです. Take turns.

Ex. 質問：「日本人の家は広いですか。」

　　答え：「いいえ、あまり広くないらしいです。」

1. 日本の夏はあついですか。	
2. 日本の高校生はよく勉強しますか。	
3. 漢字のかずは少ないですか。	
4. 日本の家はせまいですか。	
5. 日本の電車はこんでいますか。	
6. 日本的な家に住むのはかんたんですか。	
7. 日本にいい音楽がありますか。	
8. 日本のお弁当は色がきれいですか。	
9. ビールは苦いんですか。	
10. たくあんというつけ物はくさいですか。	
11. なっとうという日本の食べ物はおいしいですか。	
12. とうふはけんこう的ですか。	
13. 日本の自然は美しいですか。	

C. ペアワーク

Your family is having a party tonight and is preparing to receive guests. Ask what each person is doing and write the answers. Answer using 〜ておきます.

Ex. 質問：「あなたは何を<u>しておきます</u>か。」

答え：「私は、ごみをとっ<u>ておきます</u>。」

いちろう

ゆりえ

toy おもちゃ

1. お母さん	
2. お父さん	
3. いちろう	
4. ゆりえ	

D. ペアワーク

Ask your partner about his/her summer vacation plans. Your partner answers. Take turns.

1. 夏休みにサマースクールに行こうと思っていますか。	
2. 夏休みに働〔はたら〕こうと思っていますか。	
3. 夏休みにどこへ旅行しようと思っていますか。	
4. 夏休みに何をしようと思っていますか。	
5. 夏休みに日本語を勉強しようと思っていますか。	

八課

E. ペアゲーム：食べ物神経衰弱ゲーム

Copy the names of these Japanese foods and make two sets of cards. Play a matching game with your partner. Put all the cards face down on the table. Flip two cards. If they are the same and you can give the correct name of the dish, you keep the cards and have a chance to flip another two cards. If the two cards do not match, it will be your partner's turn. The winner is the person who has the most cards.

ご飯	みそしる	つけ物	にぎりずし
さしみ	天ぷら	どんぶり	うどん
三角むすび	ざるそば	ラーメン	とんかつ

カレーライス　　焼き肉　　焼き鳥　　お茶づけ

ぎょうざ　　焼きそば　　そうめん　　すき焼き

焼き魚　　コロッケ　　まきずし　　いなりずし

すの物　　竹の子のに物　　なっとう　　うなぎ弁当

八課

F. ペアワーク - Tic Tac Toe

Directions:

1. One person takes the O card. His/her partner takes the X card.

2. You and your partner take turns doing the following: Choose a square and tell your partner the number of that square.

3. When your partner hears the number you give, he/she will read the word/hint for that number. If you tell your partner "五番," for example, your partner reads the word/hint in square 5. If your partner says "二番," you read the word/hint in square 2.

4. Your partner answers. Your partner should give the answer that you see in the parentheses on your card.

5. Let's say that you are "O" and your partner is "X." If person O answers correctly, both players must mark an O in the numbered space on the Tic Tac Toe game sheet. If person O answers question 5 correctly, for example, both players must mark an O in space #5. If person X gives a correct answer to # 2, tell him/her that the answer is correct, and then both of you must mark an X in square # 2.

6. If you don't answer correctly, it is your partner's turn to give a number. You may ask for the same number again later if that square is still blank. If your partner gives an incorrect answer (one that is not in the parentheses), tell your partner that the answer is wrong, but do NOT give the answer. Your partner may choose the same item again later in the game. If an answer is wrong, do not mark on the game sheet. It is the other person's turn to try again.

Who wins?

1. The first person to get three in a row (horizontally, vertically, or diagonally), OR

2. The first person to answer five items correctly, OR

3. The person with the most marks (five marks) if all the squares are filled.

4. The person with the most marks wins (four to three, four to two, three to two, etc.) if both players can no longer ask for or give responses.

ゲーム＃１: What is the antonym (word of opposite meaning)?

[○ person]

1. いい （悪い）	2. 大きい （小さい）	3. 丸い （四角い）
4. 重い （かるい）	5. かたい （やわらかい）	6. 高い （安い）
7. うすい （あつい thick）	8. 明るい （くらい）	9. 早い （おそい）

[X person]

1.ほそい （太い）	2.からい （あまい）	3.広い （せまい）
4.とおい （近い）	5.お金持ち （びんぼう）	6.みじかい （長い）
7.白い （黒い）	8.うるさい （しずか）	9.新しい （古い）

ゲーム＃2：Give the appropriate food name.

[○ person]

1.白くて、やわらかい 日本の食べ物 （とうふ）	2.赤くて、小さい、 三角の かたちのくだ物 （いちご）	3.赤くて、丸い やさい （トマト）
4.あまい ちょうみりょう （さとう）	5.やさいにすとさとうを 入れた日本料理 （すの物）	6.あまくて、 チョコレートが 入っている 四角にきったデザート （ブラウニー）
7.日本人がお正月に 食べる白い食べ物 （もち）	8.ぶた肉のフライ （とんかつ）	9.グレイの色の 日本のめんnoodleの つめたい料理 （ざるそば）

[X person]

1. 黄色くて、丸くて、 くさい日本のつけ物 （たくあん）	2. 黄色くて、ほそ長い くだ物 （バナナ）	3. オレンジ色で、 ちょっとほそ長い やさい （にんじん）
4. 白くて、からい ちょうみりょう （しお）	5. ご飯にお茶をかけて 食べる食べ物 （お茶づけ）	6. パンの間に焼いた牛肉と レタスなどのやさいを 入れた アメリカの食べ物 （ハンバーガー）
7. 白くて太い 日本のめんnoodle （うどん）	8. ご飯の上にやさいと鳥肉 とたまごをかけた日本料理 （おや子どんぶり）	9. 黄色いめんnoodleが スープに入っている 中国料理 （ラーメン）

G. ペアワーク

You are at a party and have to give a toast. What words are appropriate for each situation? Match the situation on the left and the Japanese words on the right.

1. けっこんをする友達のパーティー で、何と言いますか。	

A. けんこうをいのって、 かんぱいしよう。

2. ビジネスを始める友だちの パーティーで、何と言いますか。	

B. 仕事のせいこうをいのっ て、かんぱいしよう。

3. ７０才のおばあさんのパーティー で、何と言いますか。	

C. しあわせをいのって、 かんぱいしよう。

4. 大学へ行く友達のパーティーで、 何と言いますか。	

D. 明るいしょう来をいのっ て、かんぱいしよう。

八課

262

You are looking at the Japanese restaurant menu shown on the next two pages. With your partner, look for the answers for the following questions.

1. このレストランで洋食が食べられますか。	
2. てい食の中で何が一番高いですか。	
3. てい食の中で何が一番安いですか。	
4. 子供の夕食には何をちゅうもんしたらいいでしょうか。	
5. おすしは高いですか。	
6. 和てい食を食べたいんですが、生の魚が食べられません。どれをちゅうもんしたら、いいでしょうか。	
7. ちょっとめずらしい物を食べてみたいんです。何がおいしそうですか。	
8. 変わった食べ物を食べてみませんか。何を食べてみましょうか。	
9. 私はさい食しゅぎで、お肉を食べません。天ぷらを食べたいんですが、何をちゅうもんしたらいいでしょうか。	
10. 私は今あまりおなかがすいていないし、あついから、つめたいうどんかそばを食べたいんですが、そんな物がありますか。	
11. 私はあまい物が大好きですが、デザートの中で何が一番おいしそうですか。	
12. このレストランの食べ物はけんこう的だと思いますか。	

日本料理
あじひな

定食

小鉢、ご飯、みそ汁、漬物付き

刺身定食	￥ 3,000
天ぷら定食	￥ 2,700
唐揚げ定食（魚または鳥）	
	￥ 1,800
すきやき定食	￥ 2,700
牛肉照焼き定食	￥ 2,700
幕の内	￥ 3,500
お子様セット	￥ 1,500

お寿司

小鉢、ご飯、みそ汁、漬物付き

にぎり（松）	￥ 4,000
にぎり（竹）	￥ 3,500
ちらし	￥ 3,500

和定食コース

（雪コース）
小鉢・鳥唐揚げ・すき焼き・
酢の物・みそ汁・ご飯・漬物・
アイスクリーム　　　￥ 4,000

（月コース）
小鉢・刺身・牛肉照焼き・野菜
煮物・みそ汁・ご飯・漬物・
アイスクリーム　　　￥ 4,000

（花コース）
小鉢・刺身・天ぷら・魚照焼き・
みそ汁・ご飯・漬物・
アイスクリーム　　　￥ 4,000

（花屋スペシャル）
小鉢・揚げ豆腐・刺身・
伊勢エビサラダ・
ビーフ照焼きステーキまたは
天ぷら・みそ汁・ご飯・漬物・
アイスクリーム　　　￥ 4,000

一品料理			うどん、そば		
やっこ豆腐	￥	300	肉うどん	￥	800
納豆	￥	350	月見うどん	￥	700
枝豆	￥	400	きつねうどん	￥	700
きゅうり酢の物	￥	450	天ぷらうどん	￥	850
たこ酢の物	￥	500	なべ焼きうどん	￥	1,200
野菜サラダ	￥	400	月見そば	￥	700
天ぷら盛合わせ	￥	1,000	天ぷらそば	￥	850
えび天ぷら	￥	1,000	ざるそば	￥	700
いか天ぷら	￥	800			
野菜天ぷら	￥	700	**どんぶり**		
さしみ盛合わせ	￥	2,000	みそ汁・漬物付き		
まぐろ刺身	￥	2,500	天丼	￥	1,500
いか刺身	￥	1,000	親子丼	￥	1,200
たこ刺身	￥	800	牛丼	￥	1,500
焼き魚	￥	1,000	かつ丼	￥	1,500
焼き鳥	￥	1,000	うな丼	￥	2,000
鳥照焼き	￥	800			
いか照焼き	￥	800	**デザート**		
おでん	￥	1,000	抹茶アイスクリーム	￥	500
野菜煮物	￥	500	バニラアイスクリーム	￥	500
漬物盛合わせ	￥	500	あんみつ	￥	850
お茶漬け	￥	700	ぜんざい	￥	850

I. クラスゲーム：食器をおくところ

At the bottom, there is a set of Japanese dishes and utensils that Japanese people use. Draw them in at the right position on the tray. Work with your partner. The first group of students who puts everything in its correct place is the winner.

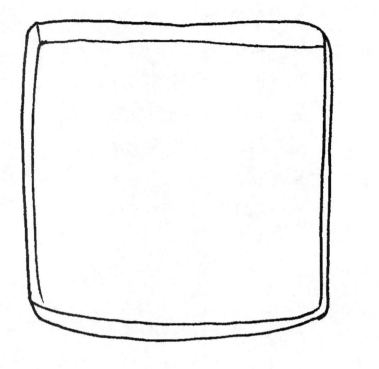

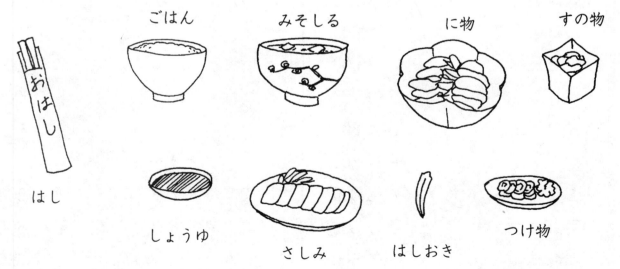

ごはん　　　みそしる　　　に物　　　す の物

はし

しょうゆ　　　さしみ　　　はしおき　　　つけ物

J. ペアワーク：クッキングショー

Look at the visual presentation on how one makes おむすび／おにぎり. Put the correct numbers in the parentheses on the next page to show the correct sequence of events.

1.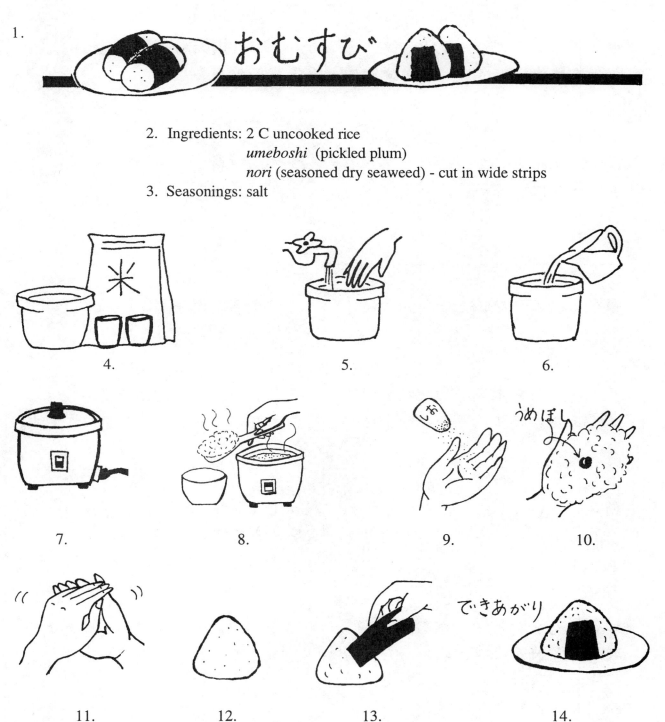

おむすび

2. Ingredients: 2 C uncooked rice
                umeboshi (pickled plum)
                nori (seasoned dry seaweed) - cut in wide strips
3. Seasonings: salt

4.

5.

6.

7.

8.

9.

10.

11.

12.

13.

14.

八課

(1.)	( )
今日はおむすびの作り方を教えましょう。	それから、お米をたきます。
( ) 最初〔さいしょ〕に、２カップのお米をすいはんきに入れます。	( ) つぎに、調味料〔ちょうみりょう〕。 しお　少々
( ) はい、出来ました。 おにぎりはお弁当に最高ですよ。	( ) まず、材料〔ざいりょう〕。 米　２カップ うめぼし　４こ のり　４まい
( ) 最後に、のりをまきます。	( ) それから、両手〔りょうて〕でおにぎりをにぎります。
( ) それから、お米をつめたい水でよくあらいます。きたない水はすてます。	( ) それから、すいはんきにつめたい水を２の所まで入れます。
( ) ぬらした(wet)手にしおをかけます。少しつめたくしたご飯を手におきます。	( ) そして、中にうめぼし(pickled plum)をおきます。
( ) すいはんきがとまったら、 ４、５分待ちます。ぬらした(wet)しゃもじ(rice paddle)で、ご飯をボールに入れます。	( ) はい、おむすびは三角のかたちになりました。

K. ペアワーク

An American is invited to dinner by a Japanese family. Act out the following conversation at the dinner table.

日本人　　：どうぞ、ごえんりょなくどうぞ。

アメリカ人：では、いただきます。

　　　　　　＜はしを持って、みそ汁を飲む。それから、野菜の煮物を

　　　　　　食べる。＞

　　　　　　この野菜は何ですか。ちょっと変わった味ですね。

日本人　　：それは、竹の子です。苦いですか。

アメリカ人：いいえ、おいしいです。

日本人　　：ご飯をどうぞ。

　　　　　　＜ご飯をアメリカ人にわたす。＞

アメリカ人：どうも。

　　　　　　＜アメリカ人はご飯をもらう。＞

　　　　　　すみません、おしょうゆを取って下さい。

日本人　　：どうぞ。

　　　　　　＜日本人はおしょうゆをアメリカ人にわたす。

　　　　　　アメリカ人はしょうゆを魚にかけて、食べる。＞

　　　　　　おかわりはいかがですか。

アメリカ人：いいえ、けっこうです。おなかがいっぱいです。

日本人　　：では、お茶漬けはいかがですか。

アメリカ人：いいえ、けっこうです。ごちそうさまでした。

八課

アドベンチャー日本語3
ＯＰＩ単語＆文法チェックリスト
8課：日本の食事

名前：＿＿＿＿＿＿＿＿＿＿

クラス：＿＿＿＿＿＿

たんご	Check	たんご	Check	ぶんぽう	Check	Error
つけ物		やわらかい		〜という〜		
あげ物		かたい		〜とか〜		
に物		和食		〜時（に）		
すの物		西洋料理		Noun Modifiers		
焼き物		かわった		〜ので		
〜物		めずらしい		〜し		
たくあん		竹の子		〜てから		
なっとう		いのる		〜と／〜たら／〜ば		
自然		えんりょする		〜やすい／〜にくい		
きせつ		ごえんりょなく		〜かもしれない		
苦い〔にがい〕		最初〔さいしょ〕		〜のような		
くさい		最後		〜のように		
けんこう的		最高		〜ようになる		
お茶づけ		かんぱい		V ないで		
焼き魚		おかわり		V（てform）＋ も		
三角		〜をとって下さい		〜だろう		
四角（い）		一石二鳥〔いっせきにちょう〕		〜そうだ		
丸（い）				N ばかり		
ざい料				〜らしい		
ちょう味料				〜ておく		
太い				V oo と思っている		
ほそい				いAdj. ＋ さ		
ほそ長い				Plain Polite		
〜をかける				Male Female		

 By the end of this lesson, you will be able to communicate the information below in the given situation. Complete the following tasks with a partner. You are expected to conduct a natural conversation using as many new vocabulary and grammatical structures as you can, while appropriately incorporating vocabulary and structures you have learned previously. Use the appropriate speech style (plain or polite) and male/female speech if appropriate. Practice the dialogue with your partner; the aim is not to memorize a dialogue, but to communicate meaningfully with your partner on the topics below.

Your teacher will randomly fill in the blanks below. Use the map in the lesson.

【Ⅲ-9 トピック 1】

Partner **A**: *Student from the U. S. in Japan*
Partner **B**: *Japanese friend*

Situation: *B calls A on the phone and they make plans for the weekend.*

B invites **A** to go to _____, which is in _____. **B** explains why they will go there. **A** asks what day it is and accepts the invitation, but does not know how to get there from the station near his/her host family's home in Nakano. **B** explains the entire route in detail as **A** asks questions or repeats the instructions back. **A** expresses some fear of possibly getting lost, but **B** says to call him/her if **A** does get lost. They agree on a meeting time and place. **A** is looking forward to this weekend.

＜ケンは、秋葉原で友達と会う約束をしたが、電車の乗り方を知らない。ホストのお母さんは、ケンと渋谷駅南口まで歩いて行き、説明してくれた。＞

　　ケン：ここから秋葉原駅まで、どう行けばいいんですか。

お母さん：この地図を見て。まず、この渋谷駅から山手線に乗って、新宿
　　　　　まで行って、新宿で中央線に乗りかえて、御茶ノ水駅まで行って、
　　　　　御茶ノ水駅で総武線に乗りかえれば、秋葉原は次の駅よ。

　　ケン：＜くりかえす。＞　切符はどうやって買うか、教えて下さい。

お母さん：券売機の地図でこの秋葉原をさがしたら、料金が分かるわ。

　　ケン：あった、あった。＜ケンは切符を券売機で買って来る。＞
　　　　　じゃあ、ちょっと心配だけど、行って来ます。

お母さん：いってらっしゃい。気をつけてね。迷子になったら、電話して。
　　　　　改札口はあっちよ。

＜ケンは新宿のホームで山手線をおりたが、中央線が分からない。＞

　　ケン：あのう、すみません。秋葉原へ行きたいんですが、中央線はどこ
　　　　　ですか。

　　駅員：7・8番線です。この階段を上がって、左へ行くと、分かります。

　　ケン：どうもありがとうございました。

＜ケンが新宿の東京方面のホームで電車を待っていると、電車が来た。＞

　　ケン：すみません、この電車は秋葉原へ行きますか。

　　駅員：いいえ、行きません。この電車で御茶ノ水まで行って、総武線に
　　　　　乗りかえて下さい。同じホームで降りたら、向かい側です。

　　ケン：秋葉原は御茶ノ水からいくつ目ですか。

　　駅員：一つ目です。

　　ケン：どうもありがとうございました。

東京の電車

Note: This is a simplified map that shows only three major train lines and one subway line.

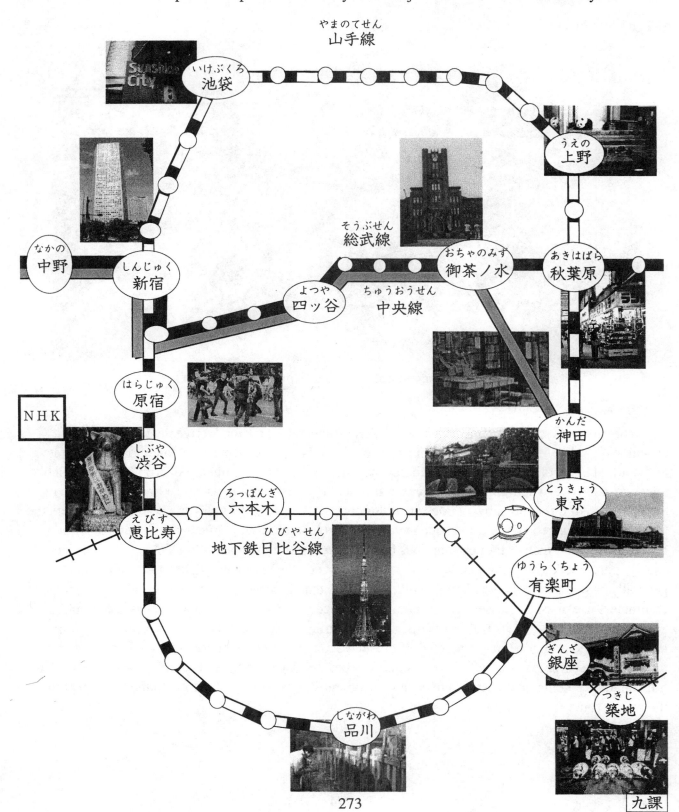

山手線
やまのてせん

Sunshine City

いけぶくろ
池袋

うえの
上野

なかの
中野

総武線
そうぶせん

おちゃのみず
御茶ノ水

あきはばら
秋葉原

しんじゅく
新宿

よつや
四ッ谷

ちゅうおうせん
中央線

NHK

はらじゅく
原宿

かんだ
神田

しぶや
渋谷

とうきょう
東京

えびす
恵比寿

ろっぽんぎ
六本木

ひびやせん
地下鉄日比谷線

ゆうらくちょう
有楽町

ぎんざ
銀座

つきじ
築地

しながわ
品川

九課

A. Train Stations in Japan

The automated ticket gates at Shinjuku Station.

The railway system in Japan is known for its efficiency, precision, convenience, safety and cleanliness. While train lines connect most major cities throughout Japan, they are most concentrated in the urban areas of Japan. Tokyo's railway system is a highly developed modern network, which may at first be overwhelming to a visitor, but it is actually quite easy to use once one is familiar with the system. All train and subway lines are color coded. For example, the Yamanote Line is green, the Chuo Line is orange and the Sobu Line is yellow. JR (Japan Railway) lines are subsidized by the government while many other private lines increase accessibility to and within Tokyo. Tickets are usually purchased at vending machines located just outside the automated ticket gates. Fares are generally posted above the vending machines on maps that indicate all destination stations. Regular commuters use discount passes. Train stations can become very crowded during peak travel times known in Japan as ラッシュアワー (rush hour). During these times, pushing is especially common and once in the train, one may find oneself crushed against a window or standing back to back or face to face with a complete stranger. If one is not familiar with one's route, one should listen carefully to train announcements, pay attention to each stop, or study computerized "maps" on the train that trace the train's route.

B. Famous Areas in Tokyo

Tokyo, the capital city of Japan, is a metropolis with a population of 11,542,468 (1998). Within Tokyo are many smaller cities. The Yamanote Line, which encircles the heart of Tokyo, connects most of the major areas in urban Tokyo. These areas possess their own unique features and attractions. Some of them are described below. Others described below are not on the Yamanote Line, but within close reach.

1. 東京駅 〔とうきょうえき〕 Tokyo Station

At the heart of the Yamanote Line lies the Imperial Palace, the official residence of the Emperor of Japan. Although it is visible and accessible from many of the stations that lie on the eastern side of the Yamanote Line, it is probably most accessible from Tokyo Station. Tokyo Station is considered the terminal station of most train and subway lines, including the bullet trains that travel to the northernmost and southernmost islands of Japan. It is said that there are at least 3,000 train and subway arrivals per day at this Grand Central Station, which is constructed of red brick to resemble the central station in Amsterdam.

Imperial Palace

Tokyo Station

新幹線 〔しんかんせん〕
Bullet train

2. 上野 〔うえの〕 Ueno

Ueno Station, located at the northeast of the Yamanote Line, is one of the largest and busiest commuter railway and subway stations in Tokyo. Now considered a middle-class district of Tokyo, Ueno is located in the older section of the city. Many older shops, restaurants, small businesses and wholesalers clutter the streets of Ueno. The most famous attractions in Ueno are the Ueno National Museum, Ueno Park and Ueno Zoo, which are clustered together a short distance from the station. Ueno Zoo houses the famous pandas, which regularly draw crowds. Ueno Park is a popular site for cherry blossom viewing parties in early April.

Panda at Ueno Zoo

九課

3. 新宿 〔しんじゅく〕 Shinjuku

Shinjuku Station is one of the largest and most complex stations in Tokyo. It is located at the western edge of the Yamanote Line and is a central stop for the Chuo Line. Several private train lines and subway lines run through or alongside the main Shinjuku Station. Shinjuku is easily identifiable by its high-rise skyscrapers located beyond the station's west exit. These buildings house offices and plush international hotels, which form one of the more recent commercial/business centers of Tokyo. Shinjuku is the home of several department stores and many shops, restaurants, coffee shops, clubs and bars. It is also known for its colorful entertainment district called Kabukicho, one of the main centers of nightlife in Tokyo. It is said that *yakuza* (organized crime operators) trace their roots to this area of Shinjuku.

Skyscraper in Shinjuku

4. 銀座 〔ぎんざ〕 Ginza

Ginza is the oldest and best-known shopping district in Japan. Located in the central area of downtown Tokyo, it is also a sophisticated entertainment center. The property values in the heart of Ginza are considered the highest in all of Japan. It is not located on the Yamanote Line, but it is well-connected to all parts of Tokyo by several subway lines and is accessible from Yurakucho Station on the Yamanote Line. On Sundays, the main street is closed to vehicular traffic so pedestrians may enjoy leisurely strolls through Ginza. The famous Kabukiza Theatre, which is used exclusively for *kabuki* performances, lies at the edge of the Ginza area, near Higashi Ginza Station.

On Sundays, the main street is closed to vehicular traffic for pedestrians in Ginza.

Kabukiza Theatre

Kabuki

5. 秋葉原 〔あきはばら〕 Akihabara

Located at the northeast of the JR Yamanote Line and also on the Sobu Line, Akihabara is the mecca for electronic goods. Literally hundreds of shops featuring the latest and best selection of electronic appliances, goods, gadgets and other electronic items, whether simple batteries or the most complex computerized systems, can be found here. One is able to shop hop, compare prices and even bargain for the lowest prices here. The lively, almost festive mood of Akihabara entices thousands of Japanese and foreigners.

Arcade of electronic goods shops

6. 渋谷 〔しぶや〕 Shibuya

In recent years, Shibuya has blossomed into a fashionable shopping, entertainment and gathering place for the young and young-at-heart. There are several department stores, a dozen theaters, countless restaurants of every variety and specialty shops galore. Shibuya Station, through which numerous subways lines, the JR Yamanote Line and other private train lines course, is known for its beloved Hachiko Statue. The bronze statue was built in memory of a dog named Hachiko, who is said to have come every evening to Shibuya Station to await the return of his master, a university professor. One evening, his master failed to return, but Hachiko faithfully arrived at Shibuya Station day after day to await his master until he himself saw his own death. The statue of Hachiko is now a popular landmark used as a favorite meeting place for Japanese.

Hachiko Statue

7. 原宿 〔はらじゅく〕 Harajuku

Harajuku is a favorite spot for the young people of Japan. It lies between Shinjuku and Shibuya on the Yamanote Line. Harajuku attracts many foreigners and tourists as there are many restaurants and specialty shops and boutiques that appeal to them. The broad tree-lined main street, which begins at the station, is blocked off to vehicles every Sunday so people may stroll freely and enjoy the music and dancing of teenagers and young adults along the street. The grand Meiji Shrine is within walking distance from the station, as is the 1964 Olympic Village, which now serves as a sports and recreation center.

Dancing youth on the streets of Harajuku

8. 御茶ノ水〔おちゃのみず〕 Ochanomizu

Ochanomizu, which lies inside the Yamanote Line circle, is on the Chuo and Sobu Lines. Its name, which literally means "tea water," refers to a nearby spring from which Tokugawa Ieyasu, a famous historical figure in Japan, drew water for tea ceremony. Like nearby Kanda, Ochanomizu is a district well populated by scholars and students. This area is sometimes called the "Latin Quarter" of Tokyo. The legendary Tokyo University, which is recognized throughout Japan as the top university in the nation, is located near Nezu Station, also in this general area.

Tokyo University

9. 神田〔かんだ〕 Kanda

Long known as the district for bookstores and the home of several universities and many schools, Kanda is located south of Akihabara and just northeast of Tokyo Station. It is at the eastern edge of the Yamanote Line, where the Chuo Line joins the Yamanote Line. Kanda is also a popular shopping area for sporting goods.

Bookstores in Kanda

10. 池袋〔いけぶくろ〕 Ikebukuro

Ikebukuro lies at the northwest section of the Yamanote Line and has recently become a center of entertainment, shopping and businesses. Several high-rise hotels are located here as are several major department stores. One of the most famous skyscrapers in Tokyo, the Sunshine 60 Building, is a 60-story building that is one of the tallest in Asia. The Sunshine City complex accommodates offices, a performance hall, an aquarium, an art museum, hotels, shopping malls and parks.

Sunshine City complex

11. 品川〔しながわ〕 Shinagawa

Located at the southwest of the Yamanote Line, Shinagawa Station is a central landmark of the area, as many trains heading to the southwestern regions of Japan run through this station. Several international hotels are located near the station. The burial site of the famous 47 Ronin is also located in the general area.

Burial site of the 47 Ronin

12. 築地〔つきじ〕 Tsukiji

Tsukiji, which lies on the Hibiya Subway Line not far from Ginza, is most famous for its early morning fish market. Fish shop owners and Japanese restaurant cooks arrive in droves before dawn to inspect and select the freshest fish of the day to sell and serve to their customers. A wholesale market for fresh produce also attracts many clients to this area.

Fish market

OTHER POPULAR ATTRACTIONS IN AND AROUND TOKYO:

13. 浅草〔あさくさ〕 Asakusa

Asakusa lies in one of the oldest and most historical sections of Tokyo. It is east of Ueno and, during the Edo Period, it grew around the famous Sensoji Temple, which is one of the oldest temples in metropolitan Tokyo. It is said that two local fishermen from a nearby neighborhood found a small statue of a Kannon, the Goddess of Mercy, in their fishing net and first enshrined it at Sensoji. The Sensoji complex is known for the Kaminari Mon (Thunder Gate), which serves as the entrance to the temple. It is famous for its huge red paper lantern, which hangs suspended from the top of the gate. The complex also includes a five-story pagoda, the main temple, the shrine itself and the colorful and bustling shopping arcade called Nakamise. The shops are a favorite stop for tourists who enjoy shopping for many traditional Japanese souvenirs from many of the shops, some of which have been in business for generations.

Sensoji Temple

14. 東京〔とうきょう〕タワー Tokyo Tower

Tokyo Tower, which is located 15 minutes west of Hamamatsucho Station on the Yamanote Line, stands 1093 feet high, taller than the Eiffel Tower. Built in 1958, it is a popular sightseeing attraction, but functions mainly as a broadcasting tower for television, radio and other public broadcasting systems for the Kanto region of Japan. There are two observation decks offering a panoramic view of Tokyo. On clear days, one is able to see Mt. Fuji and the southern Japan Alps in the distance.

Tokyo Tower

九課

15. 東京〔とうきょう〕ディズニーランド Tokyo Disneyland

Tokyo Disneyland, completed in 1983, is located about a half-hour ride from Tokyo in Chiba Prefecture. It is one and a half times larger than Disneyland in California, but it is modelled closely after its California counterpart. It includes all of the five major theme lands - - Westernland (Frontierland), Adventureland, Fantasyland, Tomorrowland and the World Bazaar (Main Street). Over 10 million people visit Tokyo Disneyland annually.

Tokyo Disneyland

16. かっぱ橋〔かっぱばし〕 Kappabashi

Kappabashi is an area east of Ueno that is known for its wholesale restaurant supply markets. It attracts foreigners who have learned that here, one can find abundant supplies and varieties of 食品サンプル (*shokuhin sanpuru*), the realistic wax or plastic food models that are used in restaurant display cases throughout Japan. Once can also purchase other restaurant supplies such as dishes, utensils, and even *sushi* chef costumes. To get to Kappabashi, one needs to take the Ginza Subway Line headed toward Asakusa and get off at Tawaramachi. It is also a five-munute walk from Sensoji Temple (see Asakusa above.)

Plastic *sushi* samples at a Kappabashi shop

1. 北　north　　　　きた　　　北口 〔きたぐち〕 North exit

　　　　　　　　　　　　　　　　北川 〔きたがわ〕 さん

　　　　　　　　　　　ホク　　　東北大学 〔とうほくだいがく〕

　　　　　　　　　　　　　　　　Tohoku University

　　　　　　　　　　　ホッ　　　北海道 〔ほっかいどう〕 Hokkaido

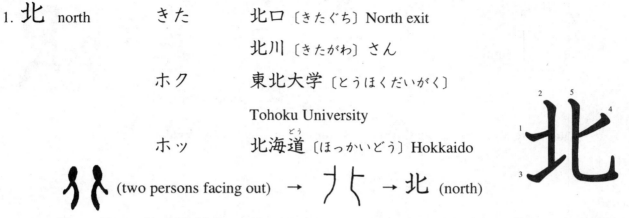

(two persons facing out) → → 北 (north)

The cold north wind blows and two persons sit back to back facing out to keep warm.

2. 南　south　　　　みなみ　　　南口 〔みなみぐち〕 South exit

　　　　　　　　　　　　　　　　南田 〔みなみだ〕 さん

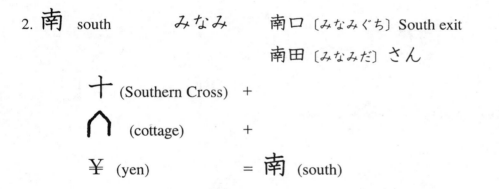

十 (Southern Cross)　+

∧ (cottage)　+

￥ (yen)　= 南 (south)

Under the Southern Cross, there is a cottage full of yen.

3. 京　capital　　　　キョウ　　　東京 〔とうきょう〕 Tokyo

　　　　　　　　　　　　　　　　京都 〔きょうと〕 Kyoto

(building on the hill; palace) → → 京 (capital)

In the capital, people's mouths are small (under control) under the roof.

九課

4. 駅 train station　　エキ　　　　東京駅 〔とうきょうえき〕 Tokyo Station

駅員 〔えきいん〕 station employee

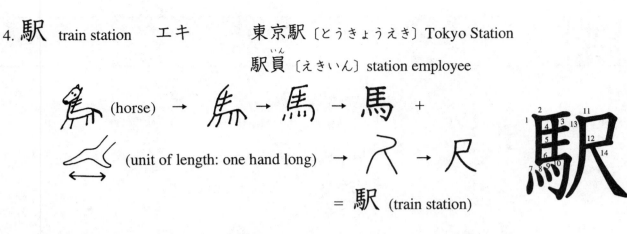

(horse) → 馬 → 馬 → 馬 +

(unit of length: one hand long) → 尺 → 尺

= 駅 (train station)

The horse was the ancient train and stopped at regular intervals.

5. 乗 to ride　　　　の（る）　　電車 〔でんしゃ〕 に乗る ride an electric car

(point) → ノ → ノ +

(to stand) → 立 → 立 +

木 (tree)　　　　　　　　　　　= 乗 (to ride)

Stand on the tree and point out where to ride.

6. 地 ground　　　チ　　　　　地下 〔ちか〕 underground

地図 〔ちず〕 map

土 (soil)　+

せ (world = せかい) = 地 (ground)

The soil of the world (せかい) makes the ground.

7. 鉄 iron   テツ   地下鉄〔ちかてつ〕 subway

     金 (metal)   +

     ⸜ (point)   +

     二 (two)   +

     人 (person) → 失 (to lose something) = 鉄 (iron)

The metal those two persons lost is iron.

8. 図 chart   ズ   地図〔ちず〕 map

                    ト   図書館〔としょかん〕 library

     ☐ (boundary; fence)   +

     ツ (*Katakana* TSU)   +

     ◊ (dot)   = 図 (chart)

On this chart, there are many markings within the boundary.

9. 道 road, way   みち   道をまっすぐ行く go straight along the road

                                道子〔みちこ〕さん Michiko (girl's name)

                    トウ   神道〔しんとう〕 *Shinto* (Japanese religion)

                    ドウ   北海道〔ほっかいどう〕 Hokkaido

                                書道〔しょどう〕 calligraphy

                                剣道〔けんどう〕 *kendo*

     自 (oneself)   = 首 (neck) +

go back and forth   = 道 (way)

My neck knows which way to go.

283

10. 歩 to walk　　ある（く）　　　　歩いて行く　to go by walking
　　　　　　　　　ホ、ポ　　　　　　散歩〔さんぽ〕する　to take a walk

足 (to stop) → 凵 → 止 → 止 ＋

少 (a little; a few)　　　　　　　　　　＝ 歩 (to walk)

When I stop a few times, it is not running, but walking.

歩

11. 動 to move　　うご（く）　　　　車は動きませんでした。　The car did not move.
　　　　　　　　　ドウ　　　　　　　自動車〔じどうしゃ〕car
　　　　　　　　　　　　　　　　　　動物園〔どうぶつえん〕zoo
　　　　　　　　　　　　　　　　　　運動会〔うんどうかい〕athletic event

重 (is heavy)　＋

power → カ → カ → カ ＝ 動 (to move)

You can move heavy things with strength.

動

12. 働 to work　　はたら（く）　　　父は銀行で働いています。
　　　　　　　　　　　　　　　　　　My father is working at a bank.

a person → イ ＋

動 (to move)　　＝　働 (to work)

A person moves one's body to work.

働

13. 円 yen;　　　　　エン　　　　百円玉〔ひゃくえんだま〕 one hundred yen coin

circle　　　　　　　　千円〔せんえん〕 one thousand yen

一万円〔いちまんえん〕 ten thousand yen

∧ (cottage) ＋ ⊔⊔ (window) ＝ 円 (yen)

Like a cottage, the round Japanese yen has windows.

【読みかえの漢字】

1. 明　is bright　　あか（るい）　＊　明るい部屋〔へや〕 a bright room

☆　　　　　明日〔あした〕 tomorrow

メイ　　　　説明〔せつめい〕して下さい。 Please explain it.

2. 売　to sell　　う（る）　＊　売っています。 They are selling it.

バイ　　　　券売機〔けんばいき〕 ticket vending machine

＊ Previously introduced.

【読めればいい漢字】

1. 〜線　　　- せん　　　　　　〜line

2. 橋　　　　はし／- ばし　　　bridge

3. 病院　　　びょういん　　　　hospital

4. 新幹線　　しんかんせん　　　bullet train

5. 中央線　　ちゅうおうせん　　Chuo (Central) Line [orange-colored train line in

Tokyo]

Let's review previous vocabulary!

A. めいし　Nouns

1. 電車	electric train	11. きっぷ	ticket
2. 友達	friend	12. 心ぱい	a worry
3. 乗り方〔のりかた〕	how to board	13. どこ	where?
4. ホスト	host	14. かいだん	steps; stairs
5. お母さん	(someone else's) mother	15. 左	left
6. ここ	here	16. おなじ	same
7. 地図〔ちず〕	map	17. いくつ目	which (in order)?
8. つぎ	next	18. 一つ目	first
9. 駅〔えき〕	train station	19. むこう	other side; beyond
10. あっち	over there [informal equiv. of あちら]		

B. どうし Verbs

20. 会う〔G1 あいます／あって〕　　　　　　　　　to meet

21. 知らない〔G1 しる／しって〕　　　　　　　　do not know

22. 歩いて行き〔G1 あるいていく／あるいていきます〕　to go by foot

23. 〜てくれた〔G2 くれる／くれます〕　　　　　did something (for my in-group)

24. 見て〔G2 みる／みます〕　　　　　　　　　　to look

25. 乗って〔G1 のります／のって〕　　　　　　　to ride

26. 行き〔G1 いく／いきます〕　　　　　　　　　to go

27. 買う〔G1 かいます／かって〕　　　　　　　　to buy

28. 教えて下さい〔G2 おしえる／おしえます〕　　please teach/show me

29. さがしたら〔G1さがす／さがします〕　　　　when you look for it

30. 分かる〔G1 わかります／わかって〕　　　　　to understand

31. 来る〔IR きます／きて〕　　　　　　　　　　to come

32. 電話して〔IR でんわする／でんわします〕　　to make a phone call

33. おりた〔G2 おります／おりて〕　　　　　　　got off

34. 行きたいんです〔G1 いく／いきます〕　　　　to want to go (you know)

35. 上がって〔G1 あがる／あがります〕　　　　　to go up

36. 下りて〔G2 おりる／おります〕　　　　　　　to go down

37. 行くと〔G1 行きます／行って〕　　　　　　　if (he) goes

38. 待っていると〔G1 まちます／まつ〕　　　　　if (he) is waiting

39. とまります〔G1 とまる／とまって〕 it will stop
40. おりたら〔G2 おりる／おります〕 when (you) get off

C. そのほか　Others
41. 〜から　　　　　　　　　　　　from 〜
42. 〜まで　　　　　　　　　　　　to 〜
43. まず　　　　　　　　　　　　　First of all
44. 〜けど、　　　　　　　　　　　〜, but

D. Expressions
45. どう行けばいいんですか。　　　How should I go?
46. あった、あった。　　　　　　　I found it.
47. じゃあ、　　　　　　　　　　　Well then,
48. 行って来ます。　　　　　　　　[Used by a family member who leaves home for the day. lit., I'll go and come back.]
49. いってらっしゃい。　　　　　　[Used by a family member who sees off another family member for the day. lit., Go and return.]
50. 気をつけてね。　　　　　　　　Be careful.
51. あのう、すみません。　　　　　Uhh . . . excuse me.
52. どうもありがとうございました。 Thank you very much [for a past event or gift received in the past].

九課

Activity A

1.
あきはばら＜秋葉原＞_{は　ばら}　N　Akihabara [a district in Tokyo]
秋葉原で安い電気製品を買うことが出来る。_{は　ばら　　　　　　せいひん} You can buy cheap electric goods at Akihabara.

2.
しぶや＜渋谷＞_{しぶや}　N　Shibuya [a district in Tokyo]
渋谷のハチ公の所で会おう。_{しぶや} Let's meet at (the place of) Hachiko (a famous statue of a dog).

3.
しんじゅく＜新宿＞_{じゅく}　N　Shinjuku [a district in Tokyo]
新宿駅は一日に百万人が使うそうだ。_{じゅく} I heard that one million people per day use Shinjuku Station.

4.
おちゃノみず＜御茶ノ水＞_お　N　Ochanomizu [a district in Tokyo]
御茶ノ水という駅で降りると、東大まではバスに乗って行かなければならない。_{お　　　　　　　　　　　　　　　　　　　　　お} When you get off at Ochanomizu Station, you have to ride a bus to Tokyo University (top national university.)

5.
うえの＜上野＞_の　N　Ueno [a district in Tokyo]
パンダで有名な動物園は、上野駅にある。_の The zoo famous for pandas is in Ueno.

6.
ぎんざ＜銀座＞　N　Ginza [a district in Tokyo]
歌舞伎を見たければ、銀座へ行かなければならない。_{ぶ　き} If you want to see the *kabuki*, you should go to Ginza.

7.  とうきょうえき＜東京駅＞　N　Tokyo Station

東京から京都へ新幹線で行きたければ、東京駅へ行かなければなら

ない。 If you want to go to Kyoto from Tokyo, you have to go to Tokyo Station.

8.  かんだ＜神田＞　N　Kanda [a district in Tokyo]

神田という所は昔から古本屋がたくさんあることで有名だ。 The place

called Kanda has long been famous for its many second-hand bookstores.

9.  はらじゅく＜原宿＞　N　Harajuku [a district in Tokyo]

原宿の竹下通りは若い人たちが好きな所だ。 Takeshita Street in Harajuku is

a place that young people like.

10.  いけぶくろ＜池袋＞　N　Ikebukuro [a district in Tokyo]

池袋のサンシャイン６０というビルはとてもおもしろそうだ。 The

building called Sunshine 60 in Ikebukuro seems to be very interesting.

11.  しながわ＜品川＞　N　Shinagawa [a district in Tokyo]

品川は、東京の南にあって、「忠臣蔵」の泉岳寺というお寺がある。

Shinagawa is in southern Tokyo and there is a temple called Sengakuji known for

Chushingura (The 47 *Ronin*).

12.  しんかんせん＜新幹線＞　N　bullet train

新幹線はとても速くて便利だ。　 The bullet trains are very fast and convenient.

13.  かぶきざ＜歌舞伎座＞　N　*kabuki* theater

歌舞伎は、歌舞伎座へ行くと、見ることが出来る。 If you go to the

kabuki theater, you can see the *kabuki*.

14.  てんのう＜天皇＞　N　Emperor

天皇は東京の皇居という所にいらっしゃる。 The Emperor is at a place called

the Imperial Palace in Tokyo.

Activity B

15.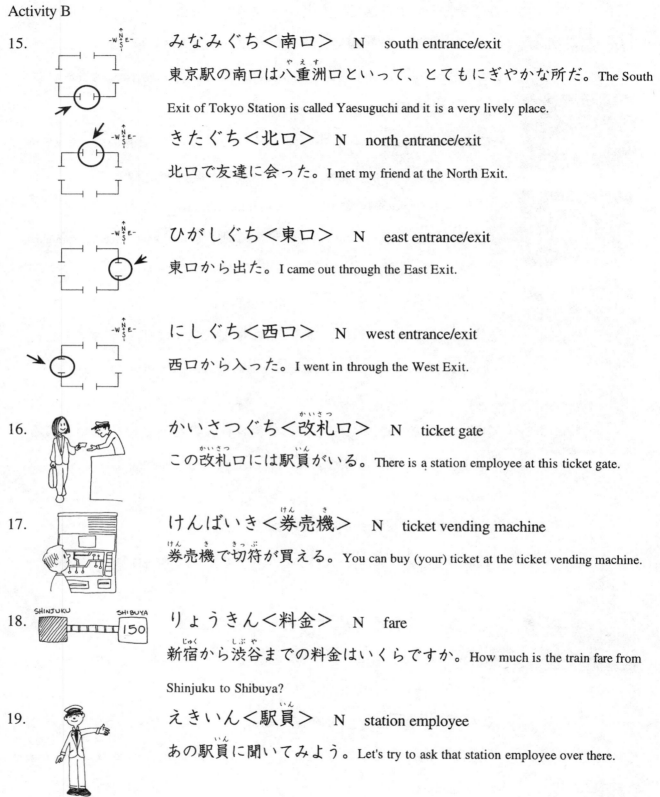

みなみぐち＜南口＞　N　south entrance/exit

東京駅の南口は八重洲口といって、とてもにぎやかな所だ。The South

Exit of Tokyo Station is called Yaesuguchi and it is a very lively place.

きたぐち＜北口＞　N　north entrance/exit

北口で友達に会った。I met my friend at the North Exit.

ひがしぐち＜東口＞　N　east entrance/exit

東口から出た。I came out through the East Exit.

にしぐち＜西口＞　N　west entrance/exit

西口から入った。I went in through the West Exit.

16. かいさつぐち＜改札口＞　N　ticket gate

この改札口には駅員がいる。There is a station employee at this ticket gate.

17. けんばいき＜券売機＞　N　ticket vending machine

券売機で切符が買える。You can buy (your) ticket at the ticket vending machine.

18. りょうきん＜料金＞　N　fare

新宿から渋谷までの料金はいくらですか。How much is the train fare from

Shinjuku to Shibuya?

19. えきいん＜駅員＞　N　station employee

あの駅員に聞いてみよう。Let's try to ask that station employee over there.

20.  ホーム　N　platform

ホームのベンチに座って、電車を待とう。Let's sit on the bench at the platform and wait for the electric train.

21.  JR ［ジェイアール］　N　Japan Railway

JRのレールパスを持っていれば、日本の旅行はとても便利だ。
If you have a JR rail pass, travelling in Japan is very convenient.

Activity C

22.  どうやって（＝どう）　N　How (to do something)?

どうやって切符を買えばいいんですか。How should I buy the tickets?

23.  パンダ　N　panda

パンダは中国から来た。Pandas came from China.

24. はくぶつかん＜博物館＞　N　museum

上野の博物館はすばらしいそうだ。I heard that the museum in Ueno is wonderful.

Activity D　　No new vocabulary.

Activity E

25. せつめい＜説明＞　N　an explanation

せつめいをする＜説明をする＞　V3　to explain

その日本人はどうやってお寺に行けるか説明してくれた。That Japanese explained to me how to get to the temple.

26. やくそく＜約束＞　N　a promise

やくそくをする＜約束をする＞　V3　to make a promise

友達と七時に会う約束をした。I promised to meet with my friend at 7:00.

九課

27.  くりかえす＜繰り返す＞　V1　to repeat

その日本人は私の分からないところを繰り返して言ってくれた。The Japanese repeated to me what I do not understand.

28.  まいごになる＜迷子になる＞　V1　to get lost

東京で迷子になって、困った。I got lost in Tokyo and was troubled.

Activity F

29.  のりば＜乗り場＞　N　place of embarkment; place one gets in a vehicle　タクシー乗り場はどこですか。Where is the place where I (can) get in a taxi?

30.  ビル　N　building; high rise

兄の会社は、ビルの十五階にあります。My older brother's company is on the 15th floor of the building.

31.  ガソリンスタンド　N　gas station

ガソリンスタンドに寄って、ガソリンを買おう。Let's drop by the gas station and buy some gas.

32. 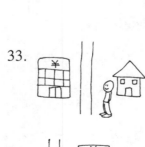 ポスト　N　mailbox [on the street for mailing letters]

ゆうんびんばこ＜郵便箱＞　N　mailbox [at house and office for receiving mail]

ポストは郵便局の前にある。There is a mailbox in front of the post office.

33. むかいがわ＜向かい側＞　N　other side (of)

銀行は家の向かい側にある。The bank is on the other side of our house.

34. てまえ＜手前＞　N　this side (of)

銀行の手前にガソリンスタンドがあり、向こうに喫茶店がある。

There is a gas station on this side of the bank and a coffee shop on the other side.

35.  つきあたり＜突き当たり＞　N　end (of a street)

この道の突き当たりに田中さんの家がある。 Tanaka's house is at the end of this street.

Activity G & H

36.  のりかえる＜乗りかえる＞　V2　to change (buses, trains, airplanes, etc.)

２番のバスから８番のバスに乗りかえた。I changed from the #2 bus to the #10 bus.

37. やまのてせん＜山手線＞　N　Yamanote Line [green-colored train line in Tokyo]　山手線はとても便利だ。The Yamanote Line is very convenient.

38. ちゅうおうせん＜中央線＞　N　Chuo (Central) Line [orange-colored train line in Tokyo]　中央線で新宿から御茶ノ水まで行った。

I went from Shinjuku to Ochanomizu by the Chuo Line.

39. そうぶせん＜総武線＞　N　Sobu Line [yellow-colored train line in Tokyo]　御茶ノ水で中央線から総武線に乗りかえた。I transferred at Ochanomizu from the Chuo Line to the Sobu Line.

40. ～ばんせん＜～番線＞　N　track number ～

次の大阪行きの新幹線は８番線から出る。The next bullet train bound for Osaka leaves from Track Number 8.

41. ～ほうめん＜～方面＞　N　～ direction

東京方面の新幹線は７番線に入る。The bullet train travelling in the Tokyo direction will come in on Track Number 7.

【オプショナル単語】

1.  とっきゅう（でんしゃ）＜特急（電車）＞ N special express train (stops at major stations only)

特急電車は大きい駅だけに止まる。The special express trains stop at only the big stations.

2.  きゅうこう（でんしゃ）＜急行（電車）＞ N express train (stops at all major and other smaller stations)

急行電車は少し大きい駅にも止まる。The express trains stop at some slightly bigger stations, too.

3. かいそく（でんしゃ）＜快速（電車）＞ N rapid train (another name for 急行)

快速は急行と同じだ。The *kaisoku* and the *kyuko* are the same.

4. ふつう（でんしゃ）＜普通（電車）＞ N local train (stops at every stop)

普通電車は全部の駅に止まる。The local trains stop at all the stations.

5. かくえき（でんしゃ）＜各駅（電車）＞ N local train (stops at every stop)

各駅電車と普通電車は同じだ。The *kakueki* and the *futsu* are the same.

A. 〜か（どうか）　　　　whether or not; if (〜 or not)

This construction is used when one expresses uncertainty about a certain condition, event or fact. When the optional どうか is used, the embedded question has to be a yes-no question. If it is not used, then the question can be either a yes-no question or a WH-question. Typical final verbs include, among others, verbs of knowing, examining, understanding, asking, remembering and deciding. Use the plain form before か. だ is omitted after な adjectives and nouns.

Verb	食べる			eat, will eat
	食べない			do not eat; will not eat
	食べた			ate
	食べなかった			did not eat
い Adjective	高い			is expensive
	高くない			is not expensive
	高かった			was expensive
	高くなかった	＋か		was not expensive
な Adjective	好き	＋かどうか		like
	好きじゃない or 好きではない			do not like
	好きだった			liked
	好きじゃなかった or 好きではなかった			did not like
Noun	学生			is a student
	学生じゃない or 学生ではない			is not a student
	学生だった			was a student
	学生じゃなかった or 学生ではなかった			was not a student

1. 田中さんがパーティーに来る<u>かどうか</u>知りません。

> I do not know if Mr. Tanaka will come to the party.

2. 田中さんがパーティーに来る<u>か来ないか</u>知りません。

> I do not know if Mr. Tanaka will come to the party or not.

3. この本がおもしろい<u>かどうか</u>よく知りません。

> I do not really know whether this book is interesting.

4. 日本の物が<u>高いか安いか</u>よく知りません。

> I do not really know whether things in Japan are expensive or cheap.

5. 東京の電車料金が<u>高いか高くないか</u>よく知りません。

> I do not know whether the electric train fare in Tokyo is expensive or not.

6. ジョンさんはテニスが上手<u>かどうか</u>よく知りません。

> I do not know whether Jon is skillful at tennis.

7. 東京駅までいくら<u>か</u>知っていますか。

       Do you know how much it is to Tokyo Station?

8. <u>いつ</u>日本語の試験がある<u>か</u>おぼえていますか。

       Do you remember when we will have our Japanese exam?

9. 秋葉原<ruby>原<rt>はばら</rt></ruby>まで<u>どうやって</u>行く<u>か</u>教えて下さい。

       Please tell me how to get to Akihabara.

B. Review: 　～と、
               ～たら、
               ～ば、

All of the above can be expressed as "If . . ." Although they may be interchangeable in usage, there are certain restrictions on each.

a. **Verb (Dictionary/ NAI form - Nonpast Plain form) ＋ と、Sentence 2。**

    いAdjective (-い/-くない - Nonpast Plain form) ＋ と、Sentence 2。

    なAdjective (だ/-ではない - Nonpast Plain form) ＋ と、Sentence 2。

    Noun　　　　(だ/-ではない - Nonpast Plain form) ＋ と、Sentence 2。

    Normally used when stating fact, mathematical or scientific principles. Is not generally used when expressing opinion or information of a personal nature.

    1. 右に<u>まがると</u>、大きいデパートがあります。

       If you turn right, there is a large department store.

    2. 冬に<u>なると</u>、雪がふります。

       When it becomes winter, it will snow.

b. **Verb (TA form/ NAKATTA) ＋ら、Sentence 2。**

    いAdjective (-かった/-くなかった - Past Plain form) ＋ら、Sentence 2。

    なAdjective (だった/-ではなかった - Past Plain form) ＋ら、Sentence 2。

    Noun　　　　(だった/-ではなかった - Past Plain form) ＋ら、Sentence 2。

    Used to make general statements, often of a more personal nature. Sentence 2 (the main clause) may express volition, suggestion, invitation, request, permission, prohibition or opinion.

    Though it is considered a conditional, ーたら is also often expressed as "When."

    3. 早く<u>終わったら</u>、買い物に行きましょう。

       If we finish early, let's go shopping.

    4. お天気が<u>良かったら</u>、家へ来て下さい。

       When the weather is good, please come to my house.

c. **Verb (-ば)、Sentence 2。**

    いAdjective (-ば)、Sentence 2。

    なAdjective (なら)、Sentence 2。

    Noun　　　　(なら)、Sentence 2。

    Used in hypothetical statements, i.e., "if and only if . . ."

    5. 雨が<u>ふらなければ</u>、ピクニックをします。

       If and only if it does not rain, we will have a picnic.

    6. <u>安ければ</u>、人々は買います。People will buy it only if it is inexpensive.

C. Review: Particles

1. **Particle の**

　　Modifying noun + の + main noun [modifier]

　　　　Ex. 東京駅の北口　　　　　　　The north exit of Tokyo Station.
　　　　　　二番目の駅　　　　　　　　The second station

2. **Particle で**

　　A. Place + で + action verb ["at, in"]

　　　　Ex. 部屋で読む。　　　　　　　I read in the room.
　　　　　　こうさてんでとまる。　　　I stop at the intersection.

　　B. Tool/Means + で　["by means of"]

　　　　Ex. 電車で行く。　　　　　　　I will go by electric train.
　　　　　　えんぴつで書く。　　　　　I will write with a pencil.

3. **Particle に**

　　Location/Target + に　["to," "toward"]

　　に is used to indicate movement toward a goal or destination, such as with direction verbs
　　(ex. 行く，帰る, etc.), as well as 入る，乗る, etc.)

　　　　Ex. 東京に行く。　　　　　　　I will go to Tokyo.
　　　　　　左にまがる。　　　　　　　I will turn to the left.
　　　　　　バスに乗りかえる。　　　　I transfer to the bus.
　　　　　　教室に入る。　　　　　　　I will enter the classroom.

4. **Particle を**

　　A. Direct object + を　[object marker]

　　　　Ex. お水を飲む。　　　　　　　I drink water.
　　　　　　本を読む。　　　　　　　　I will read a book.
　　　　　　バスを待つ。　　　　　　　I will wait for the bus.

　　B. Route/Place + を　["from," "out of"]

　　を is used to mark the place from which one gets off or leaves. Use with such verbs as
　　おりる, 出る, etc.

　　　　Ex. 車をおりる。　　　　　　　I will get out of the car.
　　　　　　家を出る。　　　　　　　　I will leave home.
　　　　　　高校をそつぎょうする。　　I will graduate from high school.

　　C. Route/Place+ を　["through," "along"]

　　　　Ex. この道を行く。　　　　　　I will go along this street.
　　　　　　橋をわたる。　　　　　　　I will cross the bridge.
　　　　　　かいだんを上がる。　　　　I will go up the stairs.

5. **Particle と**

　　Person/Object + と　["with," "in association with"]

　　　　Ex. 友達と行く。　　　　　　　I will go with my friend.

九課

A. ペアワーク：どこへ行ったらいいでしょうか。

You want to know where you can do the following activities in Tokyo. Write the name of the station where you must go to in order to get to the correct places/activities. Mark the places on the train map of Tokyo in this lesson.

したい事	駅名〔えきめい〕
1. コンピューターや電気製品〔せいひん〕がとても安いそうですが、どこですか。	
2. 高いビルがたくさんあって、東京の西のにぎやかな所だそうですが、買物やディスコも出来るそうです。夜も大変にぎやかだと聞きました。どこですか。	
3. サンシャイン６０という東京でとても高いビルへ行ってみたいんです。	
4. ハチ公の犬のどうぞう(statue)を見てみたいんです。	
5. わかい人たちがたくさんおもしろいかっこうをしておどったりしているって聞いたんですが、どこですか。スターのしゃしんやポスターもあるそうですね。	
6. かぶきを見に行きたいんですが、かぶきざはどこにありますか。	
7. 新幹線に乗って、京都〔きょうと〕に旅行したいんですが、新幹線はどこから出ていますか。	
8. パンダがいる動物園や博物館〔はくぶつかん〕があるそうですが、どこですか。	
9. "ちゅうしんぐら(47 Ronin)"という話で有名なお寺はどこですか。	
10. 古本を売っている所で有名だそうですが、どこですか。	
11. とても広い魚のマーケットが朝早くあるそうですが、どこですか。	
12. 天皇〔てんのう〕が住んでいらっしゃる所はどこですか。	

B. ペアワーク

The following pictures show the sequence of buying tickets, getting on a train and reaching one's destination. Match the pictures with the correct captions that follow. Write the correct letter in the parentheses.

1. (　　)

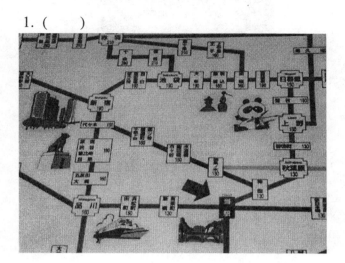

2. (　　)

3. (　　)

4. (　　)

5. (　　)

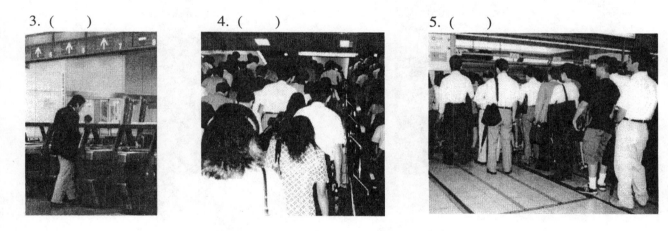

6. (　　)

7. (　　)

8. (　　)

9. (　　)

10. (　　)

11. (　　)

12. (　　)

A. JRの電車が来ました。

B. 南口から出ます。

C. 電車の駅の地図を見、料金をしらべます。

D. 電車に乗ってから、寝たり本を読んだりする人もいます。

E. かいだんを上がり、ホームに行きます。

F. 改札口〔かいさつぐち〕できっぷを入れ、駅の中に入ります。

G. 電車に乗っている人を駅員〔えきいん〕が手つだいます。

H. ホームで電車を待っています。

I. この改札口〔かいさつぐち〕からは外に出られませんから、
　ほかの改札口〔かいさつぐち〕へ行かなければなりません。

J. 券売機〔けんばいき〕にお金を入れ、きっぷを買います。

K. 電車からおります。

L. かいだんを下りて行きます。

C. ペアワーク

You ask your partner the following questions, but he/she does not know the answers and tells you so. Take turns.

Ex.　A:「今日、日本語の宿題がありますか。」

　　　B:「さあ、日本語の宿題がある<u>かどうか</u>、知りません。」

1. 日本は今、あついでしょうか。
2. いつ日本語の試験がありますか。
3. 先生はあまい物がお好きですか。
4. 博物館〔はくぶつかん〕は東京のどこにありますか。
5. くうこうまでどうやってバスで行けますか。
6. 名古屋〔なごや〕は何で有名ですか。
7. 来年、学校はいつから始まりますか。
8. 日本のデパートで売っている物は安いですか。
9. どこでパンダを見ることが出来ますか。
10. どうすれば日本語が上手になりますか。

D. ペアワーク：「〜と〜」のふくしゅうゲーム

Copy the following cards and cut them out. Put the stack up cards face down or spread the cards on the table face down. One person picks up one card and makes a sentence using the 〜と〜 sentence pattern. If the person makes up a correct sentence, he/she keeps the card. If the sentence is wrong, he/she has to return the card. Set a time limit for thinking about and making up a sentence. The winner is the person who collects the most cards.

Ex. 　「たくさん<u>書くと</u>、えんぴつがみじかくなります。」

九課

E. ペアワーク：どうすればいいでしょうか。

With your partner, take turns making suggestions for the following problems. Use the example below as a guide for your conversations.

A：「日本語のクラスでAのせいせきがほしいんですよ。どうすれば

いいでしょうか。」

B：「もっとよく勉強すれば、いいでしょう。」

1. 日本語をもっと上手に話したいんですが、どうすればいいでしょうか。	
2. すう学の先生のせつ明がよく分からないんです。どうすればいいでしょうか。	
3. スポーツでいつもおそく家へ帰るので、宿題をする時間がないんです。どうすればいいでしょうか。	
4. 友達がいつもやくそくの時間に来ないんです。どうすればいいでしょうか。	
5. 知らない所を旅行すると、いつもまい子になるんですよ。どうすればいいでしょうか。	
6. 日本語のテープをくりかえして聞いていますが、それでも分からないんですよ。どうすればいいでしょうか。	
7. 日本語のクラスにおすしを持って行くんですが、作り方を知らないんですよ。どうすればいいでしょうか。	
8. 今年の夏に日本へ行くんですが、あまりお金がないんですよ。どうすればいいでしょうか。	

F. ペアワーク：Directionのふくしゅうゲーム

Read the directions on the next page to your partner. Your partner will follow the directions using the map below and finds your location. Start from location ◎ each time. Take turns. Give directions to the four locations listed on the next page. Your partner follows the directions and checks if they were correct or not. Take turns.

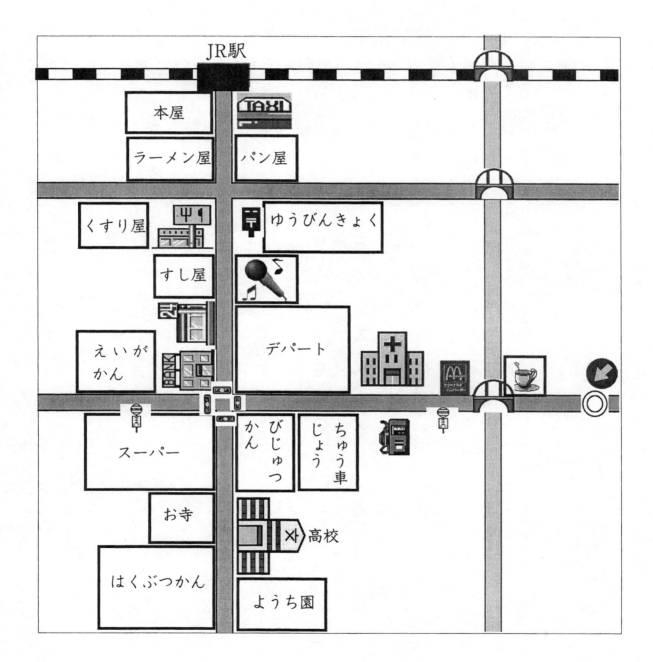

場所〔ばしょ〕	行き方
	橋の手前にあります。
	この道をまっすぐ行くと、橋のむこうの右にあります。
	橋をわたって、この道をまっすぐ行って、つぎの交差点〔こうさてん〕で右にまがって、その道をまっすぐ行くと、また交差点〔こうさてん〕がありますが、もっとまっすぐ行って、その道のつきあたりにあります。
	橋をわたって、この道をまっすぐ行って、つぎの交差点〔こうさてん〕で左にまがります。道の左がわの二番目の建物〔たてもの〕です。
	橋をわたって、この道をまっすぐ行って、つぎの交差点〔こうさてん〕の信号〔しんごう〕でむこうににわたって、右にまがります。道の左がわの二番目の建物〔たてもの〕です。
	橋をわたると、右に病院がありますが、その向い側〔むかいがわ〕にあります。
	橋をわたって、この道をまっすぐ行って、つぎの交差点〔こうさてん〕で右にまがって、まっすぐ行くと、つぎの交差点〔こうさてん〕の左の角〔かど〕にあります。
すし屋	
銀行	
ポスト	
タクシー乗り場	

G. ペアワーク：何番線のホーム？

This photo is the ticket gate at Shinjuku Station. After you go though the ticket gate, you must locate the correct platform to catch your train. The numbers in the photo such as 13 and 14 indicate track numbers. Write the line number you must go to in order to reach the destinations based on information given on the following page.

１３   １４

行き先〔いきさき〕 Destination	何番線？
1. 渋谷〔しぶや〕	
2. 池袋〔いけぶくろ〕	
3. 東京駅	
4. 中野〔なかの〕	
5. 秋葉原〔あきはばら〕	
6. 上野〔うえの〕	

漢字：方面〔ほうめん〕

新宿〔しんじゅく〕駅

御茶ノ水・東京方面 For Ochanomizu & Tokyo	オレンジ	中央線 快速 Chuo Line (Rapid)	**8**

中野・高尾方面 For Nakano & Takao	オレンジ	中央線 快速 Chuo Line (Rapid)	**9**

中野・三鷹方面 For Nakano & Mitaka	きいろ	総武線 Sobu Line	**10**

御茶ノ水・秋葉原・西船橋方面 For Ochanomizu & Akihabara & Nishifunabashi	きいろ	総武線 Sobu Line	**11**

渋谷・品川方面 For Shibuya & Shinagawa	みどり	山手線内回り Yamanote Line	**12**

池袋・上野方面 For Ikebukuro & Ueno	みどり	山手線外回り Yamanote Line	**13**

改札口〔かいさつぐち〕

九課

H. ペアワーク：電車の乗り方

Using the JR Tokyo railroad map on p. 273, give directions to the destinations below. Use the following dialogue as a guide. Take turns.

Ex. 渋谷〔しぶや〕 → 秋葉原〔あきはばら〕

＜渋谷で＞

A:「あのう...すみません。ちょっとうかがいますが、秋葉原まで
　　どうやって行けばいいか、教えて下さい。」

B:「秋葉原ですね。この地図を見て下さい。まず、渋谷から山手線に
　　乗って、新宿まで行き、新宿で、東京方面の中央線に乗りかえて、
　　御茶ノ水で総武線に乗りかえれば、秋葉原は次(＃番目) の駅ですよ。

A:「渋谷から山手線に乗って、新宿まで行き、新宿で、中央線に
　　乗りかえて、御茶ノ水で総武線に乗るんですね。
　　ありがとうございました。」

B:「どういたしまして。」

	Departure	Destination
1.	中野〔なかの〕	上野〔うえの〕
2.	御茶ノ水	新宿〔しんじゅく〕
3.	中野〔なかの〕	秋葉原〔あきはばら〕
4.	御茶ノ水	池袋〔いけぶくろ〕
5.	渋谷〔しぶや〕	銀座
6.	東京	新宿〔しんじゅく〕
7.	六本木	神田〔かんだ〕
8.	原宿〔はらじゅく〕	築地〔つきじ〕

九課

ＯＰＩ単語＆文法チェックリスト

名前：＿＿＿＿＿＿＿＿＿＿＿＿

クラス：＿＿＿＿＿＿＿

9課：電車

たんご	Check	たんご	Check
どうやって		天皇〔てんのう〕	
パンダ		かぶきざ	
はく物かん			
新幹線		**山手線**	
北口		上野〔うえの〕	
南口		秋葉原〔あきはばら〕	
東口		神田〔かんだ〕	
西口		東京	
かいさつ口		品川〔しながわ〕	
けん売き		渋谷〔しぶや〕	
料金		原宿〔はらじゅく〕	
駅いん		新宿〔しんじゅく〕	
ホーム		池袋〔いけぶくろ〕	
JR		**中央線**	
せつ明する		お茶ノ水	
やくそくする		中野〔なかの〕	
くりかえす		**総武線**〔そうぶせん〕	
まい子になる		六本木	
乗りば		銀座	
むかいがわ		築地〔つきじ〕	
手前			
つきあたり			
～番線			
～方面〔ほうめん〕			
#番目の駅			

ぶんぽう	Check	Error
～という～		
～とか～		
～時（に）		
Noun Modifiers		
～ので		
～た方がいい		
～てから		
～し		
～と		
～たら		
～ば		
～かもしれない		
S1V(stem) + S2。		
～か（どうか）		
V(stem)かえる		
Particles		
Plain **Polite**		
Male **Female**		

九課

310

I. Sentence Patterns

6課

1. 弟がテレビを見ている<u>間</u>に、私は宿題をしてしまいました。

  I finished doing my homework while my younger brother was watching T.V.

2. 冬休みの<u>間</u>に、日本へ旅行するつもりです。

  I am planning to take a trip to Japan during winter vacation.

3. 長い<u>間</u>、私は日本料理を食べていません。

  I have not eaten Japanese food for a long time.

4. 静（しず）かな<u>間</u>、よく勉強出来ました。 I could study well while it was quiet.

5. 姉は、いつも音楽を聞き<u>ながら</u>、勉強しています。

  My older sister always studies while she listens to music.

6. あの俳優（はいゆう）は三度目の結婚（けっこん）を<u>した</u>そうです。

  I heard that that actor got married for the third time.

7. 新聞によると、この冬はとても寒（さむ）い<u>そうだ</u>よ。

  According to the newspaper, (I understand that) it will be very cold this winter.

8. 日本人は食べた<u>後で</u>、「ごちそうさま。」と言います。

  Japanese say "GOCHISOSAMA" after eating.

9. このクラスの<u>後で</u>、お昼（しょ）を一緒に食べましょう。

  Let's eat lunch together after this class.

10. この<u>後で</u>、何をしますか。 What are you going to do after this?

11. 日本人は食べる<u>前</u>に、「いただきます。」と言います。

  Japanese say "ITADAKIMASU" before they eat.

12. 冬休みの<u>前</u>に、ビデオを貸（か）して下さい。

  Please lend me some videos before winter vacation.

7課

1. BA form / NAKEREBA form if ～/if not ～

  日本語が<u>話せれ</u>ば、旅行は楽しいです。 If you can speak Japanese, the trip will be fun.

  あなたが<u>行かなけれ</u>ば、私も行きません。 If you won't go, I won't go either.

  もし<u>安けれ</u>ば、買います。 If it is cheap, I will buy it.

  映画が好き<u>なら</u>、おもしろい映画をたくさん知っているはずです。

  If he likes movies, he should know lots of interesting movies.

311

<u>学生</u>なら、安いですよ。 If you are a student, it is cheap.

2. 友子さん<u>からの</u>電話はいつもとても長いんです。

Telephone calls from Tomoko are always very long.

3. パーティーの食べ物はもう買って<u>あります</u>。 The food for the party has already been bought.

4. 明日、雨が降る<u>かもしれません</u>。 It might rain tomorrow.

5. 昨日おそく家へ<u>帰り</u>、すぐ寝ました。

I returned home late yesterday and went to bed immediately.

8課

1. 弟は毎日テレビゲーム<u>ばかり</u>しています。

My younger brother is playing only computer games every day.

2. ベンさんは来年日本へ行く<u>らしい</u>です。

It seems that Ben is going to Japan next year.

3. 明日、パーティーをするので、今日食べ物を買って<u>おきました</u>。

Since we are going to have a party tomorrow, I bought food today ahead of time.

4. 大学に行っても、日本語を<u>勉強しよう</u>と思っています。

I am thinking of studying Japanese even when I go to college.

9課

1. 田中さんがパーティーに来る<u>かどうか</u>、知りません。

I do not know if Mr. Tanaka will come to the party or not.

2. 田中さんがパーティーに来る<u>か来ないか</u>、知りません。

I do not know if Mr. Tanaka will come or will not come to the party.

3. 東京駅までいくら<u>か</u>、知っていますか。

Do you know how much it is to Tokyo Station?

4. <u>いつ</u>日本語の試験がある<u>か</u>、おぼえていますか。

Do you remember when we are having our Japanese exam?

5. 右に<u>まがると</u>、大きいデパートがあります。

If you turn right, there will be a large department store.

6. 早く<u>終わったら</u>、買い物に行きましょう。 If we finish early, let's go shopping.

7. 雨が<u>降らなければ</u>、ピクニックをします。

If and only if it does not rain, we will have a picnic.

十課

312

II. 動詞 Verbs, い Adjectives and な Adjectives

[The Roman numerals preceding each word indicate the volume in which the word was introduced. I = Lev. 1
II = Level 2. Arabic numerals indicate the lesson from Volume 3 where the word was first introduced.]

A. Verbs
Group 1 Verbs

-む	-ぬ	-ぶ	-う	-つ
I のむ	I しぬ	I あそぶ	I いう	I かつ
I よむ			I あう （会)	I たつ
I やすむ			I かう	I まつ
II すむ			I うたう	II もつ
II かむ			I もらう	
II こむ			II ならう	
6 たのしむ			II ちがう	
			II すう	
			II はらう	
			II あらう	
			II てつだう	
			II ちがう	
			II (TE) しまう	
			II おもう	
			II うかがう	
			II わらう	
			1 つかう	
			2 かよう	
			6 つきあう	

[The Roman numerals preceding each word indicate the volume in which the word was introduced. I = Lev. 1
II = Level 2. Arabic numerals indicate the lesson from Volume 3 where the word was first introduced.]

-る		-く	-ぐ	-す
I おわる	2 やる do	I きく	I およぐ	I はなす
I わかる	3 (ふろに)はいる	I かく （書）	2 ぬぐ	I だす
I しる	3 はる （貼）	I 行く		I かす
I ふとる	3 うけとる	I あるく		II スピードをだす
I とる	3 こまる	II はたらく		II かえす
I かえる	4 (〜が)みつかる	II はく		II ゴミをだす
I ある	4 (stem)おわる	II つく		II かくす
I がんばる	6 おどる	II おく put, leave		II ふきとばす
I はしる	6 にんきがある	II かぜを　ひく		II あいす
I すわる	6 なくなる	II ピアノを　ひく		4 さがす
I やる	7 かざる	II むかえに行く		4 おもいだす
I つくる	7 あがる	II とりに行く		4 やくす
II かぶる	8 いのる	II うごく		7 こわす
II とまる　（止）	8 かわった	II すく		7 なおす
II まがる	9 まいごになる	II かく （描）		9 くりかえす
II のる		II なく		
II いらっしゃる		2 (はを)みがく		
II かわる		4 (じしょを)ひく		
II おくる （送）		6 (トランペットを)ふく		
II ふる		6 (ドラムを)たたく		
II かかる		7 おちつく		
II うる		8 (〜て)おく		
II はじまる		8 やく		
II おわる				
II とりにかえる				
II むかえにかえる				
II よる （寄）				
II なる				
II わたる				
II きる （切）				
II おこる （怒）				
II しかる				

Group 2 Verbs

-E		One ひらがな	Special
I はじめる	1 かえる	I みる	I おきる
I みえる	2 はきかえる	I ねる	II かりる
I きこえる	2 やめる	I いる	II おりる （降）
I たべる	2 (パーマを)かける	II きる	II できる
I やせる	3 (しけんを)うける	II でる	II -すぎる
I つかれる	4 まちがえる	6 (part of body)	3 (シャワーを)あびる
I まける	4 (〜を)みつける	をしている	7 おりる （下）
I みせる	4 (Verb Stem)はじめる	8 にる （煮）	
I あける	4 (Verb Stem)つづける		
I しめる	4 しらべる		
I わすれる	6 わかれる		
I くれる	7 かける		
I あげる	7 (〜が)こわれる		
II うまれる	7 たてる		
II つとめる	8 つける （漬）		
II こたえる	8 かける		
II (めがねを)かける			
II (ごみを)すてる			
II きをつける			
II おしえる			
II でかける			
II (でんわを)かける			
II まちがえる			
II おぼえる			
II さしあげる			
II くらべる			
II いれる			
II つける			
II かたづける			
II たすける			

十課

Group 3 Irregular Verbs

I　くる	I　する	1　かんしゃ（を）する
II　むかえにくる	I　べんきょう（を）する	1　せんこう（を）する
II　とりにくる	I　タイプ（を）する	2　りゅうがく（を）する
	I　りょこう（を）する	2　（お）けしょう（を）する
	I　かいもの（を）する	3　せわ（を）する
	I　しょくじ（を）する	3　はっぴょう（を）する
	I　でんわ（を）する	3　そうだん（を）する
	I　れんしゅう（を）する	4　はつおん（を）する
	II　アルバイト（を）する	6　せいこう（を）する
	II　けっこん（を）する	7　けいけん（を）する
	II　ホームステイ（を）する	7　せいざ（を）する
	II　しょうかい（を）する	8　まる（を）する
	II　じこしょうかい（を）する	8　えんりょする
	II　しつもん（を）する	9　せつめい（を）する
	II　アクセサリーを　する	9　やくそく（を）する
	II　うんてん（を）する	
	II　しんぱい（を）する	
	II　シートベルトを　する	
	II　けんか（を）する	
	II　thing に　する	
	II　よやく（を）する	
	II　ちゅうもん（を）する	
	II　ごちそう（を）する	
	II　そうじ（を）する	
	II　せんたく（を）する	
	II　りょうり（を）する	
	II　うんどう（を）する	
	II　おうえん（を）する	
	II　ゆうしょう（を）する	
	II　げきをする	
	II　あつくする	
	II　きれいにする	
	II　さんぽ（を）する	
	II　りこん（を）する	
	II　かんしゃ（を）する	

Japanese 1 Verbs

[The numbers preceding each word indicate the lesson and section in which the word was introduced in *Adventures in Japanese 1*.]

1-4 はじめます	to begin; start	10-1 います	exist (animate)
1-4 おわります	to finish	10-1 あります	exist (inanimate)
2-1 わかります	to understand	11-2 あります	to have
2-1 しりません	do not know	12-1 しにます	to die
2-1 みえます	can see	12-2 やすみます	to rest; be absent
2-1 きこえます	can hear	12-2 (くすりを)のみます	to take (medicine)
2-1 いいます	to say	12-2 つかれています	to be tired
4-1 はなします	to speak; talk	12-3 かちます	to win
4-2 たべます	to eat	12-3 まけます	to lose
4-2 のみます	to drink	12-4 がんばります	to do one's best
4-4 よみます	to read	12-5 あいます	to meet
4-4 ききます	to listen; hear; ask	12-5 れんしゅう（を）します	to practice
4-4 します	to do	12-5 はしります	to run
4-4 べんきょう（を）します	to study	13-2 すわります	to sit
4-5 みます	to see; watch; look	13-2 たちます	to stand
4-5 かきます	to write	13-2 だします	to turn in
4-5 タイプ（を）します	to type	13-2 みせます	to show
6-4 ふとっています	is fat	13-2 あけます	to open
6-4 やせています	is thin	13-2 しめます	to close
6-4 としを　とっています	is old (age)	13-2 しずかにします	to quiet (down)
7-3 いきます	to go	13-2 いいます	to say
7-3 きます	to come	13-2 まちます	to wait
7-3 かえります	to return (place)	13-2 かいます	to buy
7-3 おきます	to get up; wake up	14-3 わすれます	to forget
7-3 ねます	to go to bed; sleep	14-3 (〜が)いります	need 〜
7-4 あるいて　いきます	to go on foot	14-3 かします	to lend
7-4 あるいて　きます	to come on foot	15-1 うたいます	to sing
7-4 あるいて　かえります	to return on foot	15-2 くれます	to give (me)
7-5 スポーツを　します	to play sports	15-2 もらいます	to receive, get
7-5 パーティー をします	to have a party	15-3 あげます	to give (to equal)
7-5 りょこう（を）します	to travel	15-3 やります	to give (to inferior)
7-5 かいもの（を）します	to shop	15-5 あそびます	to play (for fun)
7-5 しょくじ（を）します	to have a meal, dine	15-5 およぎます	to swim
7-5 でんわ（を）します	to make a phone call	15-5 ゲームをします	to play a game
		15-5 つくります	to make
		15-5 (しゃしんを)とります	to take (picture)

十課

Japanese 2 Verbs

[The numbers preceding each word indicate the lesson and section in which the word was introduced in *Adventures in Japanese 2.*]

2-1	Place で うまれる	G2	to be born in (place)
2-1	Place に すんで いる	G1	to be living in (place)
2-1	Place に つとめて いる	G2	to be employed at (place)
2-1	Place で はたらく	G1	to work at (place)
2-1	Place で アルバイト（を）する	IR	to work part-time at (place)
2-1	Person と けっこん（を）する	IR	to marry (a person)
2-1	もって いる	G1	to have
2-1	しっている	G1	to know
2-1	しらない	G1	do not know
2-1	ならう	G1	to learn
2-1	ホームステイを する	IR	to do a homestay
2-3	しょうかい（を）する	IR	to introduce
2-3	じこしょうかい（を）する	IR	to introduce oneself
2-4	ちがう	G1	to differ; is wrong
2-4	しつもん（を）する	IR	to ask a question
2-4	こたえる	G2	to answer
3-1	きる	G2	to wear [above the waist]
3-1	はく	G1	to wear [at or below the waist]
3-1	する	IR	to wear [accessories]
3-1	かぶる	G1	to wear [on the head]
3-1	かける	G2	to wear [glasses]
3-2	いけません	G2	won't do; must not do
3-2	かまいません	G1	I do not mind if . . .
3-2	たばこを すう	G1	to smoke cigarettes
3-2	ガムを かむ	G1	to chew gum
3-2	ごみを すてる	G2	to litter; throw away garbage
3-2	うんてん（を）する	IR	to drive
3-2	Person に あう	G1	to meet (a person)
3-2	Person に 聞く	G1	to ask (a person)
3-3	かりる	G2	to borrow
3-3	きを つける	G2	to be careful
3-4	Thing が 見える	G2	(Thing) can be seen
3-4	Thing が 聞こえる	G2	(Thing) can be heard
4-1	おしえる	G2	to teach
4-2	とまる	G1	to stop
4-2	まがる	G1	to turn
4-2	スピードを だす	G1	to speed

十課

318

4-2	しんぱいを　する	IR	to worry
4-3	Vehicle に　のる	G1	to ride (vehicle); to get on
4-3	Vehicle から／を　おりる	G2	to get off; to get out (vehicle)
4-3	シートベルトを　する	IR	to wear a seatbelt
4-3	出かける	G2	to go out
4-3	Place を　出る	G2	to leave (a place)
4-3	Place に　つく	G1	to arrive (at a place)
4-4	けんか（を）する	IR	to fight
5-1	Thing に　する	IR	to decide on (thing)
5-2	よやく（を）する	IR	to make a reservation
5-2	ちゅうもん（を）する	IR	to order
5-2	おく	G1	to put; leave
5-2	はらう	G1	to pay
5-3	ごちそう（を）する	IR	to treat someone
5-3	かえす	G1	to return (something)
6-1	かぜを　ひく	G1	to catch a cold
6-1	ひく	G1	to play (string instrument)
6-1	Thing が　出来る	G2	can do (thing)
6-2	（でんわを）かける	G2	to make a phone call
6-2	いらっしゃいます［いらっしゃる］	G1	to exist [polite equiv. of います]
6-2	まちがえる	G2	to make a mistake
6-2	かわりました［かわる］	G1	It's me. [lit., We've changed over.]
6-3	クラス／うんてんめんきょを　とる	G1	to take (a class); get (a driver's license)
6-3	おぼえる	G2	to memorize
7-1	おくる	G1	to send; mail
7-2	（あめ／ゆきが）ふる	G1	to (rain/snow) fall
7-3	そうじ（を）する	IR	to clean (house, room)
7-3	せんたく（を）する	IR	to do laundry
7-3	りょうり（を）する	IR	to cook
7-3	あらう	G1	to wash
7-3	てつだう	G1	to help
7-3	ごみを　だす	G1	to take out the garbage
9-1	Person に　さしあげる	G2	to give (to a superior)
9-2	くらべる	G2	to compare
9-2	ちがう	G1	is different; is wrong
9-4	いれる	G2	to put in ～
9-4	かかる	G1	to require (tax); to take (time)
9-4	うる	G1	to sell
10-1	うんどう（を）する	IR	to exercise
10-1	（しあいに）出る	G2	to play (a game)
10-1	おうえん（を）する	IR	to cheer

十課

10-1	（〜が） はじまる	G1	(something) begins; starts
10-1	（〜が） おわる	G1	(something) finishes; ends
10-2	（Placeに） よる	G1	to stop by; drop by (a place)
10-2	（Person を） むかえに行く	G1	to go to pick up (a person)
10-2	（Person を） むかえに来る	IR	to come to pick up (a person)
10-2	（Person を） むかえにかえる	G1	to return to pick up (a person)
10-2	（Object を） とりに行く	G1	to go to pick up (an object)
10-2	（Object を） とりに来る	IR	to come to pick up (an object)
10-2	（Object を） とりにかえる	G1	to return to pick up (an object)
10-3	ゆうしょう （を） する	IR	to win a championship
10-4	ドキドキしている	IR	to be excited, be nervous
11-2	（Thing を） かくす	G1	to hide (a thing)
11-2	ふきとばす	G1	to blow away
11-2	（Thing が） うごく	G1	(thing) moves
11-2	Verb (TE) しまう	G1	to do 〜 completely
11-4	おもう	G1	to think
12-1	げきをする	IR	to give (put on) a (stage) play
12-1	〜に なる	G1	to become 〜
13-1	うかがう	G1	to ask; inquire [Polite equiv. of きく]
13-2	〜を わたる	G1	to cross; go over 〜
13-4	こんでいる	G1	to be crowded
13-4	すいている	G1	not to be crowded; is empty
14-2	きる	G1	to cut
14-2	あつくする	IR	to make hot; to heat
14-2	きれいにする	IR	to make clean; to clean
14-4	〜すぎる	G2	to exceed; too 〜
14-4	〜が 出来た	G2	〜 is ready; 〜 is done
14-4	（Object を） （Thing に） つける	G2	to dip (object) in (thing)
14-4	かたづける	G2	to clean up; put away
15-1	さんぽ （を） する	IR	to take a walk
15-1	わらう	G1	to smile; laugh
15-1	なく	G1	to cry
15-1	おこる	G1	to become angry
15-1	しかる	G1	to scold
15-1	りこん （を） する	IR	to divorce
15-3	たすける	G2	to rescue; help
15-4	かんしゃ （を） する	IR	to appreciate; thank
15-4	あいしている	G1	to love

Japanese 3 Verbs

[Arabic numerals preceding each word indicate the lesson in which the word was introduced in *Adventures in Japanese 3*.]

III-1	そつぎょうする	IR	to graduate
III-1	(Subject を)せんこうする	IR	to major in (a subject)
III-1	食べよう	G2	let's eat
III-1	かえる	G2	to change (something)
III-1	つかう	G1	to use
III-2	かよう	G1	to commute
III-2	りゅうがくする	IR	to study abroad
III-2	やる	G1	to do [informal form of する]
III-2	パーマをかける	IR	to perm (one's hair)
III-2	（お）けしょうをする	IR	to apply make-up
III-2	ぬぐ	G1	to remove clothing [i.e., shoes, dress, hat]
III-2	はきかえる	G2	to change [i.e., shoes, pants, etc.]
III-2	やめる	G2	to quit; discontinue
III-3	（はを）みがく	G1	to brush teeth
III-3	（シャワーを）あびる	G2	to take a shower
III-3	（ふろに）はいる	G1	to take a bath
III-3	はる	G1	to paste; glue; attach
III-3	うけとる	G1	to receive
III-3	せわをする	IR	to take care of
III-3	はっぴょうする	IR	to present; announce
III-3	（しけんを）うける	G2	to take (an exam)
III-3	そうだんする	IR	to consult
III-3	こまる	G1	to be troubled
III-3	（ペットを）かう	G1	to raise a pet
III-3	そんけいする	IR	to respect
III-4	まちがえる	G2	to make mistakes
III-4	（じしょを）ひく	G1	to look up a word (in a dictionary)
III-4	さがす	G1	to look for; search for
III-4	（〜が）見つかる	G1	(something) is found [intransitive]
III-4	（〜を）見つける	G2	to find (an object) [transitive]
III-4	Verb stem + はじめる	G2	to begin doing 〜
III-4	Verb stem + おわる	G1	to finish doing 〜
III-4	Verb stem + つづける	G2	to continue/keep doing 〜
III-4	しらべる	G2	to check; investigate
III-4	おもいだす	G1	to recall

十課

III-4	やくす	G1	to translate
III-4	はつおんする	IR	to pronounce
III-6	おどる	G1	to dance
III-6	（トランペットを）ふく	G1	to blow (a trumpet)
III-6	（ドラムを）たたく	G1	to beat (a drum)
III-6	（part of body を）している	G2	to have (part of body)
III-6	にんきがある	G1	to be popular
III-6	せいこうする	IR	to succeed
III-6	わかれる	G2	to separate
III-6	なくなる	G1	to pass away; die [polite form of しぬ]
III-6	たのしむ	G1	to enjoy
III-6	（〜と）つきあう	G1	to associate with 〜
III-7	けいけんする	IR	to experience
III-7	かける	G2	to hang
III-7	かざる	G1	to decorate
III-7	（〜が）こわれる	G2	(something) breaks [intransitive]
III-7	（〜を）こわす	G1	to break (object) [transitive]
III-7	なおす	G1	to fix
III-7	あがる	G1	to step up
III-7	おりる	G2	to go down
III-7	おちつく	G1	to become calm
III-7	せいざする	IR	to sit properly
III-7	たてる	G2	to build
III-8	つける	G2	to soak; dip
III-8	（〜て）おく	G1	to do (something in advance)
III-8	にる	G2	to boil (in broth); simmer
III-8	やく	G1	to grill; roast; bake; toast; fry
III-8	まるをする	IR	to circle
III-8	かける	G2	to pour over; sprinkle
III-8	いのる	G1	to pray
III-8	えんりょする	IR	to hesitate; be reserved
III-9	まいごになる	G1	to get lost

B. い Adjectives

Japanese 1 い Adjectives

あつい	hot	うつくしい	beautiful
さむい	cold	ひろい	spacious; wide
ずずしい	cool	せまい	narrow; small (space)
いい	good	ちかい	near
たかい	tall; high	とおい	far
ひくい	short (height); low	むずかしい	difficult
よい	good	やさしい	easy
わるい	bad	たのしい	fun, enjoyable
大きい	big	おもしろい	interesting
小さい	small	つまらない	boring; uninteresting
ながい	long	ひどい	terrible
みじかい	short (length)	うれしい	happy
あかい	red	かなしい	sad
しろい	white	おおい	many
くろい	black	すくない	few; a little
あおい	blue	(〜が)ほしい	want (something)
きいろい	yellow	いたい	sore; painful
ちゃいろい	brown	ねむい	sleepy
わかい	young	つよい	strong
きびしい	strict	よわい	weak
やさしい	kind; nice	たかい	expensive
きたない	dirty	やすい	cheap
かわいい	cute	おいしい	delicious; tasty
うるさい	noisy	まずい	not tasty
はやい	early	すごい	terrific; terrible
おそい	late	すばらしい	wonderful
いそがしい	busy	つめたい	cold (to the touch)
あたらしい	new	あたたかい	warm
ふるい	old (not for person's age)		

Japanese 2 い Adjectives

2-4	ただしい	correct; right	14-3	あまい	sweet
4-3	あぶない	dangerous	14-3	しおからい	salty
4-3	こわい	scary	14-3	からい	salty; spicy
11-1	あかるい	bright	14-3	すっぱい	sour
11-1	くらい	dark	14-4	きもちがわるい	unpleasant; uncomfortable
11-1	えらい	great (for people)	14-4	きもちがいい	pleasant; comfortable
14-2	うすい	thin (for objects)			
14-2	あつい （厚）	thick			

十課

Japanese 3 い Adjectives

3	つらい	hard; bitter; painful	8	くさい	smelly
4	V-stemやすい	easy to do ~	8	しかくい	square (shaped)
4	V-stemにくい	hard to do ~	8	まるい	round
5	さびしい	lonely	8	ふとい	thick (in width, size)
5	なつかしい	nostalgic	8	ほそい	thin; slender
5	うらやましい	envious	8	ほそながい	long and thin
7	おもい	heavy	8	かたい	hard; tough
7	かるい	light (in weight)	8	やわらかい	soft; tender
8	にがい	bitter	8	めずらしい	rare; unusual

Conjugation of い Adjectives

Function	Formal form	Informal form	Meaning
nonpast	あついです	あつい	is hot
neg. nonpast	あつくないです or あつくありません	あつくない	is not hot
past	あつかったです	あつかった	was hot
neg. past	あつくなかったです or あつくありませんでした	あつくなかった	was not hot
pre-noun	あつい　おちゃ		hot tea
conjunction	あつくて、おいしいです。		It is hot and tasty.

Conjugation of irregular い adjective: いい

Function	Formal form	Informal form	Meaning
nonpast	いいです	いい	is good
neg. nonpast	よくないです or よくありません	よくない	is not good
past	よかったです	よかった	was good
neg. past	よくなかったです or よくありませんでした	よくなかった	was not good
pre-noun	いい　ひと		good person
conjunction	あたまが　よくて、せが　たかいです。		He is smart and tall.

C. な Adjectives

Japanese 1 な Adjectives

げんき	healthy; fine	苦手〔にがて〕	be weak in
だめ	no good	きれい	pretty; clean; neat
好き	like	しずか	quiet
大好き	like very much; love	じゃま	is a hindrance; nuisance; is in my way
きらい	dislike		
大きらい	dislike a lot; hate	ゆうめい	famous
上手	skillful; be good at	大変〔たいへん〕	hard; difficult
下手	unskillful; be poor at	大丈夫〔だいじょうぶ〕	all right
とくい	be strong in; can do well	大事〔だいじ〕	important

Japanese 2 な Adjectives

3-2	じゆう	free; liberal	9-2	いろいろ	various
4-3	あんぜん	safe	11-1	びんぼう	poor
6-1	へん	strange; weird; unusual	15-2	ひま	free (time)

Japanese 3 な Adjectives

3	へいわ	peaceful	5	しあわせ	happy; fortunate
3	とくべつ	special	5	にぎやか	lively
3	らく	comfortable	7	とうようてき	Eastern style
4	かんたん	simple	7	せいようてき	Western style
4	ふくざつ	complicated	7	でんとうてき	traditional
4	めちゃくちゃ	messy; confusing; incorrect	8	けんこうてき	healthy

Conjugation of な Adjectives

Function	Formal form	Informal form	Meaning
nonpast	すきです	すきだ	like
neg. nonpast	すきではありません or すきじゃありません	すきではない or すきじゃない	do not like
past	すきでした	すきだった	liked
neg. past	すきではありませんでした or すきじゃありませんでした	すきではなかった or すきじゃなかった	did not like
pre-noun	すきなひと		person I like
conjoining	すきで、まいにち　たべます。		I like it and eat it every day.

III. Adverbs, question words, sentence interjectives, particles, clause particles, copula (plain form), dependent nouns, expressions, counters.

[The numbers preceding each word indicate the volume and lesson in which the word or expression was introduced.]

A. Adverbs

I-4	よく + Verb	well; often		II-7	ぜひ	by all means
I-4	すこし	a little		II-9	もっと	more
I-4	ちょっと	a little		II-9	ずっと	by far
I-4	ときどき	sometimes		II-9	りょう方〔ほう〕	both
I-4	たいてい	usually		II-9	一番	the most
I-4	いつも	always		II-10	そのころ	around that time
I-5	とても	very		II-11	ガリガリ	chew away; gnaw
I-5	まあまあ	so, so		II-11	いっしょうけんめい	with one's utmost effort
I-5	あまり + Neg.	(not) very		II-11	とうとう	finally; at last
I-5	ぜんぜん + Neg.	(not) at all		II-13	まっすぐ	straight
I-10	また	again		II-14	うすく	thin
I-10	たくさん	a lot; many		II-14	あつく	thick
I-10	すこし	a few; a little		II-14	はんぶんに	in half
I-12	はやく	early		II-14	まず	first of all
I-12	おそく	late		II-14	はじめに	at the beginning
I-14	もう + Positive	already		II-14	つぎに	next
I-14	まだ + Neg.	(not) yet		II-14	おわりに	at the end
I-14	ぜんぶ	everything		II-15	ニコニコ	smilingly
I-14	もう(いっぱい)	(one) more (cup)		II-15	ずっと	throughout; all the time
I-15	もうすぐ	very soon		II-15	たまに	occasionally; once in a while
II-2	まだ + Aff.	still		II-15	そのとき	at that time
II-2	もう + Neg.	(not) any more		III-2	ほとんど	almost; mostly
II-2	とくに	especially		III-3	ずいぶん	quite; fairly
II-3	ぜったい(に)	absolutely		III-4	なかなか + Neg.	(not) easily
II-3	本当〔ほんとう〕に	truly; really		III-4	さいきん	recently
II-4	はやく	fast; early		III-7	もし	if
II-4	きゅうに	suddenly		III-8	さいしょに	at first
II-4	けっして + Neg.	never		III-8	さいごに	at last; finally
II-5	だいたい	roughly		III-8	さいこうに	the most
II-5	ほかに	besides				
II-6	何度〔なんど〕も	many times				
II-6	もちろん	of course				

B. Interrogatives (Question Words)

I-1 なに, なん	what?	I-7 いつ	when?
I-2 なんまい	how many (sheets)?	I-7 なんじ	what time?
I-2 いくつ	how many (general things)?	I-7 なんぷん	how many minutes?
I-3 だれ	who?	I-11 なぜ, どうして	why?
I-3 なんにん	how many (people)?	I-13 (お)いくら	how much?
I-3 なんさい	how old?	I-13 どれ	which one?
I-3 (お)いくつ	how old?	I-13 どの〜	which ~ ?
I-3 なんねんせい	what grade?	I-13 いかが	how? [Formal]
I-3 どこ	where?	II-5 どちら？	which way? [Formal]
I-3 なにじん	what nationality?	II-6 どのぐらい？	how much? how long?
I-3 なんがつ	what month?	II-9 どっち？	which (one of two)? [Informal]
I-4 なにご	what language?	II-9 どちら？	which [one of two)? [Formal]
I-5 どんな〜	what kind of 〜 ?	II-9 どれ？	which one (of three or more)?
I-5 なにいろ	what color?	III-9 どうやって？	how? [Informal]
I-7 なんようび	what day of the week?		

C. Sentence Conjunctives and Interjectives

I-1 はい	Here. [In response to roll call.]	II-4 ううん	No [Informal]
I-1 はい or ええ	Yes	II-5 う〜ん	Yummm . . .
I-1 いいえ	No	II-9 さあ	Well . . .
I-2 ええと...	Let me see . . .	II-11 えっ	What?
I-2 あのう	Well . . .	II-11 いや（っ）	No [Stronger negation than いいえ.]
I-3 そして	And	II-11 だから	Therefore [Informal]
I-4 でも	But	II-11 ですから	Therefore [Formal]
I-6 それとも	Q1 or Q2?	II-13 ああ	Oh!
I-7 それから	And then	II-15 しかし	However [Formal equiv. of でも]
I-11 それに	Besides, moreover	III-3 たとえば	For example
I-14 これから	From now (on)		
I-14 じゃ、	Well then [informal]		
I-14 では、	Well then [formal]		
II-3 ところで	By the way		
II-4 うん	Yes [Informal]		

十課

D. Particles

I-1 は	Topic particle
I-1 Sentence + か。	Question-ending particle
I-1 Sentence + ねえ。	Sentence final particle expressing admiration, surprise or exclamation
I-3 の	Possessive and descriptive particle
I-3 と	and [Noun <u>and</u> Noun only]
I-3 も	also; too [replaces を, が, は]
I-4 で	at; in (place) [with action verb]
I-4 と （いっしょに）	(together) with
I-4 tool + で	by; with; on; in
I-6 Sentence + ね。	Sentence final particle for seeking agreement or confirmation
I-6 Sentence + よ。	Sentence final particle for emphasis or exclamation
I-7 specific time + に	at; on
I-7 place + へ／に	to [with direction verb]
I-7 activity + に	to; for (activity)
I-7 transportation + で	by [with direction verb]
I-10 Location + に + Existence Verb	in; at
I-11 ～から～まで	from ～ to ～
I-14 （ふたつ）で	for (two) [totalizing particle]
I-14 （フォーク）で	with; by; by means of
I-15 ～や～ （など）	～ and ～, etc.
II-2 ～について [P+V]	about ～
II-3 ～だけ	only
II-4 を	along; through
II-5 ～に～	～ and ～ (as a set)
II-6 S1+け(れ)ど、 S2.	Although; Though S1, S2.
II-6 Sentence+が	[Softens the statement.]
II-6 ～で	because of ～
II-6 に	per
II-6 も	as many/long as
II-9 AとBで	between A and B
II-9 ～より	more than ～
II-9 ～ほど + Neg.	(not) as ～ as
II-9 （～の中）で	among ～
II-10 (time) までに	by (a certain time)
II-11 「 」と	[Quotation particle]
III-1 N1 という N2 [P+V]	N2 called N1

[The numbers preceding each word indicate the volume and lesson in which the word or expression was introduced.]

III-1 〜しか + Neg. only; nothing but 〜

III-1 〜って [informal form of quotation particle と]

III-1 Sentence+の？ [female sentence ending particle]

III-1 Sentence + なの？ [female sentence ending particle]

III-1 Sentence + か？ [male informal sentence ending particle]

III-1 Sentence + かい？ [male informal sentence ending particle]

III-2 Sentence + かな。 I wonder if 〜. [used by male and female]

III-2 Sentence + かしら。 I wonder if 〜. [used by female]

III-2 N1 とか N2 N1 and N2 (among others)

III-2 〜として [P+V] as 〜; for 〜

III-6 〜によると [P+V+P] according to 〜

III-6 N1 のような N2 [P+N] N2 like N1

III-8 〜ばかり only 〜

E. Clause Particles

I-5 〜が、〜 〜, but 〜

I-11 〜から、〜 〜, so 〜

III-3 〜ので、 since 〜; because 〜

III-3 〜のに、 in spite of 〜; although 〜

III-3 〜し、 besides; what's more

III-3 〜て（から）、 after 〜

III-6 〜あいだに、 while 〜

III-6 (Verb stem form) ながら、 while 〜 (a person's simultaneous or concurrent actions]

III-6 (Verb dic. form) まえに、 before 〜

III-6 (Verb TA form) あとで、 after 〜

F. Copula (Plain form)

II-11 (Noun/なAdj.) だ [Plain form of です]

II-11 (Noun/なAdj.) だった [Plain form of でした]

III-1 (Noun/なAdj.) だろう probably is [Plain form of でしょう]

G. Sentence Ending

III-1 〜てくれ [male informal form of 〜て下さい]

III-3 〜てくださいます (superior) do 〜 for me

III-6 [Plain form +]そうだ I heard that 〜

十課

[The numbers preceding each word indicate the volume and lesson in which the word or expression was introduced.]

III-7 [Plain form +] かもしれない   might; may ～

III-8 [Plain form +] らしい   It seems that ～

III-8 [OO form +] と思っている   I am thinking of doing ～

H. Dependent Nouns (Suffixes)

I-1 ～せんせい	Mr./Mrs./Ms./Dr.
I-1 ～さん	Mr./Mrs./Ms.
I-3 ～がつうまれ	born in (month)
I-7 ～はん	half past ～
I-7 ～ころ、ごろ	about ～ (time)
I-7 ～まえ	before ～
I-7 ～すぎ	after ～
I-12 ～たち	[plural for animate objects]
I-13 ～くらい，ぐらい	about [not for specific time]
I-15 ～ねんうまれ	born in (year)
II-2 ～ちゃん	used instead of ～さん for small, cute children or animals
II-13 ～がわ	～ side
II-14 ～かた	how to ～
II-15 ～まえ	～ ago

I. Dependent Nouns (Suffixes)

I-2 この～	this ～
I-2 その～	that ～
I-2 あの～	that ～ over there
I-3 ご～	[polite]
I-3 お～	[polite]
II-10 あと～	～ more
II-11 ある～	a certain ～

J. Expressions

I-1	はじめまして。	How do you do?
I-1	どうぞよろしく。	Nice to meet you.
I-1	おはよう。	Good morning.
I-1	おはようございます。	Good morning. [Polite]
I-1	こんにちは。	Hello. Hi.
I-1	さようなら。	Good-bye.
I-1	はじめましょう。	Let's begin.
I-1	きりつ。	Stand. [used at ceremonies]
I-1	れい。	Bow. [used at ceremonies]
I-1	ちゃくせき。	Sit. [used at ceremonies]
I-1	（お）やすみです。	～ is absent.
I-1	ちこくです。	～ is tardy.
I-1	はやく。	Hurry!

十課

330

[The numbers preceding each word indicate the volume and lesson in which the word or expression was introduced.]

I-1	おわりましょう。	Let's finish.
I-1	すみません。もういちどおねがいします。	Excuse me. One more time please.
I-1	すみません。ゆっくりおねがいします。	Excuse me. Slowly please.
I-1	ちょっとまってください。	Please wait a minute.
I-1	どうもありがとうございます。	Thank you very much.
I-1	どういたしまして。	You are welcome.
I-1	はい、そうです。	Yes, it is.
I-1	いいえ、そうではありません。or いいえ、そうじゃありません。	No, it is not.
I-1	あついですねえ。	It's hot!
I-1	さむいですねえ。	It's cold!
I-1	すずしいですねえ。	It is cool!
I-1	そうですねえ。	Yes, it is!
I-1	おげんきですか。	How are you?
I-1	はい、げんきです。	Yes, I am fine.
I-2	わかりますか。	Do you understand?
I-2	しりません。	I do not know.
I-2	見えません。	I cannot see.
I-2	聞こえません。	I cannot hear.
I-2	Treeは　日本語で何と言いますか。	How do you say "tree" in Japanese?
I-2	～を　ください。	Please give me ~.
I-2	はい、どうぞ。	Here, please (take it).
I-3	そうですか。	Is that so?
I-3	～は？	How about ~?
I-5	そうですねえ...	Let me see . . .
I-7	こんばんは。	Good evening.
I-11	どうですか。	How is it?
I-11	それはいいですねえ。	How nice! [for a future event]
I-11	それはよかったですねえ。	How nice! [for a past event]
I-11	それはざんねんですねえ。	How disappointing! [for a future event]
I-11	それはざんねんでしたねえ。	How disappointing! [for a past event]
I-12	どうしましたか。	What happened?

十課

I-12 かわいそうに。	How pitiful! [to inferior]
I-12 がんばって。	Do your best. Good luck.
I-13 すわってください。	Please sit down.
I-13 たってください。	Please stand up.
I-13 だしてください。	Please turn (it) in.
I-13 みせてください。	Please show (it) to me.
I-13 まどをあけてください。	Please open the window.
I-13 ドアをしめてください。	Please close the door.
I-13 しずかにしてください。	Please be quiet.
I-13 もういちど言ってください。	Please say it one more time.
I-13 ちょっと待ってください。	Please wait a minute.
I-13 すみません。	Excuse me. [to get attention]
I-13 いくらですか。	How much is it?
I-13 いかがですか。	How is it? [polite]
I-13 わあ！	Wow!
I-14 おなかがすきました／ペコペコです。	I am hungry.
I-14 のどがかわきました／カラカラです。	I am thirsty.
I-14 いいえ、まだです。	No, not yet.
I-14 いいえ、けっこうです。	No, thank you.
I-14 ～を　かしてください。	Please lend me ～.
I-14 いただきます。	[expression before meal]
I-14 ごちそうさま。	[expression after meal]
I-14 おなかがいっぱいです。	I am full.
I-14 じゃ、またあとで。	Well then, see you later.
I-14 バイバイ。	Bye-bye.
I-15 (お)たんじょうびおめでとう(ございます)。	Happy Birthday!
I-15 おめでとう(ございます)。	Congratulations!
I-15 (～を)たのしみにしています。	I am looking forward to (something).
I-15 はい、チーズ。	Say "cheese."
I-15 はい、ピース。	Say "peace."
II-5 いらっしゃいませ。	Welcome.
II-5 どうぞ　こちらへ。	This way, please.
II-5 ほかに　何か。	Anything else?
II-5 それだけです。	That is all.
II-5 すみません。	Excuse me.

II-6	ぐあいが　わるいです。	I don't feel well.
II-6	ストレスが　いっぱいです。	I am stressed.
II-6	（お）きのどくに。	I'm sorry. [Sympathy]
II-6	もしもし	Hello. [Telephone]
II-6	るすです。	No one is at home.
II-6	はなし中 [ちゅう]です。	The line is busy.
II-6	しかたが　ありません。	It can't be helped.
II-7	あけまして　おめでとうございます。	Happy New Year!
II-9	お好きですか。	Do you like it? [Polite expression of 好きですか]
II-9	何を　さしあげましょうか。	May I help you? [lit., What shall I give you?]
II-9	ありがとうございました。	Thank you very much. [Used after a deed has been done]
II-9	また　どうぞ。	Please come again.
II-10	それは　いいかんがえです。	That's a good idea.
II-10	うそです（よ）。	It is a lie (you know).
II-10	うそでしょう？	Are you kidding? Are you serious?
II-10	じょうだんです（よ）。	It's a joke (you know). I'm just kidding.
II-10	やったあ！	We did it!
II-10	ばんざい！	Hurray!
II-10	かった！　かった！	(We) won! (We) won!
II-11	とんでもない（です）。	How ridiculous! That's impossible!
II-11	なるほど。	Indeed! I see!
II-13	あのう...　ちょっとうかがいますが...	Excuse me . . . I have a question.
II-13	どのぐらい　かかりますか。	How long does it take? [time]
II-13	どのぐらい　ありますか。	How far is it? [distance]
II-14	〜が　出来ました。	〜 is ready. 〜 is done.
III-1	こちらこそ。	It is I, not you. [emphasis]
III-1	いってきます	[Used by a family member who leaves home for the day.]
III-1	いってらっしゃい。	[Used by a family member who sends off another family　member for the day.]
III-1	ただいま。	I'm home. [Used by a family member who has come home.]
III-1	お帰りなさい。	Welcome home. [Used by a family member who welcome another family member home.]
III-1	おやすみ（なさい）。	Good night.
III-1	おさきに。	Excuse me for going/doing something first.
III-1	しつれいします。	Excuse me, I must be going now. [Used when one must leave a place. lit., I will be rude.]
III-1	しつれいしました。	I am sorry to have inconvenienced you, or for a rude act I have committed.
III-3	どうしたら、いいですか。	What should I do?
III-3	おひさしぶりです。	I have not seen you for a long time.

十課

[The numbers preceding each word indicate the volume and lesson in which the word or expression was introduced.]

III-3	おかげさまで。	Thanks to you . . .
III-3	おせわになりました。	Thank you for your kind help.
III-4	どういういみですか。	What does it mean?
III-4	〜といういみです。	It means 〜.
III-8	かんぱい。	Cheers!
III-8	ごえんりょなく、どうぞ。	Without reservation/hesitation, please.
III-8	おかわりは？	Will you have seconds?
III-8	〜をとってください。	Excuse me. Please pass me 〜.

K. Proverbs

I-5	じゅうにんといろ＜十人十色＞	Ten men, ten colors.
I-10	かえるの子はかえる	A frog's child is a frog.
I-10	ねこにこばん	To give a gold coin to a cat.
I-10	さるも木からおちる	Even monkeys fall from trees.
I-11	みっかぼうず	A three days monk.
I-12	ばかにつけるくすりはない	There is no medicine for stupidity.
II-2	いしのうえにもさんねん	Sitting on a stone for as long as three years makes anything possible.
II-2	となりのはなはあかい	Flowers next door are red.
II-9	はなよりだんご	Sweet rice dumplings rather than flowers.
II-10	まけるがかち	Defeat is a win.
II-15	うみよりふかい母のあい	Mother's love is deeper than the ocean.
III-1	ちりもつもれば山となる	Dust amassed will make a mountain.
III-2	二度あることは三度ある	If something happens twice, it will happen three times.
III-7	ごうにいれば、ごうにしたがえ	When in a village, follow do as the villagers do. (When in Rome, do as the Romans do.)
III-8	いっせきにちょう	Killing two birds with one stone.

L. Counters

[The numbers in the upper right corner indicate the volume and lesson in which the counter was introduced.]

	II-5	II-5 %	II-9 Floors			
1	いっこ	いっパーセント	いっかい	いちまい	ひとつ	ひとり
2	にこ	にパーセント	にかい	にまい	ふたつ	ふたり
3	さんこ	さんパーセント	さんがい	さんまい	みっつ	さんにん
4	よんこ	よんパーセント	よんかい	よんまい	よっつ	よにん
5	ごこ	ごパーセント	ごかい	ごまい	いつつ	ごにん
6	ろっこ	ろくパーセント	ろっかい	ろくまい	むっつ	ろくにん
7	ななこ	ななパーセント	ななかい	ななまい	ななつ	ななにん
8	はっこ	はっパーセント	はっかい	はちまい	やっつ	はちにん
9	きゅうこ	きゅうパーセント	きゅうかい	きゅうまい	ここのつ	きゅうにん
10	じ(ゅ)っこ	じ(ゅ)っパーセント	じ(ゅ)っかい	じゅうまい	とお	じゅうにん
?	なんこ？	なんパーセント？	なんがい？	なんまい？	いくつ？	なんにん？

	Age I-3	Months I-3	Grade I-3	Hours I-7	Minutes I-7	Points II-10
1	いっさい	いちがつ	いちねんせい	いちじ	いっぷん	いってん
2	にさい	にがつ	にねんせい	にじ	にふん	にてん
3	さんさい	さんがつ	さんねんせい	さんじ	さんぷん	さんてん
4	よんさい	しがつ	よねんせい	よじ	よんふん	よんてん
5	ごさい	ごがつ		ごじ	ごふん	ごてん
6	ろくさい	ろくがつ		ろくじ	ろっぷん	ろくてん
7	ななさい	しちがつ		ななじ	ななふん	ななてん
8	はっさい	はちがつ		はちじ	はっぷん	はってん
9	きゅうさい	くがつ		くじ	きゅうふん	きゅうてん
10	じ(ゅ)っさい	じゅうがつ		じゅうじ	じ(ゅ)っぷん	じ(ゅ)ってん
11		じゅういちがつ		じゅういちじ		
12	20 はたち	じゅうにがつ		じゅうにじ		
?	なんさい？	なんがつ？	なんねんせい？	なんじ？	なんぷん？	なんてん？

335

[The numbers in the upper right corner indicate the volume and lesson in which the counter was introduced.]

	Degree(s); time(s) 〜ど II-6	No. of minute(s) 〜分（間） II-6	No. of hour(s) 〜時間 II-6	No. of day(s) 〜日（間） II-6
1	いちど	いっぷん（かん）	いちじかん	いちにち
2	にど	にふん（かん）	にじかん	ふつか（かん）
3	さんど	さんぷん（かん）	さんじかん	みっか（かん）
4	よんど	よんふん（かん）	よじかん	よっか（かん）
5	ごど	ごふん（かん）	ごじかん	いつか（かん）
6	ろくど	ろっぷん（かん）	ろくじかん	むいか（かん）
7	ななど	ななふん（かん）	ななじかん	なのか（かん）
8	はちど	はっぷん（かん）	はちじかん	ようか（かん）
9	きゅうど	きゅうふん（かん）	くじかん	ここのか（かん）
10	じゅうど	じ（ゅ）っぷん（かん）	じゅうかん	とおか（かん）
?	なんど？	なんぷん（かん）？	なんじかん？	なんにち（かん）？

	No. of week(s) 〜週間 II-6	No. of month(s) 〜か月 II-6	No. of year(s) 〜年（間） II-6	No. 〜 〜ばん II-10
1	いっしゅうかん	いっかげつ	いちねん（かん）	いちばん
2	にしゅうかん	にかげつ	にねん（かん）	にばん
3	さんしゅうかん	さんかげつ	さんねん（かん）	さんばん
4	よんしゅうかん	よんかげつ	よねん（かん）	よんばん
5	ごしゅうかん	ごかげつ	ごねん（かん）	ごばん
6	ろくしゅうかん	ろっかげつ	ろくねん（かん）	ろくばん
7	ななしゅうかん	ななかげつ	ななねん（かん）	ななばん
8	はっしゅうかん	はっかげつ	はちねん（かん）	はちばん
9	きゅうしゅうかん	きゅうかげつ	きゅうねん（かん）	きゅうばん
10	じ（ゅ）っしゅうかん	じ（ゅ）っかげつ	じゅうねん（かん）	じゅうばん
?	なんしゅうかん？	なんかげつ？	なんねん（かん）？	なんばん？

[The numbers in the upper right corner indicate the volume and lesson in which the counter was introduced.]

	rank ～い II-10	～stroke(s) ～かく III-3	～ time(s) ～かい III-4	～*tatami* ～じょう III-7
1	いちい	いっかく	いっかい	いちじょう
2	にい	にかく	にかい	にじょう
3	さんい	さんかく	さんかい	さんじょう
4	よい	よんかく	よんかい	よじょう
5	ごい	ごかく	ごかい	ごじょう
6	ろくい	ろっかく	ろっかい	ろくじょう
7	なない	ななかく	ななかい	ななじょう
8	はちい	はっかく	はっかい	はちじょう
9	きゅうい	きゅうかく	きゅうかい	きゅうじょう
10	じゅうい	じ(ゅ)っかく	じ(ゅ)っかい	じゅうじょう
?	なんい？	なんかく？	なんかい？	なんじょう？

漢字リスト

Hiragana is used for *KUN* (Japanese) readings and *katakana* for *ON* (Chinese) readings.

I-1 3課   ☆ Special reading   * Previously introduced.   * * For recognition only.

1. 一   one   ひと   一つ〔ひとつ〕one (general object)
                  イチ   一月〔いちがつ〕January
                  ☆   一日〔ついたち〕the first day of the month

2. 二   two   ふた   二つ〔ふたつ〕two (general objects)
                  ニ   二月〔にがつ〕February
                  ☆   二日〔ふつか〕the second day of the month

3. 三   three   みっ   三つ〔みっつ〕three (general objects)
                            三日〔みっか〕the third day of the month
                  サン   三月〔さんがつ〕March

4. 四   four   よ（っ）   四つ〔よっつ〕four (general objects)
                            四日〔よっか〕the fourth day of the month
                  よん   四本〔よんほん〕four (long objects)
                  シ   四月〔しがつ〕April

5. 五   five   いつ   五つ〔いつつ〕five (general objects)
                            五日〔いつか〕the fifth day of the month
                  ゴ   五月〔ごがつ〕May

I-1 4課

6. 六   six   むっ   六つ〔むっつ〕six (general objects)
                  ☆   六日〔むいか〕the sixth day of the month
                  ロク   六月〔ろくがつ〕June

7. 七   seven   なな   七つ〔ななつ〕seven (general objects)
                  なの   七日〔なのか〕the seventh day of the month

漢字   338

		シチ	七月 〔しちがつ〕 July
8.	八 eight	やっ	八つ 〔やっつ〕 eight (general objects)
		よう	八日 〔ようか〕 the eighth day of the month
		ハチ	八月 〔はちがつ〕 August
9.	九 nine	ここの	九つ 〔ここのつ〕 nine (general objects)
			九日 〔ここのか〕 the ninth of the month
		キュウ	九十 〔きゅうじゅう〕 90
		ク	九月 〔くがつ〕 September
10.	十 10	とお	十日 〔とおか〕 the 10th day of the month
		ジュウ	十月 〔じゅうがつ〕 October

I-15課

11.	月 moon	ガツ	一月 〔いちがつ〕 January
		ゲツ	月曜日 〔げつようび〕 Monday
12.	日 sun; day	ひ	その日 〔ひ〕 that day
		び	月曜日 〔げつようび〕 Monday
		か	十四日 〔じゅうよっか〕 the 14th of the month
		ニチ	日曜日 〔にちようび〕 Sunday
13.	火 fire	カ	火曜日 〔かようび〕 Tuesday
14.	水 water	みず	お水 〔みず〕 water
		スイ	水曜日 〔すいようび〕 Wednesday
15.	木 tree	き	おおきい木 a big tree
		モク	木曜日 〔もくようび〕 Thursday
16.	金 gold	かね	お金 money
		キン	金曜日 〔きんようび〕 Friday
17.	土 soil	ド	土曜日 〔どようび〕 Saturday

18. 口 mouth くち, ぐち

19. 目 eye め

20. 人 person ひと あの人 that person

ニン 三人〔さんにん〕 three people

ジン アメリカ人 American

☆ 一人〔ひとり〕 one (person)

二人〔ふたり〕 two (persons)

21. 本 origin; book もと 山本〔やまもと〕さん

中本〔なかもと〕さん

川本〔かわもと〕さん

木本〔きもと〕さん

ホン 本をよむ to read a book

日本〔にほん or にっぽん〕Japan

ポン 一本〔いっぽん〕 one (long object)

ボン 三本〔さんぼん〕 three (long objects)

22. 今 now いま 今、一時です。It's now 1 o'clock.

今田〔いまだ〕さん

コン 今月〔こんげつ〕 this month

今週〔こんしゅう〕 this week

☆ 今日〔きょう〕 today

今年〔ことし〕 this year

23. 年 year とし 今年〔ことし〕 this year

毎年〔まいとし〕 every year

ネン 毎年〔まいねん〕 every year

来年〔らいねん〕 next year

去年 〔きょねん〕 last year

一年 〔いちねん〕 one year

四年生 〔よねんせい〕 fourth grader

二〇〇三年 〔にせんさんねん〕 the year 2003

24. 私　I; me　　　わたし　　　私は　中本です。I am Nakamoto.

わたくし

25. 曜　day of the week　よう　　日曜日 〔にちようび〕 Sunday

月曜日 〔げつようび〕 Monday

火曜日 〔かようび〕 Tuesday

水曜日 〔すいようび〕 Wednesday

木曜日 〔もくようび〕 Thursday

金曜日 〔きんようび〕 Friday

土曜日 〔どようび〕 Saturday

何曜日 〔なんようび〕 What day of the week?

Ⅱ-3課

26. 上　above　　　うえ　　　上田 〔うえだ〕 さん

目上 〔めうえ〕 の人 superiors

27. 下　under　　　した　　　木下 〔きのした〕 さん

くだ　　　食べて下さい。Please eat.

28. 大　big　　　　おお　　　大きい人 a big person

大下 〔おおした〕 さん

大月 〔おおつき〕 さん

タイ　　　大変 〔たいへん〕 hard; difficult; very

ダイ　　　大学 〔だいがく〕 college

大好き to like very much

29. 小　small　　　ちい(さい)　小さい人 a small person

341

漢字

		ショウ	小学生 〔がくせい〕 elementary school student
			小学校 〔がっこう〕 elementary school
30.	夕 early evening	ゆう	夕方 〔がた〕 late afternoon, early evening
31.	何 what	なに	何人 〔なにじん〕 What nationality?
		なん	何人 〔なんにん〕 How many people?
			何月 〔なんがつ〕 What month?
			何曜日 〔なんようび〕 What day of the week?
			何日 〔なんにち〕 What day of the month?
32.	中 inside; middle	なか	中本 〔なかもと〕 さん
			中口 〔なかぐち〕 さん
			今中 〔いまなか〕 さん
		チュウ	中学 〔ちゅうがく〕 junior high school
			中学生 〔ちゅうがくせい〕 junior high school student
			中国 〔ちゅうごく〕 China
			中国人 〔ちゅうごくじん〕 Chinese person
33.	外 outside	そと	家の外 〔いえ〕 outside the house
		ガイ	外国 〔がいこく〕 foreign country
			外国人 〔がいこくじん〕 foreigner
			外国語 〔がいこくご〕 foreign language

Ⅱ-4課

34.	行 go	い（く）	行きます to go
		コウ	旅行 〔りょこう〕 します to travel
			銀行 〔ぎんこう〕 bank
35.	来 come	き（ます）	来て下さい。 Please come.
			よく出来ました。 〔て〕 He/she/they did well.

漢字

		く（る）	来る to come
		こ（ない）	来ないで下さい。 Please do not come.
		ライ	来年〔らいねん〕 next year
			来月〔らいげつ〕 next month
			来週〔らいしゅう〕 next week
36.	子 child	こ	子ども child
37.	車 vehicle	くるま	車にのる to ride in a car
		シャ	自動車 car
			自転車 bicycle
			電車 electric train
			外車〔がいしゃ〕 foreign car
38.	学 study	ガク	学生〔がくせい〕 college student
			小学生〔しょうがくせい〕 elementary school student
			中学生〔ちゅうがくせい〕 junior high school student
			大学〔だいがく〕 college
		ガッ	学校〔がっこう〕 school
39.	校 school	コウ	学校〔がっこう〕 school
			中学校〔ちゅうがっこう〕 junior high school
			小学校〔しょうがっこう〕 elementary school
			高校〔こうこう〕 high school
			高校生〔こうこうせい〕 high school student
40.	見 look; see	み（る）	見ます to look
41.	良 is good	よい	良くないです is not good
42.	食 eat	た（べる）	食べましょう。 Let's eat.
		ショク	食事をします to have a meal
			夕食〔ゆうしょく〕 supper

漢字

外食〔がいしょく〕eating out

43. 川　river　　　かわ　　　　川口〔かわぐち〕さん

　　　　　　　　　　がわ　　　　小川〔おがわ〕さん

44. 山　mountain　　やま　　　　山口〔やまぐち〕さん

　　　　　　　　　　　　　　　　山本〔やまもと〕さん

　　　　　　　　　　　　　　　　大山〔おおやま〕さん

　　　　　　　　　　　　　　　　小山〔こやま〕さん

　　　　　　　　　　　　　　　　中山〔なかやま〕さん

　　　　　　　　　　　　　　　　山下〔やました〕さん

　　　　　　　　　　サン　　　　富士山〔ふじさん or ふじやま〕Mt. Fuji

45. 出　go out　　　で（る）　　出かけます to leave

　　　　　　　　　　　　　　　　出て下さい。Please go out.

　　　　　　　　　　　　　　　　よく出来ました。　He/she/they did well.

　　　　　　　　　　　　　　　　出口〔でぐち〕exit

　　　　　　　　　　だ（す）　　出して下さい。Please turn it in.

　　　　　　　　　　　　　　　　スピードを出す to speed up

46. 先　first; previous　セン　　先生 teacher

　　　　　　　　　　　　　　　　先月〔せんげつ〕last month

　　　　　　　　　　　　　　　　先週 last week

47. 生　be born　　　う（まれる）生まれました was born

　　　person　　　　セイ　　　　先生〔せんせい〕teacher

　　　　　　　　　　　　　　　　学生〔がくせい〕college student

　　　　　　　　　　　　　　　　生徒〔せいと〕K-12 student

48. 父　father　　　ちち　　　　父 one's own father

　　　　　　　　　　とう　　　　お父さん someone else's father

漢字
344

49. 母	mother	はは	母 one's own mother
		かあ	お母さん someone else's mother
50. 毎	every	マイ	毎日 every day
			毎月 〔まいつき〕 every month
			毎年 〔まいねん or まいとし〕 every year
			毎週 every week
			毎食 〔まいしょく〕 every meal
51. 書	write	か（く）	書いて下さい。 Please write.
	writing	ショ	教科書 textbook
			辞書 dictionary
			図書館 library
			書道 calligraphy

II - 6課

52. 手	hand	て	右手 right hand
			左手 left hand
			苦手 is weak at
		☆	上手 〔じょうず〕 skillful
			下手 〔へた〕 unskillful
53. 耳	ear	みみ	右耳 right ear
			左耳 left ear
			小さい耳 small ears
54. 門	gate	モン	学校 〔がっこう〕 の門 school gate
			家の門 gateway to a house
55. 聞	listen; hear	き（く）	聞きます to listen; hear; ask
		ブン	新聞 newspaper
56. 女	female	おんな	女の人 〔おんなのひと〕 woman; lady

女の子 〔おんなのこ〕 girl

女の学生 〔おんなのがくせい〕 female student

57. 好 like　　　す（き）　　　大好〔だいす〕き like very much

58. 田 rice field　　た　　　田中〔たなか〕さん

中田〔なかた〕さん

田口〔たぐち〕さん

だ　　　金田〔かねだ〕さん

山田〔やまだ〕さん

上田〔うえだ〕さん

59. 男 male　　　おとこ　　　男の人 man

男の子 boy

男の学生 〔がくせい〕 male student

II - 7 課

60. 言 say　　　い（う）　　　もう一度言って下さい。 Please say it again.

61. 語 language　　ゴ　　　日本語〔にほんご〕 Japanese language

英語〔えいご〕 English language

外国語〔がいこくご〕 foreign language

中国語〔ちゅうごくご〕 Chinese language

何語〔なにご〕 What language?

語学〔ごがく〕 language study

62. 寺 temple　　てら　　　寺に行く to go to the temple

寺田〔てらだ〕さん

寺山〔てらやま〕さん

寺本〔てらもと〕さん

でら　　　山寺〔やまでら〕 temple in the mountains

ジ　　　本願寺〔ほんがんじ〕 Honganji Temple

漢字　　　346

63. 時 time; o'clock とき 時々〔ときどき〕sometimes

ジ 何時〔なんじ〕What time?

一時間〔いちじかん〕one hour

64. 間 between; あいだ 学校〔がっこう〕と家〔いえ〕の間

among; between school and my house.

interval カン 時間〔じかん〕time

一時間〔いちじかん〕one hour

65. 分 minute わ(かる) 分かりません。I do not understand.

フン 二分〔にふん〕two minutes

プン 六分〔ろっぷん〕six minutes

ブン 半分〔はんぶん〕a half

66. 正 correct ただ（しい） 正しいです is correct

ショウ お正月〔しょうがつ〕New Year

正田〔しょうだ〕さん

67. 家 house いえ 大きい家 a big house

カ 家族 family

68. 々 [pluralizer] 時々〔ときどき〕sometimes

木々〔きぎ〕trees

山々〔やまやま〕mountains

日々〔ひび〕days

人々〔ひとびと〕people

家々〔いえいえ〕houses

Ⅱ-9課

69. 白 white しろ 白いシャツ a white shirt

白木屋〔しろきや〕Shirokiya Department Store

ハク 白人〔はくじん〕Caucasian

70.	百	hundred	ヒャク	百人 〔ひゃくにん〕 100 people
			ビャク	三百 〔さんびゃく〕 300
			ピャク	六百 〔ろっぴゃく〕 600
				八百 〔はっぴゃく〕 800
71.	千	thousand	セン	二千 〔にせん〕 2,000
				八千 〔はっせん〕 8,000
			ゼン	三千 〔さんぜん〕 3,000
72.	万	ten thousand	マン	一万 〔いちまん〕 10,000
				十万 〔じゅうまん〕 100,000
				百万 〔ひゃくまん〕 one million
73.	方	person [polite]	かた	あの方 that person [polite]
		alternative	ホウ	この方が好きです。 I like this better.
				両方 〔りょうほう〕 both
74.	玉	ball; coin	たま	玉田 〔たまだ〕 さん
				玉川 〔たまかわ〕 さん
				玉城 〔たましろ〕 さん
			だま	お年玉 〔としだま〕 New Year's monetary gift
				十円玉 〔じゅうえんだま〕 10 yen coin
				目玉 〔めだま〕 eyeball
75.	国	country	くに, ぐに	どこの国 Which country?
				国本 〔くにもと〕 さん
			コク, ゴク	外国 〔がいこく〕 foreign country
				韓国 〔かんこく〕 Korea
				中国 〔ちゅうごく〕 China
76.	安	cheap	やす (い)	安い本 a cheap book
				安田 〔やすだ〕 さん

77. 高　expensive;　たか（い）　高い家〔たかいいえ〕an expensive house

　　　high　　　　　　　　　　　高田〔たかた/たかだ〕さん

　　　　　　　　　　　　　　　　高山〔たかやま〕さん

　　　　　　　　　　　　　　　　高木〔たかき/たかぎ〕さん

　　　　　　　コウ　　　　　　　高校〔こうこう〕high school

　　　　　　　　　　　　　　　　高校生〔こうこうせい〕high school student

II-10課

78. 牛　cow　　　うし　　　牛がいる。There are cows.

　　　　　　　ギュウ　　　　　　牛肉〔ぎゅうにく〕beef

　　　　　　　　　　　　　　　　牛乳〔ぎゅうにゅう〕milk (cow)

79. 半　half　　　ハン　　　　　半分〔はんぶん〕a half

　　　　　　　　　　　　　　　　五時半〔ごじはん〕5:30 (time)

*3. 手　hand　　　て *　　　　　大きい手 big hands

　　　　　　　シュ　　　　　　　バスケット選手 basketball player

　　　　　　　☆*　　　　　　　上手〔じょうず〕skillful

　　　　　　　　　　　　　　　　下手〔へた〕unskillful

80. 友　friend　　とも　　　　　友達〔ともだち〕friend

　　　　　　　　　　　　　　　　友子〔ともこ〕さん

81. 帰　return　　かえ（る）　　家〔いえ〕へ帰る return home

82. 待　wait　　　ま（つ）　　　待って下さい。Please wait.

83. 持　have; hold　も（つ）　　持っています。I have it.

84. 米　rice　　　こめ　　　　　米を買う to buy rice

　　　　　　　　　　　　　　　　米屋 rice shop

85. 番　number　　バン　　　　　一番〔いちばん〕No. 1

86. 事　matter　　こと　　　　　どんな事 What kind of things?

　　　　　　　ごと　　　　　　　仕事〔しごと〕job

漢字

		ジ	食事〔しょくじ〕meal
			大事〔だいじ〕important
			事務所〔じむしょ〕office

87.	雨	rain	あめ	雨がふっています。 It is raining.
88.	電	electricity	デン	電話 telephone
				電気 electricity
				電車〔でんしゃ〕electric train
89.	天	heaven	テン	天ぷら *tenpura*
				天どん *tenpura donburi*
90.	気	spirit	キ	天気〔てんき〕weather
				病気 illness
				合気道 *aikido*
				お気の毒に。 I'm sorry. [sympathy]
91.	会	meet	あ（う）	会いましょう。 Let's meet.
			カイ	会社〔かいしゃ〕company
				社会〔しゃかい〕social studies; society
				教会〔きょうかい〕church
92.	話	talk	はな（す）	話して下さい。 Please speak.
			はなし	お話 story
			ばなし	昔話〔むかしばなし〕folk tale
			ワ	電話〔でんわ〕telephone
				会話〔かいわ〕conversation
93.	売	sell	う（る）	売っていますか。 Are they selling?
94.	読	read	よ（む）	本を読む to read a book

漢字

95. 右　right　　　　みぎ　　　右手〔みぎて〕right hand

　　　　　　　　　　　　　　　　右目〔みぎめ〕right eye

　　　　　　　　　　　　　　　　右耳〔みぎみみ〕left ear

　　　　　　　　　　　　　　　　右田〔みぎた〕さん

96. 左　left　　　　　ひだり　　左手〔ひだりて〕left hand

　　　　　　　　　　　　　　　　左目〔ひだりめ〕left eye

　　　　　　　　　　　　　　　　左耳〔ひだりみみ〕left ear

97. 入　put in　　　　い（れる）　入れて下さい。Please put it in.

　　　enter　　　　　はい（る）　入って下さい。Please enter.

　　　　　　　　　　いり　　　　入口〔いりぐち〕entrance

98. 物　thing　　　　もの　　　　食べ物〔たべもの〕food

　　　　　　　　　　　　　　　　飲み物 a drink

　　　　　　　　　　　　　　　　建物 building

　　　　　　　　　　　　　　　　着物 kimono (things to wear)

　　　　　　　　　　　　　　　　買い物 shopping

　　　　　　　　　　　　　　　　読み物〔よみもの〕things to read

　　　　　　　　　　ブツ　　　　動物 animal

　　　　　　　　　　　　　　　　動物園 zoo

99. 名　name　　　　な　　　　　名前 name

　　　　　　　　　　メイ　　　　有名〔ゆうめい〕famous

100. 前　front; before　まえ　　　名前〔なまえ〕name

　　　　　　　　　　　　　　　　家の前〔いえのまえ〕front of the house

　　　　　　　　　　　　　　　　前田〔まえだ〕さん

　　　　　　　　　　　　　　　　前川〔まえかわ〕さん

　　　　　　　　　　ゼン　　　　午前〔ごぜん〕a. m.

101. 戸　door　　　　と　　　　　　　戸を閉めて下さい。Please close the door.

戸田〔とだ〕さん

戸口〔とぐち〕さん

戸川〔とがわ〕さん

ど　　　　　　　木戸〔きど〕さん

102. 所　place　　　ところ　　　　しずかな所 a quiet place

どころ　　　　田所〔たどころ〕さん

ショ　　　　　住所〔じゅうしょ〕address

事務所〔じむしょ〕office

103. 近　near　　　ちか（い）　　近い所〔ところ〕a nearby place

川近〔かわちか〕さん

II-14課

104. 立　stand　　　た（つ）　　　立って下さい。Please stand.

リツ　　　　　起立〔きりつ〕Stand up.

105. 作　make　　　つく（る）　　作って下さい。Please make (it).

サク　　　　　作文 composition

作田〔さくだ〕さん

作本〔さくもと〕さん

106. 肉　meat　　　にく　　　　　肉を食べる〔にくをたべる〕to eat meat

牛肉〔ぎゅうにく〕beef

豚肉〔ぶたにく〕pork

鳥肉〔とりにく〕chicken

焼き肉〔やきにく〕yakiniku

筋肉〔きんにく〕muscle

107. 魚　fish　　　さかな

108. 多　many　　　おお（い）　　人が多いです。There are many people.

			タ	多分〔たぶん〕probably
109.	少	few	すく（ない）	人が少ないです。There are few people.
			すこ（し）	少し食べました。I ate a little.
110.	古	old	ふる（い）	古い車〔くるま〕old car
				古川〔ふるかわ〕さん
				古本〔ふるもと〕さん
				古田〔ふるた〕さん
111.	新	new	あたら（しい）	新しい本〔ほん〕a new book
			シン	新聞〔しんぶん〕newspaper
				新幹線〔しんかんせん〕bullet train
*47.	生	be born	う（まれる）	* 日本で生まれました。I was born in Japan.
			なま	生卵〔なまたまご〕raw egg
			セイ*	先生〔せんせい〕teacher
				学生〔がくせい〕college student

II-15課

112.	才	～years old	サイ	十六才〔じゅうろくさい〕16 years old
113.	心	heart; mind	こころ	心がきれいです good-hearted
			シン	心配しないで下さい。Please do not worry.
114.	思	think	おも（う）	いいと思います。I think it is good.
115.	休	rest; absent	やす（む）	学校を休んでいます is absent from school
				お休み holiday; day off
116.	買	buy	か（う）	買いたいです。I want to buy it.
				買い物〔かいもの〕shopping
117.	早	early	はや（い）	早い is early
				早見〔はやみ〕さん

漢字

早川〔はやかわ〕さん

118. 自　oneself　ジ　自分〔じぶん〕の車 one's own car
　　　　　　　　　　自動車〔じどうしゃ〕car
　　　　　　　　　　自転車〔じてんしゃ〕bicycle
　　　　　　　　　　自由〔じゆう〕free

119. 犬　dog　いぬ　白〔しろ〕い犬 a white dog

120. 太　fat　ふと（る）　太っています is fat

121. 屋　store　や　本屋〔ほんや〕bookstore
　　　　　　　　　　パン屋 bakery
　　　　　　　　　　白木屋〔しろきや〕Shirokiya Department Store
　　　　　　　　　　部屋〔へや〕room

[III-1課]

122. 漢　China　カンジ　漢字 Chinese characters

123. 字　character; writing　ジ　漢字〔かんじ〕Chinese characters

124. 姉　older sister　あね　姉の本 my older sister's book
　　　　　　　　　　ねえ　お姉さん (someone's) older sister

125. 妹　younger sister　いもうと　妹の名前 my younger sister's name
　　　　　　　　　　妹さん someone else's younger sister

126. 兄　older brother　あに　兄の車 my older brother's car
　　　　　　　　　　にい　お兄さん someone's older brother

127. 弟　younger brother　おとうと　弟の本 my younger brother's book
　　　　　　　　　　弟さん someone else's younger brother
　　　　　　　　　　☆　兄弟〔きょうだい〕siblings

128. 朝　morning　あさ　朝御飯〔あさごはん〕breakfast
　　　　　　　　　　毎朝〔まいあさ〕every morning
　　　　　　　　　　朝日新聞〔あさひしんぶん〕Asahi Newspaper

漢字　354

		チョウ	朝食〔ちょうしょく〕breakfast
		☆	今朝〔けさ〕this morning
129.	昼 daytime	ひる	昼御飯〔ひるごはん〕lunch
		チュウ	昼食〔ちゅうしょく〕lunch
130.	明 is bright	あか（るい）	明るい所〔あかるいところ〕a bright place
		☆	明日〔あした〕tomorrow
131.	去 past	キョ	去年〔きょねん〕 last year
132.	銀 silver	ギン	銀行〔ぎんこう〕bank
			銀のネックレス a silver necklace
133.	仕 to serve	シ	仕事〔しごと〕job
			仕方〔しかた〕がない It cannot be helped.
*48.	父 father	ちち*	父の仕事〔しごと〕my father's job
		とう*	お父さん someone else's father
		フ	祖父 my own grandfather
*49.	母 mother	はは*	母の名前〔なまえ〕my mother's name
		かあ*	お母さん someone else's mother
		ボ	祖母 my own grandmother
*46.	先 first, previous	セン*	先生〔せんせい〕teacher
			先月〔せんげつ〕last month
		さき	お先に。 Excuse me for going/doing something first.

**1.	家族	かぞく	family
**2.	友達	ともだち	friend
**3.	質問	しつもん	question
**4.	答え	こたえ	answer
**5.	宿題	しゅくだい	homework

355

漢字

＊＊ 6. 試験　　　しけん　　　exam

＊＊ 7. 昨日　　　きのう　　　yesterday

Ⅲ-2課

134. 公 public　　　コウ　　　公園 park

　　　　　　　　　　　　　　公立〔こうりつ〕public

135. 文 writing; composition ブン　　文化〔ぶんか〕culture

　　　　　　　　　　　　　　作文〔さくぶん〕composition

　　　　　　　　　　　　　　文学〔ぶんがく〕literature

136. 化 to take the form of　カ　　化学〔かがく〕chemistry

　　　　　　　　　　　　　　文化〔ぶんか〕culture

　　　　　　　　　　　ケ　　化粧する to apply make-up

137. 花 flower　　　はな　　　花屋〔はなや〕flower shop

138. 海 ocean; sea; beach　うみ　　海へ行く to go to the beach

　　　　　　　　　　　カイ　　海外〔かいがい〕overseas

　　　　　　　　　　　　　　日本海〔にほんかい〕Sea of Japan

139. 旅 travel　　　リョ　　　旅行〔りょこう〕travel

　　　　　　　　　　　　　　海外旅行〔かいがいりょこう〕overseas travel

　　　　　　　　　　　　　　修学旅行〔しゅうがくりょこう〕study tour

140. 教 to teach　　おし（える）　教えて下さい。 Please teach me.

　　　　　　　　　キョウ　　　教室 classroom

　　　　　　　　　　　　　　教科書〔きょうかしょ〕textbook

　　　　　　　　　　　　　　教会〔きょうかい〕church

　　　　　　　　　　　　　　キリスト教 Christianity

141. 室 room　　　シツ　　　教室〔きょうしつ〕classroom

142. 後 behind; after　うし（ろ）　車〔くるま〕の後ろ behind the car

　　　　　　　　　あと　　　学校の後で〔がっこうのあとで〕after school

漢字

356

		ゴ	午後 p. m.
			放課後 after school
143. 午	noon	ゴ	午前一時〔ごぜんいちじ〕 1:00 a. m.
			午後一時〔ごごいちじ〕 1:00 p. m.
144. 着	to wear	き（る）	シャツを着る to wear a shirt
			着物〔きもの〕 Japanese traditional *kimono*
	to arrive	つ（く）	学校に着く to arrive at school
145. 知	to get to know	し（る）	知りません。 I do not know.
*24. 私	I; private	わたし*	私は山本です。 I am Yamamoto.
		わたくし*	
		シ	私立〔しりつ or わたくしりつ〕 private
*59. 男	male	おとこ*	男の子〔おとこのこ〕 boy
			男の人〔おとこのひと〕 man
		ダン	男子〔だんし〕 boy
*56. 女	female	おんな*	女の子〔おんなのこ〕 girl
			女の人〔おんなのひと〕 woman; lady
		ジョ	女子〔じょし〕 girl
			男女共学〔だんじょきょうがく〕 co-educational
*36. 子	child	こ*	子供 child(ren)
		シ	男子〔だんし〕 boy
			女子〔じょし〕 girl
*97. 入	to enter	はい（る）*	入って下さい。 Please enter.
	to put in	い（れる）*	さとうを入れる to put sugar in
		いり*	入口〔いりぐち〕 entrance
		ニュウ	入学〔にゅうがく〕 to enter a school
*34. 行	to go	い（く）*	学校へ行く to go to school

漢字

		コウ＊	旅行〔りょこう〕 travel
		ギョウ	行事〔ぎょうじ〕 event
＊＊ 8.	生徒	せいと	student [non-college]
＊＊ 9.	問題	もんだい	problem
＊＊10.	教科書	きょうかしょ	textbook
＊＊11.	公園	こうえん	park
＊＊12.	一度	いちど	one time; once
＊＊13.	図書館	としょかん	library

Ⅲ-3課

146. 春 spring　　　はる　　　春休み〔はるやすみ〕 spring vacation

春子さん Haruko

147. 夏 summer　　　なつ　　　夏休み〔なつやすみ〕 summer vacation

夏時間〔なつじかん〕 summer time

148. 秋 autumn; fall　あき　　　秋山さん Mr. Akiyama

秋田さん Mr. Akita

秋中さん Mr. Akinaka

秋子さん Akiko (Japanese girl's name)

149. 冬 winter　　　ふゆ　　　冬休み〔ふゆやすみ〕 winter vacation

冬時間〔ふゆじかん〕 winter time

150. 雪 snow　　　ゆき　　　雪がふる to snow

151. 元 healthy　　ゲン　　　元気〔げんき〕 fine; be in a good health

152. 飲 to drink　の（む）　飲み物〔のみもの〕 a drink

153. 体 body　　　からだ　　　大きい体 a big body

タイ　　　体育 physical education

体育館 gym

154. 音 sound　　　おと　　　うるさい音 noisy sound

漢字　　　　　358

			オン	音楽 music
155.	楽	enjoyable	たの（しい）	楽しい is enjoyable
		comfortable	らく	楽ないす comfortable chair
			ガク	音楽〔おんがく〕 music
156.	糸	thread; string	いと	糸こんにゃく shredded *konnyaku*
157.	紙	paper	かみ	白い紙〔しろいかみ〕 white paper
			がみ	手紙〔てがみ〕 letter
*47.	生	be born	う（まれる）*	日本で生まれました。 I was born in Japan.
			なま*	生卵〔なまたまご〕 raw egg
		person	セイ*	先生〔せんせい〕 teacher
				学生〔がくせい〕 student
			ショウ	一生懸命〔いっしょうけんめい〕 utmost efforts
**14.	世話		せわ	care
**15.	生活		せいかつ	life; living
**16.	体育		たいいく	P.E.
**17.	様		さま	polite equivalent of -さん
**18.	変		へん	strange; weird; unusual
**19.	大変		たいへん	hard; difficult

Ⅲ-4課

158.	英	British;	エイ	英語〔えいご〕 English
		excellent		英国〔えいこく〕 England
				英文学〔えいぶんがく〕 British literature
159.	草	grass	くさ	みどりの草 green grass
160.	林	small forest	はやし	林さん
				林田〔はやしだ〕さん
			ばやし	小林〔こばやし〕さん

漢字

中林〔なかばやし〕さん

外林〔そとばやし〕さん

161. 森 forest　　もり　　森さん

森田〔もりた〕さん

小森〔こもり〕さん

大森〔おおもり〕さん

中森〔なかもり〕さん

森本〔もりもと〕さん

162. 台 counter　　タイ　　台湾〔たいわん〕 Taiwan

ダイ　　一台の車〔いちだいのくるま〕 one car

台所〔だいどころ〕 kitchen

163. 始 start; begin　　はじ（める）　　始める to begin

164. 終 end; finish　　お（わる）　　終わりましょう。 Let's finish.

165. 使 to use　　つか（う）　　車を使う to use a car

辞書の使い方〔じしょのつかいかた〕

166. 勉 to endeavor　　ベン　　勉強〔べんきょう〕 study

ガリ勉〔ガリべん〕 study fervently

167. 強 strong　　つよ（い）　　強いチーム a strong team

キョウ　　勉強〔べんきょう〕 study

168. 回 - time(s)　　カイ　　二回〔にかい〕 two times

169. 週 week　　シュウ　　今週〔こんしゅう〕 this week

先週〔せんしゅう〕 last week

来週〔らいしゅう〕 next week

毎週〔まいしゅう〕 every week

週末〔しゅうまつ〕 weekend

一週間〔いっしゅうかん〕 one week

漢字　　　　　360

*103. 近 near	ちか（い）*	学校〔がっこう〕に近い close to school
	キン	最近〔さいきん〕 recently
* 64. 間 between; among	あいだ*	学校〔がっこう〕と家〔いえ〕の間
		between school and my house
interval	カン*	時間〔じかん〕 time
	ま	間違える to make a mistake
**20. 本当	ほんとう	true; real
**21. 最近	さいきん	recent; recently
**22. 違う	ちがう	is different; is wrong
**23. 辞書	じしょ	dictionary
**24. ～君	～くん	[a suffix usually attached to boys' names]
**25. 週末	しゅうまつ	weekend

Ⅲ-6課

170. 映 reflection; projection	エイ	映画 movie
		映画館 movie theater
171. 画 picture	ガ	映画〔えいが〕 movie
		漫画〔まんが〕 cartoons, comics
stroke(s)	カク	この漢字は何画〔なんかく〕ですか。
		How many strokes is this *kanji*?
172. 歌 song; to sing	うた	歌を歌う to sing a song
	カ	歌手〔かしゅ〕 singer
		校歌〔こうか〕 school song
173. 晩 evening; night	ばん	今晩〔こんばん〕 tonight
		毎晩〔まいばん〕 every night
		晩ご飯〔ばんごはん〕 dinner
174. 夜 night	よる	夜 night

漢字

175.	黒	black	くろ	黒い髪の毛 black hair
				白黒映画〔しろくろえいが〕 black and white movie
			コク	黒人〔こくじん〕 black person
				黒板〔こくばん〕 blackboard
176.	茶	tea	チャ	お茶 tea; tea ceremony
				茶色〔ちゃいろ〕 brown
			サ	喫茶店 coffee shop
177.	飯	cooked rice	ハン	ご飯 cooked rice; meal
				朝御飯〔あさごはん〕 breakfast
				昼御飯〔ひるごはん〕 lunch
				晩御飯〔ばんごはん〕 dinner
178.	足	foot	あし	大きい足 big feet
179.	長	is long	なが（い）	長いお話〔ながいおはなし〕 a long story
				長山〔ながやま〕さん
		chief	チョウ	校長先生〔こうちょうせんせい〕 school principal
				社長〔しゃちょう〕 company president
180.	走	to run	はし（る）	走りました。 I ran.
181.	起	to get up; to wake up	お（きる）	六時〔ろくじ〕に起きました。 I woke up at 6:00.
182.	寝	to sleep	ね（る）	早〔はや〕く寝ました。 I went to sleep early.

** 26.	有名	ゆうめい	famous
** 27.	番組	ばんぐみ	(T.V.) program
** 28.	女性	じょせい	female
** 29.	男性	だんせい	male
** 30.	曲	きょく	musical piece; song
** 31.	子供	こども	child

漢字

362

** 32. 選手	せんしゅ	(sports) player	
** 33. 彼	かれ	he; him; boyfriend	
** 34. 彼女	かのじょ	she; her; girlfriend	

Ⅲ-7課

183. 東 east	ひがし	東口 〔ひがしぐち〕 East exit	
		東山 〔ひがしやま〕 さん	
	トウ	東京 〔とうきょう〕 Tokyo	
184. 西 west	にし	西口 〔にしぐち〕 West exit	
		西田 〔にしだ〕 さん	
		西川 〔にしかわ〕 さん	
	セイ	西洋 〔せいよう〕 the West	
185. 洋 ocean	ヨウ	東洋 〔とうよう〕 the East; Asia	
		西洋 〔せいよう〕 the West	
		洋子 〔ようこ〕 さん	
186. 和 Japanese; harmony	ワ	和食 〔わしょく〕 Japanese food	
		和室 〔わしつ〕 Japanese-style room	
		和英辞典 〔わえいじてん〕 Japanese-English dictionary	
		英和辞典 〔えいわじてん〕 English-Japanese dictionary	
187. 部 part club	ブ	全部 〔ぜんぶ〕 all	
		部活 〔ぶかつ〕 club activity	
	ヘ	部屋 〔へや〕 room	
188. 美 beautiful	うつく(しい)	美しい庭 a beautiful garden	
	ビ	美術 〔びじゅつ〕 fine arts	
		美人 〔びじん〕 a beautiful woman	
189. 広 is spacious	ひろ (い)	広い家 〔いえ〕 a spacious house	
		広島 Hiroshima	

漢字

					広田〔ひろた〕さん
					広中〔ひろなか〕さん
190.	内	inside	うち		内にお上〔あ〕がり下さい。
					内田〔うちだ〕さん
					山内〔やまうち〕さん
			ナイ		家内〔かない〕one's own wife
191.	主	main	シュ		主人〔しゅじん〕one's own husband
					ご主人〔しゅじん〕someone else's husband
192.	住	to live	す（む）		日本に住んでいる。I am living in Japan.
			ジュウ		住所〔じゅうしょ〕address
193.	開	to open	あ（ける）		窓を開けて下さい。Please open the window.
194.	閉	to close	し（める）		戸〔と〕を閉めて下さい。Please close the door.
*47.	生	be born	う（まれる）*		日本で生まれました。I was born in Japan.
			なま*		生卵〔なまたまご〕raw egg
		person	セイ*		先生〔せんせい〕teacher
					学生〔がくせい〕student
			ショウ*		一生懸命〔いっしょうけんめい〕utmost efforts
		arrange (flowers)	い（ける）		生け花〔いけばな〕flower arrangement
*26.	上	to go up	あ（がる）		階段を上がる to go up the stairs
		top; above	うえ*		山の上〔やまのうえ〕top of the mountain
			ジョウ*		上手〔じょうず〕skillful
*27.	下	to go down	お（りる）		山を下りる to go down the mountain
		under	した*		車の下〔くるまのした〕under the car
		to give	くだ（さい）*		お水〔みず〕を下さい。Please give me some water.
			ヘ*		下手〔へた〕unskillful

漢字

*66. 正 is correct　　セイ　　　　　　正座〔せいざ〕する　to sit properly

　　　　　　　　　ただ（しい）＊　正しいです It is correct.

　　　　　　　　　ショウ＊　　　　お正月〔しょうがつ〕New Year's

*182. 寝 to sleep　　シン　　　　　　寝室〔しんしつ〕bedroom

　　　　　　　　　ね（る）＊　　　早〔はや〕く寝ました。I went to sleep early.

**36. ～階　　　　～かい／がい　　- floor

**37. ～的　　　　～てき　　　　　[suffix for - ic, -al, -ish, - style]

**38. 全部　　　　ぜんぶ　　　　　everything

**39. 座る　　　　すわる　　　　　to sit

**40. 正座する　　せいざする　　　to sit properly

III - 8 課

195. 竹 bamboo　　たけ　　　　　　竹の子〔たけのこ〕bamboo shoot

　　　　　　　　　　　　　　　　　竹田〔たけだ〕さん

　　　　　　　　　　　　　　　　　竹本〔たけもと〕さん

　　　　　　　　　　　　　　　　　竹内〔たけうち〕さん

196. 鳥 bird　　　　とり　　　　　　鳥肉〔とりにく〕chicken; poultry

　　　　　　　　　　　　　　　　　焼き鳥〔やきとり〕grilled chicken on skewers

　　　　　　　　　チョウ　　　　　一石二鳥〔いっせきにちょう〕

　　　　　　　　　　　　　　　　　Kill two birds with one stone.

197. 色 color　　　いろ　　　　　　何色〔なにいろ〕what color?

　　　　　　　　　　　　　　　　　茶色〔ちゃいろ〕brown

198. 赤 red　　　　あか　　　　　　赤い車〔くるま〕red car

　　　　　　　　　　　　　　　　　赤ちゃん a baby

199. 青 blue　　　あお　　　　　　青い海〔うみ〕blue ocean

　　　　　　　　　　　　　　　　　青木〔あおき〕さん

　　　　　　　　　　　　　　　　　青色〔あおいろ〕blue (color)

漢字

200.	黄 yellow	き	黄色 〔きいろ〕 yellow (color)	
			黄色い花 〔きいろいはな〕 yellow flowers	
201.	風 wind	かぜ	強い風 〔つよいかぜ〕 strong wind	
	～ style	フウ	和風 〔わふう〕 Japanese-style	
			洋風 〔ようふう〕 Western-style	
			台風 〔たいふう〕 typhoon	
		フ	風呂 〔ふろ〕 Japanese bath	
202.	味 flavor; taste	あじ	いい味 good taste	
			味の素 MSG (monosodium glutamate; a flavor-enhancer for food)	
		ミ	趣味はテニスです My hobby is tennis.	
			何という意味ですか What does it mean?	
203.	料 materials	リョウ	料理する to cook	
			授業料 tuition	
			材料 〔ざいりょう〕 ingredients	
			調味料 〔ちょうみりょう〕 seasonings	
204.	理 arrangement	り	日本料理 〔にほんりょうり〕 Japanese cooking	
			料理屋 〔りょうりや〕 (Japanese) restaurant	
			料理人 〔りょうりにん〕 a cook	
205.	由 a reason	ユウ	自由 〔じゆう〕 free, liberal	
206.	重 is heavy	おも（い）	重い本 heavy books	
			重 〔おも〕 さ weight	
*118.	自 oneself	ジ*	自分の車 〔じぶんのくるま〕 one's own car	
		シ	自然 〔しぜん〕 nature	
**40.	自然	しぜん	nature	
**41.	焼く	やく	to grill; roast; bake; toast; fry	

**42. 苦手　　　にがて　　　be weak in

**43. 丸　　　　まる　　　　circle

**44. 三角　　　さんかく　　triangle

**45. 四角　　　しかく　　　square

**46. 弁当　　　べんとう　　box lunch

**47. 最～　　　さい～　　　the most ～

Ⅲ-9課

207. 北　north　　きた　　　北口〔きたぐち〕North exit

　　　　　　　　　　　　　北川〔きたがわ〕さん

　　　　　　　　ホク　　　東北大学〔とうほくだいがく〕Tohoku University

　　　　　　　　ホッ　　　北海道〔ほっかいどう〕Hokkaido

208. 南　south　　みなみ　南口〔みなみぐち〕South exit

　　　　　　　　　　　　　南田〔みなみだ〕さん

209. 京　capital　キョウ　東京〔とうきょう〕Tokyo

　　　　　　　　　　　　　京都〔きょうと〕Kyoto

210. 駅　train station　エキ　東京駅〔とうきょうえき〕Tokyo Station

　　　　　　　　　　　　　駅員〔えきいん〕station employee

211. 乗　to ride　の（る）　電車〔でんしゃ〕に乗る to ride an electric train

212. 地　ground　チ　　　地下〔ちか〕underground

　　　　　　　　　　　　　地図〔ちず〕map

213. 鉄　iron　　テツ　　　地下鉄〔ちかてつ〕subway

214. 図　chart　　ズ　　　　地図〔ちず〕map

　　　　　　　　ト　　　　図書館〔としょかん〕library

215. 道　road; way　みち　道をまっすぐ行く to go straight on the road

　　　　　　　　　　　　　道子〔みちこ〕さん Michiko (girl's name)

　　　　　　　　トウ　　　神道〔しんとう〕Shinto (Japanese religion)

367

漢字

		ドウ	北海道〔ほっかいどう〕Hokkaido
			書道〔しょどう〕calligraphy
			剣道〔けんどう〕*kendo*
216.	歩 to walk	ある（く）	歩いて行く　to go by walking
		ホ、ポ	散歩〔さんぽ〕する to take a walk
217.	動 to move	うご（く）	車は動きませんでした。The car did not move.
		ドウ	自動車〔じどうしゃ〕car
			動物園〔どうぶつえん〕zoo
			運動会〔うんどうかい〕athletic event
218.	働 to work	はたら（く）	父は銀行で働いています。
			My father is working at a bank.
219.	円 yen; circle	エン	百円玉〔ひゃくえんだま〕one hundred yen coin
			千円〔せんえん〕one thousand yen
			一万円〔いちまんえん〕ten thousand yen
*130.	明 is bright	あか（るい）*	明るい部屋〔へや〕a bright room
		☆	明日〔あした〕tomorrow
		メイ	説明〔せつめい〕して下さい。Please explain it.
*93.	売 to sell	う（る）*	売っています。They are selling it.
		バイ	券売機〔けんばいき〕ticket vending machine
**48.	〜線	- せん	〜line
**49.	橋	はし／- ばし	bridge
**50.	病院	びょういん	hospital
**51.	新幹線	しんかんせん	bullet train
**52.	中央線	ちゅうおうせん	Chuo (Central) Line [orange-colored train line in Tokyo]

漢字

JAPANESE-ENGLISH & ENGLISH-JAPANESE WORD LIST

Abbreviations of Grammatical References

A		い Adjective: atsui, takai, shiroi
Adv		Adverb: totemo, amari, sukoshi
C		Copula: desu, de, na
D		Derivative
	Da	Adjectival Derivative: -tai
	Dv	Verbal Derivative: masu, mashoo, masen
Exp		Expression
N		Noun
	Na	な Adjective: kirei, joozu, suki, yuumei
	Nd	Dependent Noun: -doru, -han
	Ni	Interrogative Noun: dare, doko, ikura
	N	Noun: hana, kuruma, enpitsu
PN		Pre-Noun: donna, kono, ano
P		Particle: de, e, ni
Pc		Clause Particle: kara, ga
SI		Sentence Interjective: anoo, eeto
SP		Sentence Particle: ka, yo, ne, nee
V		Verb
	V1	Verb (group) 1: ikimasu, hanashimasu, nomimasu
	V2	Verb (group) 2: tabemasu, nemasu, imasu
	V3	Verb (group) 3 [irregular verb]: kimasu, shimasu

Japanese	Volume-Lesson #	Word type	English
\<A\>			
Aa ああ	2-13	SI	Oh!
abunai あぶない＝危ない	2-4	A	(is) dangerous
abura あぶら＝油	2-14	N	oil
achira あちら	2-5	N	over there [polite equiv. of あそこ]
	2-9	N	that one over there [polite equiv. of あれ]
agaru あがる＝上がる／あがります	3-7	V1	(to) step up
agemasu あげます	1-15	V2	(to) give (to equal)
ai あい＝愛	2-15	N	love; affection
-aida (ni) ―あいだ(に)＝―間(に)	3-6	N+P	While ～
aida あいだ＝間	2-2	N	between
aishite iru あいしている＝愛している／あいします	2-15	V1	(to be in) love
aisukuriimu アイスクリーム	2-4	N	ice cream
aji あじ＝味	2-14	N	taste; flavor
aka あか＝赤	1-5	N	red
akachan あかちゃん＝赤ちゃん	2-2	N	baby
akai あかい＝赤い	1-6	A	(is) red
akarui あかるい＝明るい	2-11	A	(is) bright
Akemashite omedetoo (gozaimasu).あけましておめでとうございます ＝明けましておめでとうございます	2-7	Exp	[New Year's greeting]
akeru あける＝開ける／あけます	1-13	V2	(to) open
akete kudasai あけてください＝開けて下さい	1-2	Exp	Please open.
aki あき＝秋	1-12	N	autumn; fall
Akihabara あきはばら＝秋葉原	3-9	N	Akihabara [a city in Tokyo]
amai あまい＝甘い	2-14	A	(is) sweet
amari + Neg. あまり + Neg.	1-5	Adv	(not) very
ame あめ＝飴	1-2	N	candy
ame あめ＝雨	1-1	N	rain
amerika アメリカ	1-3	N	U.S.
amerikajin アメリカじん＝アメリカ人	1-3	N	U.S. citizen
ana あな＝穴	2-11	N	hole
anata あなた	1-2	N	you
anatano あなたの	1-2	N	yours
ane あね＝姉	1-3	N	(own) older sister
ani あに＝兄	1-3	N	(own) older brother
ano ～ あの ～	1-2	PN	that ～ over there
anoo . . . あのう . . .	1-2	SI	let me see . . . well . . .
anzen あんぜん＝安全	2-4	Na	(is) safe
ao あお＝青	1-5	N	blue
	2-4	N	green [traffic light]

aoi あおい=青い	1-6	A	(is) blue
arau あらう=洗う/あらいます	2-7	V1	(to) wash
are あれ	1-1	N	that one over there
Arigatoo. ありがとう。	1-1	Exp	Thank you. (informal)
Arigatoo gozaimashita. ありがとうございました。 =有難うございました。	2-9	Exp	Thank you very much. [used after one has received something, or after a deed has been done.]
Arigatoo gozaimasu. ありがとうございます。	1-1	Exp	Thank you very much.
aru 〜 ある 〜	2-11	PN	(a) certain 〜
aru ある/あります	1-10	V1	there is (inanimate object); exist
	1-11	V1	have
(place で) arubaito(o) suru アルバイト(を)する	2-2	V3	(to) work part-time (at 〜)
aruku あるく=歩く/あるきます	1-7	V1	(to) walk
asa あさ=朝	1-4	N	morning
asagohan あさごはん=朝御飯	1-4	N	breakfast
asatte あさって=明後日	1-11	N	(the) day after tomorrow
ashi あし=脚	1-6	N	leg
ashi あし=足	1-6	N	foot
ashita あした=明日	1-4	N	tomorrow
asobu あそぶ=遊ぶ/あそびます	1-15	V1	(to) play; amuse [not used for sports & music]
asoko あそこ	1-2	N	over there
atama あたま=頭	1-6	N	head
atarashii あたらしい=新しい	1-10	A	(is) new
atatakai あたたかい=暖かい	1-14	A	(is) warm
(TA form) ato de -あとで=-後で	3-6	N+P	After S1, S2.
(〜no) ato de (〜の) あとで=(〜の) 後で	1-12	P+N+P	after 〜
ato 〜 あと〜=後〜	2-10	PN	〜 more
atsui あつい=暑い	1-1	A	(is) hot [temperature]
atsui あつい=厚い	2-14	A	(is) thick
atsuku suru あつくする=熱くする	2-14	V3	(to) make hot; (to) heat
atsuku あつく=厚く	2-14	Adv	thick
(place で) (person に) au あう=会う/あいます	1-12	V1	(to) meet (someone) (at a place)

<B>

baggu バッグ	2-3	N	bag
Baibai. バイバイ。	1-14	Exp	Good bye.
-bakari 〜ばかり	3-8	Nd	only 〜
-ban - ばん=- 番	2-10	Nd	Number -
ban ばん=晩	1-4	N	evening
bangohan ばんごはん=晩御飯	1-4	N	dinner; supper
bangumi ばんぐみ=番組	3-6	N	(T.V.)program
-banme - ばんめ=- 番目	2-13	Nd	[in order]

-bansen 〜ばんせん＝〜番線	3-9	N	track number 〜
Banzai! ばんざい！＝万歳！	2-10	Exp	Hurray!
baree(booru) バレー(ボール)	1-5	N	volleyball
basho ばしょ＝場所	2-10	N	place; location
basu バス	1-7	N	bus
basuketto(booru) バスケット(ボール)	1-5	N	basketball
basutei バスてい＝バス停	2-13	N	bus stop
beddo ベッド	1-10	N	bed
bengoshi べんごし＝弁護士	1-3	N	lawyer
benkyoo (o) suru べんきょう(を)する＝勉強(を)する	1-4	V3	(to) study
benri べんり＝便利	3-7	Na	convenient
bentoo べんとう＝弁当	1-14	N	box lunch
beranda ベランダ	3-7	N	veranda
bideo ビデオ	1-4	N	video
biiru ビール	2-4	N	beer
bijutsu びじゅつ＝美術	1-11	N	art
bijutsukan びじゅつかん＝美術館	2-13	N	art museum
binboo びんぼう＝貧乏	2-11	Na	poor
biru ビル	3-9	N	building
boku ぼく＝僕	1-1	N	I [used by males]
bokutachi ぼくたち＝僕達	1-12	N	we [used by males]
boorupen ボールペン	1-2	N	ballpoint pen
booshi ぼうし＝帽子	1-2	N	cap; hat
bukatsu(doo) ぶかつ(どう)＝部活(動)	3-2	N	club activity
bun ぶん＝文	3-4	N	sentence
bungaku ぶんがく＝文学	3-1	N	literature
bunka ぶんか＝文化	3-2	N	culture
bushu ぶしゅ＝部首	3-4	N	classifier
buta ぶた＝豚	1-10	N	pig
butaniku ぶたにく＝豚肉	2-14	N	pork
butsuri ぶつり＝物理	3-1	N	physics
byooin びょういん＝病院	1-3	N	hospital
byooki びょうき＝病気	1-12	N	illness; sickness

<C>

(o)cha (お)ちゃ＝(お)茶	1-4	N	tea
chairo ちゃいろ＝茶色	1-5	N	brown
chairoi ちゃいろい＝茶色い	1-6	A	(is) brown
chakuseki ちゃくせき＝着席	1-1	Exp	Sit.
- chan - ちゃん	2-2	Nd	[Used instead of - さん when addressing or referring to young, small or cute animals or children.]
(o)chazuke (お)ちゃづけ＝(御)茶漬け	3-11	N	tea poured over a bowl of rice, eaten with garnishes

chichi ちち＝父	1-3	N	(own) father
chichi no hi ちちのひ＝父の日	1-15	N	Father's Day
chigau ちがう＝違う/ちがいます	2-2	V1	(is) wrong; (to) differ
chiimu チーム	1-12	N	team
chiisai ちいさい＝小さい	1-6	A	(is) small
chika ちか＝地下	2-9	N	basement
chikai ちかい＝近い	1-10	A	(is) near; close
chikaku ちかく＝近く	2-2	N	vicinity; nearby
chikara ちから＝力	2-11	N	power; strength; ability
chikatetsu ちかてつ＝地下鉄	1-7	N	subway
Chikoku desu. ちこくです。＝遅刻です。	1-1	Exp	(He/She) is tardy; late
chippu チップ	2-5	N	tip
chiri mo tsumoreba yama to naru	3-1	Prov	"Dust amassed will make a
ちりもつもればやまとなる＝塵も積れば山となる			mountain."
chizu ちず＝地図	2-13	N	map
chokoreeto チョコレート	2-5	N	chocolate
choomiryoo ちょうみりょう＝調味料	3-8	N	seasonings
chooshoku ちょうしょく＝朝食	3-1	N	breakfast
chotto ちょっと	1-4	Adv	a little [more informal than すこし]
Chotto matte kudasai.	1-1	Exp	Please wait a minute.
ちょっとまってください。＝ちょっと待って下さい。			
Chotto ukagaimasu ga ... ちょっとうかがいますが ...	2-13	Exp	I have a question.
chuugaku ちゅうがく＝中学	1-3	N	intermediate school
chuugaku ichinensei	1-3	N	seventh grader
ちゅうがくいちねんせい＝中学一年生			
chuugaku ninensei	1-3	N	eighth grader
ちゅうがくにねんせい＝中学二年生			
chuugaku sannensei	1-3	N	freshman; ninth grader
ちゅうがくさんねんせい＝中学三年生			
chuugakusei ちゅうがくせい＝中学生	1-3	N	intermediate school student
chuugoku ちゅうごく＝中国	1-3	N	China
chuugokugo ちゅうごくご＝中国語	1-4	N	Chinese language
chuukyuu ちゅうきゅう＝中級	3-4	N	intermediate level
chuumon (o) suru ちゅうもん(を)する＝注文(を)する	2-5	V3	(to) order
(Go) chuumon wa.	2-5	Exp	What is your order? May I take
ごちゅうもんは。＝御注文は。			your order?
Chuuoosen ちゅうおうせん＝中央線	3-9	N	Chuo (Central) Line [orange
			colored train line in Tokyo]
chuushajoo ちゅうしゃじょう＝駐車場	2-13	N	parking lot
chuushoku ちゅうしょく＝昼食	3-1	N	lunch
<D>			
da だ	2-11	C	[plain form of a copula です]
- dai - だい＝ - 台	10-3	Nd	[counter for mechanized goods]

daidokoro だいどころ＝台所	2-14	N	kitchen
daigaku だいがく＝大学	1-12	N	college; university
daigakusei だいがくせい＝大学生	1-12	N	college student
daiji だいじ＝大事	1-12	Na	important
daijoobu だいじょうぶ＝大丈夫	1-12	Na	all right
daikirai だいきらい＝大嫌い	1-5	Na	dislike a lot; hate
daisuki だいすき＝大好き	1-5	Na	like very much; love
daitai だいたい	2-5	Adv	generally
dakara だから	2-11	SI	Therefore [Informal]
- dake - だけ	2-3	Nd	only ～
dame だめ	1-2	Na	no good
dansei だんせい＝男性	3-6	N	male
danshikoo だんしこう＝男子校	3-2	N	boy's school
dansu ダンス	1-5	N	dance; dancing
dare だれ＝誰	1-3	Ni	who?
daroo だろう	3-1	C	probably is [informal form of でしょう]
Dashite kudasai. だしてください。＝出して下さい。	1-2	Exp	Please turn in.
dasu だす＝出す／だします	1-13	V1	(to) turn in; hand in
	2-4	V1	(to) stick out; submit; take out
(gomi o) dasu ゴミをだす＝ゴミを出す	2-7	V1	(to) take out (the garbage)
datta だった	2-11	C	[plain form of a copula でした]
de で	1-14	C	[Te form of copula です]
～ de で	2-9	P	between; among
(place) de で (+ action verb)	1-4	P	at; in (a place)
(counter) de で	1-14	P	[totalizing particle]
(means) de で	1-7	P	by; with; on; in
(reason) de で	2-6	P	because of (reason)
(～ no naka ～のなか＝～の中) de で	2-9	P	among ～
deguchi でぐち＝出口	2-13	N	exit
(place を／から) dekakeru でかける＝出かける／でかけます	2-4	V2	(to) leave; go out (from a place)
(～ga) dekimashita (～が) できました＝出来ました	2-14	V2	(～ is) ready; (～ is) done
(～ ga) dekiru できる＝出来る／できます	2-6	V2	(be) able to do ～
Demo でも	1-4	SI	But [used at the beginning of a sentence]
denkiseihin でんきせいひん＝電気製品	3-7	N	electric goods
densha でんしゃ＝電車	1-7	N	electric train
denshimeeru でんしメール＝電子メール	3-3	N	e-mail
denshirenji でんしレンジ＝電子レンジ	3-7	N	microwave oven
dentoo でんとう＝伝統	3-7	N	tradition
dentooteki でんとうてき＝伝統的	3-7	Na	traditional
denwa でんわ＝電話	1-4	N	telephone

denwa o kakeru でんわをかける＝電話をかける/かけます			
	2-6	V2	(to) make a phone call
denwabangoo でんわばんごう＝電話番号	1-15	N	telephone number
depaato デパート	1-7	N	department store
(event ni) deru (しあいに)でる＝(event に)出る/でます			
	2-10	V2	(to) participate (in an event)
(place を) deru でる＝出る/でます	2-4	V2	(to) leave (a place)
-deshoo でしょう [falling intonation]	2-7	C	probably ～
-deshoo でしょう [rising intonation]	2-7	C	Isn't it ～?
desu です	1-1	C	am; is; are
Desukara ですから	2-11	SI	Therefore [formal]
Dewa では	1-14	Exp	Well then [formal]
dezaato デザート	2-14	N	dessert
dezain デザイン	2-9	N	design
- do - ど＝- 度	2-6	Nd	- degree(s); - time(s)
doa ドア	1-10	N	door
dochira どちら	2-5	Ni	where? [polite equiv. of どこ]
	2-9	Ni	which (one of two)? [polite]
dochiramo どちらも ＋ neg.	2-9	N	neither; not either
doitsu ドイツ	1-3	N	Germany
doitsugo ドイツご＝ドイツ語	1-4	N	German language
dokidoki suru ドキドキする	2-10	V3	(become) excited; (become) nervous
doko どこ	1-3	Ni	where?
dokodemo どこでも	3-1	Ni+P	anywhere
dokoemo ＋ neg. どこへも ＋ neg.	7-5	Ni+P	(not to) anywhere
dokusho どくしょ＝読書	1-5	N	reading
donna ～ どんな～	1-5	PN	what kind of ～?
dono - どの -	1-13	Nd	which ～?
donogurai どのぐらい	2-6	Ni	about how long/far/often?
Donogurai arimasu ka. どのぐらい ありますか。	2-13	Exp	How far is it? [distance]
Donogurai desu ka. どのぐらいですか。	2-13	Exp	How long/far is it?
Donogurai kakarimasu ka. どのぐらい かかりますか。			
	2-13	Exp	How long does it take? [time]
Doo desu ka. どうですか。	1-11	Exp	How is it? [informal]
Doo itashimashite. どういたしまして。	1-1	Exp	You are welcome.
Doo iu imi desu ka. どういういみですか。 ＝どういう意味ですか。			
	3-4	Exp	What does it mean?
Doo shimashita ka. どうしましたか。	1-12	Exp	What happened?
Doo shitara ii desu ka. どうしたら、いいですか。	3-3	Exp	What should I do?
doobutsuen どうぶつえん＝動物園	2-13	N	zoo
Doomo どうも。	1-1	Exp	Thank you.
dooshite? どうして?	1-11	Ni	why?
doo yatte どうやって （＝どう）	3-9	N	how?

Doozo kochira e. どうぞこちらへ。	2-5	Exp	This way, please.
Doozo yoroshiku. どうぞ　よろしく。	1-1	Exp	Nice to meet you.
doraibaa ドライバー	2-4	N	driver
dore どれ	1-13	Ni	which one?
	2-9	Ni	which one (of three or more)?
- doru - ドル	1-13	Nd	- dollar(s)
dotchi どっち	2-9	Ni	which (one of two)? [informal]
doyoobi どようび＝土曜日	1-7	N	Saturday

<E>

e え＝絵	1-5	N	painting; drawing
E えっ	2-11	SI	Huh?
(place) e へ	1-7	P	to (place)
Ee ええ	1-1	SI	Yes [informal]
Eeto . . . ええと . . .	1-2	SI	Let me see . . . Well . . .
eiga えいが＝映画	1-5	N	movie
eigakan えいがかん＝映画館	2-3	N	movie theater
eigo えいご＝英語	1-4	N	English
eiwajiten えいわじてん＝英和辞典	3-4	N	English-Japanese dictionary
eki えき＝駅	2-13	N	train station
ekiin えきいん＝駅員	3-9	N	station employee
emu-saizu エムサイズ	1-14	N	medium size
- en - えん＝ - 円	1-13	Nd	- yen
enjinia エンジニア	1-3	N	engineer
enpitsu えんぴつ＝鉛筆	1-2	N	pencil
enpitsukezuri えんぴつけずり＝鉛筆削り	1-10	N	pencil sharpener
enryo suru えんりょする＝遠慮する	3-8	V3	(to) hesitate; (to) be reserved
(Go) enryo naku doozo.	3-8	Exp	Without reservation/hesitation,
（ご）えんりょなく、どうぞ。			please (have some).
erai えらい＝偉い	2-11	A	(is) great (person)
eru-saizu エルサイズ	1-14	N	large size
esu-saizu エスサイズ	1-14	N	small size

<F>

fooku フォーク	1-14	N	fork
fuben ふべん＝不便	3-7	Na	inconvenient
fukitobasu ふきとばす＝吹き飛ばす/ふきとばします	2-11	V1	(to) blow away
fuku ふく＝服	2-3	N	clothing
(toranpetto o) fuku （トランペットを）ふく＝吹く/ふきます			
	3-6	V1	(to) blow (a trumpet)
Fukuoka ふくおか＝福岡	2-1	N	Fukuoka
fukuro ふくろ＝袋	2-9	N	(paper) bag
fukuzatsu ふくざつ＝複雑	3-4	Na	complicated
- fun - ふん＝ - 分	1-7	Nd	- minute(s)
fune ふね＝船	1-7	N	boat; ship

furaidopoteto フライドポテト	1-14	N	french fries
furansu フランス	1-3	N	France
furansugo フランスご=フランス語	1-4	N	French language
furu ふる=降る/ふります	2-7	V1	(rain; snow) fall
furui ふるい=古い	1-10	A	(is) old [not for person's age]
futago ふたご=双児	2-15	N	twin
futari ふたり=二人	1-3	N	two (persons)
futatsu ふたつ=二つ	1-2	N	two [general counter]
futoi ふとい=太い	3-8	A	(is) thick (in width; size)
futon ふとん=布団	3-7	N	(Japanese) bedding
futoru ふとる=太る/ふとります	1-6	V1	(to get) fat
futotte imasu ふとっています=太っています	1-6	V1	(is) fat
futsuka ふつか=二日	1-11	N	(the) second day of the month
futsuu ふつう=普通	3-3	N	ordinary; average; regular
futtobooru フットボール	1-5	N	football
fuusen ふうせん=風船	1-15	N	balloon
fuyu ふゆ=冬	1-12	N	winter

\<G\>

(subject) ga が	1-7	P	[subject particle]
(Sentence 1) ga が、(Sentence 2)	1-5	Pc	(S1), but (S2)
(Sentence) ga... が...	2-6	Ps	[Softens the statement.]
gaikokugo がいこくご=外国語	1-11	N	foreign language
gakki がっき=学期	3-2	N	semester
gakkoo がっこう=学校	1-3	N	school
gakusei がくせい=学生	1-3	N	student [college]
gamu ガム	2-3	N	gum
ganbaru がんばる=頑張る/がんばります	1-12	V1	(to) do one's best
Ganbatte. がんばって。=頑張って。	1-12	Exp	Good luck.
gareeji ガレージ	1-10	N	garage
garigari ガリガリ	2-11	Adv	chew away; gnaw[onomatopoetic]
gasorinsutando ガソリンスタンド	3-9	N	gas station
- gatsu umare - がつうまれ= - 月生まれ	1-3	Nd	born in (- month)
- gawa 〜がわ=〜側	2-13	Nd	(〜) side
geemu ゲーム	1-15	N	game
geemu o suru ゲームをする	1-15	V3	(to) play a game
geki げき=劇	2-12	N	(stage) play
geki o suru げきをする=劇をする	2-12	V3	(to) give/put on a (stage) play
genkan げんかん=玄関	3-7	N	entrance way; foyer
(o)genki (お)げんき=(お)元気	1-1	Na	fine; healthy [polite]
(O)genki desu ka. おげんきですか。=お元気ですか。	1-1	Exp	How are you?
getsuyoobi げつようび=月曜日	1-7	N	Monday
gin ぎん=銀	2-15	N	silver
giniro ぎんいろ=銀色	1-5	N	silver (color)

ginkoo ぎんこう＝銀行	2-2	N	bank
Ginza ぎんざ＝銀座	3-9	N	Ginza [a city in Tokyo]
gitaa ギター	1-5	N	guitar
go ご＝五	1-1	N	five
go-juu ごじゅう＝五十	1-1	N	fifty
gochisoo (o) suru ごちそう(を)する	2-5	V3	(to) treat (someone)
Gochisoosama. ごちそうさま＝御馳走様	1-14	Exp	[after a meal]
gogatsu ごがつ＝五月	1-3	N	May
gogo ごご＝午後	1-7	N	p. m.
gohan ごはん＝ご飯	1-4	N	(cooked) rice
gokiburi ごきぶり	1-10	N	cockroach
gomi ごみ	1-2	N	rubbish
gomibako ごみばこ＝ごみ箱	1-10	N	trash can
Goo ni ireba goo ni shitagae. ごうにいればごうにしたがえ ＝郷に入れば郷に従え	3-7	Prov	When in a village, do as the villagers do. (When in Rome do as the Romans do.)
goraku ごらく＝娯楽	3-5	N	entertainment
- goro - ごろ	1-7	Nd	about (time)
gorufu ゴルフ	1-5	N	golf
goryooshin ごりょうしん＝御両親	2-2	N	(someone else's) parents [polite]
goshujin ごしゅじん＝ご主人	3-5	N	(someone else's) husband
gozen ごぜん＝午前	1-7	N	a. m.
guai ga warui ぐあいがわるい＝具合が悪い	2-6	A	condition is bad; feel sick
- gurai - ぐらい	1-13	Nd	about 〜 [Not used for time.]
gurei グレイ	1-5	N	grey
gyooji ぎょうじ＝行事	3-2	N	event(s)
gyuuniku ぎゅうにく＝牛肉	2-14	N	beef
gyuunyuu ぎゅうにゅう＝牛乳	1-4	N	(cow's) milk

\<H\>

ha は＝歯	1-6	N	tooth
hachi はち＝八	1-1	N	eight
hachigatsu はちがつ＝八月	1-3	N	August
hachijuu はちじゅう＝八十	1-1	N	eighty
(e)hagaki （え）はがき＝（絵）葉書	3-3	N	(picture) postcard
haha no hi ははのひ＝母の日	1-15	N	Mother's Day
haha はは＝母	1-3	N	(my) mother
Hai. はい。	1-3	Exp	Yes. [used in response to roll call]
	1-6	SI	Yes
Hai doozo. はい、どうぞ。	1-2	Exp	Here, you are.
Hai, chiizu. はい、チーズ。	1-15	Exp	Say, "Cheese."
Hai, piisu. はい、ピース。	1-15	Exp	Say, "Peace."
(furo ni) hairu (ふろに)はいる＝(風呂に)入る/はいります	3-3	V1	(to) take (a bath)
(place に) hairu はいる＝入る/はいります	2-4	V1	(to) enter (a place)

haiyuu はいゆう＝俳優	3-5	N	actor
(something が) hajimaru はじまる＝始まる/はじまります			
	2-10	V1	(something will) begin; start
hajime ni はじめに＝始めに	2-14	Adv	(at the) beginning
Hajimemashite. はじめまして。	1-1	Exp	How do you do?
Hajimemashoo. はじめましょう。＝始めましょう。	1-4	Exp	Let's begin.
(V stem) hajimeru (V Stem) ＋はじめる＝始める/はじめます			
	3-4	V2	(to) begin doing ～
(something を) hajimeru はじめる＝始める/はじめます			
	2-10	V2	(someone) begins (something) [transitive]
hajimete はじめて＝始めて	2-7	N	(for the) first time
hakikaeru はきかえる＝履き替える/はきかえます			
	3-2	V2	(to) change [i.e., shoes, pants, etc.]
hako はこ＝箱	2-9	N	box
haku はく＝履く/はきます	2-3	V1	(to) wear [at or below the waist]
hakubutsukan はくぶつかん＝博物館	3-9	N	museum
- han - はん＝ - 半	1-7	Nd	- half
hana はな＝花	1-10	N	flower
hana はな＝鼻	1-6	N	nose
hanabi o suru はなびをする＝花火をする	2-7	V3	(to do) fireworks
hanashichuu はなしちゅう＝話し中	2-6	Exp	line is busy
hanasu はなす＝話す/はなします	1-4	V1	(to) speak; talk
hanaya はなや＝花屋	1-13	N	flower shop
hanbaagaa ハンバーガー	1-14	N	hamburger
hanbun ni はんぶんに＝半分に	2-14	Adv	(in) half
happyoo suru はっぴょうする＝発表する	3-3	V3	(to) present; announce
Harajuku はらじゅく＝原宿	3-9	N	Harajuku [a city in Tokyo]
harau はらう＝払う/はらいます	2-5	V1	(to) pay
hare はれ＝晴れ	2-7	N	clear (weather)
haru はる＝貼る/はります	3-3	V1	(to) paste; glue; attach
haru はる＝春	1-12	N	spring
(o) hashi (お)はし＝(お)箸	1-14	N	chopsticks
hashi はし＝橋	2-13	N	bridge
hashiru はしる＝走る/はしります	1-12	V1	(to) run
hatachi はたち＝二十歳	1-3	N	twenty years old
(place で) hataraku はたらく＝働く/はたらきます	2-2	V1	work (at ～)
hatsuka はつか＝二十日	1-11	N	(the) twentieth day of the month
hatsuon はつおん＝発音	3-4	N	pronunciation
hatsuon suru はつおんする＝発音する	3-4	V3	(to) pronounce
hayai はやい＝早い	1-7	A	(is) early
hayaku はやく＝早く	1-12	Adv	early
hayaku はやく＝速く	2-4	Adv	fast; quickly

Hayaku. はやく。＝速く。	1-4	Exp	Hurry!
(Dic./NAI) hazu desu はずです	2-6	Nd	I expect that he/she will do/will not do; He/She is expected to do/not to do.
heiwa　へいわ＝平和	3-2	N/Na	peace; peaceful
hen へん＝変	2-6	Na	strange; weird; unusual
hen へん＝辺	2-13	N	area
heta へた＝下手	1-5	Na	unskillful; (be) poor at
heya へや＝部屋	1-10	N	room
hi ひ＝日	1-15	N	day
hidari ひだり＝左	2-2	N	left side
hidoi ひどい＝酷い	1-11	A	(is) terrible
higashi ひがし＝東	2-1	N	east
higashiguchi ひがしぐち＝東口	3-9	N	east entrance/exit
hige ひげ＝髭	1-6	N	beard; moustache
- hiki - ひき＝ - 匹	1-10	Nd	[counter for small animals]
hikooki ひこうき＝飛行機	1-7	N	airplane
(jisho o) hiku （じしょを）ひく＝（辞書を）引く／ひきます	3-4	V1	(to) look up a word (in a dictionary)
hiku ひく＝弾く／ひきます	2-6	V1	(to) play (a string instrument)
hikui ひくい＝低い	1-6	A	(is) short (height)
hima ひま＝暇	2-15	Na	(is) free (time)
hiroi ひろい＝広い	1-10	A	(is) wide; spacious
Hiroshima ひろしま＝広島	2-1	N	Hiroshima
(o)hiru （お）ひる＝（お）昼	1-4	N	daytime
hirugohan ひるごはん＝昼御飯	1-4	N	lunch
hito ひと＝人	1-10	N	person
hitori ひとり＝一人	1-3	N	one (person)
hitorikko ひとりっこ＝一人っ子	2-15	N	only child
hitotsu ひとつ＝一つ	1-2	N	one [general counter]
〜 hodo ほど + Neg.	2-9	P	(not) as 〜 as
hoka ほか	2-9	N	other
Hoka ni nani ka. ほかになにか。＝ほかに何か。	2-5	Exp	Anything else?
Hokkaidoo ほっかいどう＝北海道	2-1	N	Hokkaido
hon ほん＝本	1-2	N	book
Honshuu ほんしゅう＝本州	2-1	N	Honshu
hontoo ほんとう＝本当	1-3	N	true
Hontoo desu ka. ほんとうですか。＝本当ですか。	2-3	Exp	(Is it) true/real?
hontoo ni ほんとうに＝本当に	2-3	Adv	really; truly
honya ほんや＝本屋	1-13	N	bookstore
(〜 no) hoo （〜の）ほう＝（〜の）方	2-9	N	〜 is more [alternative]
hookago ほうかご＝放課後	3-2	N	after school
-hoomen 〜ほうめん＝方面	3-9	N	〜 direction
hoomu ホーム	3-9	N	platform

hoomuruumu ホームルーム	1-11	N	homeroom
hoomusutei o suru ホームステイをする	2-2	V3	do a homestaty
(something が) hoshii ほしい＝欲しい	1-11	A	want (something)
hosoi ほそい＝細い	3-8	A	(is) thin; slender
hosonagai ほそながい＝細長い	3-8	A	(is) thin and long
hotondo ほとんど	3-2	Adv	almost; mostly
hottodoggu ホットドッグ	1-14	N	hotdog
hyaku ひゃく＝百	1-1	N	hundred
hyaku-man ひゃくまん＝百万	1-13	N	(one) million

<I>

- i - い＝- 位	2-15	Nd	[rank]
ichi いち＝一	1-1	N	one
ichiban いちばん＝一番	2-9	Adv	the most
ichigakki いちがっき＝一学期	3-2	N	first semester
ichigatsu いちがつ＝一月	1-3	N	January
ichigo いちご＝苺	2-14	N	strawberry
ie いえ＝家	2-2	N	house
ii いい	1-2	A	(is) good
Ii desu nee. いいですねえ。	1-11	Exp	How nice! [on a future event]
Iie いいえ	1-1	SI	No [formal]
Iie, kekkoo desu. いいえ、けっこうです。	1-14	Exp	No, thank you.
ijime いじめ	3-2	N	bullying
ijimeru いじめる	3-2	V2	(to) bully; (to) treat someone harshly
Ikaga desu ka. いかがですか。＝如何ですか。	1-13	Ni	how about ～? [Polite form of どうですか]
ike いけ＝池	1-10	N	pond
ikebana いけばな＝生け花	3-7	N	flower arrangement
Ikebukuro いけぶくろ＝池袋	3-9	N	Ikebukuro [a city in Tokyo]
ikemasen いけません	2-3	V2	won't do; must not do
iken いけん＝意見	3-3	N	opinion
iku いく＝行く／いきます	1-7	V1	(to) go
(o)ikura (お)いくら	1-13	Ni	how much?
ikutsu いくつ	1-2	Ni	how many? [general counter]
(o)ikutsu (お)いくつ	1-3	Ni	how old?
ima いま＝今	1-3	N	now
ima いま＝居間	3-7	N	living room; family room
imi いみ＝意味	3-4	N	meaning
(-to iu) imi desu (～という)いみです。＝(～という)意味です。	3-4	Exp	It means ～.
imooto いもうと＝妹	1-3	N	(my) younger sister
imootosan いもうとさん＝妹さん	1-3	N	(someone's) younger sister
(o)inori (お)いのり＝(お)祈り	3-8	N	prayer
inoru いのる＝祈る／いのります	3-8	V1	(to) pray
inu いぬ＝犬	1-10	N	dog

Irasshaimase. いらっしゃいませ。	2-5	Exp	Welcome. [formal]
irassharu/irasshaimasu いらっしゃる/いらっしゃいます	2-6	V1	(to) exist; be (for animate) [polite form of いる]
(- ni) ireru いれる＝入れる/いれます	2-9	V2	(to) put in 〜
iriguchi いりぐち＝入口	2-13	N	entrance
iro いろ＝色	1-5	N	color
iroiro いろいろ	2-9	Na	various
iru いる/います	1-10	V2	there is (animate object); exist
iru いる＝要る/いります	1-14	V1	need
isha いしゃ＝医者	1-3	N	(medical) doctor [informal]
isogashii いそがしい＝忙しい	1-7	A	(is) busy
Isseki nichoo. いっせきにちょう＝一石二鳥	3-8	Prov	Kill two birds with one stone.
issho ni いっしょに＝一緒に	1-4	Adv	together
isshookenmei いっしょうけんめい＝一生懸命	2-11	Adv	(with one's) utmost effort
isu いす＝椅子	1-10	N	chair
Itadakimasu. いただきます。	1-14	Exp	[before a meal]
itai いたい＝痛い	1-12	A	(is) painful; sore
itoko いとこ	1-15	N	cousin
itokonnyaku いとこんにゃく ＝糸こんにゃく	2-14	N	shredded *konnyaku* [grey or transparent tuber root gelatin]
itsu いつ	1-7	Ni	when?
itsudemo いつでも	3-1	Ni+P	anytime
itsuka いつか＝五日	1-11	N	(the) fifth day of the month
itsumo いつも	1-4	Adv	always
itsutsu いつつ＝五つ	1-2	N	five [general counter]
Ittekimasu. いってきます。＝行って来ます。	3-1	Exp	[Used by a family member who leaves home for the day.]
Itterasshai. いってらっしゃい＝行ってらっしゃい。	3-1	Exp	[Used by a family member who sends off another family member for the day.]
iu いう＝言う/いいます	1-13	V1	(to) say
iya(tt) いや(っ)	2-11	SI	No [stronger negation than いいえ]
iyaringu イヤリング	2-3	N	earrings

<J>

Ja じゃ	1-14	Exp	Well then [informal]
jaketto ジャケット	1-13	N	jacket
jama じゃま＝邪魔	1-6	Na	hindrance; nuisance; is in the way
- ji - じ＝ - 時	1-7	Nd	- o'clock
jibun じぶん＝自分	2-15	N	oneself
jidoosha じどうしゃ＝自動車	1-7	N	car; vehicle
jikan じかん＝時間	2-10	N	time
- jikan - じかん＝ - 時間	2-6	Nd	- hour(s)

jikoshookai(o) suru じこしょうかい(を)する＝自己紹介(を)する
	2-2	V3	(to) do a self-introduction
jimusho じむしょ＝事務所	1-10	N	office
jinja じんじゃ＝神社	2-7	N	shrine (Shinto)
jisho じしょ＝辞書	1-2	N	dictionary
jitensha じてんしゃ＝自転車	1-7	N	bicycle
jiyuu じゆう＝自由	2-3	Na	free; liberal
jogingu ジョギング	1-5	N	jogging
- joo - じょう＝- 畳	3-7	C	[counter for tatami]
joodan じょうだん＝冗談	2-10	N	(a) joke
jookyuu じょうきゅう＝上級	3-4	N	advanced level
joozu じょうず＝上手	1-5	Na	skillful; (be) good at
josei じょせい＝女性	3-6	N	female
joshikoo じょしこう＝女子校	3-2	N	girl's school
joyuu じょゆう＝女優	3-6	N	actress
JR J R〔ジェイアール〕	3-9	N	Japan Railway
jugyoo じゅぎょう＝授業	1-11	N	class; instruction
jugyooryoo じゅぎょうりょう＝授業料	3-2	N	tuition
juku じゅく＝塾	3-2	N	cram school
juu じゅう＝十	1-1	N	ten
juu じゅう＝銃	3-2	N	gun
juu-go じゅうご＝十五	1-1	N	fifteen
juu-hachi じゅうはち＝十八	1-1	N	eighteen
juu-ichi じゅういち＝十一	1-1	N	eleven
juu-ku じゅうく＝十九	1-1	N	nineteen
juu-kyuu じゅうきゅう＝十九	1-1	N	nineteen
juu-man じゅうまん＝十万	1-13	N	hundred thousand
juu-nana じゅうなな＝十七	1-1	N	seventeen
juu-ni じゅうに＝十二	1-1	N	twelve
juu-roku じゅうろく＝十六	1-1	N	sixteen
juu-san じゅうさん＝十三	1-1	N	thirteen
juu-shi じゅうし＝十四	1-1	N	fourteen
juu-shichi じゅうしち＝十七	1-1	N	seventeen
juu-yokka じゅうよっか＝十四日	1-11	N	(the) fourteenth day of the month
juu-yon じゅうよん＝十四	1-1	N	fourteen
juugatsu じゅうがつ＝十月	1-3	N	October
juuichigatsu じゅういちがつ＝十一月	1-3	N	November
juunigatsu じゅうにがつ＝十二月	1-3	N	December
juusho じゅうしょ＝住所	1-15	N	address
juusu ジュース	1-4	N	juice

<K>
| ka か | 1-1 | SP | [question particle] |
| - ka? ーか？ | 3-1 | SP | [male informal sentence ending |

particle]kaapetto カーペット	3-7	N	carpet
kabe かべ＝壁	2-11	N	wall
kabukiza かぶきざ＝歌舞伎座	3-9	N	Kabuki theater
kaburu かぶる/かぶります	2-3	V2	(to) wear [on or draped over the head]
kado かど＝角	2-4	N	corner
kaeru かえる＝帰る/かえります	1-7	V1	(to) return (to a place)
kaeru かえる＝変える/かえます	3-1	V2	(to) change (something)
kaesu かえす＝返す/かえします	2-5	V1	(to) return (something)
kafeteria カフェテリア	1-4	N	cafeteria
kagaku かがく＝科学	1-11	N	science
kagaku かがく＝化学	3-1	N	chemistry
-kagetsu - かげつ＝ - か月	2-6	Nd	- month(s)
kagi かぎ＝鍵	2-4	N	key
- kai/- gai - かい/- がい＝- 階	1-9	Nd	- floor
- kai - かい＝- 回	3-4	Nd	- time(s)
- kai? ーかい？	3-1	SP	[male informal sentence ending particle]
kaidan かいだん＝階段	3-7	N	stairs
kaigairyokoo かいがいりょこう＝海外旅行	3-2	N	overseas travel
kaimono かいもの＝買い物	1-7	N	shopping
kaimono (o) suru かいもの(を)する＝買い物(を)する	1-7	V3	(to) shop
kaisatsuguchi かいさつぐち＝改札口	3-9	N	ticket gate
kaisha かいしゃ＝会社	1-7	N	company
kaishain かいしゃいん＝会社員	1-3	N	company employee
kaji かじ＝家事	3-3	N	household chore; housework
kakaru かかる/かかります	2-9	V1	(to) require; to take (time)
kakeru かける/かけます	2-3	V2	(to) wear [glasses]
kakeru かける/かけます	3-8	V2	(to) pour over; sprinkle
kakeru かける＝掛ける/かけます	3-7	V2	(to) hang
kakijun かきじゅん＝書き順	3-4	N	stroke order
kakko ii かっこいい＝格好いい	3-3	A	(is) good looking
-kaku - かく＝- 画	3-4	N	- stroke(s)
kaku かく＝書く	1-4	V1	(to) write
(e o) kaku (えを)かく＝(絵を)描く	2-15	V1	(to) draw; paint a picture
kakusu かくす＝隠す/かくします	2-11	V1	(to) hide (something)
kamaimasen かまいません	2-3	V1	(I) do not mind if . . .
kamera カメラ	1-15	N	camera
kami (no ke) かみ(のけ)＝髪(の毛)	1-6	N	hair
kami かみ＝紙	1-2	N	paper
-kamo shirenai -かもしれない	3-7	E	might; may
kamoku かもく＝科目	1-11	N	subject
(gamu o) kamu （ガムを）かむ/かみます	2-3	V1	(to) chew gum
-kana. ーかな。	3-2	SP	(I) wonder if ～ [used by male and female]

kanai かない＝家内	3-6	N	(own) wife
kanashii かなしい＝悲しい	1-11	A	(is) sad
Kanda かんだ＝神田	3-9	N	Kanda [a city in Tokyo]
(o) kane (お)かね＝(お)金	1-2	N	money
(o) kanemochi (お)かねもち＝(お)金持ち	2-11	N	rich person
kanjijiten かんじじてん＝漢字辞典	3-4	N	kanji dictionary
(o) kanjoo (お)かんじょう＝(お)勘定	2-5	N	(a) check; bill
kankoku かんこく＝韓国	1-3	N	Korea
kankokugo かんこくご＝韓国語	1-4	N	Korean language
kanningu カンニング	3-2	N	cheating
kanojo かのじょ＝彼女	3-6	N	she; her; girlfriend
Kanpai! かんぱい！＝乾杯	3-8	Exp	Cheers!
kansha (o) suru かんしゃ(を)する＝感謝(を)する	2-15	V3	(to) appreciate; thank
kantan かんたん＝簡単	3-4	Na	simple
kantoku かんとく＝監督	3-6	N	(movie) director; (baseball) manager
kao かお＝顔	1-6	N	face
～ kara ～から	1-11	P	from ～
～ kara ～ made ～から～まで	2-13	P	from ～ to ～
(sentence) kara ～から	1-4	Pc	because ～; since ～; ～ so
karada からだ＝体	1-6	N	body
karai からい＝辛い	2-14	A	(is) salty; (is) spicy
kare かれ＝彼	3-6	N	he; him; boyfriend
kareeraisu カレーライス	2-5	N	curry rice
kariru かりる＝借りる/かります	2-3	V2	(to) borrow; (to) rent (from)
karui かるい＝軽い	3-7	A	(is) light (in weight)
-kashira. 一かしら。	3-2	SP	(I) wonder if ～ [used by female]
kashu かしゅ＝歌手	3-6	N	singer
kasu かす＝貸す/かします	1-14	V1	(to) lend, (to) rent (to)
～kata ～かた＝ ～方	1-10	Nd	person [polite form of ひと]
(Verb stem +) kata かた＝方	2-14	N	how to do ～
katachi かたち＝形	3-4	N	shape
katai かたい＝硬い	3-8	A	(is) hard; tough
katazukeru かたづける＝片付ける	2-14	V2	(to) clean up; put away
katsu かつ＝勝つ/かちます	1-12	V1	(to) win
Katta! Katta! かった！かった！＝勝った！勝った！	2-10	Exp	(We) won! (We) won!
kau かう＝買う/かいます	1-13	V1	(to) buy
kawa かわ＝川	1-7	N	river
kawaii かわいい＝可愛い	1-6	A	(is) cute
Kawaisoo ni. かわいそうに＝可愛そうに	1-12	Exp	How pitiful.
Kawarimashita かわりました。＝代わりました。	2-6	Exp	It's me. [lit., We've changed over.]
kawaru かわる＝代わる/かわります	2-6	V1	(to) change over
kawatta かわった＝変わった	3-8	V1	(is) different; odd; unusual

kayoobi かようび＝火曜日	1-7	N	Tuesday
kayou　かよう＝通う／かよいます	3-2	V	(to) commute
kazaru かざる＝飾る／かざります	3-7	V1	(to) decorate
kaze かぜ＝風邪	1-12	N	(a) cold
kaze かぜ＝風	2-7	N	wind
kaze o hiku かぜをひく＝風邪を引く	2-6	V1	(to) catch a cold
kazoku かぞく＝家族	1-3	N	(my) family
(go)kazoku (ご)かぞく＝(御)家族	1-3	N	(someone's) family
kazu かず＝数	3-4	N	amount
(sentence) kedo けど	2-6	Pc	Although ～
keikan けいかん＝警官	2-4	N	police officer
keiken suru けいけんする＝経験する	3-7	V3	(to) experience
keitaidenwa　けいたいでんわ＝携帯電話	3-3	N	cellular phone
keizai けいざい＝経済	3-4	N	economics
(person と) kekkon (o) suru けっこん(を)する＝結婚(を)する	2-2	V3	(is) married (to ～)
kenbaiki けんばいき＝券売機	3-9	N	ticket vending machine
kendoo　けんどう＝剣道	3-2	N	kendo [Japanese fencing]
kenka (o) suru けんか(を)する＝喧嘩(を)する	2-4	V3	(to) fight
kenkoo けんこう＝健康	3-8	N	health
kenkooteki けんこうてき＝健康的	3-8	Na	healthy
(sentence) keredo けれど	2-6	Pc	Although ～
kesa けさ＝今朝	1-12	N	this morning
keshigomu けしごむ＝消しゴム	1-2	N	eraser [rubber]
(o)keshoo o suru　(お)けしょうをする＝(お)化粧をする	3-2	V3	(to) apply make-up
kesshite + Neg. けっして＋Neg.	2-4	Adv	never
ki き＝木	1-10	N	tree
ki o tsukeru きをつける＝気をつける	2-3	V2	(to be) careful
kibishii きびしい＝厳しい	1-6	A	(is) strict
kiiro きいろ＝黄色	1-5	N	yellow
kiiroi きいろい＝黄色い	1-6	A	(is) yellow
kikoemasen きこえません＝聞こえません	1-2	V2	cannot hear
kikoemasu きこえます＝聞こえます	1-2	V2	can hear
(something が) kikoeru きこえる＝聞こえる	2-3	V2	～ can be heard
kiku きく＝聞く／ききます	1-4	V1	(to) listen, hear
(person に) kiku きく＝聞く	2-3	V1	(to) ask (someone)
kimochi ga ii きもちがいい＝気持ちがいい	2-14	A	(is) pleasant; comfortable
kimochi ga warui きもちがわるい＝気持ちが悪い	2-14	A	(is) unpleasant; uncomfortable
kin きん＝金	2-15	N	gold
kiniro きんいろ＝金色	1-5	N	gold (color)
(O)kinodoku ni. (お)きのどくに。＝(お)気の毒に。	2-6	Exp	I am sorry. [sympathy - formal]
kinoo きのう＝昨日	1-4	N	yesterday
kinyoobi きんようび＝金曜日	1-7	N	Friday
kippu きっぷ＝切符	1-15	N	ticket

J-E

kirai きらい=嫌い	1-5	Na	dislike
kirei ni suru きれいにする	2-14	V3	(to) make clean; (to) clean
kirei きれい	1-6	Na	pretty; clean; neat; nice
kirisutokyoo キリストきょう=キリスト教	2-7	N	Christianity
Kiritsu. きりつ。=起立。	1-1	Exp	Stand.
kiru きる=切る/きります	2-14	V1	(to) cut; slice
kiru きる=着る/きます	2-3	V2	(to) wear [above the waist or on the entire body]
kisetsu きせつ=季節	3-8	N	season
kisoku きそく=規則	2-3	N	rule; regulation
kissaten きっさてん=喫茶店	1-13	N	coffee shop
kita きた=北	2-1	N	north
kitaguchi きたぐち=北口	3-9	N	north entrance/exit
kitanai きたない	1-6	A	dirty; messy
kitte きって=切手	3-3	N	stamp
- ko - こ =- 個	2-5	Nd	[general counter]
kochira こちら	1-3	N	this one [polite equiv. of これ to introduce a person]
	2-5	N	here [polite equiv. of ここ]
	2-9	N	this one [polite equiv. of これ]
Kochirakoso. こちらこそ。	3-1	Exp	(It is) I, (not you.) [emphasis]
kodomo こども=子供	1-10	N	child
koe こえ=声	1-6	N	voice
koko ここ	1-2	N	here
kokonoka ここのか=九日	1-11	N	(the) ninth day of the month
kokonotsu ここのつ=九つ	1-2	N	nine [general counter]
kokoro こころ=心	1-6	N	heart
komaasharu コマーシャル	3-6	N	commercial
komaru こまる=困る/こまります	3-3	V1	(be) troubled
komu こむ=込む/こみます	2-13	V1	(to) get crowded
Konban wa. こんばんは。=今晩は。	1-7	Exp	Good evening.
konban こんばん=今晩	1-7	N	tonight
konbini コンビニ	2-13	N	convenience store
konde iru こんでいる=込んでいる	2-13	V1	(is) crowded
kongakki こんがっき=今学期	3-2	N	this semester
kongetsu こんげつ=今月	1-12	N	this month
konkuuru コンクール	2-15	N	competition [music]
Konnichi wa. こんにちは。	1-1	Exp	Hello; Hi.
kono naka de このなかで=この中で	2-9	PN+N+P	among these
kono ～ この ～	1-2	PN	this ～
konpyuutaa コンピューター	1-4	N	computer
konsaato コンサート	1-15	N	concert
konshuu こんしゅう=今週	1-11	N	this week

Koobe こうべ＝神戸	2-1	N	Kobe
kooen こうえん＝公園	2-2	N	park
koohii コーヒー	1-4	N	coffee
kookoo こうこう＝高校	1-3	N	high school
kookoo ichinensei こうこういちねんせい＝高校一年生			
	1-3	N	hight school sophomore; tenth grader
kookoo ninensei こうこうにねんせい＝高校二年生			
	1-3	N	high school junior; eleventh grader
kookoo sannensei こうこうさんねんせい＝高校三年生			
	1-3	N	high school senior; twelfth grader
kookoosei こうこうせい＝高校生	1-3	N	high school student
koora コーラ	1-4	N	cola (drink)
kooritsu こうりつ＝公立	3-2	N	public
koosaten こうさてん＝交差点	2-13	N	intersection
kooshuudenwa こうしゅうでんわ＝公衆電話	2-13	N	public phone
kootsuujiko こうつうじこ＝交通事故	2-4	N	traffic accident
koppu コップ	1-14	N	cup
kore これ	1-1	N	this one
korekara これから	1-14	SI	from now on
(time) koro ころ	1-7	Nd	about (time)
koshoo こしょう＝胡椒	2-14	N	pepper
kotae こたえ＝答え	2-2	N	answer
kotaeru こたえる＝答える／こたえます	2-2	V2	(to) answer
koto こと＝事	1-5	N	thing [intangible]
kotoba ことば＝言葉	2-15	N	words; language
kotoshi ことし＝今年	1-15	N	this year
kotowaza ことわざ＝諺	3-1	N	proverb
kowai こわい＝恐い	2-4	A	(is) scary
(〜 ga) kowareru 〜がこわれる＝壊れる	3-7	V2	(to) break [intransitive verb]
(〜 o) kowasu 〜をこわす＝壊す	3-7	V1	(to) break [transitive verb]
(o)kozukai (お)こづかい＝(お)小遣い	3-2	N	allowance
ku く＝九	1-1	N	nine
kubi くび＝首	1-6	N	neck
kuchi くち＝口	1-6	N	mouth
kudamono くだもの＝果物	2-14	N	fruit
(〜を)kudasai ください＝下さい	1-2	Exp	please give me 〜.
(-te) kudasaimasu（〜て）くださいます＝下さいます	3-3	E	(superior) do 〜 for me
kugatsu くがつ＝九月	1-3	N	September
kumo くも＝雲	2-11	N	cloud
kumori くもり＝曇り	2-7	N	cloudy (weather)
kun(yomi) くん（よみ）＝訓（読み）	3-4	N	Japanese reading (of a *kanji*)
kuni くに＝国	2-9	N	country; nation

kuraberu くらべる＝比べる/くらべます	2-9	V2	(to) compare
kurai くらい＝暗い	2-11	A	(is) dark
- kurai - くらい	1-13	Nd	about ～ [not for time]
kurasu クラス	1-11	N	class; instruction
kurejitto kaado クレジットカード	2-9	N	credit card
kureru くれる/くれます	1-15	V2	(to) give (to me or to my family)
kurikaesu くりかえす＝繰り返す	3-9	V1	(to) repeat
kurisumasu クリスマス	2-7	N	Christmas
kurisumasukaado クリスマスカード	2-7	N	Christmas card
kurisumasutsurii クリスマスツリー	2-7	N	Christmas tree
kuro くろ＝黒	1-5	N	black
kuroi くろい＝黒い	1-6	A	(is) black
kuru くる＝来る/きます	1-7	V3	(to) come
kuruma くるま＝車	1-7	N	car; vehicle
kusa くさ＝草	3-2	N	grass
kusai くさい＝臭い	3-8	A	(is) smelly
kusuri くすり＝薬	1-12	N	medicine
kutsu くつ＝靴	1-13	N	shoes
kutsushita くつした＝靴下	2-3	N	socks
kuukoo くうこう＝空港	2-13	N	airport
kyaku きゃく＝客	3-7	N	customer; guest
kyakuma きゃくま＝客間	3-7	N	room where guests are received
kyandii キャンディ	2-5	N	candy
kyanpu キャンプ	1-7	N	camp
kyoku きょく＝曲	3-5	N	musical piece; song
kyonen きょねん＝去年	1-15	N	last year
kyoo きょう＝今日	1-4	N	today
kyoodai きょうだい＝兄弟	1-3	N	(my) sibling(s)
(danjo) kyoogaku (だんじょ)きょうがく＝(男女)共学	3-2	N	co-educational
kyooiku きょういく＝教育	3-2	N	education
kyookai きょうかい＝教会	2-7	N	church
kyookasho きょうかしょ＝教科書	1-2	N	textbook
kyoomi きょうみ＝興味	3-4	N	(personal) interest
kyooshitsu きょうしつ＝教室	1-10	N	classroom
Kyooto きょうと＝京都	2-1	N	Kyoto
kyuu ni きゅうに＝急に	2-4	Adv	suddenly
kyuu きゅう＝九	1-1	N	nine
kyuu-juu きゅうじゅう＝九十	1-1	N	ninety
kyuukyuusha きゅうきゅうしゃ＝救急車	2-4	N	ambulance
kyuuryoo きゅうりょう＝給料	3-5	N	salary; pay
Kyuushuu きゅうしゅう＝九州	2-1	N	Kyushu

<M>

maamaa まあまあ	1-5	Adv	so, so

machi まち＝町	2-13	N	town
machigaeru まちがえる＝間違える／まちがえます	2-6	V2	(to) make a mistake
mada まだ + Aff.	2-2	Adv	still
mada まだ + Neg.	1-14	Adv	(not) yet
Mada desu. まだです。	1-14	Exp	Not yet.
～ made ～まで	1-11	P	to ～; until ～
(time) made ni までに	2-10	P	by (a certain time)
mado まど＝窓	1-10	N	window
mae まえ＝前	1-3	N	before
mae まえ＝前	2-2	N	front
～mae ～まえ＝ ～前	1-7	Nd	before ～
(dic. form) mae ni (dic. form)まえに＝-前に	3-5	N+P	Before S1, S2.
(～no) mae ni （～の）まえに＝（～の）前に	1-12	P+N+P	before ～
(place で/を) magaru まがる＝曲がる／まがります	2-4	V1	(to) turn at/along (place)
-mai -まい＝-枚	1-2	Nd	[counter for flat objects]
maigakki まいがっき＝毎学期	3-2	N	every semester
maigo ni naru まいごになる＝迷子になる	3-9	V1	(to) get lost
mainen まいねん＝毎年	1-15	N	every year
mainichi まいにち＝毎日	1-4	N	everyday
maishuu まいしゅう＝毎週	1-11	N	every week
maitoshi まいとし＝毎年	1-15	N	every year
maitsuki まいつき＝毎月	1-12	N	every month
majime まじめ＝真面目	3-3	Na	(is) serious
makeru まける＝負ける／まけます	1-12	V2	(to) lose
(ichi)man (いち)まん＝(一)万	1-13	N	ten thousand
manga まんが＝漫画	3-4	N	comics
maru まる＝丸	3-8	N	circle
maru o suru まるをする＝丸をする	3-8	V3	(to) circle
marui まるい＝丸い	3-8	A	(is) round
-masen ka -ませんか	1-7	Dv	won't you do ～? [invitation]
-mashoo -ましょう	1-7	Dv	let's do ～. [suggestion]
massugu まっすぐ	2-13	Adv	straight
mata また＝又	1-10	Adv	again
(Ja) mata ato de. (じゃ)またあとで。	1-14	Exp	(Well,) see you later.
Mata doozo. またどうぞ。	2-9	Exp	Please come again.
matsu まつ＝待つ／まちます	1-13	V1	(to) wait
mayaku まやく＝麻薬	3-2	N	drugs
mazu まず	2-14	SI	first of all
mazui まずい	1-13	A	(is) unappetizing; is tasteless
me め＝目	1-6	N	eye
mechakucha めちゃくちゃ	3-4	Na	messy; confusing; incorrect
megane めがね＝眼鏡	2-3	N	eyeglasses
menyuu メニュー	2-5	N	menu

mezurashii めずらしい＝珍しい	3-8	A	(is) rare; unusual
michi みち＝道	2-4	N	street; road
midori みどり＝緑	1-5	N	green
miemasen みえません＝見えません	2-1	V2	cannot see
miemasu みえます＝見えます	2-1	V2	can see
(something が) mieru みえる＝見える	2-3	V2	～ can be seen
(ha o) migaku (はを)みがく＝歯を磨く／みがきます	3-3	V1	(to) brush teeth
migi みぎ＝右	2-2	N	right side
mijikai みじかい＝短い	1-6	A	(is) short [not for height]
mikka みっか＝三日	11-1	N	(the) third day of the month
mimi みみ＝耳	1-6	N	ear
minami みなみ＝南	2-1	N	south
minamiguchi みなみぐち＝南口	3-9	N	south entrance/exit
minasan みなさん＝皆さん	1-15	N	everyone [polite address form]
minna みんな＝皆	1-15	N	everyone
(Verb TE form ＋) miru みる	2-5	Dv	try to (do)
miru みる＝見る／みます	1-4	V2	(to) watch; look; see
miruku ミルク	1-4	N	(cow's) milk
(o)mise (お)みせ＝(お)店	1-13	N	store
miseru みせる＝見せる／みせます	1-13	V2	(to) show
Misete kudasai. みせてください。＝見せて下さい。	1-2	Exp	Please show.
(o)misoshiru(お)みそしる＝(お)味噌汁	2-5	N	soup flavored with miso
Mite kudasai. みてください。＝見て下さい。	1-2	Exp	Please look.
(～ ga) mitsukaru みつかる＝見つかる／みつかります	3-4	V1	(to be) found [intransitive]
(～ o) mitsukeru みつける＝見つける／みつけます	3-4	V2	(to) find [transitive]
mittsu みっつ＝三つ	1-2	N	three [general counter]
(o)miyage (お)みやげ＝(お)土産	2-9	N	souvenir gift
(o)mizu (お)みず＝(お)水	1-4	N	water
～mo ～も (＋ Aff.)	1-3	P	too; also
～mo ～も (＋ Neg.)	1-3	P	either
(counter) mo も	2-6	P	as many/long as ～
mochiron もちろん	2-6	SI	of course
mokuyoobi もくようび＝木曜日	1-7	N	Thursday
mon もん＝門	2-3	N	gate
mondai もんだい＝問題	2-6	N	problem
mono もの＝物	1-5	N	thing [tangible]
moo もう＋ Aff.	1-14	Exp	already
moo もう＋ Neg.	2-2	Adv	(not) any more
moo (ippai) もう(いっぱい)＝もう(一杯)	1-14	Adv	(one) more (cup)
moo ichido もういちど＝もう一度	1-1	Adv	one more time
moo sugu もうすぐ	1-15	Adv	very soon
morau もらう／もらいます	1-15	V1	(to) receive; get from
moshi もし	3-7	Adv	If

Moshi moshi. もしもし。	2-6	Exp	Hello. (on the phone)
motsu もつ＝持つ/もちます	2-2	V1	(to) have; hold; carry
motte iku もっていく＝持って行く/もっていきます	2-7	V1	(to) take (something)
motte kaeru もってかえる＝持って帰る/もってかえります	2-7	V1	(to) take/bring (something) back home
motte kuru もってくる＝持って来る/もってきます	2-7	V3	(to) bring (something)
motto もっと	2-9	Adv	more
muika むいか＝六日	1-11	N	(the) sixth day of the month
(person を) mukae ni iku むかえにいく＝迎えに行く/むかえにいきます	2-10	V1	(to) go to pick up (person)
(person を) mukae ni kaeru むかえにかえる＝迎えに帰る/むかえにかえります	2-10	V1	(to) return to pick up (person)
(person を) mukae ni kuru むかえにくる＝迎えに来る/むかえにきます	2-10	V3	(to) come to pick up (someone)
mukaigawa むかいがわ＝向かい側	3-9	N	other side (of)
mukashibanashi むかしばなし＝昔話	2-11	N	folk tale
mukashimukashi むかしむかし＝昔々	2-11	N	long, long ago
mukoo むこう＝向こう	2-13	N	other side; beyond
murasaki むらさき＝紫	1-5	N	purple
mushiatsui むしあつい＝蒸し暑い	1-1	A	(is) hot and humid
(o)musubi (お)むすび	1-14	N	riceball
musuko むすこ＝息子	2-11	N	(own) son
musukosan むすこさん＝息子さん	2-11	N	(someone else's) son
musume むすめ＝娘	2-11	N	(own) daughter; young lady
musumesan むすめさん＝娘さん	2-11	N	(someone else's) daughter; young lady [polite]
muttsu むっつ＝六つ	1-2	N	six [general counter]
muzukashii むずかしい＝難しい	1-11	A	(is) difficult

\<N\>

nabe なべ＝鍋	2-14	N	pot; pan
- nado - など	1-15	Nd	～ etc.
nagai ながい＝長い	1-6	A	(is) long
(V stem form+) nagara ーながら	3-6	Rc	While ～ [Describing a person's simultaneous or concurrent actions]
Nagoya なごや＝名古屋	2-1	N	Nagoya
Naha なは＝那覇	2-1	N	Naha [a city in Okinawa]
naifu ナイフ	1-14	N	knife
naka なか＝中	2-2	N	inside
nakanaka + Neg. なかなか + Neg.	3-4	Adv	(not) easily ～
-nakereba narimasen -なければなりません	2-5	Dv	have to (do); should (do)
naku なく＝泣く/なきます	2-15	V1	(to) cry
nakunaru なくなる＝亡くなる/なくなります	3-6	V1	(to) pass away; die [polite form of しぬ]

-nakutemo iidesu -なくてもいいです	2-5	Dv	do not have to (do); no need to (do)
nama tamago なまたまご＝生卵	2-14	N	raw egg
namae なまえ＝名前	1-3	N	name
(o)namae おなまえ＝御名前	1-3	N	(someone's) name [polite]
nan なん＝何	1-1	Ni	what?
nan-bai なんばい＝何杯	1-14	Ni	how many cups?
nan-gatsu なんがつ＝何月	1-3	Ni	what month?
nan-nensei なんねんせい＝何年生	1-3	N	what grade?
nan-nichi なんにち＝何日	1-11	Ni	(the) what day of the month?
nan-nin なんにん＝何人	1-3	Ni	how many people?
nan-sai なんさい＝何歳, 何才	1-3	Ni	how old?
nan-satsu なんさつ＝何冊	1-15	Ni	how many [bound objects]?
nan-yoobi なんようび＝何曜日	1-7	Ni	what day of the week?
nana なな＝七	1-1	N	seven
nana-juu ななじゅう＝七十	1-1	N	seventy
nanatsu ななつ＝七つ	1-2	N	seven [general counter]
nanbiki なんびき＝何匹	1-10	Ni	how many [small animals]?
nanbon なんぼん＝何本	1-10	Ni	how many [long cylindrical objects]?
nandai なんだい＝何台	1-10	Ni	how many [mechanized goods]?
nandemo なんでも＝何でも	3-1	Ni+P	anything
nandomo なんども＝何度も	2-6	Adv	many times
nani なに＝何	1-1	Ni	what?
Nani o sashiagemashoo ka. なにをさしあげましょうか。＝何を差し上げましょうか。			
	2-9	Exp	May I help you?
nani-jin なにじん＝何人	1-3	Ni	what nationality?
nanigo なにご＝何語	1-4	Ni	what language?
naniiro なにいろ＝何色	1-5	N	what color?
nanika なにか＝何か	2-15	N	something
nanimo なにも＝何も＋Neg.	1-4	Ni+P	(not) anything
nanji なんじ＝何時	1-7	Ni	what time?
-nano? ーなの？	3-1	SP	[female sentence ending particle]
nanoka なのか＝七日	1-11	N	(the) seventh day of the month
nanwa なんわ＝何羽	1-10	Ni	how many [birds]?
naosu なおす＝直す/なおします	3-7	V1	(to) fix
napukin ナプキン	1-14	N	napkin
Nara なら＝奈良	2-1	N	Nara
narau ならう＝習う/ならいます	2-2	V1	(to) learn
nareetaa ナレーター	2-11	N	narrator
narimasen なりません	2-5	V1	(it) won't do
(〜に) naru なる/なります	2-12	V1	(to) become 〜
naruhodo なるほど	2-11	Exp	Indeed! I see!
natsu なつ＝夏	1-12	N	summer
natsukashii なつかしい＝懐かしい	3-6	A	(is) nostalgic

nattoo なっとう＝納豆	3-8	N	fermented soybeans
naze なぜ	1-11	Ni	why?
(sentence +) ne ね	1-6	SP	isn't it? [sentence ending particle]
(o)nedan (お)ねだん＝(お)値段	2-9	N	price
nekkuresu ネックレス	2-3	N	necklace
neko ねこ＝猫	1-10	N	cat
nemui ねむい＝眠い	1-12	A	(is) sleepy
- nen - ねん＝ - 年	1-15	Nd	- year
- nen(kan) - ねんかん＝ - 年間	2-6	Nd	- year(s)
nengajoo ねんがじょう＝年賀状	2--7	N	New Year's card
neru ねる＝寝る／ねます	1-7	V2	(to) sleep; go to bed
netsu ねつ＝熱	1-12	N	fever
nezumi ねずみ＝鼠	1-10	N	mouse
〜 ni 〜 に	2-6	P	per 〜
〜 ni 〜 〜 に〜	2-5	P	〜 and 〜 (as a set)
ni に＝二	1-1	N	two
(place) ni に (+ direction verb)	1-7	P	to (place)
(place) ni に (+ existence verb)	1-10	P	in; at (place)
(specific time) ni に	1-7	P	at (specific time)
(activity) ni に	1-7	P	for (activity)
- ni tsuite 〜について	2-2	P+V	about
- ni yoruto 〜によると	3-6	P+V+P	according to 〜
ni-juu にじゅう＝二十	1-1	N	twenty
- nichi - にち＝ - 日	1-11	Nd	day of the month
- nichi(kan) - にち(かん)＝- 日(間)	2-6	Nd	- day(s)
nichiyoobi にちようび＝日曜日	1-7	N	Sunday
Nido aru koto wa sando aru. にどあることはさんどある＝二度あることは三度ある			
	3-2	Prov	If something happens twice, it will happen three times.
nigai にがい＝苦い	3-8	A	(is) bitter
nigate にがて＝苦手	1-5	Na	(be) weak in
nigatsu にがつ＝二月	1-3	N	February
(o)nigiri (お)にぎり	1-14	N	riceball
nigirizushi にぎりずし＝握り鮨	2-5	N	sushi rice shaped in bite-sized rectangles topped with fish, roe, shellfish, vegetables or egg
nigiyaka にぎやか＝賑やか	3-6	NA	lively; bustling
nihon にほん＝日本	1-3	N	Japan
(-wa) nihongo de nan to iimasu ka. (-は)にほんごでなんといいますか。			
	1-1	Exp	How do you say 〜 in Japanese?
nihongo にほんご＝日本語	1-4	N	Japanese language
nihonjin にほんじん＝日本人	1-3	N	Japanese citizen
nijuu-yokka にじゅうよっか＝二十四日	1-11	N	(the) twenty-fourth day of the month

nikaidate にかいだて＝二階建て	3-7	N	two story house
nikoniko ニコニコ	2-15	Adv	smilingly [onomatopoetic]
(V stem) nikui (Verb Stem) ＋にくい	3-4	A	(is) hard to do 〜
nikuudon にくうどん＝肉うどん	2-5	N	udon topped with beef
nimono にもの＝煮物	3-8	N	boiled (in broth) foods
- nin - にん＝ - 人	1-3	Nd	[counter for people]
ninjin にんじん＝人参	3-1	N	carrot
ninki ga aru にんきがある＝人気がある	3-6	V1	(be) popular
nioi におい＝臭い	2-7	N	smell; fragrance
niru にる＝煮る/にます	3-8	V2	(to) boil (in broth); simmer
nishi にし＝西	2-1	N	west
nishiguchi にしぐち＝西口	3-9	N	west entrance/exit
niwa にわ＝庭	1-10	N	garden; yard
no の	1-3	P	[possessive and descriptive particle]
-no? 〜の？	3-1	SP	[female sentence ending particle]
-node 〜ので	3-3	Rc	since 〜; because 〜; so
nodo のど＝喉	1-6	N	throat
Nodo ga karakara desu. のどがカラカラです。＝喉がカラカラです。	1-14	Exp	I am thirsty.
Nodo ga kawakimashita. のどがかわきました。＝喉が渇きました。	1-14	Exp	I got thirsty.
nomimono のみもの＝飲み物	1-5	N	(a) drink
nomu のむ＝飲む/のみます	1-4	V1	(to) drink
	1-12	V1	take (medicine)
-noni 〜のに	3-3	Rc	in spite of 〜; although 〜 [reverse result]
nooto ノート	1-2	N	notebook
noriba のりば＝乗り場	3-9	N	place of embarkment; place one gets on a vehicle
(vehicle に) noru のる＝乗る/のります	2-4	V1	(to) ride
nugu ぬぐ＝脱ぐ/ぬぎます	3-2	V1	(to) remove clothing [i.e., shoes, dress, hat]

\<O\>

o を	2-4	P	through; along
oba おば＝叔母	3-1	N	(one's own) aunt
obaasan おばあさん	1-3	N	grandmother; elderly woman
obasan おばさん	1-15	N	aunt; middle aged woman
oboeru おぼえる＝覚える/おぼえます	2-6	V2	(to) memorize
ocha おちゃ＝お茶	1-4	N	tea
Ochanomizu おちゃノみず＝御茶ノ水	3-9	N	Ochanomizu [a city in Tokyo]
ochitsuku おちつく＝落ち着く/おちつきます	3-7	V1	(to) become calm
odori おどり＝踊り	3-6	N	dance
odoru おどる＝踊る/おどります	3-6	V1	(to) dance

Ohayoo gozaimasu. おはようございます。	1-1	Exp	Good morning. [formal]
Ohayoo. おはよう。	1-1	Exp	Good morning. [informal]
ohisama おひさま＝お日様	2-11	N	sun [polite]
Ohisashiburi desu. おひさしぶりです。	3-3	Exp	(I) have not seen you for a long time.
oishasan おいしゃさん＝御医者さん	1-3	N	(medical) doctor [polite form of いしゃ]
oishii おいしい＝美味しい	1-13	A	(is) delicious
oji おじ＝叔父	3-1	N	(one's own) uncle
ojiisan おじいさん	1-3	N	grandfather; elderly man
ojisan おじさん	1-15	N	uncle; man
okaasan おかあさん＝お母さん	1-3	N	(someone's) mother
Okaerinasai. おかえりなさい。 ＝お帰りなさい。	3-1	Exp	Welcome home. [Used by a family member who welcomes another family member home.]
Okagesama de. おかげさまで。＝お陰様で。	3-3	Exp	Thanks to you ...
Okawari おかわり＝お代わり	3-8	N	second serving
Okawari wa? おかわりは？＝お代わりは？	3-8	Exp	Will you have seconds?
Okinawa おきなわ＝沖縄	2-1	N	Okinawa
okiru おきる＝起きる／おきます	1-7	V2	(to) wake up; get up
okoru おこる＝怒る／おこります	2-15	V1	(to become) angry
(-te) oku （〜て）おく／おきます	3-8	V1	(to) do (something in advance)
oku おく＝置く／おきます	2-5	V1	(to) put; leave
okuru おくる＝送る／おくります	2-7	V1	(to) send; mail
okusan おくさん＝奥さん	3-6	N	(someone else's) wife
Omedetoo gozaimasu. おめでとうございます	1-15	Exp	Congratulations.
omoi おもい＝重い	3-7	A	(is) heavy
omoidasu おもいだす＝思い出す／おもいだします	3-4	V2	(to) recall
omoshiroi おもしろい＝面白い	1-11	A	(is) interesting; (is) funny
(-oo to) omotte iru (-ooと) おもっている＝思っている	3-8	V1+V1	(I am) thinking of doing
omou おもう＝思う／おもいます	2-11	V1	(to) think
on (yomi) おん（よみ）＝音（読み）	3-4	N	Chinese reading (of a kanji)
onaji おなじ＝同じ	2-9	N	same
onaka おなか＝お腹	1-6	N	stomach
Onaka ga ippai desu. おなかがいっぱいです＝お腹が一杯です	1-14	Exp	(I am) full.
Onaka ga pekopeko desu. おなかがペコペコです。＝お腹がペコペコです。	1-14	Exp	I am hungry.
Onaka ga sukimashita. おなかがすきました。＝お腹が空きました。	1-14	Exp	I got hungry.
ondo おんど＝温度	2-7	N	temperature
oneesan おねえさん＝お姉さん	1-3	N	(someone's) older sister
Onegaishimasu. おねがいします。＝御願いします。	1-1	Exp	Please. [request]
ongaku おんがく＝音楽	1-5	N	music
oniisan おにいさん＝お兄さん	1-3	N	(someone's) older brother

onna no hito おんなのひと=女の人	1-10	N	woman; lady
onna no ko おんなのこ=女の子	1-10	N	girl
onna おんな=女	1-10	N	female
ooen (o) suru おうえん(を)する=応援(を)する	2-10	V3	(to) cheer
ooi おおい=多い	1-11	A	(are) many, much
ookii おおきい=大きい	1-6	A	(is) big
orenji (iro) オレンジいろ=オレンジ色	1-5	N	orange (color)
(kaidan を) oriru おりる=下りる/おります	3-7	V2	(to) go down (stairs)
(vehicle から/を) oriru おりる=降りる	2-4	V2	(to) get off (vehicle)
Osaka おおさか=大坂	2-1	N	Osaka
Osaki ni. おさきに。=お先に。	3-1	Exp	Excuse me for going/doing something first.
Osewa ni narimashita. おせわになりました。=お世話になりました。			
	3-3	Exp	Thank you for your kind help.
oshieru おしえる=教える/おしえます	2-4	V2	(to) teach; to show (how)
oshimai おしまい	2-11	N	(the) end
osoi おそい=遅い	1-7	A	(is) late
osoku おそく=遅く	1-12	Adv	late
Osoku narimashita. おそくなりました。=遅くなりました。	2-14	Exp	Sorry to be late.
Osuki desu ka. おすきですか。=お好きですか。	2-9	Exp	Do you like it? [polite]
otaku おたく=お宅	2-6	N	(someone's) house; residence [polite]
oto おと=音	3-3	N	sound
otoko おとこ=男	1-10	N	male
otoko no hito おとこのひと=男の人	1-10	N	man
otoko no ko おとこのこ=男の子	1-10	N	boy
otona おとな=大人	2-14	N	adult
otonashii おとなしい	3-3	A	(is) quiet (refers to people only)
otoosan おとうさん=お父さん	1-3	N	(someone's) father
otooto おとうと=弟	1-3	N	(my) younger brother
otootosan おとうとさん=弟さん	1-3	N	(someone's) younger brother
otoshidama おとしだま=お年玉	2-7	N	money received mainly by children from adults at New Year's
ototoi おととい=一昨日	1-11	N	(the) day before yesterday
otsuri おつり=お釣	2-9	N	change (from a larger unit of money)
owari ni おわりに=終わりに	2-14	Adv	(at the) end
Owarimashoo. おわりましょう。=終わりましょう。	1-4	Exp	Let's finish.
(V stem) owaru (V Stem) ＋おわる=終わる=おわります	3-4	V1	(to) finish doing ～
(～ を) owaru おわる=終わる/おわります	2-10	V1	(someone will) finish (something) [transitive]
(～ が) owaru おわる=終わる=おわります	2-10	V1	(something) finishes; ends [intransitive]
oyako donburi おやこどんぶり=親子丼	2-5	N	chicken and egg over a bowl of steamed rice
Oyasumi. お休み（なさい）=おやすみ（なさい）。	3-1	Exp	Good night.

oyogu およぐ=泳ぐ/およぎます	1-15	V1	(to) swim

<P>

paama o kakeru パーマをかける/かけます	3-2	V2	(to) perm (one's hair)
-paasento -パーセント	2-5	Nd	percent
paatii パーティー	1-7	N	party
- pai - ぱい= - 杯	1-14	Nd	cupful; glassful; bowlful; spoonful
pan パン	1-4	N	bread
panda パンダ	3-9	N	panda
pantsu パンツ	1-13	N	pants
pasupooto パスポート	2-3	N	passport
patokaa パトカー	2-4	N	patrol car
petto o kau ペットをかう=飼う/かいます	3-3	V1	(to) raise a pet
piano ピアノ	1-5	N	piano
piasu ピアス	2-3	N	pierced earrings
pikunikku ピクニック	1-7	N	picnic
pinku ピンク	1-5	N	pink
piza ピザ	1-14	N	pizza
- pon - ぽん= - 本	1-10	Nd	[counter for long cylindrical objects]
posuto ポスト	3-9	N	mail box
potetochippu ポテトチップ	2-4	N	potato chips
purezento プレゼント	1-15	N	present
puroyakyuu プロやきゅう=プロ野球	3-6	N	professional baseball
puuru プール	1-10	N	pool

<R>

raamen ラーメン	2-5	N	Chinese noodle soup
raigakki らいがっき=来学期き	3-2	N	next semester
raigetsu らいげつ=来月	1-12	N	next month
rainen らいねん=来年	1-15	N	next year
raishuu らいしゅう=来週	1-11	N	next week
raisukaree ライスカレー	2-5	N	curry rice
rajio ラジオ	1-4	N	radio
raku らく=楽	3-3	NA	(is) comfortable
-rashii 〜らしい	3-8	Da	(It) seems that 〜
Rei. れい。=礼。	1-1	Exp	Bow.
(o)rei （お）れい=（お）礼	3-3	N	thanks; gratitude; appreciation
(o)reijoo （お）れいじょう=（お）礼状	3-3	N	thank you letter
reizooko れいぞうこ=冷蔵庫	3-7	N	refrigerator
reji レジ	2-5	N	cash register
rekishi れきし=歴史	3-1	N	history
renshuu (o) suru れんしゅう(を)する=練習(を)する	1-12	V3	(to) practice
repooto レポート	1-4	N	report; paper
resutoran レストラン	1-7	N	restaurant
rika りか=理科	3-1	N	science

rikon (o) suru りこん(を)する＝離婚(を)する	2-15	V3	(to) divorce
rokkaa ロッカー	1-10	N	locker
roku ろく＝六	1-1	N	six
roku-juu ろくじゅう＝六十	1-1	N	sixty
rokugatsu ろくがつ＝六月	1-3	N	June
rusu るす＝留守	2-6	N	(is) not at home
ryokoo (o) suru りょこう(を)する＝旅行(を)する	1-7	V3	(to) travel
ryokoo りょこう＝旅行	1-7	N	trip, traveling
ryoo りょう＝寮	2-2	N	dormitory
ryoohoo りょうほう＝両方	2-9	N	both
ryookin りょうきん＝料金	3-9	N	fare
ryoori (o) suru りょうり(を)する＝料理(を)する	2-7	V3	(to) cook
ryooshin りょうしん＝両親	2-2	N	(own) parents
ryuugaku suru りゅうがくする＝留学する	3-2	V3	(to) study abroad

<S>

Saa ... さあ...	2-9	SI	Well ... [Used when one does not know or is unsure of an answer.]
sabishii さびしい＝寂しい	3-6	A	(is) lonely
sagasu さがす＝探す／さがします	3-4	V1	(to) look for; search for
- sai - さい＝- オ, - 歳	1-3	Nd	[counter for age]
saifu さいふ＝財布	2-5	N	wallet
saigo さいご＝最後	3-8	N	(the) last; final
saigo ni さいごに＝最後に	3-8	Adv	(at) last; finally
saikin さいきん＝最近	3-4	Adv	recently; recent
saikoo さいこう＝最高	3-8	N	(the) best
saikoo ni さいこうに＝最高に	3-8	Adv	(the) most
saisho さいしょ＝最初	3-8	N	(the) first
saisho ni さいしょに＝最初に	3-8	Adv	first of all
saizu サイズ	1-14	N	size
sakana さかな＝魚	1-10	N	fish
(o)sake (お)さけ＝(お)酒	2-14	N	rice wine; liquor in general
sakkaa サッカー	1-5	N	soccer
samui さむい＝寒い	1-1	A	(is) cold (temperature)
samurai さむらい＝侍	3-6	N	(Japanese) warrior
- san - さん	1-1	Nd	Mr./Mrs./Ms.
san さん＝三	1-1	N	three
san-juu さんじゅう＝三十	1-1	N	thirty
sandoitchi サンドイッチ	1-14	N	sandwich
sangatsu さんがつ＝三月	1-3	N	March
sangurasu サングラス	2-3	N	sunglasses
sankaku さんかく＝三角	3-8	N	triangle
sanpo (o) suru さんぽ(を)する＝散歩(を)する	2-15	V3	(to) take a walk
Sapporo さっぽろ＝札幌	2-1	N	Sapporo

(o)sara おさら＝お皿	1-14	N	plate; dishes
sarada サラダ	1-14	N	salad
(superior ni に) sashiageru さしあげる＝差し上げる／さしあげます			
	2-9	V2	(to) give (to a superior)
satoo さとう＝砂糖	2-14	N	sugar
- satsu - さつ＝ - 冊	1-15	Nd	[counter for bound objects]
Sayoonara. さようなら。	1-1	Exp	Good-bye.
se(i) せ(い)＝背	1-6	N	height
seeru(chuu) セール中	2-9	N	(for) sale
seetaa セーター	2-3	N	sweater
seifuku せいふく＝制服	2-3	N	(school) uniform
seikaku せいかく＝性格	3-3	N	personality
seikatsu せいかつ＝生活	3-3	N	life; living
seikoo せいこう＝成功	3-5	N	success
seikoo suru せいこうする＝成功する	3-5	V3	(to) succeed
seiseki せいせき＝成績	1-11	N	grade
seito せいと＝生徒	1-3	N	student [non-college]
seiyoo ryoori せいようりょうり＝西洋料理	3-8	N	Western-style cooking
seiyooteki せいようてき＝西洋的	3-7	NA	Western style
seiza suru せいざする＝正座する	3-7	V3	(to) sit properly
sekai せかい＝世界	2-9	N	world
semai せまい＝狭い	1-10	A	(is) narrow; small (room)
sen せん＝千	1-13	N	thousand
Sendai せんだい＝仙台	2-1	N	Sendai
sengakki せんがっき＝先学期	3-2	N	last semester
sengetsu せんげつ＝先月	1-12	N	last month
senkoo suru せんこうする＝専攻する	3-1	V3	(to) major (in)
sensei せんせい＝先生	1-1	N	teacher; Mr./Mrs./Ms./Dr.
senshu せんしゅ＝選手	2-10	N	(sports) player
senshuu せんしゅう＝先週	1-11	N	last week
sentaku (o) suru せんたく(を)する＝洗濯(を)する	2-7	V3	(to do) laundry
- sento - セント	1-13	Nd	- cent(s)
setsumei せつめい＝説明	3-9	N	(an) explanation
setsumei o suru せつめいをする＝説明をする	3-9	V3	(to) explain
sewa o suru せわ（を）する＝世話（を）する	3-3	V3	(to) take care of ～
shakai しゃかい＝社会	1-11	N	social studies; society
shashin しゃしん＝写真	1-2	N	photo
shatsu シャツ	1-13	N	shirt
shawaa o abiru シャワーをあびる／あびます	3-3	V2	(to) take a shower
-shi - し、	3-4	Rc	besides; what's more
shi し＝四	1-1	N	four
shi し＝市	2-9	N	city
shiai しあい＝試合	1-12	N	(sports) game

shiawase しあわせ＝幸せ	3-6	NA	happy (life); fortunate
shibafu しばふ＝芝生	3-2	N	lawn
Shibuya しぶや＝渋谷	3-9	N	Shibuya [a city in Tokyo]
shichi しち＝七	1-1	N	seven
shichi-juu しちじゅう＝七十	1-1	N	seventy
shichigatsu しちがつ＝七月	1-3	N	July
shigatsu しがつ＝四月	1-3	N	April
(o)shigoto (お)しごと＝(お)仕事	1-3	N	job
shiitoberuto o suru シートベルトをする	2-4	V3	(to) wear a seat belt
-shika -しか+Neg.	3-1	P	only ～ [emphasis]
shika しか＝鹿	3-10	N	deer
shikaku しかく＝四角	3-11	N	square
shikakui しかくい＝四角い	3-11	A	(is) square (shaped)
shikaru しかる＝叱る／しかります	2-15	V1	(to) scold
Shikashi しかし	2-15	SI	However [formal equivalent of でも]

Shikata ga arimasen/nai. しかたがありません／ない。＝仕方がありません／ない。

	2-6	Exp	(It) cannot be helped.
shiken しけん＝試験	1-2	N	exam
shiken o ukeru しけんをうける＝試験を受ける／うけます	3-3	V2	(to) take an exam
Shikoku しこく＝四国	2-1	N	Shikoku
shima しま＝島	2-9	N	island
(verb TE) shimau しまう／しまいます	2-11	V1	(to) do ～ completely [regret, criticism]
shimeru しめる＝閉める／しめます	1-13	V2	(to) close
Shimete kudasai. しめてください。＝閉めて下さい。	1-1	Exp	Please close.
Shinagawa しながわ＝品川	3-9	N	Shinagawa [a city in Tokyo]
shinbun しんぶん＝新聞	1-4	N	newspaper
shingoo しんごう＝信号	2-4	N	traffic lights
Shinjuku しんじゅく＝新宿	3-9	N	Shinjuku [a city in Tokyo]
shinkansen しんかんせん＝新幹線	3-9	N	bullet train
shinpai (o) suru しんぱい(を)する＝心配(を)する	2-4	V3	(to) worry
shinseki しんせき＝親戚	1-15	N	relatives
shinsetsu しんせつ＝親切	3-3	Na	(is) kind
shinshitsu しんしつ＝寝室	3-7	N	bedroom
shinu しぬ＝死ぬ／しにます	1-12	V1	(to) die
shio しお＝塩	2-14	N	salt
shiokarai しおからい＝塩辛い	2-14	A	(is) salty
shiraberu しらべる＝調べる／＝しらべます	3-4	V2	(to) check; (to) investigate
shirimasen しりません＝知りません	1-2	V1	do not know
shiritsu しりつ＝私立	3-2	N	private
shiro しろ＝白	1-5	N	white
shiroi しろい＝白い	1-6	A	(is) white
shita した＝下	2-2	N	under; below
(part of body o) shite iru (part of body を) している	3-6	V	have (part of body)

shitsumon しつもん＝質問	2-2	N	question
shitsumon (o) suru しつもん(を)する＝質問(を)する	2-2	V3	(to) ask a question
Shitsurei shimashita. しつれいしました。＝失礼しました。	3-1	Exp	(I am) sorry to have inconvenienced you, or for a rude act I have committed.
Shitsurei shimasu. しつれいします。＝失礼します。	3-1	Exp	Excuse me, I must be going now. I am about to trouble you. [lit., I will be rude]
shitte iru しっている＝知っている	2-2	V1	(to) know
shizen しぜん＝自然	3-8	N	nature
shizuka しずか＝静か	1-6	Na	quiet
shizuka ni suru しずかにする＝静かにする	1-13	V3	quiet down
Shizuka ni shite kudasai. しずかにしてください＝静かにして下さい			
	1-2	Exp	Please be quiet.
shokuji しょくじ＝食事	1-7	N	meal; dining
shokuji (o) suru しょくじ（を）する＝食事（を）する	1-7	V3	(to) dine; have a meal
shokyuu しょきゅう＝初級	3-4	N	beginner level
(o)shoogatsu (お)しょうがつ＝(お)正月	2-7	N	New Year
shooji しょうじ＝障子	3-7	N	shoji (rice paper) door
shookai (o) suru しょうかい(を)する＝紹介(を)する	2-2	V3	(to) introduce
shoomeisho しょうめいしょ＝証明書	2-3	N	I. D.
shoorai しょうらい＝将来	2-14	N	future
shootesuto しょうテスト＝小テスト	1-2	N	quiz
shootopantsu ショートパンツ	2-3	N	shorts
shootsu ショーツ	2-3	N	shorts
shufu しゅふ＝主婦	1-3	N	housewife
shujin しゅじん＝主人	3-6	N	(own) husband
shukudai しゅくだい＝宿題	1-2	N	homework
shumi しゅみ＝趣味	1-5	N	hobby
shuu しゅう＝州	2-9	N	state
- shuukan - しゅうかん＝- 週間	2-6	Nd	- week(s)
shuumatsu しゅうまつ＝週末	1-11	N	weekend
soba そば＝傍	2-2	N	by; nearby
sobo そぼ＝祖母	3-1	N	(one's own) grandmother
sochira そちら	2-5	N	there [polite equiv. of そこ]
	2-9	N	that one [polite equiv. of それ]
sofu そふ＝祖父	3-1	N	(one's own) grandfather
sokkusu ソックス	2-3	N	socks
soko そこ	1-2	N	there
sonkei suru そんけいする＝尊敬する	3-3	V3	(to) respect
sono koro そのころ＝その頃	2-10	PN+N	around that time
sono toki そのとき＝その時	2-15	N	at that time
sono ～ その ～	1-2	PN	that ～
-soo da ーそうだ	3-6	Nd+ C	(I) heard that ～

(Stem form +) soo desu -そうです	2-5	SI	looks ～
Soo desu ka. そうですか。	1-3	Exp	Is that so?
Soo desu. そうです。	1-1	Exp	It is.
Soo desu nee . . . そうですねえ...	1-5	Exp	Let me see . . .
Soo dewa arimasen. そうではありません。	1-1	Exp	It is not so. [formal]
Soo ja arimasen. そうじゃありません。	1-1	Exp	It is not so. [informal]
Soobusen そうぶせん＝総武線	3-9	N	Sobu Line [yellow colored train line in Tokyo]
soodan suru そうだんする＝相談する	3-3	V3	(to) consult
sooji (o) suru そうじ(を)する＝掃除(を)する	2-7	V3	(to) clean up
sore それ	1-1	N	that one
Sore wa ii kangae desu. それはいいかんがえです。＝それはいい考えです。	2-10	Exp	That is a good idea.
Soredake desu. それだけです。	2-5	Exp	That's all.
Sorekara それから	1-7	SI	And then
Soreni それに	1-11	SI	Moreover; Besides
Soretomo それとも	1-6	SI	(Question 1). Or (Question 2)
Soshite そして	1-3	SI	And [Used at the beginning of a sentence.]
soto そと＝外	1-10	N	outside
(school o) sotsugyo suru そつぎょうする＝卒業する	3-1	V3	(to) graduate (from school)
sotsugyooshiki そつぎょうしき＝卒業式	3-2	N	graduation ceremony
su す＝酢	2-14	N	vinegar
subarashii すばらしい＝素晴らしい	1-13	A	(is) wonderful
- sugi - すぎ＝ - 過ぎ	1-7	Nd	after ～
(Stem form +) sugiru すぎる＝過ぎる/すぎます	2-14	V2	too ～
sugoi すごい＝凄い	1-13	A	(is) terrible, terrific
suiei すいえい＝水泳	1-5	N	swimming
suite iru すいている/すいています	2-13	V1	(is) not crowded; (is) empty
suiyoobi すいようび＝水曜日	1-7	N	Wednesday
sukaato スカート	2-3	N	skirt
suki すき＝好き	1-5	Na	like
sukiyaki すきやき＝鋤焼き	2-14	N	*sukiyaki*
sukoa スコア	2-10	N	score
sukoshi すこし＝少し	1-4	Adv	a little [formal]
	1-10	Adv	a few; a little
suku すく	2-13	V1	(to) get empty; be empty
sukunai すくない＝少ない	1-11	A	is few; little
sukuurubasu スクールバス	2-4	N	school bus
Sumimasen. すみません	1-1	Exp	Excuse me.
	1-13	Exp	Excuse me. [to get attention]
(place に) sumu すむ＝住む/すみます	2-2	V1	live (in ～)
sunakkubaa スナックバー	1-4	N	snack bar

sunomono すのもの＝酢の物	3-8	N	vinegared vegetables
supein スペイン	1-3	N	Spain
supeingo スペインご＝スペイン語	1-4	N	Spanish language
supiido o dasu スピードをだす＝出す／だします	2-4	V1	(to) speed
supootsu スポーツ	1-5	N	sports
suppai すっぱい＝酸っぱい	2-14	A	(is) sour
supuun スプーン	1-14	N	spoon
suru する／します	1-4	V3	(to) do
suru する／します	2-3	V3	(to) wear [accessories]
(something に) suru する／します	2-5	V3	(to) decide on ～
Suruto すると	2-13	SI	Thereupon
sushiya すしや＝寿司屋	1-13	N	*sushi* shop/bar
(gomi o) suteru (ごみを)すてる／すてます	2-3	V2	(to) litter; (to) throw away (garbage)
Sutoresu ga ippai desu. ストレスがいっぱいです。	2-6	Exp	(is) very stressed
sutoroo ストロー	1-14	N	straw
(tabako o) suu (たばこを)すう／すいます	2-3	V1	(to) smoke cigarettes
suugaku すうがく＝数学	1-11	N	math
suupaa スーパー	1-13	N	supermarket
suwaru すわる＝座る／すわります	1-13	V1	(to) sit
Suwatte kudasai. すわってください。＝座って下さい。	1-2	Exp	Please sit.
suzushii すずしい＝涼しい	1-1	A	(is) cool [temperature]

\<T\>

tabako たばこ	2-3	N	tobacco; cigarettes
tabemono たべもの＝食べ物	1-5	N	food
taberu たべる＝食べる／たべます	1-4	V2	(to) eat
tabeyoo たべよう＝食べよう	3-1	V2	let's eat [informal form of 食べましょう]
tabun たぶん＝多分	2-7	Adv	probably
- tachi - たち＝ - 達	1-12	Nd	[suffix for animate plurals]
Tadaima. ただいま。	3-1	Exp	(I'm) home. [Used by a family member who has come home.]
tadashii ただしい＝正しい	2-2	A	(is) correct
～ tai ～ ～たい～＝～対 ～	2-10	PN	～ to ～; ～ vs. ～
(Verb stem +) tai -たい	1-12	Da	want (to do)
taihen たいへん＝大変	1-11	Na	hard; difficult
taiiku たいいく＝体育	1-11	N	P.E.
taiikukan たいいくかん＝体育館	2-10	N	gym
taipu (o) suru タイプ(を)する	1-4	V3	(to) type
taitei たいてい＝大抵	1-4	Adv	usually
takai たかい＝高い	1-6	A	(is) tall
	1-13	A	(is) expensive
takenoko たけのこ＝竹の子	3-8	N	bamboo shoot
takusan たくさん＝沢山	1-10	Adv	a lot; many
takushii タクシー	1-7	N	taxi

takuwan たくわん＝沢庵	3-8	N	pickled turnip
tama ni たまに	2-15	Adv	occasionally; once in a while
tamago たまご＝卵	2-14	N	egg
(o)tanjoobi (お)たんじょうび＝(お)誕生日	1-11	N	birthday
tanoshii たのしい＝楽しい	1-11	A	(is) fun; enjoyable
(〜を)tanoshimi ni shite imasu (-を)たのしみにしています＝(-を)楽しみにしています			
	1-15	Exp	I am looking forward to (something).
tanoshimu たのしむ＝楽しむ/たのしみます	3-6	V1	(to) enjoy
tasukeru たすける＝助ける/たすけます	2-15	V2	(to) rescue; (to) help
(doramu o) tataku （ドラムを）たたく/たたきます	3-5	V1	(to) beat (a drum)
tatami たたみ＝畳	3-7	N	straw mat
tatemono たてもの＝建物	1-10	N	building
tateru たてる＝建てる/たてます	3-7	V1	(to) build
tatoeba たとえば＝例えば	3-4	SI	For example
tatsu たつ＝立つ/たちます	1-13	V1	(to) stand
Tatte kudasai. たってください。＝立って下さい。	1-2	Exp	Please stand.
-te (kara) -て（から）、	3-4	V+P	After 〜
te て＝手	1-6	N	hand
(o)tearai (お)てあらい＝(お)手洗い	1-10	N	bathroom; restroom
teeburu テーブル	1-2	N	table
teepu テープ	1-4	N	tape
tegami てがみ＝手紙	1-4	N	letter
tekisuto テキスト	1-2	N	textbook
-tekure ーてくれ	3-1	E	[male informal form of ーて下さい]
temae てまえ＝手前	3-9	N	this side (of)
-ten - てん＝ - 点	2-10	Nd	- point(s)
tenisu テニス	1-5	N	tennis
(o)tenki (お)てんき＝(お)天気	1-1	N	weather
tenkiyohoo てんきよほう＝天気予報	3-6	N	weather forecast
tennoo てんのう＝天皇	3-9	N	Emperor
(o)tera (お)てら＝(お)寺	2-7	N	temple (Buddhist)
terebi テレビ	1-4	N	T.V.
terebigeemu テレビゲーム	1-5	N	video game
tetsudau てつだう＝手伝う/てつだいます	2-7	V3	(to) help
tiishatsu Tシャツ	2-3	N	T-shirt
tisshu ティッシュ	1-2	N	tissue
to と	1-3	P	and [used between two nouns]
to と＝戸	1-10	N	door
(quotation) to と	2-11	P	[quotation particle]
to (issho ni) と(いっしょに)	1-4	P	with (person)
(N1) to iu (N2) N1 という N2	3-2	P+V	N2 called N1
(o)toire (お)トイレ	1-10	N	bathroom; restroom
(N1) toka (N2) N1 とか N2 (とか)	3-2	P	(N1) and (N2) (among others)

tokei とけい＝時計	1-13	N	watch, clock
～toki ～とき＝～時	2-15	N	time; when ～
tokidoki ときどき＝時々	1-4	Adv	sometimes
tokoro ところ	3-2	N	point
tokoro ところ＝所	2-2	N	place
Tokorode ところで	2-3	SI	By the way
toku ni とくに＝特に	2-2	Adv	especially
tokubetsu とくべつ＝特別	3-3	NA	special
tokui とくい＝得意	1-5	Na	(be) strong in; can do well
Tokyo とうきょう＝東京	2-1	N	Tokyo
(place で/に) tomaru とまる＝止まる/とまります	2-4	V1	(to) stop
tomodachi ともだち＝友達	1-4	N	friend
tonari となり＝隣	2-2	N	next to
Tondemonai. とんでもない。	2-11	Exp	How ridiculous! That's impossible!
tonkatsu とんかつ＝豚カツ	2-5	N	pork cutlet
too とお＝十	1-2	N	ten [general counter]
tooi とおい＝遠い	1-10	A	(is) far
tooka とおか＝十日	1-11	N	(the) tenth day of the month
tooku とおく＝遠く	2-2	N	far away
Tookyooeki とうきょうえき＝東京駅	3-9	N	Tokyo Station [a station in Tokyo]
toori とおり＝通り	2-13	N	street; avenue
tootoo とうとう	2-11	Adv	finally; at last [after much effort]
tooyooteki とうようてき＝東洋的	3-7	Na	Eastern style
toraberaazu chekku トラベラーズチェック	2-9	N	traveler's check
toranpu トランプ	1-5	N	(playing) cards
tori とり＝鳥	1-10	N	bird
(thing を) tori ni iku とりにいく＝取りに行く/とりにいきます	2-10	V1	(to) go to pick up (something)
(thing を) tori ni kaeru とりにかえる＝取りに帰る/とりにかえります	2-10	V1	(to) return to pick up (something)
(thing を) tori ni kuru とりにくる＝取りに来る/とりにきます	2-10	V3	(to) come to pick up (something)
toriniku とりにく＝鳥肉	2-14	N	chicken (meat)
toru とる＝取る	1-15	V1	(to) take; get
toshi o totte iru としをとっている＝年を取っている	1-6	V1	(is) old (person's, animal's age)
-toshite ～として	3-2	P+V	as ～; for ～
toshokan としょかん＝図書館	1-4	N	library
totemo とても	1-5	Adv	very
(～ o) totte kudasai. (～を)とってください。＝取って下さい。	3-8	Exp	Excuse me. Please pass me ～.
tsugi つぎ＝次	1-11	N	next
tsugi ni つぎに＝次に	2-14	Adv	next
tsuitachi ついたち＝一日	1-11	N	(the) first day of the month

tsukaremashita つかれました＝疲れました　　　1-12　V2　(became) tired
tsukarete imasu つかれています＝疲れています1-12　V2　(is) tired
tsukau　つかう＝使う／つかいます　　　3-1　V1　(to) use
tsukemono つけもの＝漬け物　　　3-8　N　pickled vegetable
(object を thing に) tsukeru つける／つけます 2-14　V2　(to) dip (object in thing)
tsukeru つける＝漬ける／つけます　　　3-8　V2　(to) soak; dip
tsukiatari つきあたり＝突き当たり　　　3-9　N　end (of a street)
(-to) tsukiau (〜と) つきあう／つきあいます3-6　V1　(to) associate with 〜
(place に) tsuku つく＝着く／つきます　　2-4　V1　(to) arrive (at a place)
tsukue つくえ＝机　　　1-10　N　desk
tsukurikata つくりかた＝作り方　　　2-14　N　how to make
tsukuru つくる＝作る／つくります　　　1-15　V1　(to) make
tsumaranai つまらない　　　1-11　A　(is) boring, uninteresting
tsumetai つめたい＝冷たい　　　1-14　A　cold (to the touch)
(Dic./NAI) tsumori desu つもりです　　2-6　Nd　plan to do/do not plan to do
tsurai つらい＝辛い　　　3-3　A　(is) hard; bitter; painful
tsurete iku つれていく＝連れて行く／つれていきます 2-7　V1　(to) take (animate)
tsurete kaeru つれてかえる＝連れて帰る／つれてかえります
　　　　　　　　　　　　　　　2-7　V1　(to) take/bring (animate) back home
tsurete kuru つれてくる＝連れて来る／つれてきます 2-7　V3　(to) bring (animate)
(place に) tsutomeru つとめる＝勤める 2-2　V2　(is) employed (at 〜)
tsuyoi つよい＝強い　　　1-12　A　(is) strong
(V stem) tsuzukeru (V Stem) ＋つづける＝続ける／つづけます
　　　　　　　　　　　　　　　3-4　V2　(to) continue/keep doing 〜
-tte 一って　　　3-1　P[informal form of quotation particle と]
<U>
uchi うち　　　1-4　N　house
uchi うち＝内　　　3-7　N　inside
udon うどん　　　2-5　N　thick white noodles in broth
ue うえ＝上　　　2-2　N　on; top
Ueno うえの＝上野　　　3-9　N　Ueno [a city in Tokyo]
(object が) ugoku うごく＝動く／うごきます2-11　V1　(something) move [intransitive]
ukagau うかがう＝伺う／いかがいます 2-13　V1　(to) ask [polite equiv. of 聞く]
uketoru うけとる＝受け取る／うけとります　　3-3　V1　(to) receive
(place で) umareru うまれる＝生まれる／うまれます 2-2　V2　(be) born (in 〜)
umi うみ＝海　　　1-7　N　beach; ocean; sea
Un うん　　　2-4　SI　Yes [informal]
undoo (o) suru うんどう(を)する＝運動(を)する 2-10　V3　(to) exercise
undoo うんどう＝運動　　　2-10　N　sports
undoogutsu うんどうぐつ＝運動靴　　　2-10　N　sports shoes
undoojoo うんどうじょう＝運動場　　　2-10　N　athletic field
unten (o) suru うんてん(を)する＝運転(を)する 2-3　V3　(to) drive
untenmenkyo うんてんめんきょ＝運転免許　　　2-3　N　driver's license

　　　J-E

untenshu うんてんしゅ＝運転手	2-4	N	driver
urayamashii うらやましい＝羨ましい	3-6	A	envious
ureshii うれしい＝嬉しい	1-11	A	(is) glad; happy
uru うる＝売る／うります	2-9	V1	(to) sell
urusai うるさい	1-6	A	(is) noisy
ushiro うしろ＝後ろ	2-2	N	back, behind
uso うそ＝嘘	2-10	N	(a) lie
Uso deshoo. うそでしょう。	2-10	Exp	Are you kidding? Are you serious?
usui うすい＝薄い	2-14	A	(is) thin [referring to something]
usuku うすく＝薄く	2-14	Adv	thin
uta うた＝歌	1-5	N	song; singing
utau うたう＝歌う／うたいます	1-15	V1	(to) sing
utsukushii うつくしい＝美しい	1-10	A	(is) beautiful
Uun う〜ん	2-5	SI	Yummm…
Uun ううん	2-4	SI	No [informal]
uwasa うわさ	3-6	N	rumor

<W>

wa は	1-1	P	[particle marking the topic of the sentence]
-wa -わ＝-羽	1-10	Nd	[counter for birds]
Waa わあ	1-13	SI	Wow!
waakushiito ワークシート	1-2	N	worksheet
waeijiten わえいじてん＝和英辞典	3-4	N	Japanese-English dictionary
wakai わかい＝若い	1-6	A	(is) young
wakareru わかれる＝別れる／わかれます	3-6	V2	(to) separate
wakaru わかる＝分かる／わかります	1-2	V1	(to) understand
wanpiisu ワンピース	2-3	N	dress
warau わらう＝笑う／わらいます	2-15	V1	(to) smile; laugh
warui わるい＝悪い	1-6	A	(is) bad
washitsu わしつ＝和室	3-7	N	Japanese-style room
washoku わしょく＝和食	3-8	N	Japanese meal
wasureru わすれる＝忘れる／わすれます	1-14	V2	(to) forget
(place を) wataru わたる＝渡る／わたります	2-13	V1	(to) cross; go over
watashi わたし＝私	1-1	N	I (used by anyone informally)
watashino わたしの＝私の	1-2	N	mine
watashitachi わたしたち＝私達	1-12	N	we
weitaa ウェイター	2-5	N	waiter
weitoresu ウェイトレス	2-5	N	waitress
wookuman ウォークマン	1-4	N	walkman

<Y>

(N1) ya や (N2)	1-15	P	(N1) and (N2), etc.
yakiniku やきにく＝焼肉	2-5	N	meat grilled on fire
yakitori やきとり＝焼き鳥	2-5	N	grilled skewered chicken

yakizakana やきざかな＝焼き魚	3-8	N	grilled fish
yaku やく＝焼く/やきます	3-8	V1	(to) grill; roast; bake; toast; fry
yaku やく＝訳	3-4	N	translation
yakusoku o suru やくそくをする＝約束をする	3-9	V3	(to make a) promise or agreement
yakusoku やくそく＝約束	3-9	N	(a) promise; agreement
yakusu やくす＝訳す/やくします	3-4	V1	(to) translate
yakyuu やきゅう＝野球	1-5	N	baseball
yama やま＝山	1-7	N	mountain
Yamanotesen やまのてせん＝山手線	3-9	N	Yamanote Line [green colored train line in Tokyo]
yameru やめる＝辞める/やめます	3-2	V2	(to) quit; discontinue
yaru やる/やります	3-2	V1	(to) do [informal form of する]
yaru やる/やります	1-15	V2	(to) give (to inferior)
yasai やさい＝野菜	2-14	N	vegetable
yasashii やさしい＝易しい	1-11	A	(is) easy
yasashii やさしい＝優しい	1-6	A	(is) nice, kind
yasete iru やせている＝痩せている/やせています	1-6	V2	(is) thin (person, animal)
(V stem) yasui (Verb Stem) ＋やすい	3-4	A	(is) easy to do ～
yasui やすい＝安い	1-13	A	(is) cheap
(o)yasumi (お)やすみ＝(お)休み	1-7	N	day off; vacation
(o)yasumi desu (お)やすみです＝(お)休みです	1-1	Exp	(is) absent
yasumijikan やすみじかん＝休み時間	1-11	N	(a) break
(～を) yasumu やすむ＝休む/やすみます	1-12	V1	(be) absent (from ～)
yasumu やすむ＝休む/やすみます	1-12	V1	(to) rest
Yattaa. やったあ。	2-10	Exp	We did it!
yattsu やっつ＝八つ	1-2	N	eight [general counter]
yawarakai やわらかい＝柔らかい	3-8	A	(is) soft; tender
(sentence) yo よ	1-6	SP	you know [sentence ending particle]
yoi よい＝良い	1-6	A	(is) good
yojoohan よじょうはん＝四畳半	3-7	N	4 1/2-mat room
Yokatta desu nee. よかったですねえ。＝良かったですねえ。	1-11	Exp	How nice! [on a past event]
yokka よっか＝四日	1-11	N	(the) fourth day of the month
yoku よく	1-4	Adv	well; often
Yoku dekimashita. よくできました。＝良く出来ました。	1-2	Exp	Well done.
yomu よむ＝読む/よみます	1-4	V1	(to) read
yon よん＝四	1-1	N	four
yon-juu よんじゅう＝四十	1-1	N	forty
Yonde kudasai. よんでください。＝読んで下さい。	1-2	Exp	Please read.
(N1 no) yoo na N2 (N1の)ようなN2	3-6	P+Nd+C	N2 like N1
yoochien ようちえん＝幼稚園	3-1	N	kindergarten
yooka ようか＝八日	1-11	N	(the) eighth day of the month
yooshitsu ようしつ＝洋室	3-7	N	Western-style room

yooshoku ようしょく＝洋食	3-8	N	Western style meal
- yori - より	2-9	P	more than ～
yoru よる＝夜	1-4	N	night
(place に) yoru よる＝寄る／よります	2-10	V1	(to) stop by; drop by (a place)
yottsu よっつ＝四つ	1-2	N	four [general counter]
yowai よわい＝弱い	1-12	A	(is) weak
yoyaku (o) suru よやく(を)する＝予約(を)する	2-5	V3	(to) make a reservation
yubi ゆび＝指	1-6	N	finger; toe
yubiwa ゆびわ＝指輪	2-3	N	ring
yuka ゆか＝床	2-4	N	floor
yuki ゆき＝雪	2-7	N	snow
yukkuri ゆっくり	1-1	Adv	slowly
yume ゆめ＝夢	3-3	N	dream
yunifoomu ユニフォーム	2-10	N	(sports) uniform
yuube ゆうべ	1-12	N	last night
yuubinkyoku ゆうびんきょく＝郵便局	2-13	N	post office
yuugata ゆうがた＝夕方	1-4	N	late afternoon; early evening
yuumei ゆうめい＝有名	1-10	Na	famous
yuushoku ゆうしょく＝夕食	3-1	N	dinner, supper
yuushoo suru ゆうしょうをする＝優勝をする	2-10	V3	(to) win a championship

<Z>

zabuton ざぶとん＝座布団	3-7	N	floor cushion
zairyoo ざいりょう＝材料	3-8	N	ingredients
Zannen deshita nee. ざんねんでしたねえ。＝残念でしたねえ。	1-11	Exp	How disappointing! [on a past event]
Zannen desu ga … ざんねんですが 残念ですが …	2-6	Exp	I'm sorry, but …
Zannen desu nee. ざんねんですねえ。 ＝残念ですねえ。	1-11	Exp	How disappointing! [on a future event]
zarusoba ざるそば	2-5	N	buckwheat noodle dish
zasshi ざっし＝雑誌	1-4	N	magazine
zehi ぜひ＝是非	2-7	Adv	by all means; definitely
zeikin ぜいきん＝税金	2-9	N	tax
zenbu de ぜんぶで＝全部で	1-14	N	for everything
zenbu ぜんぶ＝全部	1-14	N	everything
zenzen (+ Neg.) ぜんぜん＝全然	1-5	Adv	(not) at all
zettai ni ぜったいに＝絶対に	2-3	Adv	absolutely
zubon ズボン	2-3	N	(long) pants
zuibun ずいぶん＝随分	3-3	Adv	quite; fairly
zutto ずっと	2-15	Adv	throughout; all the time

ENGLISH-JAPANESE WORD LIST

English	Volume-Lesson #	Word type	Japanese
\<A\>			
ability	2-11	N	ちから＝力
(be) able to do ～	2-6	V2	(～が) できる＝出来る[できます]
about (time)	1-7	Nd	～ころ; ～ごろ
about how long/far/often?	2-6	Ni	どのぐらい
about ～ [Not used for time]	1-13	Nd	～くらい; ～ぐらい
about ～ [topic]	2-2	P+V	～について
(be) absent (from ～)	1-12	V2	(～を)やすむ＝休む[やすみます]
(He/She is) absent.	1-4	Exp	(お)やすみです。＝(お)休みです。
absolutely	2-3	Adv	ぜったいに＝絶対に
according to ～	3-6	P+V+P	～によると
actor	3-6	N	はいゆう＝俳優
actress	3-6	N	じょゆう＝女優
address	1-15	N	じゅうしょ＝住所
adult	2-14	N	おとな＝大人
advanced level	3-4	N	じょうきゅう＝上級
affection	2-15	N	あい＝愛
after (an event)	1-12	P+N+P	～のあとで＝～の後で
after (time)	1-7	Nd	～すぎ＝～過ぎ
After ～	3-4	V+P	-te (kara) -て（から）、
After S1	3-6	N+P	(TA form)あとで＝-後で
after school	3-2	N	ほうかご＝放課後
again	1-10	Adv	また＝又
airplane	1-7	N	ひこうき＝飛行機
airport	2-13	N	くうこう＝空港
Akihabara [a city in Tokyo]	3-9	N	あきはばら＝秋葉原
all right	1-12	Na	だいじょうぶ＝大丈夫
all the time	2-15	Adv	ずっと
allowance	3-2	N	(お)こづかい＝(お)小遣い
almost; mostly	3-2	Adv	ほとんど
along	2-4	P	を
already	1-14	Exp	もう(+aff.)
alternative	2-9	N	(～の) ほう＝方
Although ～	2-6	Pc	～けど; ～けれど
always	1-4	Adv	いつも
a. m.	1-7	N	ごぜん＝午前
ambulance	2-4	N	きゅうきゅうしゃ＝救急車
among these	2-9	PN+N+P	このなかで＝この中で
among ～	2-9	P	(～のなか＝～の中) で
amount	3-4	N	かず＝数

English	Lesson	Type	Japanese
amuse [not used for sports & music]	1-15	V1	あそぶ＝遊ぶ[あそびます]
(N1) and (N2) (among others)	3-2	P	N1 とか N2 (とか)
(Noun1) and (Noun2), etc.	1-15	P	(N1) や (N2) など
and [used between two nouns]	1-3	P	(N1) と (N2)
And [used only at the beginning of a sentence]	1-3	SI	そして
And then	1-7	SI	それから
(to become) angry	2-15	V1	おこる＝怒る[おこります]
answer	2-2	N	こたえ＝答え
(to) answer	2-2	V2	こたえる＝答える[こたえます]
(not) any more	2-2	Adv	もう＋Neg.
anyplace	3-1	Ni+P	どこでも
Anything else?	2-5	Exp	ほかになにか。＝ほかに何か。
(not) anything	1-4	Ni+P	なにも＝何も＋Neg.
anything	3-1	Ni+P	なんでも＝何でも
anytime	3-1	Ni+P	いつでも
(not to) anywhere	1-7	Ni+P	どこへも＋Neg.
(to) apply make-up	3-2	V3	(お)けしょうをする＝(お)化粧をする [(お)けしょうをします]
(to) appreciate	2-15	V3	かんしゃ(を)する＝感謝(を)する[かんしゃ (を)します]
approximately	2-6	Adv	だいたい
April	1-3	N	しがつ＝四月
area	2-13	N	へん＝辺
around that time	2-10	PN+N	そのころ＝その頃
(to) arrive (at a place)	2-4	V1	(place に) つく＝着く[つきます]
art museum	2-13	N	びじゅつかん＝美術館
art	1-11	N	びじゅつ＝美術
as many/long as ～	2-6	P	(counter) も
(not) as ～ as	2-9	P	～ほど (＋Neg.)
as ～; for ～	3-2	P+V	～として
(to) ask (someone)	2-3	V1	(person に) きく＝聞く[ききます]
ask [polite equiv. of 聞く]	2-13	V1	うかがう＝伺う[うかがいます]
(to) ask a question	2-2	V3	しつもん(を)する＝質問(を)する[しつもん (を)します]
(to) associate with ～	3-6	V1	(～と) つきあう[つきあいます]
at (location) [with existence verb]	1-10	P	に [with existence verb]
at (place) [with action verb]	1-4	P	で [with action verb]
at (specific time)	1-7	P	(specific time) に
(not) at all	1-5	Adv	ぜんぜん＝全然＋Neg.
at last [after much effort]	2-11	Adv	とうとう
at that time	2-15	N	そのとき＝その時
athletic field	2-10	N	うんどうじょう＝運動場
August	1-3	N	はちがつ＝八月

English	Lesson	Type	Japanese
aunt	1-15	N	おばさん
(one's own) aunt	3-1	N	おば＝叔母
autumn	1-12	N	あき＝秋
avenue	2-13	N	とおり＝通り
\<B\>			
baby	2-2	N	あかちゃん＝赤ちゃん
back	2-2	N	うしろ＝後ろ
(is) bad	1-6	A	わるい＝悪い
bag	1-2	N	バッグ
(paper) bag	2-9	N	ふくろ＝袋
balloon	1-15	N	ふうせん＝風船
ballpoint pen	1-2	N	ボールペン
bamboo shoot	3-8	N	たけのこ＝竹の子
bank	2-2	N	ぎんこう＝銀行
baseball	1-5	N	やきゅう
basement	2-9	N	ちか＝地下
basketball	1-5	N	バスケット(ボール)
bathroom	1-10	N	(お)トイレ; (お)手洗い
be (for animate) [polite equiv. of いる]	2-6	V1	いらっしゃる [いらっしゃいます]
beach	1-7	N	うみ＝海
beard	1-6	N	ひげ＝髭
(to) beat (a drum)	3-6	V1	（ドラムを）たたく[たたきます]
(is) beautiful	1-10	A	うつくしい＝美しい
because of (noun)	2-6	P	(noun) で
because	1-11	Pc	(reason) から; ので
(to) become calm	3-7	V1	おちつく＝落ち着く[おちつきます]
become ～	2-12	V1	(～ に) なる [なります]
bed	1-10	N	ベッド
(Japanese) bedding	3-7	N	ふとん＝布団
bedroom	3-7	N	しんしつ＝寝室
beef	2-14	N	ぎゅうにく＝牛肉
beer	2-4	N	ビール
before	1-3	N	まえ＝前
before (not time)	1-12	P+N+P	～のまえに＝ ～の前に
before (time)	1-7	Nd	～まえ＝ ～前
Before S1	3-6	N+P	(dic. form)まえに＝-前に
begin (something)	1-4	V2	(～ を) はじめる＝始める [はじめます]
(to) begin doing ～	3-4	V2	(V Stem) ＋はじめる＝始める[はじめます]
beginner level	3-4	N	しょきゅう＝初級
(at the) beginning	2-14	Adv	はじめに＝始めに
(something) begins	2-10	V1	(～ が) はじまる＝始まる [はじまります]
behind	2-2	N	うしろ＝後ろ
below	2-2	N	した＝下

Besides [used at the beginning of a sentence]　1-11　SI　それに
besides; what's more	3-4	Rc	-し、
(the) best	3-8	N	さいこう＝最高
between [comparison]	2-9	P	～で
between [location]	2-2	N	あいだ＝間
beyond	2-13	N	むこう＝向こう
bicycle	1-7	N	じてんしゃ＝自転車
big	1-6	A	おおきい＝大きい
bill	2-5	N	(お)かんじょう＝(お)勘定
bird	1-10	N	とり＝鳥
birthday	1-11	N	(お)たんじょうび＝(お)誕生日
(is) bitter	3-8	A	にがい＝苦い
black	1-5	N	くろ＝黒
(is) black	1-6	A	くろい＝黒い
(to) blow (a trumpet)	3-6	V1	（トランペットを）ふく＝吹く[ふきます]
(to) blow away	2-11	V1	ふきとばす＝吹き飛ばす [ふきとばします]
blue	1-5	N	あお＝青
(is) blue	1-6	A	あおい＝青い
boat	1-7	N	ふね＝船
body	1-6	N	からだ＝体
(to) boil (in broth); simmer	3-8	V2	にる＝煮る[にます]
boiled (in broth) foods	3-8	N	にもの＝煮物
book	1-2	N	ほん＝本
bookstore	1-13	N	ほんや＝本屋
boring	1-11	A	つまらない
(be) born (in ～)	2-2	V2	(place で)うまれる＝生まれる [うまれます]
born in (month)	1-3	Nd	- がつうまれ＝- 月生まれ
(to) borrow	2-3	V2	かりる＝借りる [かります]
both	2-9	N	りょうほう＝両方
Bow.	1-1	Exp	れい。＝礼。
-bowlful	1-14	Nd	- ぱい＝- 杯
box	2-9	N	はこ＝箱
box lunch	1-14	N	べんとう＝弁当
boy	1-10	N	おとこのこ＝男の子
boy's school	3-2	N	だんしこう＝男子校
bread	1-4	N	パン
(a) break	1-11	N	やすみじかん＝休み時間
(something) breaks	3-7	V2	(～が) こわれる＝壊れる[こわれます] [intransitive]
(to) break (something)	3-7	V1	(～を) こわす＝壊す[こわします] [transitive]
breakfast	1-4	N	あさごはん＝朝御飯
	3-1	N	ちょうしょく＝朝食
bridge	2-13	N	はし＝橋

(is) bright	2-11 A	あかるい＝明るい
(to) bring (animate)	2-7 V3	つれてくる＝連れて来る [つれてきます]
(to) bring (something)	2-7 V3	もってくる＝持って来る [もってきます]
brown	1-5 N	ちゃいろ＝茶色
(is) brown	1-6 A	ちゃいろい＝茶色い
(to) brush (teeth)	3-3 V1	(はを)みがく＝(歯を)磨く[みがきます]
buckwheat noodle dish	2-5 N	ざるそば
(to) build	3-7 V1	たてる＝建てる[たてます]
building	1-10 N	たてもの＝建物　　　3-9　N　ビル
bullet train	3-9 N	しんかんせん＝新幹線
bullying	3-2 N	いじめ
(to) bully	3-2 V2	いじめる
bus	1-7 N	バス
bus stop	2-13 N	バスてい＝バス停
(is) busy	1-7 A	いそがしい＝忙しい
but	1-5 Pc	(sentence 1) が, (sentence 2)
But [used at the beginning of the sentence.]	1-4 SI	でも
(to) buy	1-13 V1	かう＝買う [かいます]
by (a certain time)	2-10 P	(time) までに
by (means)	1-4 P	(means) で
by all means	2-7 Adv	ぜひ＝是非
by far	2-9 Adv	ずっと
By the way	2-3 SI	ところで
by	2-2 N	そば＝傍

<C>

cafeteria	1-4 N	カフェテリア
camera	1-15 N	カメラ
camp	1-7 N	キャンプ
can do well	1-5 Na	とくい＝得意
candy	1-2 N	あめ＝飴; キャンディ
(It) cannot be helped.	2-6 Exp	しかたがありません。＝仕方がありません。
cannot hear	1-2 V2	きこえません＝聞こえません
cannot see	1-2 V2	みえません＝見えません
cap; hat	2-3 N	ぼうし＝帽子
car	1-7 N	くるま＝車; じどうしゃ＝自動車
(playing) cards	1-5 N	トランプ
(to be) careful	2-3 V2	きをつける＝気をつける [きをつけます]
carpet	3-7 N	カーペット
carrot	3-1 N	にんじん＝人参
(to) carry	2-2 V1	もつ＝持つ [もちます]
cash register	2-5 N	レジ
cat	1-10 N	ねこ＝猫
(to) catch a cold	2-6 V1	かぜをひく＝風邪を引く [ひきます]

cellular phone	3-3 N	けいたいでんわ=携帯電話
cent(s)	1-13 Nd	- セント
(a) certain ～	2-11 PN	ある ～
chair	1-10 N	いす=椅子
change (from a larger unit of money)	2-9 N	おつり=お釣
(to) change (something)	3-1 V2	かえる=変える[かえます] [transitive]
(to) change [i.e., shoes, pants, etc.]	3-2 V2	はきかえる=履き替える[はきかえます]
(to) change over	2-6 V1	かわる=代わる [かわります]
(is) cheap; inexpensive	1-13 A	やすい=安い
cheating	3-2 N	カンニング
(a) check; bill	2-5 N	(お)かんじょう =(お)勘定
(to) check; (to) investigate	3-4 V2	しらべる=調べる [しらべます]
(to) cheer	2-10 V3	おうえん(を)する =応援(を)する[おうえん(を)します]
Cheers!	3-8 Exp	かんぱい！=乾杯
chemistry	3-1 N	かがく=化学
chew away	2-11 Adv	ガリガリ
(to) chew gum	2-3 V1	（ガムを） かむ[かみます]
chicken (meat)	2-14 N	とりにく=鳥肉
chicken and egg over a bowl of steamed rice	2-5 N	おやこどんぶり=親子丼
child	1-10 N	こども=子供
China	1-3 N	ちゅうごく=中国
Chinese language	1-4 N	ちゅうごくご=中国語
Chinese noodle soup	2-5 N	ラーメン
Chinese reading (of a *kanji*)	3-4 N	おん(よみ)=音(読み)
chocolate	2-5 N	チョコレート
chopsticks	1-14 N	(お)はし=(お)箸
Christianity	2-7 N	キリストきょう=キリスト教
Christmas	2-7 N	クリスマス
Christmas card	2-7 N	クリスマスカード
Christmas tree	2-7 N	クリスマスツリー
Chuo (Central) Line [orange colored train line in Tokyo]	3-9 N	ちゅうおうせん=中央線
church	2-7 N	きょうかい=教会
cigarettes	2-3 N	たばこ
circle	3-8 N	まる=丸
(to) circle	3-8 V3	まるをする=丸をする[まるをします]
city	2-9 N	し=市
class	1-11 N	じゅぎょう=授業; クラス
classifier	3-4 N	ぶしゅ=部首
classroom	1-10 N	きょうしつ=教室
(to) clean up	2-7 V3	そうじ(を)する =掃除(を)する[そうじ(を)します]
(to) clean up; put away	2-14 V2	かたづける=片付ける[かたづけます]

(is) clean	1-6	Na	きれい
(to) clean	2-14	V3	きれいにする[きれいにします]
clear (weather)	2-7	N	はれ＝晴れ
clock; watch	1-13	N	とけい＝時計
(to) close	1-13	V2	しめる＝閉める[しめます]
close; near	1-10	A	ちかい＝近い
(Please) close.	1-2	Exp	しめてください。＝閉めて下さい。
clothing	2-3	N	ふく＝服
cloud	2-11	N	くも＝雲
cloudy (weather)	2-7	N	くもり＝曇り
club activity	3-2	N	ぶかつ(どう)＝部活(動)
co-educational	3-2	N	(だんじょ)きょうがく＝(男女)共学
cockroach	1-10	N	ごきぶり
coffee shop	1-13	N	きっさてん＝喫茶店
coffee	1-4	N	コーヒー
cola (drink)	1-4	N	コーラ
(a) cold	1-12	N	かぜ＝風邪
(is) cold (temperature)	1-1	A	さむい＝寒い
(is) cold (to the touch)	1-14	A	つめたい＝冷たい
college	1-12	N	だいがく＝大学
college student	1-12	N	だいがくせい＝大学生
color	1-5	N	いろ＝色
(to) come	1-7	V3	くる＝来る[きます]
(to) come to pick up (someone)	2-10	V3	(person を) むかえにくる＝迎えに来る [むかえにきます]
(to) come to pick up (something)	2-10	V3	(something を) とりにくる＝取りに来る [とりにきます]
(is) comfortable	2-14	A	きもちがいい＝気持ちがいい
(is) comfortable	3-3	Na	らく＝楽
comics	3-4	N	まんが＝漫画
commercial	3-6	N	コマーシャル
(to) commute	3-2	V	かよう＝通う[かよいます]
company	1-7	N	かいしゃ＝会社
company employee	1-3	N	かいしゃいん＝会社員
(to) compare	2-9	V2	くらべる＝比べる[くらべます]
competition [music]	2-15	N	コンクール
complicated	3-4	Na	ふくざつ＝複雑
computer	1-4	N	コンピューター
concert	1-15	N	コンサート
condition is bad (not well)	2-6	A	ぐあいがわるい＝具合が悪い
Congratulations.	1-15	Exp	おめでとうございます。
(to) consult (someone)	3-3	V3	(someone に)そうだん(を)する＝相談(を)する [そうだん(を)します]

(to) continue/keep doing ～	3-4 V2	(V Stem) ＋つづける＝続ける[つづけます]
convenience store	2-13 N	コンビニ
(is) convenient	3-7 NA	べんり＝便利
(to) cook	2-7 V3	りょうり(を)する＝料理(を)する [りょうり(を)します]
cool [temperature]	1-1 A	すずしい＝涼しい
corner	2-4 N	かど＝角
(is) correct	2-2 A	ただしい＝正しい
country	2-9 N	くに＝国
cousin	1-15 N	いとこ
cram school	3-2 N	じゅく＝塾
credit card	2-9 N	クレジットカード
(to) cross (over) ～	2-13 V1	(～を) わたる＝渡る[わたります]
(to get) crowded	2-13 V1	こむ＝込む[こみます]
(is) crowded	2-13 V1	こんでいる＝込んでいる[こんでいます]
(to) cry	2-15 V1	なく＝泣く[なきます]
culture	3-2 N	ぶんか＝文化
cup	1-14 N	コップ
- cupful	1-14 Nd	- ぱい＝ - 杯
curry rice	2-5 N	カレーライス; ライスカレー
(floor) cushion	3-7 N	ざぶとん＝座布団
customer; guest	3-7 N	きゃく＝客
(to) cut	2-14 V1	きる＝切る[きります]
cute	1-6 A	かわいい＝可愛い
<D>		
dance	1-5 N	ダンス
	3-6 N	おどり＝踊り [traditional]
(to) dance	3-6 V1	おどる＝踊る[おどります]
dancing	1-5 N	ダンス
(is) dangerous	2-4 A	あぶない＝危ない
(is) dark	2-11 A	くらい＝暗い
(own) daughter	2-11 N	むすめ＝娘
(someone else's) daughter	2-11 N	むすめさん＝娘さん
(the) day after tomorrow	1-11 N	あさって＝明後日
(the) day before yesterday	1-11 N	おととい＝一昨日
day of the month	1-11 Nd	- にち＝ - 日
day	1-15 N	ひ＝日
day off	1-7 N	(お)やすみ＝(お)休み
- day(s)	2-6 Nd	-にち(かん)＝-日(間)
daytime	1-4 N	(お)ひる＝(お)昼
December	1-3 N	じゅうにがつ＝十二月
decide on ～	2-5 V3	(something に) する[します]
(to) decorate	3-7 V1	かざる＝飾る[かざります]

definitely	2-7	Adv	ぜひ＝是非
- degree(s)	2-6	Nd	- ど＝-度
(is) delicious	1-13	A	おいしい＝美味しい
department store	1-7	N	デパート
design	2-9	N	デザイン
desk	1-10	N	つくえ＝机
dessert	2-14	N	デザート
dictionary	1-2	N	じしょ＝辞書
(to) die	1-12	V1	しぬ＝死ぬ[しにます]
(to) differ	2-2	V1	ちがう＝違う[ちがいます]
(is) different	2-9	V1	ちがう＝違う[ちがいます]
(is) different; odd; unusual	3-8	V1	かわった＝変わった
(is) difficult	1-11	A	むずかしい＝難しい
difficult; hard	1-11	Na	たいへん＝大変
(to) dine; have a meal	1-7	V3	しょくじをする＝食事をする[しょくじをします]
dining	1-7	N	しょくじ＝食事
dinner	1-4	N	ばんごはん＝晩御飯
	3-1	N	ゆうしょく＝夕食
(to) dip (object in thing)	2-14	V2	(object を thing に) つける[つけます]
- direction	3-9	N	〜ほうめん＝〜方面
(movie) director; (baseball) manager	3-5	N	かんとく＝監督
(is) dirty	1-6	A	きたない
dishes	1-14	N	(お)さら＝(お)皿
dislike	1-5	Na	きらい＝嫌い
dislike a lot	1-5	Na	だいきらい＝大嫌い
(to) divorce	2-15	V3	りこん(を)する＝離婚(を)する[りこん(を)します]
(to) do	1-4	V3	する[します]
(to) do [informal form of する]	3-2	V1	やる[やります]
do a homestay	2-2	V3	ホームステイをする[ホームステイをします]
do a self-introduction	2-2	V3	じこしょうかい(を)する＝自己紹介(を)する[じこしょうかい(を)します]
do not have to (do)	2-5	Dv	-なくてもいいです
do not know	1-2	V1	しりません＝知りません
(I) do not mind if . . .	2-3	V1	かまいません
do one's best	1-12	V1	がんばる＝頑張る[がんばります]
Do you like it? [polite]	2-9	Exp	おすきですか。＝お好きですか。
(to) do 〜 completely [regret]	2-11	V1	(verb TE) しまう[しまいます]
(superior) do 〜 for me	3-3	E	(〜て) くださいます＝下さいます
(medical) doctor	1-3	N	いしゃ＝医者
(medical) doctor [polite]	1-3	N	おいしゃさん＝御医者さん
dog	1-10	N	いぬ＝犬
dollar(s)	1-13	Nd	-ドル
(〜 is) done	2-14	V2	(〜が) できました＝出来ました

door	1-10	N	ドア; と＝戸
dormitory	2-2	N	りょう＝寮
(to) draw (a picture)	2-15	V1	(えを) かく＝描く[かきます]
drawing	1-5	N	え＝絵
dream	3-3	N	ゆめ＝夢
dress	2-3	N	ワンピース
(a) drink	1-5	N	のみもの＝飲み物
(to) drink	1-4	V2	のむ＝飲む[のみます]
(to) drive	2-3	V3	うんてん(を)する＝運転(を)する[うんてん(を)します]
driver	2-4	N	うんてんしゅ＝運転手; ドライバー
driver's license	2-3	N	うんてんめんきょ＝運転免許
(to) drop by (a place)	2-10	V1	(place に) よる＝寄る[よります]
drugs	3-2	N	まやく＝麻薬
Dust amassed will make a mountain.	3-1	Prov	ちりもつもればやまとなる ＝塵も積れば山となる

<E>

e-mail	3-3	N	でんしメール＝電子メール
ear	1-6	N	みみ＝耳
early [used with a verb]	1-12	Adv	はやく＝早く
early evening	1-4	N	ゆうがた＝夕方
(is) early	1-7	A	はやい＝早い
early	2-4	Adv	はやく＝早く
earrings	2-3	N	イヤリング
(not) easily ～	3-4	Adv	なかなか＋ Neg.
east	2-1	N	ひがし＝東
east entrance/exit	3-9	N	ひがしぐち＝東口
Eastern style	3-7	Na	とうようてき＝東洋的
(is) easy	1-11	A	やさしい＝易しい
(is) easy to do ～	3-4	A	(Verb Stem) ＋やすい
(to) eat	1-4	V2	たべる＝食べる[たべます]
economics; economy	3-4	N	けいざい＝経済
education	3-2	N	きょういく＝教育
egg	2-14	N	たまご＝卵
eight	1-1	N	はち＝八
eight [general counter]	1-2	N	やっつ＝八つ
eighteen	1-1	N	じゅうはち＝十八
(the) eighth day of the month	1-11	N	ようか＝八日
eighth grader	1-3	N	ちゅうがくにねんせい＝中学二年生
eighty	1-1	N	はちじゅう＝八十
(not) either	2-9	N	どちらも＋ Neg.
elderly man	1-3	N	おじいさん
elderly woman	1-3	N	おばあさん

electric goods	3-7	N	でんきせいひん＝電気製品
electric train	1-7	N	でんしゃ＝電車
eleven	1-1	N	じゅういち＝十一
eleventh grader	1-3	N	こうこうにねんせい＝高校二年生
Emperor	3-9	N	てんのう＝天皇
(is) employed (at 〜)	2-2	V2	(place に) つとめる＝勤める[つとめます]
(is) empty	2-13	V1	すいている[すいています]
(to become) empty	2-13	V1	すく[すきます]
end (of a street)	3-9	N	つきあたり＝突き当たり
(something) ends	2-10	V1	(〜が) おわる＝終わる[おわります] [intransitive]
(the) end	2-11	N	おしまい
(at the) end	2-14	Adv	おわりに＝終わりに
engineer	1-3	N	エンジニア
English language	1-4	N	えいご＝英語
English-Japanese dictionary	3-4	N	えいわじてん＝英和わ辞典
(to) enjoy	3-6	V1	たのしむ＝楽しむ[たのしみます]
(is) enjoyable	1-11	A	たのしい＝楽しい
(to) enter (a place)	2-4	V1	(place に) はいる＝入る[はいります]
entertainment	3-6	N	ごらく＝娯楽
entrance way; foyer	3-7	N	げんかん＝玄関
entrance	2-13	N	いりぐち＝入口
envious	3-6	A	うらやましい＝羨ましい
eraser [rubber]	1-2	N	けしごむ＝消しゴム
especially	2-2	Adv	とくに＝特に
(N1 and N2) etc.	1-15	Nd	(N1) や (N2) など
evening	1-4	N	ばん＝晩
event(s)	3-2	N	ぎょうじ＝行事
every month	1-12	N	まいつき＝毎月
every semester	3-2	N	まいがっき＝毎学期
every week	1-11	N	まいしゅう＝毎週
every year	1-15	N	まいとし＝毎年; まいねん＝毎年
everyday	1-4	N	まいにち＝毎日
everyone [polite address form]	1-15	N	みなさん＝皆さん
everyone	1-15	N	みんな＝皆
everything	1-14	N	ぜんぶ＝全部
exam	1-2	N	しけん＝試験
(is) excited	2-10	V3	ドキドキする[ドキドキします]
Excuse me for going/doing something first.	3-1	Exp	おさきに。＝お先に。
Excuse me. I must be going now.	3-1	Exp	しつれいします。＝失礼します。
Excuse me. (apology)	1-1	Exp	すみません。
Excuse me. (to get attention)	1-13	Exp	すみません。
(to) exercise	2-10	V3	うんどう(を)する＝運動(を)する[うんどう(を)します]
(to) exist [polite]	2-6	V1	いらっしゃる [いらっしゃいます]

exit	2-13	N	でぐち＝出口
(I) expect that he/she will do/will not do. He/She is expected to do/not to do			
	2-6	Nd	(Dic./NAI)はずです
(is) expensive	1-13	A	たかい＝高い
(to) experience	3-7	V3	けいけんする＝経験する[けいけんします]
(to) explain	3-9	V3	せつめいをする＝説明をする[せつめいします]
(an) explanation	3-9	N	せつめい＝説明
eye	1-6	N	め＝目
eyeglasses	1-2	N	めがね＝眼鏡

<F>

face	1-6	N	かお＝顔
fall (season)	1-12	N	あき＝秋
(rain, snow) fall	2-7	V1	ふる＝降る[ふります]
(my) family	1-3	N	かぞく＝家族
(someone's) family	1-3	N	ごかぞく＝御家族
famous	1-10	Na	ゆうめい＝有名
far away	2-2	N	とおく＝遠く
(is) far	1-10	A	とおい＝遠い
fare	3-9	N	りょうきん＝料金
fast	2-4	Adv	はやく＝速く
(is) fat	1-6	V1	ふとっている＝太っている[ふとっています]
(someone's) father	1-3	N	おとうさん＝お父さん
(my) father	1-3	N	ちち＝父
Father's Day	1-15	N	ちちのひ＝父の日
February	1-3	N	にがつ＝二月
feel sick	2-6	A	ぐあいがわるい＝具合が悪い
female	3-6	N	じょせい＝女性
female; woman	1-10	N	おんな＝女
fermented soybeans	3-8	N	なっとう＝納豆
fever	1-12	N	ねつ＝熱
(a) few	1-10	Adv	すこし＝少し
(is) few	1-11	A	すくない＝少ない
fifteen	1-1	N	じゅうご＝十五
(the) fifth day of the month	1-11	N	いつか＝五日
fifty	1-1	N	ごじゅう＝五十
(to) fight	2-4	V3	けんか(を)する＝喧嘩(を)する[けんか(を)します]
finally	2-11	Adv	とうとう
(to) find (something) [transitive]	3-4	V2	(～ を) みつける＝見つける[みつけます]
fine; healthy	1-1	Na	(お)げんき＝(お)元気
finger	1-6	N	ゆび＝指
(to) finish doing ～	3-4	V1	(V Stem) ＋おわる＝終わる[おわります]
(to) finish (something)	1-1	V1	(～を) おわります＝終わります
(something) finishes [intransitive]	2-10	V1	(～が) おわる＝終わる[おわります]

English	Ref	Type	Japanese
(to do) fireworks	2-7	V3	はなび(をする)＝花火(をする)
(the) first day of the month	1-11	N	ついたち＝一日
first of all	2-14	SI	まず
first semester	3-2	N	いちがっき＝一学期
(at) first	3-8	Adv	さいしょに＝最初に
(for the) first time	2-7	N	はじめて＝始めて
(the) first	3-8	N	さいしょ＝最初
fish	1-10	N	さかな＝魚
five	1-1	N	ご＝五
five [general counter]	1-2	N	いつつ＝五つ
(to) fix	3-7	V1	なおす＝直す[なおします]
flavor	2-14	N	あじ＝味
- floor	1-9	Nd	- かい／がい＝- 階
floor	2-4	N	ゆか＝床
flower	1-10	N	はな＝花
flower arrangement	3-7	N	いけばな＝生け花
flower shop	1-13	N	はなや＝花屋
folk tale	2-11	N	むかしばなし＝昔話
food	1-5	N	たべもの＝食べ物
foot	1-6	N	あし＝足
football	1-5	N	フットボール
for (activity)	1-7	P	(activity)に
for everything	1-14	N	ぜんぶ＝全部で
For example	3-4	SI	たとえば＝例えば
foreign language	1-11	N	がいこくご＝外国語
(to) forget	1-14	V2	わすれる＝忘れる[わすれます]
fork	1-14	N	フォーク
forty	1-1	N	よんじゅう＝四十
(to be) found [intransitive]	3-4	V1	(〜 が) みつかる＝見つかる[みつかります]
four	1-1	N	し＝四; よん＝四
four [general counter]	1-2	N	よっつ＝四つ
4 1/2-mat room	3-7	N	よじょうはん＝四畳半
fourteen	1-1	N	じゅうし＝十四; じゅうよん＝十四
(the) fourteenth day of the month	1-11	N	じゅうよっか＝十四日
(the) fourth day of the month	1-11	N	よっか＝四日
fragrance	2-7	N	におい＝臭い
France	1-3	N	フランス
(is) free (time)	2-15	Na	ひま＝暇
(is) free	2-3	Na	じゆう＝自由
french fries	1-14	N	フライドポテト
French language	1-4	N	フランスご＝フランス語
freshman (9th grader)	1-3	N	ちゅうがくさんねんせい＝中学三年生
Friday	1-7	N	きんようび＝金曜日

friend	1-4	N	ともだち＝友達
from now on	1-14	SI	これから
from ～	1-11	P	～から
from ～ to ～	2-13	P	～から ～まで
front	1-2	N	まえ＝前
fruit	2-14	N	くだもの＝果物
Fukuoka	2-1	N	ふくおか＝福岡
(I am) full.	1-14	Exp	おなかがいっぱいです。＝お腹が一杯です。
(is) fun	1-11	A	たのしい＝楽しい
(is) funny	1-11	A	おもしろい＝面白い
future	2-14	N	しょうらい＝将来

\<G\>

(sports) game	1-12	N	しあい＝試合
game	1-15	N	ゲーム
garage	1-10	N	ガレージ
garden	1-10	N	にわ＝庭
gas station	3-9	N	ガソリンスタンド
gate	2-3	N	もん＝門
generally	2-5	Adv	だいたい
German language	1-4	N	ドイツご＝ドイツ語
Germany	1-3	N	ドイツ
(to) get; take	2-6	V1	とる＝取る[とります]
(to) get off (vehicle)	2-4	V2	(vehicle から/を)おりる＝降りる[おります]
(to) get up	1-7	V2	おきる＝起きる[おきます]
(to) get/receive from ～	1-15	V1	～から/に もらう[もらいます]
Ginza [a city in Tokyo]	3-9	N	ぎんざ＝ぎんざ
girl	1-10	N	おんなのこ＝女の子
girl's school	3-2	N	じょしこう＝女子校
(to) give (to a superior)	2-9	V2	(superior に) さしあげる＝差し上げる [さしあげます]
(to) give (to equal)	1-15	V2	あげる[あげます]
(to) give (to inferior)	1-15	V2	やる[やります]
(to) give (to speaker or to speaker's family)	1-15	V2	くれる[くれます]
(is) glad	1-11	A	うれしい＝嬉しい
glassful	1-14	Nd	- はい; - ばい; - ぱい＝ - 杯
(to) gnaw [onomatopoetic]	2-11	Adv	ガリガリ
(to) go	1-7	V1	いく＝行く[いきます]
(to) go down	3-7	V2	おりる＝下りる[おります]
(to) go out (from a place)	2-4	V2	(place を/から)でかける＝出かける[でかけます]
(to) go over; cross	2-13	V1	(～を) わたる＝渡る[わたります]
(to) go to bed	1-7	V2	ねる＝寝る[ねます]
(to) go to pick up (person)	2-10	V1	(person を)むかえにいく＝迎えに行く [むかえにいきます]

(to) go to pick up (something)	2-10	V1	(something を)とりにいく＝取りに行く [とりにいきます]
gold (color)	1-5	N	きんいろ＝金色
gold	2-15	N	きん＝金
golf	1-5	N	ゴルフ
(be) good at	1-5	Na	じょうず＝上手
Good evening.	1-7	Exp	こんばんは＝今晩は
(is) good looking	3-3	A	かっこいい＝格好いい
Good luck.	1-12	Exp	がんばって。＝頑張って。
Good morning. [Formal]	1-1	Exp	おはようございます。
Good morning. [Informal]	1-1	Exp	おはよう。
Good night.	3-1	Exp	お休み（なさい）＝おやすみ（なさい）。
(is) good	1-2	A	いい; よい＝良い
Good-bye. [Formal]	1-1	Exp	さようなら。
Good-bye. [Informal]	1-14	Exp	バイバイ
grade	1-11	N	せいせき＝成績
(to) graduate (school)	3-1	V3	(school を) そつぎょうする＝卒業する [そつぎょうします]
graduation ceremony	3-2	N	そつぎょうしき＝卒業式
grandfather	1-3	N	おじいさん
(one's own) grandfather	3-1	N	そふ＝祖父
grandmother	1-3	N	おばあさん
(one's own) grandmother	3-1	N	そぼ＝祖母
grass	3-2	N	くさ＝草
(is) great (person)	2-11	A	えらい＝偉い
green	1-5	N	みどり＝緑
green [traffic light]	2-2	N	あお＝青
grey	1-5	N	グレイ
(to) grill; roast; bake; toast; fry	3-8	V1	やく＝焼く[やきます]
grilled fish	3-8	N	やきざかな＝焼き魚
grilled skewered chicken	2-5	N	やきとり＝焼き鳥
guitar	1-5	N	ギター
gum	2-3	N	ガム
gun	3-2	N	じゅう＝銃
gym	2-10	N	たいいくかん＝体育館

<H>

hair	1-6	N	かみ(のけ)＝髪(の毛)
-half	1-7	Nd	-はん＝半
(in) half	2-14	Adv	はんぶんに＝半分に
hamburger	1-14	N	ハンバーガー
hand	1-6	N	て＝手
(to) hang	3-7	V2	かける＝掛ける[かけます]
happy (life); fortunate	3-6	NA	しあわせ＝幸せ

Happy New Year!	2-7	Exp	あけましておめでとうございます。
			＝明けましておめでとうございます。
(is) happy	1-11	A	うれしい＝嬉しい
Harajuku [a city in Tokyo]	3-9	N	はらじゅく＝原宿
(is) hard (difficult)	1-11	Na	たいへん＝大変
(is) hard to do ～	3-4	A	(Verb Stem) ＋にくい
(is) hard; tough (to the touch)	3-8	A	かたい＝硬い
(is) hard; bitter; painful	3-3	A	つらい＝辛い
hat	2-3	N	ぼうし＝帽子
hate	1-5	Na	だいきらい＝大嫌い
have (part of body)	3-6	V	(part of body を) している[しています]
(I) have not seen you for a long time.	3-3	Exp	おひさしぶりです。
have to (do)	2-5	Dv	-なければなりません
(to) have	1-11	V1	ある[あります]
(to) have; hold; carry	2-2	V1	もつ＝持つ[もちます]
he; him; boyfriend	3-6	N	かれ＝彼
head	1-6	N	あたま＝頭
health	3-8	N	けんこう＝健康
healthy	1-1	Na	(お)げんき＝(お)元気
	3-8	NA	けんこうてき＝健康的
(to) hear	1-4	V1	きく＝聞く[ききます]
(I) heard that ～	3-6	Nd+ C	―そうだ[―そうです]
heart (spiritual)	1-6	N	こころ＝心
(to) heat	2-14	V3	あつくする＝熱くする[あつくします]
(is) heavy	3-7	A	おもい＝重い
height	1-6	N	せ(い)＝背
Hello. [telephone]	2-6	Exp	もしもし
Hello. Hi.	1-1	Exp	こんにちは。
(to) help	2-7	V3	てつだう＝手伝う[てつだいます]
(to) help; rescue	2-15	V2	たすける＝助ける[たすけます]
here	1-2	N	ここ
here [polite equiv. of ここ]	1-2	N	こちら
Here.	1-3	Exp	はい。
Here, please (take it).	1-2	Exp	はい、どうぞ。
(to) hesitate; (to) be reserved	3-8	V3	えんりょする＝遠慮する[えんりょします]
(to) hide (something)	2-11	V1	かくす＝隠す[かくします]
high school	1-3	N	こうこう＝高校
high school student	1-3	N	こうこうせい＝高校生
hindrance	1-6	Na	じゃま＝邪魔
Hiroshima	2-1	N	ひろしま＝広島
history	3-1	N	れきし＝歴史
hobby	1-5	N	しゅみ＝趣味
Hokkaido	2-1	N	ほっかいどう＝北海道

(to) hold	2-2	V1	もつ＝持つ[もちます]
hole	2-11	N	あな＝穴
(I'm) home. [Used by a family member who has come home.] 3-1 Exp ただいま。			
homeroom	1-11	N	ホームルーム
homework	1-2	N	しゅくだい＝宿題
Honshu	2-1	N	ほんしゅう＝本州
hospital	1-3	N	びょういん＝病院
(is) hot [temperature]	1-1	A	あつい＝暑い
(is) hot and humid	1-1	A	むしあつい＝蒸し暑い
hotdog	1-14	N	ホットドッグ
-hour(s)	2-6	Nd	-じかん＝-時間
house [building]	2-2	N	いえ＝家
(someone's) house [polite]	2-6	N	おたく＝お宅
house; home	1-4	N	うち
household chore; housework	3-3	N	かじ＝家事
housewife	1-3	N	しゅふ＝主婦
How are you?	1-1	Exp	おげんきですか。＝お元気ですか。
How disappointing! [on a future event]	1-11	Exp	ざんねんですねえ。＝残念ですねえ。
How disappointing! [on a past event]	1-11	Exp	ざんねんでしたねえ。＝残念でしたねえ。
How do you do?	1-1	Exp	はじめまして。
How do you say ～ in Japanese?	1-2	Exp	～はにほんごでなんといいますか。
			＝～は日本語で何と言いますか。
How far is it? [distance]	2-13	Exp	どのぐらいありますか。
How is it? [informal]	1-11	Exp	どうですか。
How long does it take? [time]	2-13	Exp	どのぐらい　かかりますか。
How long/far is it?	2-13	Exp	どのぐらいですか。
how many [birds]?	1-10	Ni	なんわ＝何羽
how many [bound objects]?	1-15	Ni	なんさつ＝何冊
how many [long cylindrical objects]?	1-10	Ni	なんぼん＝何本
how many [mechanized goods]?	1-10	Ni	なんだい＝何台
how many [small animals]?	1-10	Ni	なんびき＝何匹
how many cups?	1-14	Ni	なんばい＝何杯
how many people?	1-3	Ni	なんにん＝何人
how many? [general counter]	1-2	Ni	いくつ
how much? [price]	1-13	Ni	おいくら
How nice! [on a future event]	1-11	Exp	いいですねえ。
How nice! [on a past event]	1-11	Exp	よかったですねえ。
how old? [age]	1-3	Ni	なんさい＝何歳; 何才; (お)いくつ
How pitiful.	1-12	Exp	かわいそうに。＝可愛そうに。
How ridiculous!	2-11	Exp	とんでもない。
how to do ～	2-14	N	(Verb stem) かた＝方
how to make	2-14	N	つくりかた＝作り方
how? [Polite exp. of どう]	1-13	Ni	いかが？

How?	3-9 N	どうやって（＝どう）
However [Formal expression of でも]	2-15 SI	しかし
Huh?	2-11 SI	えっ
hundred thousand	1-13 N	じゅうまん＝十万
hundred	1-1 N	ひゃく＝百
(I got) hungry.	1-14 Exp	おなかがすきました。＝お腹が空きました。
(I am) hungry.	1-14 Exp	おなかがペコペコです。＝お腹がペコペコです。
Hurray!	2-10 Exp	ばんざい！＝万歳！
Hurry!	1-1 Exp	はやく＝速く
(someone else's) husband	3-6 N	ごしゅじん＝ご主人
(own) husband	3-6 N	しゅじん＝主人

<I>

I (used by anyone informally)	1-1 N	わたし＝私
I (used by males)	1-1 N	ぼく＝僕
I have a question.	2-13 Exp	ちょっとうかがいますが...
I see!	2-11 Exp	なるほど
(It is) I	3-1 Exp	こちらこそ。
I. D.	2-3 N	しょうめいしょ＝証明書
ice cream	2-4 N	アイスクリーム
If	3-7 Adv	もし
If something happens twice, it will happen three times.	3-2 Prov	にどあることはさんどある＝二度あることは三度ある
Ikebukuro [a city in Tokyo]	3-9 N	いけぶくろ＝池袋
illness	1-12 N	びょうき＝病気
important	1-12 Na	だいじ＝大事
in (location)	1-10 P	(location) に
in (place) [with action verb]	1-4 P	(place) で [with action verb]
in [tool particle]	1-4 P	(tool) で
in spite of 〜; although 〜 [reverse result]	3-3 Rc	〜のに
(is) in the way	1-6 Na	じゃま＝邪魔
(is) inconvenient	3-7 Na	ふべん＝不便
Indeed!	2-11 Exp	なるほど
ingredients	3-8 N	ざいりょう＝材料
inside	2-2 N	なか＝中
	3-7 N	うち＝内
(personal) interest	3-4 N	きょうみ＝興味
(is) interesting	1-11 A	おもしろい＝面白い
intermediate level	3-4 N	ちゅうきゅう＝中級
intermediate school student	1-3 N	ちゅうがくせい＝中学生
intermediate school	1-3 N	ちゅうがく＝中学
intersection	2-13 N	こうさてん＝交差点
(to) introduce	2-2 V3	しょうかい(を)する＝紹介(を)する [しょうかい(を)をします]

(It) is not so. [formal]	1-1	Exp	そうではありません。
(It) is not so. [informal]	1-1	Exp	そうじゃありません。
island	2-9	N	しま＝島
Isn't it 〜?	2-7	C	-でしょう [rising intonation]
isn't it? [sentence ending particle]	1-6	SP	ね
(Yes,) it is.	1-1	Exp	そうです。
It's me.	2-6	Exp	かわりました。＝代わりました。 [used on the telephone]

<J>

jacket	1-13	N	ジャケット
January	1-3	N	いちがつ＝一月
Japan	1-3	N	にほん＝日本
Japan Railway	3-9	N	ＪＲ〔ジェイアール〕
Japanese citizen	1-3	N	にほんじん＝日本人
Japanese language	1-4	N	にほんご＝日本語
Japanese meal	3-8	N	わしょく＝和食
Japanese reading (of a kanji)	3-4	N	くん（よみ）＝訓（読み）
Japanese-English dictionary	3-4	N	わえいじてん＝和英辞典
Japanese-style room	3-7	N	わしつ＝和室
job	1-3	N	(お)しごと＝(お)仕事
jogging	1-5	N	ジョギング
joke	2-10	N	じょうだん＝冗談
juice	1-4	N	ジュース
July	1-3	N	しちがつ＝七月
June	1-3	N	ろくがつ＝六月
junior (in high school)	1-3	N	こうこうにねんせい＝高校二年生

<K>

kabuki theater	3-9	N	かぶきざ＝歌舞伎座
Kanda [a city in Tokyo]	3-9	N	かんだ＝神田
kanji dictionary	3-4	N	かんじじてん＝漢字辞典
kendo [Japanese fencing]	3-2	N	けんどう＝剣道
key	2-4	N	かぎ＝鍵
(Are you) kidding?	2-10	Exp	うそでしょう。
Kill two birds with one stone.	3-8	Prov	いっせきにちょう＝一石二鳥
(is) kind	1-6	A	やさしい＝優しい
(is) kind; considerate	3-3	Na	しんせつ＝親切
kindergarten	3-1	N	ようちえん＝幼稚園
kitchen	2-14	N	だいどころ＝台所
knife	1-14	N	ナイフ
(do not) know	1-1	V1	しりません＝知りません
(to) know	2-2	V1	しっている＝知っている[しっています]
Kobe	2-1	N	こうべ＝神戸
Korea	1-3	N	かんこく＝韓国

Korean language	1-4	N	かんこくご＝韓国語
Kyoto	2-1	N	きょうと＝京都
Kyushu	2-1	N	きゅうしゅう＝九州

<L>

language	2-15	N	ことば＝言葉
large size	1-14	N	エルサイズ
last month	1-12	N	せんげつ＝先月
last night	1-12	N	ゆうべ
last semester	3-2	N	せんがっき＝先学期
last week	1-11	N	せんしゅう＝先週
last year	1-15	N	きょねん＝去年
(the) last; final	3-8	N	さいご＝最後
(at) last; finally	3-8	Adv	さいごに＝最後に
late	1-12	Adv	おそく＝遅く
late afternoon	1-4	N	ゆうがた＝夕方
(is) late	1-7	A	おそい＝遅い
(to) laugh	2-15	V1	わらう＝笑う[わらいます]
(to do) laundry	2-7	V3	せんたく(を)する＝洗濯(を)する [せんたく(を)します]
lawn	3-2	N	しばふ＝芝生
lawyer	1-3	N	べんごし＝弁護士
(to) learn	2-2	V1	ならう＝習う[ならいます]
(to) leave (a place)	2-4	V2	(place を) でる＝出る[でます]
(to) leave (something)	2-5	V1	おく＝置く[おきます]
left	2-2	N	ひだり＝左
leg	1-6	N	あし＝脚
(Please) lend me.	1-14	V1	かしてください。＝貸して下さい。
Let me see ...	2-1	SI	ええと..，あのう..，そうですねえ..
Let's begin.	1-1	Exp	はじめましょう＝始めましょう
Let's do 〜. [suggestion]	1-4	Dv	-ましょう
let's eat [informal form of 食べましょう]	3-1	V2	たべよう＝食べよう
Let's finish.	1-1	Exp	おわりましょう＝終わりましょう
letter	1-4	N	てがみ＝手紙
liberal	2-3	Na	じゆう＝自由
library	1-4	N	としょかん＝図書館
(a) lie	2-10	N	うそ＝嘘
life; living	3-3	N	せいかつ＝生活
(is) light (in weight)	3-7	A	かるい＝軽い
like	1-5	Na	すき＝好き
like very much	1-5	Na	だいすき＝大好き
line is busy (phone)	2-6	Exp	はなしちゅう＝話し中
liquor (in general)	2-14	N	(お)さけ＝(お)酒
(to) listen	1-4	V1	きく＝聞く[ききます]

(Please) listen.	1-2	Exp	きいてください＝聞いて下さい
literature	3-1	N	ぶんがく＝文学
(to) litter	2-3	V2	（ごみを）すてる[すてます]
(a) little [formal]	1-4	Adv	すこし＝少し
(a) little [more colloquial than すこ し]1-4		Adv	ちょっと
(is a) little; few	1-11	A	すくない＝少ない
(to) live (in ～)	2-2	V1	(place に)すむ＝住む[すみます]
lively	3-6	Na	にぎやか＝賑やか
living room; family room	3-7	N	いま＝居間
location	2-10	N	ばしょ＝場所
locker	1-10	N	ロッカー
(is) lonely	3-6	A	さびしい＝寂しい
long ago	2-11	N	むかしむかし＝昔々
(is) long	1-6	A	ながい＝長い
(to) look for; search for	3-4	V1	さがす＝探す[さがします]
(to) look up a word (in a dictionary) 3-4		V1	（じしょを）ひく＝（辞書を）引く[ひきます]
(to) look	1-4	V2	みる＝見る[みます]
(Please) look.	1-2	Exp	みてください。＝見て下さい。
(I am) looking forward to ～.	1-15	Exp	(～を)たのしみにしています。＝(～を)楽しみにしています。
looks ～	2-5	SI	(stem)そうです
(to) lose	1-12	V2	まける＝負ける[まけます]
(to become) lost	3-9	V1	まいごになる＝迷子になる[なります]
(a) lot	1-10	Adv	たくさん＝沢山
love	2-15	N	あい＝愛
(to be in) love	2-15	V1	あいしている＝愛している[あいしています]
love; like very much	1-5	Na	だいすき＝大好き
lunch	1-4	N	ひるごはん＝昼御飯
	3-1	N	ちゅうしょく＝昼食

<M>

magazine	1-4	N	ざっし＝雑誌
mail box	3-9	N	ポスト
(to) mail	2-7	V1	おくる＝送る[おくります]
(to) major (in)	3-1	V3	せんこうする＝専攻する[せんこうします]
(to) make	1-15	V1	つくる＝作る[つくります]
(to) make a mistake	2-6	V2	まちがえる＝間違える[まちがえます]
(to) make a phone call	2-6	V2	でんわをかける＝電話をかける[でんわ(を)かけます]
(to) make a reservation	2-5	V3	よやく(を)する＝予約(を)する[よやく(を)します]
(to) make clean	2-14	V3	きれいにする[きれいにします]
male	1-10	N	おとこ＝男
male	3-6	N	だんせい＝男性
man	1-10	N	おとこのひと＝男の人

many times	2-6 Adv	なんども＝何度も
(are) many	1-11 A	おおい＝多い
many; a lot (+ verb)	1-10 Adv	たくさん＝沢山
map	2-13 N	ちず＝地図
March	1-3 N	さんがつ＝三月
(to) marry	2-2 V3	(person と) けっこん(を)する[けっこん(を)します]
math	1-11 N	すうがく＝数学
May I help you?	2-9 N	なにをさしあげましょうか。＝何を差し上げましょうか。
May	1-3 N	ごがつ＝五月
may; might	3-7 E	〜かもしれない
meal	1-7 N	しょくじ＝食事
(have a) meal	1-7 V3	しょくじをする＝食事をする[しょくじ(を)します]
meaning	3-4 N	いみ＝意味
(It) means 〜.	3-4 Exp	(〜という)いみです。＝(〜という)意味です。
meat grilled on fire	2-5 N	やきにく＝焼肉
medicine	1-12 N	くすり＝薬
medium (size)	1-14 N	エムサイズ
(to) meet	1-12 V1	あう＝会う[あいます]
(to) meet someone	2-3 V1	(person に) あう＝会う[あいます]
(to) memorize	2-6 V2	おぼえる＝覚える[おぼえます]
menu	2-5 N	メニュー
(is) messy	1-6 A	きたない
messy; confusing; incorrect	3-4 Na	めちゃくちゃ
microwave oven	3-7 N	でんしレンジ＝電子レンジ
might; may	3-7 E	〜かもしれない
(cow's) milk	1-4 N	ぎゅうにゅう＝牛乳, ミルク
(one) million	1-13 N	ひゃくまん＝百万
mine	1-2 N	わたしの＝私の
-minute(s)	1-7 Nd	-ふん＝-分
Monday	1-7 N	げつようび＝月曜日
money	1-2 N	(お)かね＝(お)金
money received mainly by children from adults at New Year's		
	2-7 N	おとしだま＝お年玉
-month(s)	2-6 Nd	-かげつ＝-か月
more	2-9 Adv	もっと
(one) more (cup)	1-14 Adv	もう(いっぱい)＝もう(一杯)
more than 〜	2-9 P	〜より
Moreover	1-11 SI	それに
morning	1-4 N	あさ＝朝
(the) most	2-9 Adv	いちばん＝一番
	3-8 Adv	さいこうに＝最高に
(my) mother	1-3 N	はは＝母

(someone's) mother	1-3 N	おかあさん=お母さん
Mother's Day	1-15 N	ははのひ=母の日
mountain	1-7 N	やま=山
mouse	1-10 N	ねずみ=鼠
moustache	1-6 N	ひげ=髭
mouth	1-6 N	くち=口
(thing) move	2-11 V1	(thing が)うごく =動く[うごきます]
movie	1-5 N	えいが=映画
movie theater	2-3 N	えいがかん =映画館
Mr./Mrs./Ms.	1-1 Nd	-さん
Mr./Mrs./Ms./Dr.(teacher, doctor, statesman)	1-1 N	-せんせい=-先生
(are) much	1-11 A	おおい=多い
museum	3-9 N	はくぶつかん=博物館
music	1-5 N	おんがく=音楽
musical piece; song	3-6 N	きょく =曲
must not do	2-3 V2	いけません
N2 called N1	3-2 P+V	N1 という N2
N2 like N1	3-6 P+Nd+C	(N1の)ような N2

<N>

Nagoya	2-1 N	なごや=名古屋
Naha	2-1 N	なは=那覇
(someone's) name	1-3 N	おなまえ=御名前
name	1-3 N	なまえ=名前
napkin	1-14 N	ナプキン
Nara	2-1 N	なら=奈良
narrator	2-11 N	ナレーター
(is) narrow; small [a place]	1-10 A	せまい=狭い
nation	2-9 N	くに =国
nature	3-8 N	しぜん=自然
(is) near	1-10 A	ちかい=近い
nearby	2-2 N	ちかく =近く; そば=傍
neat	1-6 Na	きれい
neck	1-6 N	くび=首
necklace	2-3 N	ネックレス
need 〜	1-14 V1	(〜が) いる=要る[いります]
neither	2-9 N	どちらも+ Neg.
(is) nervous	2-10 V3	ドキドキする[ドキドキします]
never + Neg.	2-4 Adv	けっして+ Neg.
New Year	2-7 N	(お)しょうがつ =(お)正月
New Year's card	2-7 N	ねんがじょう=年賀状
(is) new	1-10 A	あたらしい=新しい
newspaper	1-4 N	しんぶん=新聞
next	1-11 N	つぎ=次

	2-14	Adv	つぎに＝次に
next [location]; neighboring	2-2	N	となり＝隣
next month	1-12	N	らいげつ＝来月
next semester	3-2	N	らいがっき＝来学期
next week	1-11	N	らいしゅう＝来週
next year	1-15	N	らいねん＝来年
Nice to meet you.	1-1	Exp	どうぞよろしく。
(is) nice, kind	1-6	A	やさしい＝優しい
nice; pretty	1-6	Na	きれい
night	1-4	N	よる＝夜
nine	1-1	N	く＝九; きゅう＝九
nine [general counter]	1-2	N	ここのつ＝九つ
nineteen	1-1	N	じゅうく＝十九; じゅうきゅう＝十九
ninety	1-1	N	きゅうじゅう＝九十
(the) ninth day of the month	1-11	N	ここのか＝九日
ninth grader	1-3	N	ちゅうがくさんねんせい＝中学三年生
No [formal]	1-1	SI	いいえ
No [informal]	2-4	SI	うぅん
No [Stronger negation than いいえ.]	2-11	SI	いや(っ)
no good	1-2	Na	だめ
no need to (do)	2-5	Dv	-なくてもいいです
No, thank you.	1-14	Exp	いいえ、けっこうです。
(is) noisy	1-6	A	うるさい
north	2-1	N	きた＝北
north entrance/exit	3-9	N	きたぐち＝北口
nose	1-6	N	はな＝鼻
(is) nostalgic	3-6	A	なつかしい＝懐かしい
(is) not at home	2-6	N	るす＝留守
not yet	1-14	Exp	まだです
notebook	1-2	N	ノート
November	1-3	N	じゅういちがつ＝十一月
now	1-3	N	いま＝今
nuisance	1-6	Na	じゃま＝邪魔
number - [order]	2-10	Nd	-ばん＝-番

<O>

- o'clock	1-7	Nd	-じ＝-時
occasionally	2-15	Adv	たまに
ocean	1-7	N	うみ＝海
Ochanomizu [a city in Tokyo]	3-9	N	おちゃノみず＝御茶ノ水
October	1-3	N	じゅうがつ＝十月
of course	2-6	SI	もちろん
office	1-10	N	じむしょ＝事務所
often	1-4	Adv	よく

Oh!	2-13	SI	ああ
oil	2-14	N	あぶら＝油
Okinawa	2-1	N	おきなわ＝沖縄
(is) old (age)	1-6	V1	としをとっている＝年を取っている [としをとっています]
old (not for person's age)	1-10	A	ふるい＝古い
(my) older brother	1-3	N	あに＝兄
(someone's) older brother	1-3	N	おにいさん＝お兄さん
(my) older sister	1-3	N	あね＝姉
(someone's) older sister	1-3	N	おねえさん＝お姉さん
on; top	2-2	N	うえ＝上
once in a while	2-15	Adv	たまに
one	1-1	N	いち＝一
one (person)	1-3	N	ひとり＝一人
one [general counter]	1-2	N	ひとつ＝一つ
one more time	1-1	Adv	もういちど＝もう一度
oneself	2-15	N	じぶん＝自分
only child	2-15	N	ひとりっこ＝一人っ子
only 〜	2-3	Nd	〜だけ
only 〜	3-8	Nd	〜ばかり
only 〜 [emphasis]	3-1	Nd	〜しか＋Neg.
(to) open	1-13	V2	あける＝開ける[あけます]
(Please) open.	1-2	Exp	あけてください。＝開けて下さい。
opinion	3-3	N	いけん＝意見
Or	1-6	SI	それとも
orange (color)	1-5	N	オレンジいろ＝オレンジ色
(to) order	2-5	V3	ちゅうもん(を)する＝注文(を)する [ちゅうもん(を)します]
(What is your/May I take your) order?	2-5	Exp	ごちゅうもんは。＝御注文は。
ordinary; average; regular	3-3	N	ふつう＝普通
Osaka	2-1	N	おおさか＝大坂
other	2-9	N	ほか
other side	2-13	N	むこう＝向こう
other side (of)	3-9	N	むかいがわ＝向かい側
outside	1-10	N	そと＝外
over there [polite equiv. of あそこ]	2-5	N	あちら
over there	1-2	N	あそこ
overseas (foreign) travel	3-2	N	かいがいりょこう＝海外旅行

<P>

p. m.	1-7	N	ごご＝午後
P.E.	1-11	N	たいいく＝体育
(is) painful	1-12	A	いたい＝痛い
(to) paint (a picture)	2-15	V1	(えを)かく＝描く[かきます]

painting	1-5	N	え＝絵
pan	2-14	N	なべ＝鍋
panda	3-9	N	パンダ
pants	1-13	N	パンツ [Used by younger people.]
	2-3	N	ズボン
paper	1-2	N	かみ＝紙
paper (report)	1-4	N	レポート
(own) parents	1-2	N	りょうしん＝両親
(someone else's) parents	1-2	N	ごりょうしん＝御両親
park	2-2	N	こうえん＝公園
parking lot	2-13	N	ちゅうしゃじょう＝駐車場
(to) participate (in an event)	2-10	V2	(event に)でる＝(eventに)出る[でます]
party	1-7	N	パーティー
(to) pass away; die [polite form of しぬ]	3-6	V1	なくなる＝亡くなる[なくなります]
(Please) pass me 〜.	3-8	Exp	(〜を)とってください。＝取って下さい。
passport	2-3	N	パスポート
(to) paste; glue; attach	3-3	V1	はる＝貼る[はります]
patrol car	2-4	N	パトカー
(to) pay	2-5	V1	はらう＝払う[はらいます]
peace; peaceful	3-2	N/Na	へいわ＝平和
pencil	1-2	N	えんぴつ＝鉛筆
pencil sharpener	1-10	N	えんぴつけずり＝鉛筆削り
pepper	2-14	N	こしょう＝胡椒
per 〜	2-6	P	〜に
- percent	2-5	Nd	-パーセント
(to) perm (one's hair)	3-2	V2	パーマをかける[かけます]
person	1-10	N	ひと＝人
person [polite form of ひと]	1-10	Nd	-かた＝-方
personality	3-3	N	せいかく＝性格
photo	1-2	N	しゃしん＝写真
physics	3-1	N	ぶつり＝物理
piano	1-5	N	ピアノ
pickled turnip	3-8	N	たくわん＝沢庵
pickled vegetable	3-8	N	つけもの＝漬け物
picnic	1-7	N	ピクニック
pierced (earrings)	2-3	N	ピアス
pig	1-10	N	ぶた＝豚
pink	1-5	N	ピンク
pizza	1-14	N	ピザ
place	2-2	N	ところ＝所
place; location	2-10	N	ばしょ＝場所
place of embarkment	3-9	N	のりば＝乗り場
plan to do/do not plan to do	2-6	Nd	(Dic./NAI)つもりです

plate	1-14 N	おさら＝お皿
platform (train station)	3-9 N	ホーム
(to) play (a string instrument)	2-6 V1	ひく＝弾く[ひきます]
(to) play (for fun)	1-15 V1	あそぶ＝遊ぶ[あそびます]
(to) play (sports)	1-15 V3	する[します]
(to) play a game	1-15 V3	ゲームをする[ゲームをします]
(stage) play	2-12 N	げき＝劇
(to give/put on a stage) play	2-12 V3	げきをする＝劇をする[げきをします]
(sports) player	2-10 N	せんしゅ＝選手
(is) pleasant	2-14 A	きもちがいい＝気持ちがいい
(Here) please (take it).	1-2 Exp	はい、どうぞ
Please come again.	2-9 Exp	またどうぞ。
Please give me 〜.	1-2 Exp	〜をください＝〜を下さい
Please. [request]	1-1 Exp	おねがいします＝御願いします
point	3-2 N	ところ
- point(s) [score]	2-10 Nd	- てん＝ - 点
police officer	2-4 N	けいかん＝警官
pond	1-10 N	いけ＝池
pool	1-10 N	プール
poor	2-11 Na	びんぼう＝貧乏(be)
(be) poor at	1-5 Na	へた＝下手
(be) popular	3-6 V1	にんきがある＝人気がある[にんきがあります]
pork	2-14 N	ぶたにく＝豚肉
pork cutlet	2-5 N	とんかつ＝豚カツ
post office	2-13 N	ゆうびんきょく＝郵便局
(picture) postcard	3-3 N	（え）はがき＝（絵）葉書
pot	2-14 N	なべ＝鍋
potato chips	2-4 N	ポテトチップ
(to) pour over; sprinkle	3-8 V2	かける[かけます]
power	2-11 N	ちから＝力
(to) practice	1-12 V3	れんしゅう(を)する＝練習(を)する [れんしゅう(を)します]
(a) present	1-15 N	プレゼント
(to) present; announce	3-3 V3	はっぴょうする＝発表する[はっぴょうします]
(is) pretty	1-6 Na	きれい
price	2-9 N	(お)ねだん＝(お)値段
private	3-2 N	しりつ＝私立
probably	2-7 Adv	たぶん＝多分
probably 〜	2-7 C	-でしょう [falling intonation]
probably is [informal form of でしょう]	3-1 C	だろう
problem	2-6 N	もんだい＝問題
professional baseball	3-6 N	プロやきゅう＝プロ野球
(T.V.) program	3-6 N	ばんぐみ＝番組

(a) promise	3-9	N	やくそく＝約束
(to make a) promise	3-9	V3	やくそくをする＝約束をする[やくそくします]
(to) pronounce	3-4	V3	はつおんする＝発音する[はつおんします]
pronunciation	3-4	N	はつおん＝発音
proverb	3-1	N	ことわざ＝諺
public (institution)	3-2	N	こうりつ＝公立
public phone	2-13	N	こうしゅうでんわ＝公衆電話
purple	1-5	N	むらさき＝紫
(to) put	2-5	V1	おく＝置く[おきます]
(to) put away	2-14	V2	かたづける＝片付ける[かたづけます]
(to) put in 〜	2-9	V2	(〜 に)いれる＝入れる[いれます]

<Q>

question	2-2	N	しつもん＝質問
quickly	2-4	Adv	はやく＝速く
quiet	1-6	Na	しずか＝静か
(is) quiet (refers to people only)	3-3	A	おとなしい
(to) quiet down	1-13	V3	しずかにする＝静かにする[しずかにします]
(Please be) quiet.	1-2	Exp	しずかにしてください。＝静かにして下さい。
(to) quit; discontinue	3-2	V2	やめる＝辞める[やめます]
quite; fairly	3-3	Adv	ずいぶん＝随分
quiz	1-2	N	しょうテスト＝小テスト

<R>

radio	1-4	N	ラジオ
rain	1-1	N	あめ＝雨
(to) raise a pet	3-3	V1	ペットをかう＝飼う[かいます]
(is) rare; unusual	3-8	A	めずらしい＝珍しい
raw egg	2-14	N	なまたまご＝生卵
(to) read	1-4	V1	よむ＝読む[よみます]
(Please) read.	1-2	Exp	よんでください。＝読んで下さい。
reading	1-5	N	どくしょ＝読書
(〜 is) ready	2-14	V2	(〜 が)できました＝出来ました
really	2-3	Adv	ほんとうに＝本当に
(to) recall	3-4	V2	おもいだす＝思い出す[おもいだします]
(to) receive	1-15	V1	もらう[もらいます]
(to) receive	3-3	V1	うけとる＝受け取る[うけとります]
recently	3-4	Adv	さいきん＝最近
red	1-5	N	あか＝赤
(is) red	1-6	A	あかい＝赤い
refrigerator	3-7	N	れいぞうこ＝冷蔵庫
regulation	2-3	N	きそく＝規則
relatives	1-15	N	しんせき＝親戚
(to) remove clothing [i.e., shoes, dress, hat]	3-2	V1	ぬぐ＝脱ぐ[ぬぎます]
(to) rent (from)	2-3	V2	かりる＝借りる[かります]

(to) repeat	3-9	V1	くりかえす＝繰り返す[くりかえします]
report; paper	1-4	N	レポート
(to) require	2-9	V1	かかる[かかります]
(to) rescue	2-15	V2	たすける＝助ける[たすけます]
residence	2-6	N	おたく＝お宅
(to) respect	3-3	V3	そんけいする＝尊敬する[そんけいします]
(to) rest	1-12	V1	やすむ＝休む[やすみます]
restaurant	1-7	N	レストラン
restroom	1-10	N	(お)トイレ; (お)てあらい＝(お)手洗い
(to) return (something)	2-5	V1	かえす＝返す[かえします]
(to) return (to a place)	1-7	V1	かえる＝帰る[かえります]
(to) return to pick up (a person)	2-10	V1	(person を)むかえにかえる＝迎えに帰る [むかえにかえります]
(to) return to pick up (something)	2-10	V1	(something を)とりにかえる＝取りに帰る [とりにかえります]
rice wine	2-14	N	(お)さけ＝(お)酒
(cooked) rice	1-4	N	ごはん＝ご飯
riceball	1-14	N	おむすび; おにぎり
rich person	2-11	N	(お)かねもち＝(お)金持ち
(to) ride	2-4	V1	(vehicle に)のる＝乗る[のります]
right side	2-2	N	みぎ＝右
ring	2-3	N	ゆびわ＝指輪
river	1-7	N	かわ＝川
road	2-4	N	みち＝道
room	1-10	N	へや＝部屋
room where guests are received	3-7	N	きゃくま＝客間
(is) round	3-8	A	まるい＝丸い
rubbish	1-2	N	ごみ
rule	2-3	N	きそく＝規則
rumor	3-6	N	うわさ
(to) run	1-12	V1	はしる＝走る[はしります]
<S>			
(is) sad	1-11	A	かなしい＝悲しい
(is) safe	2-4	Na	あんぜん＝安全
salad	1-14	N	サラダ
salary; pay	3-6	N	きゅうりょう＝給料
(for) sale	2-9	N	セール中
salt	2-14	N	しお＝塩
(is) salty	2-14	A	からい＝辛い; しおからい＝塩辛い
same	2-9	N	おなじ＝同じ
sandwich	1-14	N	サンドイッチ
Sapporo	2-1	N	さっぽろ＝札幌
Saturday	1-7	N	どようび＝土曜日

(to) say	1-13 V1	いう=言う[いいます]
Say, "Cheese."	1-15 Exp	はい、チーズ。
Say, "Peace."	1-15 Exp	はい、ピース。
(is) scary	2-4 A	こわい=恐い
school	1-3 N	がっこう=学校
school bus	2-4 N	スクールバス
science	1-11 N	かがく=科学
science [school subject]	3-1 N	りか=理科
(to) scold	2-15 V1	しかる=叱る[しかります]
score	2-10 N	スコア
sea	1-7 N	うみ=海
season	3-8 N	きせつ=季節
seasonings	3-8 N	ちょうみりょう=調味料
(the) second day of the month	1-11 N	ふつか=二日
second serving	3-8 N	おかわり=お代わり
(Well then,) see you later.	1-14 Exp	(じゃ)またあとで。
(to) see	1-4 V2	みる=見る[みます]
(It) seems that ～	3-8 Da	～らしい
(to) sell	2-9 V1	うる=売る[うります]
semester	3-2 N	がっき=学期
(to) send	2-7 V1	おくる=送る[おくります]
Sendai	2-1 N	せんだい=仙台
(high school) senior	1-3 N	こうこうさんねんせい=高校三年生
sentence	3-4 N	ぶん=文
(to) separate	3-6 V2	わかれる=別れる[わかれます]
September	1-3 N	くがつ=九月
(is) serious	3-3 NA	まじめ=真面目
seven	1-1 N	しち=七; なな=七
seven [general counter]	1-2 N	ななつ=七つ
seventeen	1-1 N	じゅうしち; じゅうなな=十七
(the) seventh day of the month	1-11 N	なのか=七日
seventh grader	1-3 N	ちゅうがくいちねんせい=中学一年生
seventy	1-1 N	ななじゅう; しちじゅう=七十
shape	3-4 N	かたち=形
she; her; girlfriend	3-6 N	かのじょ=彼女
Shibuya [a city in Tokyo]	3-9 N	しぶや=渋谷
Shikoku	2-1 N	しこく=四国
Shinagawa [a city in Tokyo]	3-9 N	しながわ=品川
Shinjuku [a city in Tokyo]	3-9 N	しんじゅく=新宿
ship	1-7 N	ふね=船
shirt	1-13 N	シャツ
shoes	1-13 N	くつ=靴
shoji (rice paper) door	3-7 N	しょうじ=障子

(to) shop	1-7 V3	かいものをする＝買い物をする[かいものをします]
shopping	1-7 N	かいもの＝買い物
(is) short (height)	1-6 A	ひくい＝低い
(is) short [length]	1-6 A	みじかい＝短い
shorts	2-3 N	ショーツ; ショートパンツ
should (do)	2-5 Dv	-なければなりません
(to) show	1-13 V2	みせる＝見せる[みせます]
(Please) show.	1-2 Exp	みせてください。＝見せて下さい。
shredded konnyaku	2-14 N	いとこんにゃく＝糸こんにゃく
shrine (Shinto)	2-7 N	じんじゃ＝神社
(my) sibling(s)	1-3 N	きょうだい＝兄弟
sickness	1-12 N	びょうき＝病気
silver	2-15 N	ぎん＝銀
silver color	1-5 N	ぎんいろ＝銀色
simple	3-4 NA	かんたん＝簡単
since (reason)	1-11 Pc	(reason) から
since ～; because ～ [expected result]; so	3-3 Rc	～ので
(to) sing	1-15 V1	うたう＝歌う[うたいます]
singer	3-6 N	かしゅ＝歌手
singing	1-5 N	うた＝歌
(to) sit	1-13 V1	すわる＝座る[すわります]
(to) sit properly	3-7 V3	せいざする＝正座する[せいざします]
Sit. [ceremony]	1-4 Exp	ちゃくせき＝着席
(Please) sit.	2-2 Exp	すわってください＝座って下さい
six	1-1 N	ろく＝六
six [general counter]	1-2 N	むっつ＝六つ
sixteen	1-1 N	じゅうろく＝十六
(the) sixth day of the month	1-11 N	むいか＝六日
sixty	1-1 N	ろくじゅう＝六十
size	1-14 N	サイズ
skillful	1-5 Na	じょうず＝上手
skirt	2-3 N	スカート
(to) sleep	1-7 V2	ねる＝寝る[ねます]
(is) sleepy	1-12 A	ねむい＝眠い
(to) slice	2-14 V1	きる＝切る[きります]
slowly	1-1 Adv	ゆっくり
small size	1-14 N	エスサイズ
(is) small	1-6 A	ちいさい＝小さい
(is) small; narrow	1-10 A	せまい＝狭い
smell	2-7 N	におい＝臭い
(is) smelly	3-8 A	くさい＝臭い
(to) smile; laugh	2-15 V1	わらう＝笑う[わらいます]

smilingly [onomatopoetic]	2-15 Adv	ニコニコ
(to) smoke (cigarettes)	2-3 V1	（たばこを）すう[すいます]
snack bar	1-4 N	スナックバー
snow	2-7 N	ゆき＝雪
(sentence 1,) so (sentence 2).	1-11 Pc	(reason)から、(result)
so, so	1-5 Adv	まあまあ
(Is that) so?	1-3 Exp	そうですか。
(to) soak; dip	3-8 V2	つける＝漬ける[つけます]
Sobu Line [yellow colored train line in Tokyo]	3-9 N	そうぶせん＝総武線
soccer	1-5 N	サッカー
social studies	1-11 N	しゃかい＝社会
socks	2-3 N	くつした＝靴下；ソックス
(is) soft; tender	3-8 A	やわらかい＝柔らかい
something	2-15 N	なにか＝何か
(to do) something in advance	3-8 V1	(〜て)おく[おきます]
sometimes	1-4 Adv	ときどき＝時々
(own) son	2-11 N	むすこ＝息子
(someone else's) son	2-11 N	むすこさん＝息子さん
song	1-5 N	うた＝歌
sophomore, 10th grader	1-3 N	こうこういちねんせい＝高校一年生
(is) sore	1-12 A	いたい＝痛い
(I'm) sorry to be late.	2-14 Exp	おそくなりました。＝遅くなりました。
(I am) sorry to have inconvenienced you.	3-1 Exp	しつれいしました。＝失礼しました。
Sorry, but ...	2-6 Exp	ざんねんですが...＝残念ですが...
(I am) sorry. [Sympathy - formal]	2-6 Exp	(お)きのどくに。＝(お)気の毒に。
sound	3-3 N	おと＝音
soup flavored with miso	2-5 N	(お)みそしる＝(お)味噌汁
(is) sour	2-14 A	すっぱい＝酸っぱい
south	2-1 N	みなみ＝南
south entrance/exit	3-9 N	みなみぐち＝南口
souvenir gift	2-9 N	(お)みやげ＝(お)土産
(is) spacious	1-10 A	ひろい＝広い
Spain	1-3 N	スペイン
Spanish language	1-4 N	スペインご＝スペイン語
(to) speak	1-4 V1	はなす＝話す[はなします]
special	3-3 Na	とくべつ＝特別
(to) speed	2-4 V1	スピードをだす＝出す[だします]
(is) spicy	2-14 A	からい＝辛い
spoon	1-14 N	スプーン
-spoonful	1-14 Nd	-はい／-ぱい／-ばい＝杯
sports shoes	2-10 N	うんどうぐつ＝運動靴
sports	1-5 N	スポーツ
	2-10 N	うんどう＝運動

spring	1-12 N	はる＝春
square	3-8 N	しかく＝四角
(is) square (shaped)	3-8 A	しかくい＝四角い
stairs	3-7 N	かいだん＝階段
stamp	3-3 N	きって＝切手
(to) stand	1-13 V1	たつ＝立つ[たちます]
Stand. [ceremony]	1-1 Exp	きりつ＝起立
(Please) stand.	1-2 Exp	たってください＝立って下さい
(someone) starts (something) [transitive]	2-10 V2	(〜を) はじめる＝始める[はじめます]
(something) starts [intransitive]	2-10 V1	(〜 が) はじまる＝始まる[はじまります]
state	2-9 N	しゅう＝州
station employee	3-9 N	えきいん＝駅員
(to) step up	3-7 V1	あがる＝上がる[あがります]
still	2-2 Adv	まだ ＋ Aff.
stomach	1-6 N	おなか＝お腹
(to) stop (at a place)	2-4 V1	(place で/に)とまる＝止まる[とまります]
(to) stop by	2-10 V1	(place に)よる＝寄る[よります]
store	1-13 N	(お)みせ＝(お)店
straight	2-13 Adv	まっすぐ
strange; unusual	2-6 Na	へん＝変
straw	1-14 N	ストロー
straw mat	3-7 N	たたみ＝畳
strawberry	2-14 N	いちご＝苺
street, avenue	2-13 N	とおり＝通り
street, road	2-4 N	みち＝道
strength	2-11 N	ちから＝力
(is very) stressed	2-6 Exp	ストレスがいっぱいです。
(is) strict; severe	1-6 A	きびしい＝厳しい
stroke order	3-4 N	かきじゅん＝書き順
- stroke(s)	3-4 N	〜かく＝〜画
(be) strong in	1-5 Na	とくい＝得意
(is) strong	1-12 A	つよい＝強い
student [college]	1-3 N	がくせい＝学生
student [pre-college]	1-3 N	せいと＝生徒
(to) study	1-4 V3	べんきょうする＝勉強(を)する[べんきょう(を)します]
(to) study abroad	3-2 V3	りゅうがくする＝留学する[りゅうがくします]
subject	1-12 N	かもく＝科目
(to) submit	2-4 V1	だす＝出す[だします]
subway	1-7 N	ちかてつ＝地下鉄
success	3-6 N	せいこう＝成功
(to) succeed	3-6 V3	せいこうする＝成功する[せいこうします]
suddenly	2-4 Adv	きゅうに＝急に

sugar	2-14	N	さとう＝砂糖
sukiyaki	2-14	N	すきやき＝鋤焼き
summer	1-12	N	なつ＝夏
sun [polite]	2-11	N	おひさま＝お日様
Sunday	1-7	N	にちようび＝日曜日
sunglasses	2-3	N	サングラス
supermarket	1-13	N	スーパー
supper	1-4	N	ばんごはん＝晩御飯
	3-1	N	ゆうしょく＝夕食
sushi shop/bar	1-13	N	すしや＝寿司屋
sweater	2-3	N	セーター
(is) sweet	2-14	A	あまい＝甘い
(to) swim	1-15	V1	およぐ＝泳ぐ[およぎます]
swimming	1-5	N	すいえい＝水泳
<T>			
T-shirt	2-3	N	Tシャツ
T.V.	1-4	N	テレビ
table	2-5	N	テーブル
(to) take	1-15	V1	とる＝取る[とります]
(to) take (animate)	2-7	V1	つれていく＝連れて行く[つれていきます]
(to) take (medicine)	1-12	V1	のむ＝飲む[のみます]
(to) take (thing)	2-7	V1	もっていく＝持って行く[もっていきます]
(to) take (time)	2-9	V1	かかる[かかります]
(to) take (a bath)	3-3	V1	(ふろに)はいる＝(風呂に)入る[はいります]
(to) take a shower	3-3	V2	シャワーをあびる[あびます]
(to) take a walk	2-15	V3	さんぽ(を)する＝散歩(を)する[さんぽ(を)します]
(to) take an exam	3-3	V2	しけんをうける＝試験を受ける[うけます]
(to) take care of ～	3-3	V3	せわ(を)する＝世話(を)する[せわ(を)します]
(to) take out (the garbage)	2-7	V1	ごみをだす＝ごみを出す[だします]
(to) take out	2-4	V1	だす＝出す[だします]
(to) take/bring (animate) back home	2-7	V1	つれてかえる＝連れて帰る[つれてかえります]
(to) take/bring (thing) back home	2-7	V1	もってかえる＝持って帰る[もってかえります]
(to) talk	1-4	V1	はなす＝話す[はなします]
(is) tall	1-6	A	たかい＝高い
tape	1-4	N	テープ
(He/She is) tardy; late.	1-1	Exp	ちこくです。＝遅刻です。
taste; flavor	2-14	N	あじ＝味
tatami	3-7	N	たたみ＝畳
(counter for *tatami*)	3-7	C	～じょう＝～畳
tax	2-9	N	ぜいきん＝税金
taxi	1-7	N	タクシー
tea poured over a bowl of rice	3-8	N	(お)ちゃづけ＝(御)茶漬け

tea	1-4 N	(お)ちゃ＝(お)茶	
(to) teach	2-4 V2	おしえる＝教える[おしえます]	
teacher	1-1 N	せんせい＝先生	
team	1-12 N	チーム	
telephone	1-4 N	でんわ＝電話	
telephone number	1-15 N	でんわばんごう＝電話番号	
temperature	2-7 N	おんど＝温度	
temple (Buddhist)	2-7 N	(お)てら＝(お)寺	
ten	1-1 N	じゅう＝十	
ten [general counter]	1-2 N	とお＝十	
ten thousand	1-13 N	(いち)まん＝(一)万	
tennis	1-5 N	テニス	
(the) tenth day of the month	1-11 N	とおか＝十日	
tenth grader	1-3 N	こうこういちねんせい＝高校一年生	
(is) terrible	1-11 A	ひどい＝酷い	
(is) terrific	1-13 A	すごい＝凄い	
textbook	1-2 N	きょうかしょ＝教科書; テキスト	
Thank you.	1-1 Exp	どうも, ありがとう。	
Thank you for your kind help.	3-3 Exp	おせわになりました。＝お世話になりました。	
thank you letter	3-3 N	(お)れいじょう＝(お)礼状	
Thank you very much.	1-1 Exp	ありがとうございます。	
Thank you very much. [used after one has received something] 1-2 Exp ありがとう ございました。＝有難うございました。			
(to) thank	2-15 V3	かんしゃ(を)する＝感謝(を)する[かんしゃ (を)します]	
Thanks to you ...	3-3 Exp	おかげさまで。＝お陰様で。	
thanks; gratitude; appreciation	3-3 N	(お)れい＝(お)礼	
That is a good idea.	2-10 Exp	それはいいかんがえです。＝それはいい考え です。	
that one	1-1 N	それ	
that one [polite equiv. of それ]	2-9 N	そちら	
that one over there [polite equiv. of あれ]	2-9 N あちら		
that one over there	1-1 N	あれ	
that ～ over there	1-2 PN	あの～	
that ～	1-2 PN	その～	
That's all.	2-5 Exp	それだけです。	
That's impossible!	2-11 Exp	とんでもない（です）。	
there	1-2 N	そこ	
there [polite equiv. of そこ]	2-5 N	そちら	
there is (animate object)	1-10 V2	いる＝居る[います]	
there is (inanimate object)	1-10 V1	ある＝有る[あります]	
Therefore [Formal]	2-11 SI	ですから	
Therefore [Informal]	2-11 SI	だから	

Thereupon	2-13 SI	すると
(is) thick (in width; size)	3-8 A	ふとい＝太い
thick white noodles in broth	2-5 N	うどん
thick	2-14 Adv	あつく＝厚く
(is) thick	2-14 A	あつい＝厚い
thin	2-14 Adv	うすく＝薄く
(is) thin	2-14 A	うすい＝薄い
(is) thin (person)	1-6 V2	やせている＝痩せている[やせています]
(is) thin and long	3-8 A	ほそながい＝細長い
(is) thin; slender	3-8 A	ほそい＝細い
thing [intangible]	1-5 N	こと＝事
thing [tangible]	1-5 N	もの＝物
(to) think	2-11 V1	おもう＝思う[おもいます]
(I am) thinking of doing	3-8 V1+V1	(-ooと) おもっている＝思っている [おもっています]
(the) third day of the month	1-11 N	みっか＝三日
(I got) thirsty.	1-14 Exp	のどがかわきました。＝喉が渇きました。
(I am) thirsty.	1-14 Exp	のどがカラカラです。
thirteen	1-1 N	じゅうさん＝十三
thirty	1-1 N	さんじゅう＝三十
This is a small gift. [Used when handing someone a gift.]	3-8 Exp	これは少しですが…
this month	1-12 N	こんげつ＝今月
this morning	1-12 N	けさ＝今朝
this one	1-1 N	これ
this one [polite equiv. of これ]	1-3 N	こちら
this semester	3-2 N	こんがっき＝今学期
this side (of)	3-9 N	てまえ＝手前
This way, please.	2-5 Exp	どうぞこちらへ。
this week	1-11 N	こんしゅう＝今週
this year	1-15 N	ことし＝今年
this ～	1-2 PN	この ～
thousand	1-13 N	せん＝千
three	1-1 N	さん＝三
three [general counter]	1-2 N	みっつ＝三つ
throat	1-6 N	のど＝喉
through ～	2-4 P	～を
throughout	2-15 Adv	ずっと
(to) throw away (garbage)	2-3 V2	(ごみを) すてる[すてます]
Thursday	1-7 N	もくようび＝木曜日
ticket gate	3-9 N	かいさつぐち＝改札口
ticket	1-15 N	きっぷ＝切符
ticket vending machine	3-9 N	けんばいき＝券売機
time	2-10 N	じかん＝時間

- time(s)	2-6 Nd	- ど = - 度
- time(s)	3-4 Nd	- かい = - 回 [informal]
tip	2-5 N	チップ
(I am) tired.	1-12 Exp	つかれています。＝疲れています。
(I became) tired.	1-12 Exp	つかれました。＝疲れました。
tissue	1-2 N	ティッシュ
to (place)	1-7 P	(place) へ; (place) に
(from 〜) to 〜	1-11 P	(〜から) 〜まで
to 〜	2-13 P	〜まで
tobacco	2-3 N	たばこ
today	1-4 N	きょう＝今日
toe	1-6 N	ゆび＝指
together	1-4 Adv	いっしょに＝一緒に
Tokyo	2-1 N	とうきょう＝東京
Tokyo Station [a station in Tokyo]	3-9 N	とうきょうえき＝東京駅
tomorrow	1-4 N	あした＝明日
tonight	1-7 N	こんばん＝今晩
too 〜	2-14 V2	(stem+)すぎる＝過ぎる[すぎます]
tooth	1-6 N	は＝歯
top	2-2 N	うえ＝上
tough	3-8 A	かたい＝硬い
town	2-13 N	まち＝町
track number 〜	3-9 N	〜ばんせん＝〜番線
tradition	3-7 N	でんとう＝伝統
traditional	3-7 Na	でんとうてき＝伝統的
traffic accident	2-4 N	こうつうじこ＝交通事故
traffic lights	2-4 N	しんごう＝信号
train station	2-13 N	えき＝駅
(to) translate	3-4 V1	やくす＝訳す[やくします]
translation	3-4 N	やく＝訳
trash can	1-10 N	ごみばこ＝ごみ箱
(to) travel	1-7 V3	りょこうをする＝旅行をする[りょこう(を)します]
traveler's check	2-9 N	トラベラーズチェック
traveling	1-7 N	りょこう＝旅行
(to) treat (someone) to a meal	2-5 V3	ごちそう(を)する＝御馳走(を)する[ごちそう(を)します]
tree	1-10 N	き＝木
triangle	3-8 N	さんかく＝三角
trip	1-7 N	りょこう＝旅行
(be) troubled	3-3 V1	こまる＝困る[こまります]
true	1-3 N	ほんとう＝本当
(Is it) true/real?	2-3 Exp	ほんとうですか。＝本当ですか。

truly	2-3 Adv	ほんとうに＝本当に
try to (do)	2-5 Dv	(-て) みる[みます]
Tuesday	1-7 N	かようび＝火曜日
tuition	3-2 N	じゅぎょうりょう＝授業料
(to) turn at/along (place)	2-4 V1	(place で/を) まがる＝曲がる[まがります]
(to) turn in; hand in	1-13 V1	だす＝出す[だします]
(Please) turn in.	1-2 Exp	だしてください。＝出して下さい。
twelfth grader	1-3 N	こうこうさんねんせい＝高校三年生
twelve	1-1 N	じゅうに＝十二
(the) twentieth day of the month	1-11 N	はつか＝二十日
twenty	1-1 N	にじゅう＝二十
(the) twenty fourth day of the month	1-11 N	にじゅうよっか＝二十四日
twenty years old	1-3 N	はたち＝二十歳
twin	2-15 N	ふたご＝双児
two	1-1 N	に＝二
two (persons)	1-3 N	ふたり＝二人
two [general counter]	1-2 N	ふたつ＝二つ
two story house	3-7 N	にかいだて＝二階建て
(to) type	1-4 V3	タイプ(を)する[タイプ(を)します]

<U>

U.S.	1-3 N	アメリカ
U.S. citizen	1-3 N	アメリカじん＝アメリカ人
udon topped with beef	2-5 N	にくうどん＝肉うどん
Ueno [a city in Tokyo]	3-9 N	うえの＝上野
(is) unappetizing; tasteless	1-13 A	まずい
uncle	1-15 N	おじさん
(own) uncle	3-1 N	おじ＝叔父
(is) uncomfortable	2-14 A	きもちがわるい＝気持ちが悪い
under	2-2 N	した＝下
(to) understand	1-1 V1	わかる＝分かる[わかります]
(sports) uniform	2-10 N	ユニフォーム
uniform	2-3 N	せいふく＝制服
(is) uninteresting	1-11 A	つまらない
university	1-12 N	だいがく＝大学
(is) unpleasant	2-14 A	きもちがわるい＝気持ちが悪い
unskillful	1-5 Na	へた＝下手
unusual	2-6 Na	へん＝変
(to) use	3-1 V1	つかう＝使う[つかいます]
usually	1-4 Adv	たいてい＝大抵
(with one's) utmost effort	2-11 Adv	いっしょうけんめい＝一生懸命

<V>

| vacation | 1-7 N | (お)やすみ＝(お)休み |
| various | 2-9 Na | いろいろ |

vegetable	2-14 N	やさい＝野菜	
vehicle	1-7 N	くるま＝車; じどうしゃ＝自動車	
veranda	3-7 N	ベランダ	
very	1-5 Adv	とても	
very soon	1-15 Adv	もうすぐ	
(not) very	1-5 Adv	あまり ＋ Neg.	
vicinity	2-2 N	ちかく＝近く	
video	1-4 N	ビデオ	
video game	1-5 N	テレビゲーム	
vinegar	2-14 N	す＝酢	
vinegared vegetables	3-8 N	すのもの＝酢の物	
voice	1-6 N	こえ＝声	
volleyball	1-5 N	バレー(ボール)	

<W>

(Please) wait a minute.	1-1 Exp	ちょっとまってください。	
		＝ちょっと待って下さい。	
(to) wait	1-13 V1	まつ＝待つ[まちます]	
waiter	2-5 N	ウェイター	
waitress	2-5 N	ウェイトレス	
(to) wake up	1-7 V2	おきる＝起きる[おきます]	
(to) walk	1-7 V1	あるく＝歩く[あるきます]	
walkman	1-4 N	ウォークマン	
wall	2-11 N	かべ＝壁	
wallet	1-2 N	さいふ＝財布	
want (something)	1-11 A	(something が) ほしい＝欲しい	
want (to do)	1-12 Da	(verb stem form) -たい	
(is) warm	1-14 A	あたたかい＝暖かい	
(Japanese) warrior	3-6 N	さむらい＝侍	
(to) wash	2-7 V1	あらう＝洗う[あらいます]	
(a) watch	1-13 N	とけい＝時計	
(to) watch	1-4 V2	みる＝見る[みます]	
water	1-4 N	(お)みず＝(お)水	
we	1-12 N	わたしたち＝私達	
we [Used by males.]	1-12 N	ぼくたち＝僕達	
We did it!	2-10 Exp	やったあ！	
(be) weak in	1-5 Na	にがて＝苦手	
(is) weak	1-12 A	よわい＝弱い	
(to) wear [above the waist or on the entire body]	2-3 V2	きる ＝着る[きます]	
(to) wear [accessories]	2-3 V3	する[します]	
(to) wear [at or below the waist]	2-3 V1	はく ＝履く[はきます]	
(to) wear [glasses]	2-3 V2	(めがねを)かける[かけます]	
(to) wear [on or draped over the head]	2-3 V2	かぶる[かぶります]	
(to) wear a seat belt	2-4 V3	シートベルトをする[します]	

weather	1-1	N	(お)てんき＝(お)天気
weather forecast	3-6	N	てんきよほう＝天気予報
Wednesday	1-7	N	すいようび＝水曜日
-week(s)	2-6	Nd	-しゅうかん＝-週間
weekend	1-11	N	しゅうまつ＝週末
weird	2-6	Na	へん＝変
Welcome. [polite]	2-5	Exp	いらっしゃいませ。
(You are) welcome.	1-1	Exp	どういたしまして。
well	1-4	Adv	よく
Well done.	1-2	Exp	よくできました。＝良く出来ました。
Well ... [Used when one does not know or is unsure of the answer.]	2-9	SI	さあ...
Well ... [Used when one is unsure of the answer.]	2-1	SI	ええと...　あのう...
Well then [formal]	1-14	Exp	では
Well then [informal]	1-14	Exp	じゃ
Welcome home.	3-1	Exp	おかえりなさい。＝お帰りなさい。
west	2-1	N	にし＝西
west entrance/exit	3-9	N	にしぐち＝西口
Western style	3-7	NA	せいようてき＝西洋的
Western style meal	3-8	N	ようしょく＝洋食
Western-style cooking	3-8	N	せいようりょうり＝西洋料理
Western-style room	3-7	N	ようしつ＝洋室
what?	1-1	Ni	なに＝何; なん＝何
what color?	1-5	N	なにいろ＝何色
(the) what day of the month?	1-11	Ni	なんにち＝何日
what day of the week?	1-7	Ni	なんようび＝何曜日
What does it mean?	3-4	Exp	どういういみですか。＝どういう意味ですか。
what grade?	1-3	N	なんねんせい＝何年生
What happened?	1-12	Exp	どうしましたか。
what kind of 〜?	1-5	PN	どんな〜
what language?	1-4	Ni	なにご＝何語
what month?	1-3	Ni	なんがつ＝何月
what nationality?	1-3	Ni	なにじん＝何人
What should I do?	3-3	Exp	どうしたら、いいですか。
what time?	1-7	Ni	なんじ＝何時
when?	1-7	Ni	いつ
where?	1-3	Ni	どこ
where? [polite equiv. of どこ]	2-5	Ni	どちら
which (one of two)? [informal]	2-9	Ni	どっち
which (one of two)? [polite]	2-9	Ni	どちら
which one (of three or more)?	1-13	Ni	どれ
which 〜?	1-13	Nd	どの〜
While 〜	3-6	N+P	—あいだに＝一間に

While ～ [Describing a person's simultaneous or concurrent actions]

	3-6	Rc	(verb stem) ながら
white	1-5	N	しろ＝白
(is) white	1-6	A	しろい＝白い
who?	1-3	Ni	だれ＝誰
why?	1-11	Ni	なぜ；どうして
(is) wide	1-10	A	ひろい＝広い
(own) wife	3-6	N	かない＝家内
(someone else's) wife	3-6	N	おくさん＝奥さん
Will you have seconds?	3-8	Exp	おかわりは？＝お代わりは？
(to) win	1-12	V1	かつ＝勝つ[かちます]
(to) win a championship	2-10	V3	ゆうしょうをする＝優勝をする [ゆうしょう(を)します]
wind	2-7	N	かぜ＝風
window	1-10	N	まど＝窓
winter	1-12	N	ふゆ＝冬
with (person)	1-4	P	(person)と(いっしょに)
with (tool)	1-4	P	(tool)で

Without reservation/hesitation, please (have some).

	3-8	Exp	（ご）えんりょなく、どうぞ。
woman	1-10	N	おんなのひと＝女の人
woman (middle-aged)	1-15	N	おばさん
(We) won! (We) won!	2-10	Exp	かった！かった！＝勝った！勝った！
won't do	2-3	V2	いけません
(it) won't do	2-5	V1	なりません
Won't you do ～? [invitation]	7-1	Dv	-ませんか
(I) wonder if ～ [used by female]	3-2	SP	ーかしら。
(I) wonder if ～ [used by male and female] 3-2	SP	ーかな。
(is) wonderful	1-13	A	すばらしい＝素晴らしい
words	2-15	N	ことば＝言葉
(to) work (at ～)	2-2	V1	(place で) はたらく＝働く[はたらきます]
(to) work part-time (at ～)	2-2	V3	(place で) アルバイト(を)する [アルバイト(を)します]
worksheet	1-2	N	ワークシート
world	2-9	N	せかい＝世界
(to) worry	2-4	V3	しんぱい(を)する＝心配(を)する [しんぱい(を)します]
Wow!	1-13	SI	わあ
(to) write	1-4	V1	かく＝書く[かきます]
(Please) write.	1-2	Exp	かいてください＝書いて下さい
(is) wrong	2-2	V1	ちがう＝違う[ちがいます]

<Y>

Yamanote Line [green colored train line in Tokyo]　3-9　N　やまのてせん＝山手線

(a) yard	1-10 N	にわ＝庭
-year	1-15 Nd	-ねん＝-年
-year(s) (duration)	2-6 Nd	-ねんかん＝-年間
yellow	1-5 N	きいろ＝黄色
(is) yellow	1-6 A	きいろい＝黄色い
yen	1-13 Nd	-えん＝-円
Yes [formal]	1-1 SI	はい
Yes [informal]	2-4 SI	うん
Yes [less formal than はい]	1-1 SI	ええ
yesterday	1-4 N	きのう＝昨日
You are welcome.	1-1 Exp	どういたしまして。
you know [sentence ending particle]	1-6 SP	よ
you	1-2 N	あなた
young lady [informal]; daughter	2-11 N	むすめ＝娘
young lady [polite]; daughter	2-11 N	むすめさん＝娘さん
(is) young	1-6 A	わかい＝若い
(own) younger brother	1-3 N	おとうと＝弟
(someone's) younger brother	1-3 N	おとうとさん＝弟さん
(my) younger sister	1-3 N	いもうと＝妹
(someone's) younger sister	1-3 N	いもうとさん＝妹さん
yours	1-2 N	あなたの＝あなたの
Yummm...	2-5 SI	う～ん
<Z>		
zoo	2-13 N	どうぶつえん＝動物園

日本語１と２の漢字

I	一 いち, ひと(つ)	二 に, ふた(つ)	三 さん, みっ(つ)	四 し, よ, よん, よっ(つ)	五 ご, いつ(つ)			
	六 ろく, ろっ, むっ(つ)	七 なな, しち, なな(つ)	八 はち, はっ, やっ(つ)	九 きゅう, く, ここの(つ)	十 じゅう, じっ, じゅっ, とお			
	日 [に], にち, ひ, [び], か	月 がつ, げつ	火 か	水 みず, すい	木 き, もく	金 かね, きん	土 ど	
II 2 課	口 くち, [ぐち]	目 め	人 ひと, にん, じん	本 もと, ほん, [ぼん], [ぽん]	今 いま, こん	年 とし, ねん	私 [わたし], わたくし	曜 よう
II 3 課	上 うえ	下 した, くだ(さい)	大 おお(きい), たい, だい	小 ちい(さい), しょう	夕 ゆう	何 なに, なん	中 なか, ちゅう	外 そと, がい
II 4 課	行 い(く), こう	来 き(ます), く(る), こ らい	子 こ	車 くるま, しゃ	学 がく, [がっ]	校 こう	見 み(る)	良 よ(い)	食 た(べる), しょく
II 5 課	川 かわ, [がわ]	山 やま, さん	出 で(る), だ(す)	先 せん	生 う(まれる), せい	父 ちち, [とう]	母 はは, [かあ]	毎 まい	書 か(く), しょ
II 6 課	手 て	耳 みみ	門 もん	聞 き(く), ぶん	女 おんな	好 す(き)	田 た, [だ]	男 おとこ	
II 7 課	言 い(う)	語 ご	寺 てら, [でら], じ	時 とき, じ	間 あいだ, かん	分 わ(かる), ふん, [ぷん], ぶん	正 ただ(しい), しょう	家 いえ, か	々 [repeat]

453

Ⅱ 9 課	白 しろ, はく	百 ひゃく, [びゃく], [びゃく]	千 せん, [ぜん]	万 まん	方 かた, ほう	玉 たま, [だま]	国 くに,[ぐに] こく,[ごく]	安 やす(い)	高 たか(い), こう	
Ⅱ 10 課	牛 うし, ぎゅう	半 はん	*手 て, しゅ	友 とも	帰 かえ(る)	待 ま(つ)	持 も(つ)	米 こめ	番 ばん	事 こと,[ごと], じ
Ⅱ 11 課	雨 あめ	電 でん	天 てん	気 き	会 あ(う), かい	話 はな(す), はなし, [ばなし], わ	売 う(る)	読 よ(む)		
Ⅱ 13 課	右 みぎ	左 ひだり	入 い(れる), はい(る), [いり]	物 もの, ぶつ	名 な, めい	前 まえ, ぜん	戸 と, [ど]	所 ところ, [どころ] しょ,[じょ]	近 ちか(い)	
Ⅱ 14 課	立 た(つ), りつ	作 つく(る), さく	肉 にく	魚 さかな	多 おお(い), た	少 すく(ない), すこ(し)	古 ふる(い)	新 あたら(しい), しん	*生 う(まれる), せい, なま	
Ⅱ 15 課	才 さい	心 こころ, しん	思 おも(う)	休 やす(み)	買 か(う)	早 はや(い)	自 じ	犬 いぬ	太 ふと(る)	屋 や

* Previously introduced.

日本語 3 の漢字

III 1課	漢 かん	字 じ	姉 あね, ねえ	妹 いもうと	兄 あに, にい	弟 おとうと	朝 あさ, ちょう	昼 ひる, ちゅう
	明 あか (るい)	去 きょ	銀 ぎん	仕 し	*父 ちち, とう, ふ	*母 はは, かあ, ぼ	*先 せん, さき	家族 かぞく
	友達 ともだち	質問 しつもん	答え こたえ	宿題 しゅくだい	試験 しけん	昨日 きのう		
III 2課	公 こう	文 ぶん	化 か, け	花 はな	海 うみ, かい	旅 りょ	教 おし(える), きょう	室 しつ
	後 うし(ろ), あと, ご	午 ご	着 き(る), つ(く)	知 し (る)	*私 [わたし], わたくし, し	*男 おとこ, だん	*女 おんな, じょ	*子 こ, し
	*入 はい (る), い (れる), いり, にゅう	*行 い(く), こう, ぎょう	生徒 せいと	問題 もんだい	教科書 きょうかしょ	公園 こうえん	一度 いちど	図書館 としょかん
III 3課	春 はる	夏 なつ	秋 あき	冬 ふゆ	雪 ゆき	元 げん	飲 の (む)	体 からだ, たい
	音 おと, おん	楽 たの(しい), らく, がく	糸 いと	紙 かみ, [がみ]	*生 う(まれる), なま, せい, しょう	世話 せわ	生活 せいかつ	体育 たいいく
	様 さま	変 へん	大変 たいへん					

❋ Previously introduced.

Highlighted *kanji* are for recognition only.

III 4課	英 えい	草 くさ	林 はやし, [ばやし]	森 もり	台 たい, [だい]	始 はじ(める)	終 お(わる)	使 つか(う)
	勉 べん	強 つよ(い), きょう	回 かい	週 しゅう	*近 ちか(い), きん	*間 あいだ, かん, ま	本当 ほんとう	最近 さいきん
	違う ちがう	辞書 じしょ	～君 くん	週末 しゅうまつ				
III 6課	映 えい	画 が, かく	歌 うた, か	晩 ばん	夜 よる	黒 くろ, こく	茶 ちゃ, さ	飯 はん
	足 あし	長 なが(い), ちょう	走 はし(る)	起 お(きる), き	寝 ね(る)	有名 ゆうめい	番組 ばんぐみ	女性 じょせい
	男性 だんせい	曲 きょく	子供 こども	選手 せんしゅ	彼 かれ	彼女 かのじょ		
III 7課	東 ひがし, とう	西 にし, せい	洋 よう	和 わ	部 ぶ, へ	美 うつく(しい), び	広 ひろ(い)	内 うち, ない
	主 しゅ	住 す(む), じゅう	開 あ(ける)	閉 し(める)	*生 う(まれる), なま, せい, しょう, い(ける)	*上 あ(がる), うえ, じょう	*下 お(りる), した, くだ(さい), へ	*正 せい, ただ(しい), しょう
	*寝 ね(る), しん	～階 -かい, -がい	～的 -てき	全部 ぜんぶ	座る すわる	正座 せいざ		

*Previously introduced.

Highlighted *kanji* are for recognition only.

III 8課	竹 たけ	鳥 とり, ちょう	色 いろ	赤 あか	青 あお	黄 き	風 かぜ, ふう,[ふ]	味 あじ, み
	料 りょう	理 り	由 ゆう	重 おも(い)	*自 し,[じ]	自然 しぜん	焼く やく	苦手 にがて
	丸 まる	三角 さんかく	四角 しかく	弁当 べんとう	最〜 さい〜			
III 9課	北 きた, ほく,[ほっ]	南 みなみ	京 きょう	駅 えき	乗 の(る)	地 ち	鉄 てつ	図 ず, と
	道 みち, とう,[どう]	歩 ある(く), ほ[ぽ]	動 どう, うご(く)	働 はたら(く)	円 えん	*明 あか(るい), めい	*売 う(る), ばい	〜線 -せん
	橋 はし,[ばし]	病院 びょういん	新幹線 しんかんせん	中央線 ちゅうおうせん				

* Previously introduced.

Highlighted *kanji* are for recognition only.

Verb Conjugations

	NAI form	MASU form	Dic. form	BA form	OO form	TE form	TA form
	informal, neg., nonpast	formal, nonpast	informal, nonpast	conditional	informal, volitional		informal, past
I. Group 1 Verbs							
み	のまない nomanai	のみます nomimasu	のむ nomu	のめば nomeba	のもう nomoo	のんで nonde	のんだ nonda
に	しなない shinanai	しにます shinimasu	しぬ shinu	しねば shineba	しのう shinoo	しんで shinde	しんだ shinda
び	あそばない asobanai	あそびます asobimasu	あそぶ asobu	あそべば asobeba	あそぼう asoboo	あそんで asonde	あそんだ asonda
い	かわない kawanai	かいます kaimasu	かう kau	かえば kaeba	かおう kaoo	かって katte	かった katta
ち	またない matanai	まちます machimasu	まつ matsu	まてば mateba	まとう matoo	まって matte	まった matta
り	かえらない kaeranai	かえります kaerimasu	かえる kaeru	かえれば kaereba	かえろう kaeroo	かえって kaette	かえった kaetta
	*ない * nai	あります arimasu	ある aru	あれば areba		あって atte	あった atta
き	かかない kakanai	かきます kakimasu	かく kaku	かけば kakeba	かこう kakoo	かいて kaite	かいた kaita
	いかない ikanai	いきます ikimasu	いく iku	いけば ikeba	いこう ikoo	*いって * itte	*いった * itta
ぎ	およがない oyoganai	およぎます oyogimasu	およぐ oyogu	およげば oyogeba	およごう oyogoo	およいで oyoide	およいだ oyoida
し	はなさない hanasanai	はなします hanashimasu	はなす hanasu	はなせば hanaseba	はなそう hanasoo	はなして hanashite	はなした hanashita
II. Group 2 Verbs							
- e	たべない tabenai	たべます tabemasu	たべる taberu	たべれば tabereba	たべよう tabeyoo	たべて tabete	たべた tabeta
□	みない minai	みます mimasu	みる miru	みれば mireba	みよう miyoo	みて mite	みた mita

Special verbs: おきます get up, かります borrow, お（降）ります get off, できます can do, -すぎます too ~, シャワーをあびます shower, お（下）ります go down

III. Group 3 Irregular verbs							
する (do)	しない shinai	します shimasu	する suru	すれば sureba	しよう shiyoo	して shite	した shita
くる (come)	こない konai	きます kimasu	くる kuru	くれば kureba	こよう koyoo	きて kite	きた kita

*Exceptional form.

	NAKATTA form informal, neg., past	Potential (Group 2 verb)	(Honorific-Passive)
I. Group 1 Verbs			
み	のまなかった nomanakatta	のめる nomeru	のまれる nomareru
に	しななかった shinanakatta	しねる shineru	しなれる shinareru
び	あそばなかった asobanakatta	あそべる asoberu	あそばれる asobareru
い	かわなかった kawanakatta	かえる kaeru	かわれる kawareru
ち	またなかった matanakatta	まてる materu	またれる matareru
り	かえらなかった kaeranakatta ＊なかった * nakatta	かえれる kaereru	かえられる kaerareru
き	かかなかった kakanakatta いかなかった ikanakatta	かける kakeru いける ikeru	かかれる kakareru いかれる ikareru
ぎ	およがなかった oyoganakatta	およげる oyogeru	およがれる oyogareru
し	はなさなかった hanasanakatta	はなせる hanaseru	はなされる hanasareru
II. Group 2 Verbs			
- e	たべなかった tabenakatta	たべられる taberareru	たべられる taberareru
☐	みなかった minakatta	みられる mirareru	みられる mirareru
Special verbs: おきます get up, かります borrow, おります get off, できます can do, -すぎます too ~, シャワーをあびます shower, おりる go down			
III. Group 3 Irregular verbs			
する (do)	しなかった shinakatta	できる dekiru	される sareru
くる (come)	こなかった konakatta	こられる korareru	こられる korareru

＊Exceptional form.

459